Professions
AND THE
French State,
1700–1900

*Published under the auspices of
the Shelby Cullom Davis
Center for Historical Studies,
Princeton University*

Professions AND THE French State, 1700–1900

GERALD L. GEISON,
Editor

University of Pennsylvania Press
Philadelphia

Design by Robert Nance

Copyright © 1984 by the University of Pennsylvania Press
All rights reserved

Library of Congress Cataloging in Publication Data

Main entry under title:
Professions and the French state, 1700–1900.
   Includes bibliographical references and index.
   1. Science and state—France—History.   2. Professions
—France—History.   I. Geison, Gerald L., 1943–.
Q127.F8P76   1984   331.7′615′0944   83-14700
ISBN 0-8122-7912-3

Printed in the United States of America

*For Charles Coulston Gillispie,
who knows a lot about France
and everything
about being a professional*

Contents

Preface   ix

Introduction   1
GERALD L. GEISON

PART ONE: Engineers, Scientists, and Academics   13

1   *Bridges and Barriers: Narrowing Access and Changing Structure in the French Engineering Profession, 1800–1850*   15
JOHN H. WEISS

2   *Science, the University, and the State in Nineteenth-Century France*   66
ROBERT FOX

PART TWO: Surgeons, Physicians, and Psychiatrists   147

3   *A "Monarchical Profession" in the Old Regime: Surgeons, Ordinary Practitioners, and Medical Professionalization in Eighteenth-Century France*   149
TOBY GELFAND

4 "Moral Contagion": A Professional Ideology of
   Medicine and Psychiatry in Eighteenth-
   and Nineteenth-Century France   181
   JAN GOLDSTEIN

   PART THREE: Medical Monopoly, Professional
   Power, and Political Cultures   223

5 *The Politics of Professional Monopoly in Nineteenth-
   Century Medicine: The French Model and Its Rivals*   225
   MATTHEW RAMSEY

   Index   307

   Notes on Contributors   318

Preface

The essays gathered together here had their origins in the research seminar of the Shelby Cullom Davis Center for Historical Studies at Princeton University. The contributors were selected from a group of forty speakers who presented papers to the Davis Center during the academic years 1978–79 and 1979–80, when the Center focused on the history of the professions. A separate collection of four essays on professions and professional ideologies in America has already been published.[1] Three of the contributors to this volume (Robert Fox, Matthew Ramsey, and John Weiss) were visiting fellows at the Davis Center for at least one semester. Toby Gelfand and Jan Goldstein were invited to the Center seminar to give earlier versions of the essays published here. I participated in the seminar as a member of the faculty of the History Department at Princeton.

This volume has been long a-borning and would never have seen the light of day without the support and assistance of many people, most notably the contributors themselves, whose immense patience has served as an example for me. Faye Angelozzi and Joan Daviduk have handled with dispatch and good cheer a wealth of administrative and clerical tasks. John McGuigan has been an uncommonly supportive and penetrating editor. Ezra Suleiman offered bibliographic suggestions, as did Matthew Ramsey in abundance. All of the contributors to this volume have served as my guides in a subject all too new to me. Finally, I owe special thanks to Lawrence Stone, director of the Davis Center, for his unflagging support and encouragement, his crucial role in negotiations with the contrib-

---

1. Gerald L. Geison, ed., *Professions and Professional Ideologies in America* (Chapel Hill, 1983).

utors and the publisher, and his efforts to improve my introduction. The Davis Center provided financial support to the visiting fellows and other contributors, to me in the form of released time from teaching to edit the volume, and to the publisher in the form of a subsidy to cover a portion of the production costs. I am of course solely responsible for any lapses in editorial judgment.

G. L. G.

Princeton, New Jersey
19 June 1983

GERALD L. GEISON

Introduction

In the rapidly expanding body of scholarship on the history and historical sociology of the professions, very little focused attention has been paid to the role of the nation-state and centralized bureaucracy. The professions in France are also in need of much closer scrutiny. This volume therefore represents an important departure in two ways at once. It not only points toward two neglected avenues of research, but also takes some solid steps along them.

The reasons for the prior neglect of the state are not far to seek. They are, for the most part, a reflection of the political cultures and traditions in which scholars are embedded. The bulk of the literature on professions has been produced by British and especially American scholars, resulting in a preoccupation with Anglo-American developments, in which the state has played a relatively late, indirect, and passive role. In addition, many American scholars have found it hard to suppress the traditional Anglo-American suspicion of centralized political authority and bureaucracy, and some of them have found it impossible to imagine any close connection between the (malign) process of bureaucratization and the (benign) process of professionalization. Until very recently, it might even be said, American scholars have tended to see an inherent *opposition* between the state and professions, between government control or supervision and the "free" exercise of professional authority by autonomous individuals belonging by choice and training to sharply contained "communities of the competent."[1]

This image of free professional experts, operating independently of the central state and its bureaucracy, may have reached its apotheosis in the work of the influential "functionalist" school of American sociology, whose leading exponent was the late Talcott Parsons. In an essay of 1968,

Parsons went so far as to claim that the state, "in the relatively early modern sense of that term," had been displaced by the "professional complex," which had surpassed even capitalist or socialist modes of organization to become "the most important single component in the structure of modern societies."[2] Parsons and other functionalists saw the professions as highly effective occupational groups sharing a small cluster of attributes, including notably an intellectual foundation in the research university, and exercising authority by virtue of their expertise rather than their political power as usually conceived. On this view, professionals were outside or above ordinary politics, and they operated as autonomous experts free of any substantial relation with the state or government bureaucracy.[3]

The benign Parsonian conception of professions has lately fallen on hard times in Anglo-American scholarship. But the recent wave of anti-Parsonian literature has done little to challenge the Anglo-American image of "free" professionals. The authors of this scholarship may rail against the alleged "tyranny" of professional authority, but most of them continue to ignore the role of the state and government bureaucracy. They focus instead on the role of capitalism or class interest, treating professional groups as if they were independent agents actively engaged in the project of carving out and monopolizing markets for their services.[4] In doing so, they tend to ignore the extent to which even powerful professional groups depend ultimately on the borrowed authority of the state, even in that alleged bastion of professional power, the United States. They tend to forget, for example, that even the paradigmatically powerful American medical profession draws much of its power from state protection, however much it may fulminate against state supervision or intervention. In the mid-nineteenth century, as Matthew Ramsey reminds us in his contribution to this volume, officially qualified American doctors discovered to their dismay that the state (or, more precisely, the states) could choose to withdraw privileges that had once been bestowed upon them. Then as now, American physicians seemed surprised to discover that not everyone agreed that they should enjoy freedom from state intervention for themselves while seeking state protection from their "irregular" competitors.

But if Anglo-American studies of the professions have largely neglected the state, French (and German) scholars have shown relatively little interest in the professions as such. In part, this indifference reflects the appeal of Marxist thought for Continental scholars. The professions got short shrift from Marx himself, and they continue to pose difficulties for traditional Marxist analysis because of the problematic location of professionals within the standard classes of capitalist, landowner, and

Introduction

laborer.[5] But other factors must also be involved. In France, even non-Marxist observers, from Emile Durkheim on down, have also tended to make the professions a subsidiary category within the much broader rubric of social stratification. In French discourse, whether Marxist or not, the concept "profession" lacks some of the distinctness and salience that it holds for English and especially American scholars. In the social vocabulary of the Old Regime, "profession" was but one term in a rich and shifting "corporate idiom" that included such culturally specific terms as *corps, confrérie, communauté, état*, and *métier*.[6] If that "corporate idiom" now sounds archaic, it is nonetheless the case that French discourse continues to lack precise equivalents for the current Anglo-Saxon usage of "profession" and "professional."[7]

All of this surely reflects profound differences between Anglo-American and French political culture, including notably differences in the role and social standing of noncapitalist elites. Especially in the meritocratic ideology of "classless" America, the professions have come to be seen as the most obviously "legitimate" way to claim, attain, or retain elite status.[8] In French (and German) political culture, the social standing of noncapitalist elites has had a less distinct connection with their occupational role, and the "liberal professions" in particular have generally been perceived as a much less important social and political force.

It should therefore come as little surprise that French scholars have produced a fairly large body of literature that relates somehow to the professions but relatively little that can be brought into direct comparison or confrontation with the burgeoning Anglo-American scholarship. And despite recent signs of a developing convergence between the pertinent Anglo-American and Continental literature,[9] there has been no collective effort to treat the professions in France as a central historical problem. It is thus a signal feature of this set of essays, one by an English scholar and four by Americans, that it brings Anglo-American notions of "profession" to bear on (mainly) French historical materials covering several different professions and a broad sweep of time. Although each essay focuses on a single profession, their collective effect is to identify professionalism in France as a single large historical problem.

More than that, this collection of essays is united by a central theme and basic thrust. It situates the state where it belongs, at center stage, in any discussion of professionalization in France. And it even points toward a common conclusion: in the French context, by striking contrast to standard Anglo-American assumptions, professional "autonomy" or success often went hand in hand with "dependence" on the state and its bureaucracy. In France, professional groups in search of fiscal support, social legitimacy, and some measure of intellectual independence usually discovered that the most effective way to attain their goals was through cooperation or even "collaboration" with the central state and its bureaucracy. What follows is not so much an attempt to summarize the individual essays, let alone to capture their full richness, but rather an effort to highlight some of the ways in which each essay contributes toward this common conclusion about the relationship between the professions and the state in France.

In Part I, John Weiss and Robert Fox explore the advantages that nineteenth-century engineers and scientists enjoyed by virtue of their relation to the French state, even if the scientists sometimes failed to recognize or appreciate them. Weiss offers his study of French engineering from ca. 1800 to 1850 as an example of the role that the state has played in the persistent stratification of French society as a whole. In particular, he argues that the state educational system, theoretically open to all, has in fact operated in such a way as to perpetuate longstanding patterns of social disparity. Especially after 1820, positions in the French state bureaucracy and access to professional schools came increasingly to depend on the possession of a *baccalauréat-ès-lettres*. That was the case even for the leading engineering schools, despite the arguably tenuous connection between the actual work or functional expertise of the engineer and the classical, latinate, humanist content of the *lycée* curriculum that led to the *baccalauréat-ès-lettres*. On Weiss's account, the stratifying role of the state educational system was reinforced by the persistence into the nineteenth century of privileged state corporations of professional functionaries. In civil (as opposed to military) engineering, the most important of these *corps d'état* was the Corps des Ponts et Chaussées, which not only survived the Revolution but was officially granted a semiautonomous position within the French state by Napoleon in 1804. The *conducteurs des ponts et chaussées*, the "nonprofessional" subordinates of the *ingénieurs*, were also referred to as a *corps*, but otherwise enjoyed none of the autonomy, authority, and status of the Corps *ingénieurs*. Meanwhile, outside the state system, an ever larger number of men resembled the state-employed *conducteurs* in the sense that they were performing the functions of the civil engineer while being denied the title and status of the state *ingénieurs*. And these differences in status correlated closely with the social origins of the men who belonged to each group. In France, by contrast with the relatively fluid opportunities for "civil engineers" in England, both the state-employed *conducteurs* and the private engineers found their social mobility blocked by "professional" privileges that flowed to the Corps *ingénieurs* by virtue of their relation to the French state and its stratifying educational system.

Robert Fox's essay explores the ambiguous relation between the French state and academic scientists from the Revolution until World War I. As employees of the state with no clients in the usual sense, French academic scientists were quite nakedly dependent on the state and on ministerial conceptions of their role. Until roughly 1830, Old Regime patterns remained largely intact. Science was dominated by the small, exclusive group of well-connected *savants* who held chairs in the major institutions of the capital. Aided by a restricted but growing body of professors in the science faculties of Napoleon's creation, the Université de France, these *savants* fulfilled only one essential state function: to conduct national examinations. They also taught, but usually to audiences in search of polite culture rather than students in search of formal qualifications. Research counted for little, especially in the provincial faculties, but those who chose to do original work could at least pursue it without fear of state interference. After 1832, however, the newly established Ministry of Public Instruction became increasingly active in determining the qualifications and defining the role of scientists who held chairs in the Université. Over the next two or three decades, the tradition of independent private patronage excercised within a state system increasingly gave way to close bureaucratic control. When in the Second Empire the expanding community of academic scientists quite suddenly came to regard the ministry as too intrusive and too concerned with ideological purity along nationalist lines, would-be reformers among them seized upon two strategies for reasserting their declining autonomy. First, they invoked the needs of research and the various international disciplinary communities to which they belonged. But the crucial state administrators were only fitfully and moderately responsive to this appeal. Second, frustrated reformers, especially in the provincial faculties of science, pinned their hopes on a potentially powerful force for change: the new market for expert technical advice and trained manpower in the emerging science-based chemical and electrical industries. After 1880, in the very different political and economic climate of the Third Republic, the Ministry of Public Instruction responded to the reformers' demands by bestowing an unprecedented degree of autonomy on the faculties in both Paris and the provinces. Ironically, however, many of the reformers soon found cause to regret the shift from dependence on the state bureaucracy to dependence on local political, commercial, and industrial elites. They were now obliged to perform as public advocates and salesmen of science before audiences that were even less sympathetic to the autonomy of learning than the once-despised state bureaucracy. By the coming of World War I, it was evident to leading research scientists in France that they had become more vulnerable than ever to outside scrutiny and "interference." One corollary of this change was, in their eyes, all too obvious. As the scientific community had grown larger and more inclusive, so the quality of its research had seemed to pale by comparison with the brilliant achievements of French science in the late eighteenth and early nineteenth centuries. The stature of French science had declined and international leadership had slipped from its hands precisely when and to the extent that academic scientists had become increasingly less "dependent" on the central state.

In Part II of this collection, attention shifts from engineers and scientists to more or less marginal medical men who sought to improve their professional fortunes by appealing to the French state. Toby Gelfand's essay argues that surgeons and barber-surgeons constituted a "monarchical" profession in eighteenth-century France. On his account, the surgical profession—at once hierarchical and inclusive, bureaucratic and corporative—reflected the structure of the royal state to which it owed its existence. Beginning in the 1720s, royal legislation created a national network of surgical *communautés* over which the king's personal or *premier* surgeon officially presided, while delegating de facto authority to crown-appointed lieutenants in each surgical *communauté*. These *communautés*, corresponding for the most part to royal juridical subdivisions, effectively controlled the licensing of ordinary practitioners and the regulation of ordinary medical practice in the region. Thus certified by the state, the surgeons and barber-surgeons occupied a legitimate if modest place in the great chain of professions in the Old Regime, and they operated in de facto autonomy from their nominal superiors, the university-educated physicians. In telling this story, Gelfand disputes current conceptions of when, how, and why a legitimate medical profession emerged from the allegedly futile efforts of earlier healers. He replaces current schemes with his model of a premodern but formally organized and legitimate profession of "ordinary practitioners." In the transition to modern medicine, one sort of profession was replaced by another as the "monarchical" profession of ordinary practitioners gave way before a more collegial, homogeneous, and exclusive group of "general practitioners" who increasingly held medical degrees, shared a standardized educational background, and came from a similar and higher social class. In France, as we shall see further in Matthew Ramsey's essay, the Napoleonic state played a major role in this transformation of the medical profession.

Introduction

Jan Goldstein's essay carries the themes of this volume directly into the realm of ideas and ideology. Indeed, most of her essay consists of a bracing exercise in intellectual history, as she explicates the theory of "moral contagion" and traces its development from the eighteenth century onward. Yet she also insists that the concept of moral contagion should be seen not only or even mainly as an attempt to provide a scientific explanation of a puzzling phenomenon but more deeply as an expression of the statist orientation of French psychiatrists or *médecins-aliénistes*. At a time when psychiatrists were trying to define and legitimate their still nascent professional identity, the state and its traditions of "political medicine" exercised a powerful appeal. The concept of moral contagion, as those who espoused it often pointed out, was closely analagous to the concept of physical contagion. And the analogy could be extended in such a way that the therapeutic program for "nervous" or "psychic" epidemics seemed to require the same close alliance between medical professionals and the state that had long existed in the imposition of quarantines for plague and other contagious somatic diseases. The theory of moral contagion thus allowed medical professionals to broaden the sphere in which they could serve as "epidemic-fighters" deputized by the state and exercising the unequivocal authority that flowed to them as its agents. In the 1860s, French officials became so concerned about an epidemic of "demonic seizures" in a village in the newly annexed and politically volatile region of Savoy that they delegated to psychiatrists the full authority of the state, including even the direct use of police and military forces. The longstanding statist orientation of writers on moral contagion—with roots in the "absolutist" Old Regime—thus yielded a spectacularly explicit success during the Second Empire. Goldstein argues that, in the case study presented here, the formation of professional knowledge and the strategy of professional legitimation were thoroughly intertwined. French physicians and, later, psychiatrists, were particularly motivated to develop the theory of moral contagion—and thus to claim expertise in the treatment of collective mental disorders—because of the benefits of collaboration with the state which that theory entailed.

Part III of this volume consists of a single essay by Matthew Ramsey. It, too, concerns the medical profession and sometimes alludes to issues already addressed in the papers by Gelfand and Goldstein. But Ramsey's central theme is quite different from theirs, and his systematically comparative approach also makes his essay distinct from the rest. His chief aim is to offer a novel interpretation of professional monopoly in Western medicine. Current explanations have usually assumed that it is sufficient to point to the cognitive superiority and instrumental efficacy of modern "scientific" medicine in the late nineteenth century or to the power of the organized medical profession. Without denying that these two factors played a role, Ramsey insists throughout his essay on the importance of broader political values and institutions, especially with respect to economic freedom and regulation of trades.

What connects Ramsey's essay to the rest of this volume is his insistence that professional power, even in medicine, depends importantly on "political culture," including particularly the role of the state. In his discussion of the French case, Ramsey emphasizes that the Napoleonic state granted officially licensed practitioners a strict de jure monopoly over medical practice in 1803, long before the Pasteurian revolution in bacteriology or the other triumphs of modern "scientific" medicine. In doing so, the Napoleonic state joined the revolutionaries in rejecting the corporate institutions of the Old Regime: the state would henceforth license practitioners as individuals. At the same time, however, the state restored order in place of the brief revolutionary experiment with medical "free enterprise." Legal medical practice was henceforth restricted to state-licensed practitioners, and the state assumed full responsibility for prosecuting the unlicensed. During the Napoleonic Wars, this strict de jure model determined or greatly influenced medical legislation in the territories annexed to or conquered by France. Outside the "French sphere," which shrank after 1815, medical practice legislation was less strict. In fact, during the middle decades of the nineteenth century several countries or territories adopted a "free field" model of medical regulation, much closer in spirit to the revolutionary than the Napoleonic model. Much of Ramsey's essay is devoted to an analysis of the rise and fate of the four most prominent of these "free fields": England after 1858, the United States from around 1830 to around 1880, Germany from 1871 to 1939, and three Swiss cantons beginning in the last quarter of the nineteenth century. Despite important differences from one another, by virtue of shifting national tendencies in ideology, political alignments, and professional organization, these free fields derived from a common impulse—the liberal challenge to the institutions that had supported monopoly and inhibited free trade: privileged corporations and the bureaucracy of the paternalistic state, which used its police powers to restrict its subjects' activities for their own good. When and where liberalism was sufficiently strong, medical libertarianism could prevail, in some cases long after the rise of modern scientific medicine.

Ramsey's essay, because of its international scope, highlights the distinctive features of the French situation. It reminds us of how different professionalization looks in France as opposed to the Anglo-American context, on which so much attention has been lavished. But Ramsey also shows that even a rigid division into strong-state versus weak-state ideal types does not hold up when tested closely against the historical record. In the Germanies, despite a strong-state tradition and tight government control over the activities of the medical profession, a free field was adopted at the height of the liberal wave of the third quarter of the nineteenth century, first in Prussia and then in the Second Reich. What is more, the free field survived for decades after that wave had crested, for reasons that can be understood only through a close examination of the political contest over free enterprise in German medicine. In France, where the state controlled medical licensing, qualified physicians nonetheless remained essentially autonomous within their sphere, being allowed to practice as they wished, free (until Vichy) of any official state mechanism for professional discipline.

In this respect, medicine remained considerably more independent than a number of other French professions, including engineering and science, as shown in the essays by Fox and Weiss. Yet French physicians still owed much of their power and status to a strong centralized state. Their institutions were imposed and sustained from above, not created from below, as in the United States. Ramsey's essay thus ultimately confirms the conclusion that emerges from this volume as a whole and that deserves repeating here: in France, professional "autonomy," power, and success virtually required "dependence" on the state. John Weiss and Robert Fox establish that point in the case of nineteenth-century engineers and scientists. Toby Gelfand shows that it applies even to "lowly" surgeons and barber-surgeons in the Old Regime. Jan Goldstein confirms it in the case of a nascent profession of psychiatry. Elsewhere, Charles Gillispie draws much the same conclusion from his study of scientists and related professional groups at the end of the Old Regime.[10]

It remains to be seen whether this conclusion will prove universally applicable even for France. For it must be admitted that this volume focuses on precisely those professions—engineering, science, and medicine—that have already attracted the most attention from historians of France.[11] It does virtually nothing to repair our still woeful ignorance of the history of such major professional groups as lawyers, notaries, and architects. Even the clergy, the military, and the bureaucracy itself have gone largely unexamined, despite their conspicuous role in French history.[12] This volume thus appears at a propitious time, when interest in the history of professions in France is beginning to accelerate but before most professional groups have begun to receive proper attention and before the central issues have been settled or even very clearly defined. The opportunities for further research are thus both exciting and daunting. But in the wake of this volume, we have a right to expect that this further research will keep its eyes firmly fixed on the central role of the state in professionalization in France.

Notes

1. For a fuller discussion of this point and access to the pertinent literature, see Magali Sarfatti Larson, *The Rise of Professionalism: A Sociological Analysis* (Berkeley and Los Angeles, 1977), esp. pp. 190–99.
2. Talcott Parsons, "Professions," in *International Encyclopedia of the Social Sciences*, ed. David L. Sills (New York, 1968), 12:536–47, quotation on p. 545.
3. Ibid., including the sources cited in Parsons's bibliography, pp. 546–47; Bernard Barber, "Some Problems in the Sociology of the Professions," *Daedalus* 92 (1963): 669–86; Howard M. Vollmer and Donal L. Mills, eds., *Professionalization* (Englewood Cliffs, N.J., 1966); Wilbert E. Moore, *The Professions: Roles and Rules* (New York, 1970).
4. This image dominates even Larson's *Rise of Professionalism*, despite the care and sophistication with which she sometimes qualifies it. For other examples of the "anti-Parsonian" literature, see Jethro K. Lieberman, *The Tyranny of the Experts: How Professionals Are Closing the Open Society* (New York, 1970); Terence J. Johnson, *Professions and Power* (London, 1972), esp. pp. 22–37; E. Richard Brown, *Rockefeller Medicine Men: Medicine and Capitalism in America* (Berkeley, 1979); and Burton Bledstein, *The Culture of Professionalism: The Middle Class and the Development of Higher Education in America* (New York, 1976).
5. See Matthew Ramsey, "History of a Profession, *Annales* Style: The Work of Jacques Léonard," *Journal of Social History*, vol. 17, no. 2 (1983–84), esp. his long note 9; and the first several pages of John H. Weiss's essay in this volume, where he stresses the tendency of Marxist scholars to focus on the stratifying effect of capitalism while minimizing the role of professions and the state.
6. See William H. Sewell, Jr., "*Etat, corps*, and *ordre*: Some Notes on the Social Vocabulary of the Old Regime," *Sozialgeschichte Heute: Festschrift für Hans Rosenberg*, ed. Hans-Ulrich Wehler (Göttingen, 1974), pp. 49–68.
7. My conception of the issues covered in this paragraph and the next owes much to correspondence and discussion with the contributors to this volume, especially Matthew Ramsey and John Weiss. Among other things, in private correspondence with me, Ramsey has pointed out the need to add qualifiers or modifiers to the French terms *profession* (any occupation) and *un professionnel*

Introduction   11

(one who does something for a living) to capture their current Anglo-Saxon connotations. Weiss reports that at a recent conference in Paris on "Social Taxonomies as Ideology" the French participants repeatedly insisted that the American occupational category "professionals" was "completely meaningless" to them. Finally, it is worth noting that although Michel Foucault's notion of "disciplines" can be compared in some ways to Anglo-Saxon conceptions of "profession," Foucault does not himself develop the comparison. Given the central theme of this volume, that is unfortunate, for Foucault sees his "disciplines" as depending on collaboration with the state as well as a number of other institutions, including the nuclear family and private philanthropies. See Jan Goldstein, "Foucault among the Sociologists: The 'Disciplines' and the History of the Professions," *History and Theory*, May 1984.

8. See Bledstein, *Culture of Professionalism*.
9. This developing convergence is particularly noticeable in recent studies of professionalism in Germany. There is, for example, at least one collective effort to treat a range of professions in Germany, with abundant references to the Anglo-American literature. See the special issue of *Geschichte und Gesellschaft* 6 (1980): no. 3: *Professionalisierung in historischer Perspektive*, ed. Hans-Ulrich Weber. See also R. Steven Turner, "The *Bildungsbürgertum* and the Learned Professions in Prussia, 1770–1830: The Origins of a Class," *Histoire Sociale/Social History* 13 (1980): 105–35; and Dietrich Ruschemeyer, *Lawyers and Their Society: A Comparative Study of the Legal Profession in Germany and the United States* (Cambridge, Mass., 1973).
10. Charles C. Gillispie, *Science and Polity in France at the End of the Old Regime* (Princeton, 1980).
11. It deserves emphasizing that the contributors to this volume have themselves produced an appreciable portion of the existing literature on engineers, scientists, and doctors in France. Their essays below offer extensive references to the entire body of literature. Restricting attention here solely to books, the important studies include Gillispie, *Science and Polity*; Robert Fox and George Weisz, eds., *The Organization of Science and Technology in France, 1808–1914* (Cambridge, 1980); Toby Gelfand, *Professionalizing Modern Medicine: Paris Surgeons and Medical Science and Institutions in the Eighteenth Century* (Westport, Conn., 1980); John H. Weiss, *The Making of Technological Man: The Social Origins of French Engineering Education* (Cambridge, Mass., 1982); Terry Shinn, *L'Ecole Polytechnique, 1794–1914: Savoir scientifique et pouvoir social* (Paris, 1980); Jean-Pierre Goubert, *Malades et médecines en Bretagne, 1770–1790* (Paris, 1974); and Jacques Léonard's massive *thèse d'état*, *Les médecins de l'Ouest au XIXe siècle*, 3 vols. (Paris, 1978).
12. The still scant, if rapidly growing, literature on these professional groups includes Lenard Berlanstein, *The Barristers of Toulouse in the Eighteenth Century* (Baltimore, 1975); Jean-Pierre Royer, Renée Martinage, and Pierre Lecocq, *Juges et notables au XIXe siècle* (Paris, 1982); Jean-Louis Magnan, *Le notariat et le monde moderne* (Paris, 1979); Theodore Zeldin, *France, 1848–1945*, vol. 1 (Ox-

ford, 1973), chap. 3 (on notaries) and chap. 8 (on bureaucrats); Raymonde Moulin et al., *Les architectes: Métamorphose d'une profession libérale* (Paris, 1973); Timothy Tackett, *Priest and Parish in Eighteenth-Century France: A Social and Political Study of Curés in a Diocese of Dauphiné, 1750–1791* (Princeton, 1977); Ezra N. Suleiman, *Politics, Power, and Bureaucracy in France* (Princeton, 1974); Suleiman, *Elites in French Society: The Politics of Survival* (Princeton, 1978); and Guy Thuillier, *Bureaucratie et bureaucrates en France au XIXe siècle* (Geneva, 1980).

… PART ONE

Engineers,
Scientists,
and
Academics

1
JOHN H. WEISS

Bridges and Barriers: Narrowing Access and Changing Structure in the French Engineering Profession, 1800–1850

Although the "democratization" of French society supposedly brought by political change, industrialization, and educational reforms has long been pictured as less than pervasive, recent scholarship has begun to show just how distant France has been from meritocracy or an egalitarian distribution of rewards. The paths of social ascent have been steep and little-traveled; the sizes of the pie wedges given to various social classes have been remarkably constant. Whether one judges the process by the rate of individual advances or by the shares of groups as a whole, the pattern has been one of slow upward mobility and a constant proportion of social rewards. Adéline Daumard's studies reveal that "the pyramid of wealth remained constant" and that, especially in business elites, a relatively open access by individuals from below during the early part of the nineteenth century gave way before World War I to a tendency by the higher reaches of the *patronat* to "perennialize themselves."[1] Jane Marceau argues that even during the prosperous "modernization" in the Fourth and Fifth Republics the distribution of rewards among social groups remained the same and that "a commercial and industrial bourgeoisie remained culturally, socially, and economically dominant."[2] Monique De Saint-Martin has presented further evidence that even in the field seemingly most promising for the promotion of meritocracy, scientific education, inequalities in the patterns of access and performance continue to favor disproportionately the higher strata.[3] The problem, then, seems to be the explanation not of the change but of the persistence in the French pattern of social stratification.[4]

15

Examining the history of professions has lately gained prominence as one possible way to approach this question. Professions have often documented their conflicts over membership, exclusion, and autonomy in more explicit and precise ways than have broader groups such as classes or strata. Because claims about intellectual qualifications usually play an important role in such struggles, the study of the professions can benefit from recent research about the way cultural knowledge and cultural styles have helped to "reproduce" the social structure. Especially in the work of Pierre Bourdieu and Jean-Claude Passeron, whose *Les héritiers*, published in 1964, marked something of a new departure in French scholarly and popular thinking about the relationship between education and social stratification, attention has shifted to the way "cultural capital" (academic diplomas, cultural knowledge associated with high status) was acquired, safeguarded, and increased by families who either already possessed it or had acquired other forms of capital, economic (money and property) and social (network of social contacts).[5] Although Bourdieu and Passeron have studied other activities, such as museum visits and moviegoing, in their view the chief responsibility for promoting this preservation and accumulation of cultural capital still lies with the ostensibly meritocratic educational system. The difficulty is that their analysis does not fully explain how the educational system that transmits this culture can itself change, or how it can respond to external changes from industrialization or new state policies so as to continue to perform the same "reproducing," mobility-limiting, class-maintaining functions. In short, the role of "cultural capital" in social stratification must be tested against history.

In examining how a single profession, French engineers, became stratified during the first half of the nineteenth century, this study hopes to contribute to an understanding of how French society as a whole became stratified. My general conclusion is that the perspectives on the profession's history presented below all reveal a "narrowing": the emergence of limitations on access to recognized status as an *ingénieur* and the development of a more closed, inward-looking profession.[6]

To understand the processes that produced this result, the present study takes as its organizing principle the role of the state in social stratification. This is a surprisingly underexplored subject. Those who reject the view that the higher orders maintained their power and prestige through a benign process of integrating the population under the guidance of the dominant value orientations have focused their attention upon capitalism, rather than the state, as the main causal agent. And they have seen civil society, clearly separate from the state, as the decisive arena of combat.

Such critics have tended to depreciate the autonomous stratifying power of state action and to view the state as a manipulatable superstructure. Only recently have such writers come to suggest that "the bureaucratic phenomenon is the germ of a new and permanent class division" or to speak of "the potential autonomy of the State" and "State-created elites."[7]

The case of French engineers provides at least three tests for this latter line of argument. (1) Almost all those attending the dominant Parisian engineering schools were products of secondary education (*enseignement secondaire*). The state's control over *enseignement secondaire* allowed it to control the distribution of high-status cultural capital and to manipulate the market for that capital by changing the system of examinations and degrees. (2) The French engineering profession has lineages that extend back to the absolutist state, expressed best in the survival of the various engineering *corps*. The recasting of the *corps* structure in the nineteenth century allowed high-level government engineers to maintain their professional dominance when faced with pressures to yield some of their positions to those from below. (3) Beginning in the nineteenth century, however, not all members of the profession came to share this lineage in the same way. In a time of accelerated industrialization and political change state-employed engineers were confronted with new groups claiming the title of *ingénieur* but employed by private industry. The investigation of the stratification of French engineering, then, must deal not only with the changing nature of the state *corps*, both elites and subordinate functionaries, but also with the struggles between state and private engineers for control of the profession and the economy.

Engineers and the Classics: The Cultural Unification of the Functionary Elite

Despite its extraordinary influence on French society, the *baccalauréat* (roughly, "bachelor's degree") still awaits a comprehensive historical study. A scattering of limited treatments and collections of official documents nevertheless reveals the broad outlines of its role in French stratification during the first half of the nineteenth century. As it became the key to success in an ever-growing number of careers, the *baccalauréat-ès-lettres* also became the principal device with which a Latin-based education regained much of the influence it had lost at the end of the eighteenth century.[8] Engineering educators and their allies held out against this influence longer than their counterparts in many other fields, but by the 1850s they had lost the most important battles.

The *baccalauréat* was revived as part of the decree of 17 March 1808, which detailed the regulations of the Université Impériale de France. Articles 16 and 17 empowered the Faculties of Letters and Sciences to grant the degrees after public examinations. Article 19 provided, however, that candidates were to be examined "on what is taught in the upper classes of the *lycées*."[9] Not higher education but secondary education would determine the content of the examination, which eventually became "the coronation and confirmation of *enseignement secondaire*."[10]

The most controversial provision concerning the new degree appeared for the first time in a decree of 18 October 1818. Article 5 stipulated that before a student could be given the examination he had to produce a certificate attesting to at least two years of study in a *lycée*. Here was a clear reflection of the pressure that the *lycées* were feeling from the competition of the private *écoles secondaires*. Here also was a challenge to all those suspicious of a state monopoly on education. As the importance of the *baccalauréat* began to be appreciated, the campaign against forced attendance at *lycées* made allies of previous opponents: those who thought the *lycées* were too religious and those who thought their religion was not strict enough, those who preferred the Jesuits and those who wished to educate their children at home. In fact, the exceptions to the decree proved more productive than the central provisions: the prosperity of the *petits seminaires*, which ostensibly delivered secondary education only to future clergymen, was assured once a decree of 1809 exempted their students from both the two-year requirement and the examination fees.[11] The governments of the Restoration and the July Monarchy could never bring themselves openly to abandon the requirement. They oscillated instead between exceptions, such as for those who certified that they had studied with a "father, uncle, or brother," and attempts to limit the fraud that such exemptions facilitated.[12] The requirement of previous attendance at a *lycée* was finally abolished for good on 16 November 1849 during the educational reforms of the Second Republic that culminated in the Falloux Law.[13]

By that time, however, the *baccalauréat* had all but achieved the domination of the educational process that it holds to this day. But in its first years few seem to have taken it very seriously. The juries could test as many as eight students at a time, which made the examinations more like a small class. Only a one-half-hour oral examination was required.[14] The mathematician and educational expert Antoine Cournot recalled that "no one paid much attention to the *baccalauréat* during the Empire or the first years of the Restoration."[15] In the five years between 1810 and 1814 the Paris Faculty of Letters awarded only 490 *bachelier-ès-lettres* diplomas.[16]

As soon as the new degree was created, however, education officials began a campaign to build up its mystique and power. A circular of 5 April 1810 stipulated, for example, that the rector of the local academy (that is, the grouping of the various faculties) must attend the examinations in person in order "to give more gravity and solemnity to the proceedings." Another of 1 October 1808 stated that the degrees were awarded "in the name of the emperor," in the same manner that the Restoration later specified that they were given "in the name of the king." On 15 September 1820 the length of the examination was extended to "at least three-quarters of an hour." Each candidate was to be examined individually. The examinations were public, and the method by which the public should be informed of their occurrence was minutely specified.[17]

The power of the *baccaulauréat* rested first in its control over entrance to further education. Articles 25 through 27 of the decree of 17 March stated that the *baccalauréat-ès-lettres* degree was required for enrollment in the faculties of theology, law, and medicine.[18] At least in the case of the faculties of law and medicine, however, the requirement does not seem to have been rigorously enforced; the Restoration announced the same rule in an ordinance of 5 July 1820 as if it were an innovation.[19] The relatively small number of students who wished to obtain the more advanced degrees (*licence* and *doctorat*) offered by the faculties of letters and sciences were also required to obtain first the appropriate *baccalauréats*.[20]

The requirement to be a *bachelier* was extended to other careers as well. The original statute of 1808 had made careers in the Université the preserve of the *baccalauréat* by requiring the degree for almost all teaching and administrative posts. Even the heads of private secondary schools were required to obtain it. A decree of 9 April 1809 marked off another career by making the degree a requirement for admission to the diocesan seminaries.[21] It was also necessary to have the degree of *bachelier-ès-lettres* to be appointed conservator of a public library. Finally, the *Code universitaire* published in 1835 refers to an ordinance stipulating that all printers (*imprimeurs*) and "inspectors of the book trade" (*inspecteurs de la libraire*) must obtain the degree.[22]

These were the professions in which the *baccalauréat* came to guard the gate during the years between 1808 and 1820. Later on almost all posts in the French bureaucracy, and most other professional schools, would require at least the *baccalauréat-ès-lettres*, which thus became one of the most powerful stratifying devices in French society.

Nothing less than a general history of postrevolutionary French society would fully explain how the *baccalauréat* came to play the role that it did. What is clear is that Napoleon and his counselors, as well as their Bourbon and Orleanist successors, were determined to forge an ordered and hierarchical structure—whether corporatist, bureaucratic, or a blend of the two—out of the social "chaos" inherited from the revolutionary decade, when the liberal professions had been deprived of their corporate organizations, quacks threatened to overwhelm "legitimate" medicine, and independently minded, uncertainly qualified *école centrale* professors had replaced the clerical teaching orders.[23] The decrees on the *baccalauréat* were an integral part of the efforts to use the powers of the state to recast the French occupational structure. In his first major reorganization of the Université Napoleon decreed on 15 November 1811 that "the Council of the Université will present a plan in which it will indicate on what professions it will be appropriate to impose the obligation of taking degrees at the various faculties."[24] In the edition of his *Code universitaire* published in 1835, Ambroise Rendu, who began his career under Napoleon and survived through two more regimes as the Université's greatest expert on educational law, revealed clearly the upgrading and protecting functions of the *baccalauréat*:

Since that decree twenty-three years have passed, during which the thirst for knowledge and the need to test those who acquire it have far from diminished. On the contrary, the form of government that we owe to the Charte was marvelously appropriate to make appreciated how much a serious and solid instruction is necessary for all those who would render worthy service to king and country. The Council of the Université has occupied itself since 1814 with the execution of this order [that of 15 November 1811]. . . . By reproducing here the principal provisions of the project presented in 1814 in response to that order, we hope to provoke useful reflections on this matter and to hasten the moment when public functionaries will have one more means of surrounding themselves with all the esteem that gives them influence.[25]

Professional groups and public administrators in fact found the tactics Rendu outlined, if perhaps not the higher goals, to be the basis for "useful reflections." They soon began to impose restrictions of their own. The politician and educational official Saint-Marc Girardin complained in 1846 that the land-registry administration (*enregistrement*) had just chosen to make the *baccalauréat* a condition of employment. He failed to see how the same degree could be used as a standard for future lawyers and for lowly registry clerks. The requirement had been imposed merely as "a barrier against the crowd of position-seekers."[26]

The *baccalauréat* shaped the French hierarchies of status and power in more subtle ways. It gave a semblance of meritocratic legitimacy to the social positions of functionaries and members of the liberal professions. At the same time, the legislation and public discussion concerning the *baccalauréat* gave them an opportunity to restate and extend their claims to the most honored positions in the French occupational structure. These "noneconomic" sectors of the French bourgeois stratum were thus not simply equal and parallel to those in the commercial and industrial specialties; they were distinctly superior. Even before the empire of the *baccalauréat* had spread to such places as the land registry, the customs office, and the forestry school, the supporters of the degree had begun slowly to expand its claims to be the anointing oil of French society. In 1808 and 1809 the decrees on the *baccalauréat* had confined themselves to a matter-of-fact list of the specific occupations for which it would be required. One of the earliest decrees of Louis XVIII's reign, that of 17 February 1815, drawn up by the philosopher and *doctrinaire* (Liberal) politician Pierre Paul Royer-Collard, spoke of *baccalauréats* to be granted to those in the "ecclesiastical, political, and civil professions." Was the degree to be required of those who became deputies? Of all functionaries? Royer-Collard did not elaborate. By 13 September 1820 a statute spoke of "the degree which offers entry to the *most important* professions."[27] In 1835 Rendu explained in the following manner the inclusion in the *Code universitaire* of a large number of details about the requirements for the *baccalauréat*:

We have reproduced exactly all the variations in legislation on this important point of the first university degree, that which gives entrance to all the high careers of social life [*toutes les hautes carrières de la vie sociale*]. We appreciate how necessary it is that a law finally determine in a decisive and consistent manner all the conditions for this degree. If these conditions were conscientiously fulfilled, the *baccalauréat-ès-lettres* would offer a real safeguard [*garantie*] to society; otherwise it would only be a joke or a lie.[28]

In the speech introducing his major bill on education to the 1841 session of the Chamber of Deputies, Minister of Public Instruction Abel Villemain, a professor of literature and an enthusiastic classicist, left no doubt about the beatific powers of the degree. Secondary education, "intimately linked to our origins, our memories, and our rational genius," had been "reestablished with éclat in the most glorious days of the Empire." Only the classical *enseignement secondaire*, "summed up and verified" by the *baccalauréat*, could give the country the "elite of capable and trained minds which the social order needs." That degree assured the "methodical and regular recruitment into all elective and appointive functions, all the liberal professions, all the highest enterprises that form, so to speak, the civil staff officers [*l'état-major civil*] of the country." Such occupations required a "select fund of knowledge" and a "veritable intellectual culture."[29] Nine years later claims that the *baccalauréat* consecrated "all the high careers of social life" and "the civil staff officers of the country" were accepted even by those who regretted the degree and wished to abolish it. In the course of an attack on the state's monopoly of education the prominent political economist Frédéric Bastiat declared in 1850 that "the law of our country decides that the *most honorable* careers will be closed to those who are not *bacheliers*."[30]

Only the study of a large sample of the decisions individual families made about education could begin to establish with certainty what were the effects of this expansion of the *baccalauréat*'s mystique, certifying power, and legitimizing rhetoric. The less direct evidence available suggests that this development had four consequences:

1. For the legal professions and the state bureaucracies the degree acted as a protective device. It ostensibly guaranteed a minimum of competence among those entering the professions; it certainly restricted their numbers. The Université's administrators did not set the degree requirements for every professional group—they did not have such authority—but they could effectively limit the total number of *bacheliers* produced. Thus after a series of circulars and ordinances in 1820 and 1821 made it more difficult to gain recognition for preparation outside a state school, required that the philosophy questions be delivered in Latin, and generally suggested that the rectors had been too lax in granting degrees, the number of *baccalauréats* awarded dropped from 3,286 (the mean for the years 1819–21) to 1,777 (the mean for 1822–24).[31]

2. The *baccalauréat* served not only as a barrier but as a unifying device. To use the language employed in R. P. DeDaineville's discussion of French officeholders, the *bacheliers* became part of the same community of status.[32] The members of the noneconomic, preindustrial sectors of the bourgeoisie were drawn together by the claims made for the degree they held in common.[33] The interests of both functionaries and members of the

liberal professions were identified with the general interests of society as a whole. Both groups claimed that theirs alone were the "political and civil professions," the "most honorable," the "high careers of social life." Only the *baccalauréat* conferred membership in these noble callings. To put the matter in somewhat schematic language, the noneconomic sector implicitly rejected a parallelism of status hierarchies; its members claimed to be superior to the commercial, agricultural, and industrial professions.[34] The *baccalauréat* was only the most formal, legally sanctioned source of their superiority, of course. The claims of classical education to a monopoly on disinterested knowledge and the traditional prestige of the servant of the state were the more general factors at work. The creation of the modern *baccalauréat* supplied a more specific, manipulatable cachet at a time when all the professions were undergoing important changes in their institutional structure.

3. In the eyes of certain groups in the economic sector likely to be influenced by these claims, such as the entrepreneurial elite of Mulhouse (of which there exists a detailed study on the matter), the *baccalauréat* became a highly visible, clearly defined means to acquire this status. A degree of status could be obtained merely by attending a *lycée* or *collège* long enough to acquire a certain patina of classical learning, of course, and many sons of the bourgeoisie were to undergo the experience without receiving a degree, but the *baccalauréat* had the additional advantage of giving access to careers. A nationally sanctioned degree was a tangible product with measurable benefits; it was also a bridge across the sectoral divide. On the other hand, the value placed on that product changed over time. Raymond Oberlé's study shows that during the period with which we are concerned here, and especially the first three decades of the century, Mulhouse entrepreneurs had little interest in either classical studies or the *baccalauréat*.[35]

4. On the other hand, the *baccalauréat* only reinforced the exclusionary effect of classical studies. Families who still saw education as an investment good designed to produce economic returns wanted something more practical than the classical curriculum, but the *baccalauréat-ès-lettres*, by providing the final justification for that curriculum, instead helped to entrench the traditional program. Most of the Université's officials, as well as its teaching corps, viewed their principal task as the furtherance of classical studies. Nonclassical programs, special courses, "attached schools," and other arrangements began slowly to appear, but they had to enter through the back door. The Université considered them temporary, embarrassing concessions to the demands of the moment.

Even before the demands of the economic sector for practical education began to make themselves felt, the problem of educating engineers challenged the votaries of the *baccalauréat*. Up to 1841 a heavy majority of the students in both state and private institutions of secondary education who prepared themselves for the École Polytechnique, the indispensable key to state engineering careers, ended their classical studies at the *troisième*.[36] Although this was three years short of the end of *baccalauréat* preparation, it gave the students enough Latin to cope with the *version latine*, the brief translation exercise which the classicists had managed to add to the entrance requirements in 1804.[37] The remaining three years—and often more because candidates usually failed in their first attempt—were devoted to intensive instruction in the mathematical subjects which held the central place in the Polytechnique examination. Yet it was clear that this school was recruiting from the very social groups Rendu had hoped to make part of the Université's clientele. In December 1841 the *Gazette spéciale de l'instruction publique*, spokesman for the Ministry of Public Instruction, published the first in a series of trial balloons which argued that the truncation of the engineers' classical education could not be allowed to continue. The first of its arguments demonstrates the way the *baccalauréat*'s gatekeeping power gathered its own momentum: because the *baccalauréat* was now required for so many careers, the students who failed the Polytechnique examination (only about one-fourth of each year's six-hundred-odd candidates gained admission) would be unemployable, "a disappointment to their families," a "crowd of dissatisfied youth" whose "distressing position" was unhealthy for society.[38] Even for those who succeeded, a long diet restricted to "theorems, solutions, and formulas" could have dire psychological consequences:

These youth, accustomed to the rigorous deduction of the exact sciences, judge poorly all that does not fit the abstract formulas with which their memories and intelligence are exclusively furnished, and consequently [they judge poorly] all that serves as a basis for political, religious, and domestic society, all that gives charm in prosperity and consolation in unhappiness, all that nourishes the soul and heart and exalts the most noble passions for the Good, the Beautiful, the Just, and the Divine. These youth thus concoct a host of prejudices about the realities of the moral world in which they must live, and which certainly is not ruled by mathematical laws, about the truths of ethics and religion which should rule the acts of their disorderly will, about the beauties of literature and art which lend charm [*charme*] to men who have had a normal development and a well-directed education, and even about the political and civil laws which govern us, and which, imperfect as they may be, must be respected and obeyed if society is to survive.

Many facts can certainly be brought to the support of these assertions: it will suffice to recall that it is from among the students of our government technical schools that Saint-Simon and Fourier found their most ardent disciples.[39]

Society could maintain its equilibrium, then, only if its ruling classes had imbibed a full, *baccalauréat*-certified measure of the classical humanities. Only the acquisition of that degree, moreover, could guarantee the infusion of *charme*, with its associations of enchantment, glamour, and seductive fascination.[40] This particular bank of cultural capital apparently required a monopoly to work its beneficent effects upon society. Speaking to more mundane concerns, the *Gazette* also noted that requiring the *baccalauréat-ès-lettres* for Polytechnique entry would undoubtedly create a need to expand the advanced classes in the existing public secondary schools and to add upper grades to other schools in the state-supported system which had not yet become "full-course colleges."[41] As the Ministry of Public Instruction contemplated the expansion of its domain, institutional interests and the interests of society neatly coincided.

The campaign to add the Polytechnique to the *baccalauréat*'s trophy list did not go unchallenged.[42] Armand Carrel's oppositionist and vaguely Republican *Le National* feared a reduction in the quality of French leadership if the new requirement reduced the number of candidates for the Polytechnique.[43] Eleven heads of private secondary institutions (faced, incidentally, with the need to find instructors for advanced Latin classes) deplored the decline in both literary and classical studies that would result from the need for intensive cramming for both *baccalauréat* and Polytechnique examinations.[44]

The most extensive reply to the Ministry of Public Instruction's initiative came from A. Bobin, the official in the War Ministry's Bureau of Military Schools who was charged with supervision of the affairs of the Polytechnique.[45] In a pamphlet published in the summer of 1842 Bobin presented the case for maintaining the independence from Université requirements that the Polytechnique had enjoyed during its first glorious half-century of existence. In the first place, he argued, the requirement of the *baccalauréat-ès-lettres* would weaken the meritocratic strain in the school's recruitment.[46] The additional studies needed for the new examination could only lengthen the period of schooling, imposing an additional burden on "families of modest means," who would thereby be prevented from sending to the Polytechnique their potential contributions to the "elite of today's youth." The *baccalauréat*, moreover, was a locally graded examination, open to "the power of local influences and patterns of collusion"; the Polytechnique competitions were immune to such distortions. Even if one granted that highly developed literary skills were needed by Polytechniciens—and Bobin doubted that all men who could render the country service as *savants* and engineers were equally endowed with superior literary aptitudes—the prevailing *secondaire* curriculum was hardly the way to import such skills: "Does [the *Gazette spéciale*] really think it is essential to gorge oneself with translations of Latin authors or to consume precious time in composing bad poetry?" Far better to study the rules of composition and the "art of developing ideas," both of which were taught in the Polytechnique's own courses on French literature. Under the current system even those who never reached the school benefited by the scientific studies they had made in competing for entry:

Will they not wish to begin equally secure and lucrative careers in industry, commerce, arts, and especially agriculture, where men of knowledge and intelligence are in such short supply? Would not such fields of endeavor be honored and fecundated by these men? Let us remember the words of Monge: "the Ecole Polytechnique multiplies useful men, even outside its walls." . . . [And what will happen if unsuccessful candidates are also *bacheliers*?] Should we not fear that such men, rather than making the wisest choice by turning their scientific learning to industrial, financial, commercial, and agricultural careers, will instead fling themselves into journalism, literature, and teaching, [influenced by] a perspective which flatters the imagination of youth but which only offers it rewards as limited as they are uncertain? And if all the excess from the Polytechnique competition directed itself to the liberal careers [*les carrières libérales*], would this not give trouble? Does anyone think, by chance, that our law schools, medical schools, pharmacy schools, etc., lack customers? Are we not learning of new attempts to restrict their enrollments?

Thus little was to be feared from those with a scientific education, even the "disappointed aspirants" to the Polytechnique; they could only be useful to society. And little was to be feared from the Ecole Polytechnique, as presently constituted, but to "submit it to the yoke of the Université" would be to remove its "special, liberal character."[47] Whether he drew his inspiration from Gaspard Monge or from Henri Saint-Simon, Bobin was convinced that the technological man of the nineteenth century needed algebraic analysis more than ablative absolutes.[48]

The debate over the *baccalauréat* requirement in the Chamber of Deputies on 26 May 1842 contained many of the same themes found in Bobin or the *Gazette spéciale*, but it also revealed details about the conflict over the matter within the French government. Marshal Soult, the minister of war, had just announced that the *baccalauréat-ès-lettres* would be required of all candidates entering the Polytechnique competition after 1844. The astronomer François Arago led the counterattack against this "grave threat" to his alma mater, which he was later to call "not just a school but a social institution, one of the great achievements of the Revolution."[49] The new regulation would exclude too many capable candidates who could not afford the extra preparation. It would also introduce a damaging rigidity into the admissions system, which had developed procedures to "compensate" for deficiencies in literary ability when a candidate coupled them with "discoveries" or "outstanding scientific capacities." He claimed that without such flexibility the great mathematician Denis Poisson would never have been admitted. In describing the internal maneuvering over the new policy, he announced that both the principal governing councils of the Polytechnique, the Council of Instruction (made up of the school's faculty) and the Council on Improvements (composed of the heads of the state services supplied by the school and other scientific notables) had unanimously rejected the proposal. Never before had changes in the admissions conditions been introduced against the will of these bodies, but this time Soult had not even bothered to answer the letters they had sent him on the matter. The new policy, moreover, would allow the Ministry of Public Instruction to become the "real arbiter" of the Ecole, undermining an independence from the Université deliberately reestablished after the Revolution of 1830. In support of Arago, Paul-François Dubois, deputy from Nantes who taught literature at the Polytechnique, declared that officials in the Université had been making periodic attempts to impose the *baccalauréat* since 1838 and had heretofore been "repulsed." In his reply to Arago and Dubois at the end of the debate the minister of public instruction, Villemain, came to the support of Soult by justifying the "warning to the families" about the projected change with a succinct assertion of the degree's stratifying mission: "If we require the diploma of *bachelier-ès-lettres*, it is because we desire that the young men of the Polytechnique be able to be called one day to high social positions [*hautes positions sociales*], and that a complete program of classical studies is the best way to arrive at this result."[50]

The struggle continued, but the "warning" had its desired effect upon Polytechnique candidates and their families. Although Arago, Bobin, and their allies continued to win delays in the imposition of an absolute *baccalauréat-ès-lettres* requirement, each year the proportion of *bacheliers* entering the school increased.[51] As a compromise between imposing the degree and total opposition, the Polytechnique began to offer "extra points" (*majorations*) to candidates who had the *lettres baccalauréat*, and by 1860 three-fourths of those admitted had the degree.[52]

The classicists' *Gleichschaltung* of the dominant institution in the French engineering profession was not the last episode in the cultural unification of the French elite, however. The Polytechnique's chief rival, the Ecole Centrale des Arts and Manufactures, gave no special preference to a Latin degree: as late as the eve of World War I only 61 percent of its students had studied any Latin.[53] Nor did the other important technical schools for engineers, the *écoles d'arts et métiers*, require the classical *baccalauréat* from their students, who were of distinctly more humble backgrounds.[54] The battle continued on through the century, attaining new complexity as engineers debated not only the value of Latin in the acquisition of *culture générale* but also the role of mathematics as a surrogate for (or supplement to) Latin, as well as a host of other pedagogical options presented as part of the formation of the ideal engineer.[55]

The Corps des Ponts et Chaussées: Consolidation and Exclusion

State action influenced the constitution and outlook of French social strata not only by the way the cultural and political offensive of one ministry could influence the formation of the clientele of another. Equally important was the state's practice of establishing *corps* of professional functionaries. To suggest some of the many possible methods of investigating this phenomenon, I will consider next the case of the largest nonmilitary engineering group, the Corps des Ponts et Chaussées.

Despite the official dissolution of the corporate structure of the Old Regime by the Le Chapelier Law of 1791, the Corps of Engineers of the Ponts et Chaussées, founded in 1716, retained its integrity. The responsibility for its survival may be laid to the political skill of its patrons, Jean-Rodolphe Perronet and Lamblardie, its provision of managerial and planning functions badly needed to maintain and expand the roads and bridges upon which the Revolution marched (accomplishing this feat at far less expense than would have resulted from recourse to private entrepreneurs), and its physical dispersal throughout the Republic, which made it a weak framework for conspiracy or collective action.[56] The relatively *roturier* social profile of the Corps may also have been important: the more heavily aristocratic military engineering corps lost heavily to emigration.[57] Perhaps because they were not at the top of the Old Regime's social pyramid, Ponts et Chaussées engineers had a chance to climb a more concrete one when General Bonaparte took seventeen of them on his expedition to Egypt.[58]

When the general became emperor, he rewarded the Ponts et Chaussées engineers' continuous service by a formal reconstitution of the Corps which recognized its semiautonomous position within the French state. A decree of 25 August 1804 established the Corps des Ponts et Chaussées, composed of 5 inspectors-general, 15 divisional inspectors, 134 engineers-in-chief (responsible for departments), 306 ordinary engineers, 15 "aspirants," and 60 student engineers. The titular head of the Corps was an appointed director-general, who reported directly to both the emperor and the Ministry of the Interior. The director-general, however, also had charge of the broader Administration des Travaux Publics, which conducted a wide range of public works activities. In matters relating to the Corps he presided over weekly meetings of a General Council composed of the five inspectors-general, five divisional inspectors, and an engineer-in-chief as secretary. Any other members of the Corps who happened to be in Paris had the right to attend the meetings in a consultative capacity.[59]

During the first half of the nineteenth century the Corps became something more than a bureaucratic subculture—a "shop" with a few quirks of language, attitude, and operating procedure—something less than a completely closed society-within-a-society. The association of its members started in the barracks-style (*caserné*) life of the Ecole Polytechnique, where each class of 100 to 150 students both learned solidarity and tasted the exercise of power in the system of *bizuthage*, of which a pale reflection remains today in the treatment given to plebes by upperclassmen at West Point.[60] Such ritual subordination found its compensation, for the *bizuths*, in the awareness that Polytechniciens were the Elect of French society. Those who met again at the Ecole des Ponts et Chaussées, moreover, knew they were an elite within an elite: 73 percent of those admitted to that school between 1830 and 1879 ranked at least tenth in their Polytechnique class.[61] At the Ponts et Chaussées school, which seldom contained more than seventy students in its three classes, cadet sergeants and corporals shared responsibility for the maintenance of order with a full-time inspector of studies. Cadets could not receive visitors at the school, and any absences had to be approved by the director.[62] The long hours in the lecture halls and drafting rooms and the carefully regimented life at the school were designed to temper the young Ponts engineer's character so that he would be able to withstand the contradictory pressures and physical trials of a professionally isolated life in the provinces. The best chance to test his mettle came during the summer months, when Ponts students were assigned to projects throughout the realm.[63] In all his training he was led to expect responsibility for supervising and planning tasks involving large sums, large groups of men, and considerable political difficulties from local interests.[64]

Upon leaving the school, the young engineer found that however much he might claim (and be awarded) elite status from society at large, his aspirations would be limited, his ambition sublimated and controlled, by the long years of patient, careful effort needed to climb the widely spaced rungs of his career ladder. The greater the number of ranks within the hierarchy, of course, the more limited were one's hopes for a rapid ascent and the greater the power of those in the higher echelons to manipulate and forestall the upward mobility of those below.[65] Starting as an "aspirant engineer," a Ponts officer received in 1829 (about the middle of the period under consideration) an annual salary of 1,800 francs, the same as a *maître d'études* (proctor-tutor, usually a recent *bachelier*) at a large Parisian secondary school, 200 francs less than an ordinary lieutenant in the military engineering corps. At the end of a normal career he could expect to become an engineer-in-chief, first class, with a salary of 5,000 francs, the same as a major (*chef de bataillon*) in the military corps or the headmaster of a medium-sized provincial *collège royal*.[66] Like state-employed teachers, military officers, and certain other functionaries, however, he also had the right to a pension, usually about one-third of his final salary.[67] The engineer's advancement was regulated by annual written evaluations by his superiors, against which the means of appeal were limited.[68] However routine the engineer's duties might be, especially in his early years, the practical training that completed his "formation" was officially considered to be an affair of long duration. When engineers began to request permission to leave the Corps to take positions in private industry (railroads, for example), it was decided that a minimum of five years' service in the field was necessary before an engineer was "adequately formed."[69]

Partly as compensation for the less-than-glorious salaries and slow advancement, the nineteenth-century Corps des Ponts et Chaussées developed a professional style and ethos inspired by the military officer corps. There was a certain irony in this emulation because under the Old Regime the Ponts et Chaussées had been concerned to establish its moral superiority to the army by scrupulously avoiding the sins of young, aristocratic military officers: indebtedness for gambling and high living; mingling public and private accounts such as by paying servants from an administrative budget; insubordination; wandering from the place of duty (engineers in the nineteenth-century Corps could not leave their departments except for authorized professional reasons); and, especially, a certain indifference to the need for assiduity in the discharge of professional obligations.[70] If avoiding such behavior reaffirmed the Corps' professionalism and utility to the state in the eighteenth century, it apparently did not sufficiently distinguish engineers' mores from the ethic of the proper nineteenth-century bourgeois. Other aspects of the military-aristocratic tradition were therefore not rejected but assimilated. As in the army, marriage plans, for example, had to be presented to the General Council for approval of the betrothed's background and dowry.[71] Refusal of a duel could bring blackballing from other members.[72] Wearing the uniform was obligatory at all times, even when conditions at the workplace made doing so a real hardship.[73] Obituaries spoke of engineers who died before retirement, whether by accident, violence, or a common illness, as *morts au champ d'honneur*.[74] Most significantly, association with commercial activity was considered a derogation. Entrepreneurship by an engineer and employment by an entrepreneur in a capacity that would jeopardize the engineer's personal reputation should the enterprise fail were both forbidden.[75]

The motivations behind a final aspect of the Corps' ethos, its desire to remain detached from politics (or at least to appear as such), did not arise merely from a wish to imitate the army. Certainly the experience of the Revolution, the Empire, and the Hundred Days argued for such detachment on the part of both Ponts engineers and army officers. In the case of the engineers, however, distance from *local* politics was equally crucial and constantly encouraged by the central administration.[76] Whatever its value for the creation of a constituency, immersion in local politics—in these years, the apogee of the *notables*' power; the distinction between politics and society was not easy to draw—threatened to divide the Corps and reduce its power as a whole. A single, unified Corps, a single social presence, represented by all members regardless of their rank or antecedents, was the image to be presented to the society at large. Even individual publications were discouraged and, technically, required advance approval. All members were enjoined to prevent their colleagues from taking any actions that might bring dishonor to the Corps.[77]

An ethos stressing the unity of the Corps acted as a means of preserving that body and ensuring that its members' status derived from a single source, service to the state, and found a single mode of expression, militarized scientific professionalism. Having survived the vagaries of the Revolution, the Corps received from Napoleon a structure which it constantly sought to strengthen and to adapt to the new responsibilities and problems brought by industrialization and political changes. During the first half of the century one of the most troubling attacks against this well-guarded bureaucratic and social fortification came not from outside the walls but from those who worked alongside the engineers every day: the *conducteurs des ponts et chaussées*.

The Corps of Conducteurs, 350 strong, was established by the same decree of 25 August 1804 that created the Corps des Ponts et Chaussées. Its members were charged with all types of surveillance, control, command, and project design to which an engineer might wish to assign them. Their professional lives have a distinctly modern cast: bureaucratic routines; thwarted individual ambition; long, often arduous service; enduring boredom; modest but genuine accomplishments; and not a little quiet desperation. The decree referred to them as a *corps*, but they had none of the autonomy and collective status granted to the engineers' grouping known by the same name: no Conseil Général to protect their interests, no higher officials of their own, no special school to attend to their training. To receive appointment as *conducteurs* candidates had to be twenty-one years old, to have worked at least two years as "supernumeraries" (for a nominal salary or none at all) in the offices of engineers-in-chief or divisional inspectors, and to present proof of their ability to read, write, calculate, measure volumes, and make outline drawings.[78] As their own representatives later put it, they worked "under the orders of and in absolute dependence upon" the engineers of the Ponts et Chaussées. They could communicate with higher authorities only with the endorsement of the engineer; his name alone appeared on projects, plans, and reports.[79]

Most important, they were barred from becoming *ingénieurs*. The higher Corps was open only to graduates of the Ecole Polytechnique, the only ones eligible to enroll in the Ecole des Ponts et Chaussées. Ability, imagination, technical skill, and proven managerial talent bought nothing without the credential from the "social institution" Arago and Dubois had defended so vigorously, purchased by years of expensive *secondaire* preparation. As the assistants to the Ponts engineers the *conducteurs* felt the weight of these educational obstacles with special sharpness, not as an episode in early adulthood to be forgotten in the distractions of the daily struggle but as a permanent, intrusive part of their existence.

As the activities of the Administration des Travaux Publics expanded during the four decades following Napoleon's decree, this closed, hierarchical organization came under strain. *Ingénieurs des ponts et chaussées* simply could not carry out all the tasks for which they were personally accountable; *conducteurs* were given considerable responsibility. The first independent evidence to this effect I have as yet uncovered dates from 1833, when a prefect in the Lozère complained that *conducteurs* seemed to be in charge of planning and directing all the public works in his department, but there are good reasons for believing that the practice was much older.[80] When the need for more *conducteurs* was considered in 1833, the total of those "in the permanent brigade" *(embrigadés)* was expanded to 603 at a time when the Corps of Engineers numbered 632.[81] In addition, the Administration began hiring growing numbers of *conducteurs auxiliaires*, who had neither pension rights nor security of tenure—a useful practice in view of the fluctuating budgets of the Bourbon and Orleanist regimes.

By 1839 the *conducteurs*' professional frustration began to be noticed. In a promotional publication aimed at those who determined the Administration and Corps' budget and perquisites, Henri-Charles Emmery, a divisional inspector of the Ponts et Chaussées, proposed a characteristic bureaucratic solution to the *conducteurs*' complaints that their efforts went unrewarded because they were barred from attaining the post of *ingénieur*. Rejecting the idea that one should become an *ingénieur* without attending the Polytechnique, he proposed that a new grade of *inspecteur* be interposed between *conducteur* and *ingénieur* to which especially meritorious *conducteurs* could aspire.[82] During the following year the *conducteurs* made their first collective statement, a petition to the Chamber of Deputies signed by twenty-nine men employed in the department of the Seine (Paris and environs). They expressed only dissatisfaction with Emmery's proposal. They already had a non-*ingénieur* career ladder that was long enough: three classes of *conducteurs auxiliaires* (at salaries from 1,000 to 1,400 francs) and three classes of *conducteurs embrigadés* (1,400–1,600 francs), with four-fifths of the Corps earning between 1,000 and 1,400 francs. What grieved them most was not the excessively low pay or the lack of pensions for the auxiliaries but the "insurmountable barrier that excludes us from the ordinary conditions of all employees who serve the state." The statute denying the title of *ingénieur* to anyone who had not attended the Polytechnique was a measure "contrary to our mores and to the Charter under which we live." In other public administrations—they cited finances, direct taxes, *domaines*, navy, artillery, military engineering, water and forests, and civil architecture—one could succeed "according to the knowledge acquired outside of the special schools and the latitude granted by the regulations of the particular administration." If a "private could become a marshal of France, why must the *conducteur* be denied the prospect of becoming an engineer?" *Conducteurs,* after all, were already officially performing the functions of engineers in France and the colonies "without receiving either the titles or the salaries."[83] The picture was accurate: by 1847 there were sixty-five cases of such a situation.[84]

In the same year, 1840, Alphonse Léon, *ingénieur des ponts et chaussées,* recommended another solution to the problem of *conducteur* advancement: the maximum age of entry to the Polytechnique should be raised to twenty-one for this category of official. They could then prepare like anyone else.[85] An anonymous *conducteur* quickly replied that none of them could possibly afford the costs of preparation for entry and maintenance at the school. Besides, he asked, what would be the practical value of the theoretical knowledge that one learned at the Polytechnique and soon forgot?[86]

The Revolution of 1848 gave the *conducteurs* a chance to push their cause. Throughout the four-year history of the Second Republic, in fact, their own Administration des Travaux Publics considered the *conducteurs* a dangerous group, riddled with pockets of "socialism" and "radical ideas."[87] Their petitions to the national assemblies, however, asked not for socialism but for ways to secure the entry of especially meritorious members of their Corps into the sublime state of engineerhood.[88] They even found two radical Polytechnicien mavericks, Adolphe Charras and Louis Chassaignac de Latrade, to present a bill in their favor.[89] The real leader of the pro-*conducteur* forces, however, was the Socialist journalist and former *conducteur* François Cantagrel.[90] The forces of opposition were led by the powerful Baron Charles Dupin, Polytechnicien, prolific writer, and veteran politician, who had the notable advantage of being president of the National Assembly.[91]

The details of the parliamentary and administrative maneuvering surrounding the *conducteurs'* campaign, launched at a time when the Corps des Ponts et Chaussées was under heavy attack on several fronts, need not detain us here: suffice it to note that the initial tactics of the *conducteurs'* opposition delayed matters until the Second Republic entered its phase of repression of the Left, the prelude to the coup d'etat of 2 December 1851.[92] Purged from the National Assembly and threatened with arrest for various radical pronouncements, Cantagrel fled to Belgium in 1849.[93] Latrade "retired" to London, and Charras, who held a high position in the Republic's War Ministry, was listed as "stricken from the list" *(rayé des contrôles)* in 1852.[94]

What the *conducteurs* finally secured was a law of 30 November 1850 opening one-sixth of all new positions of *ingénieur* to those *conducteurs* who had served ten years in their own Corps and—the crucial provision—could pass a special examination. Because the administration of the examination remained in the hands of the tightly knit Corps des Ingénieurs des Ponts et Chaussées, however, the new law did not promise to bring the *conducteurs* a swarm of promotions.[95] Not a single one, in fact, became an *ingénieur* until after new regulations were passed by Napoleon III in 1868. In the meantime more *conducteurs* were officially listed as "performing the functions of engineer," and their publications and personal dossiers bespeak only new efforts to upgrade their training. As their petitions continued to show, they refused to believe that the French state could not put a marshal's baton in the knapsack of every private.

State Engineers and *Ingénieurs Civils:* Rivalry and Selective Emulation

A comprehensive exploration of the role of the Corps des Ponts et Chaussées in French social stratification would require the investigation of its relations with a number of other groups that threatened its autonomy, power, and status during the nineteenth century: architects, prefects, other elements in the Administration des Travaux Publics, members of the smaller Corps des Mines, private entrepreneurs, and parliamentary bodies. The case of the self-definition and institutional grounding of *ingénieurs civils*, however, may be the richest source of clues about the complex ways that the schools and *corps* of French state-employed engineers affected the formation and outlook of other professional groups.

To state the problem in its broadest terms, in nineteenth-century France a wide variety of individuals engaged in technological and managerial activities that might have qualified them for the title of civil (that is, nonmilitary) engineer: architects, mechanics, artisans, land surveyors, stonemasons, estate agents, and entrepreneurs in many fields.[96] It is thus a matter of considerable interest why only certain persons eventually came to be known as *ingénieurs civils*, partaking of the status connoted in France by the term *ingénieur*, the product—in part, at least—of the tradition of state service described above but now modified by the peculiarly French associations of the qualifying adjective *civil*.

The early history of "*ingénieur civil* consciousness" remains an elusive phenomenon, glimpsed only by fragmentary documentation. One source indicates that the term was in use as early as 1815,[97] but the first systematic discussion of the matter I have as yet located appeared in one of the "journals of useful knowledge" whose burgeoning was a characteristic aspect of the publishing history of the early decades of the nineteenth century: the *Journal du génie civil, des sciences, et des arts à l'usage des ingénieurs, constructeurs de vaisseaux, des mines, des ponts et chaussées, des mécaniciens; des architectes, des sculpteurs, des peintres, des entrepreneurs de maçonnerie, de charpente, de serrurerie, de peinture et de tous les artistes qui contribuent par leurs connaissances aux constructions civiles.*[98] The fourth issue of the journal, published in the fall of 1829, carried a letter from an anonymous Monsieur X, *ingénieur des ponts et chaussées*, which deserves quotation at length:

Sir, I notice that in various articles published by your journal, you frequently employ the expression *civil* engineer, and even some of your collaborators *appear to have* that title. I do not have a very clear idea of the profession which that denomination might befit. In short, what is a civil engineer?

As far as I can judge, upon careful reflection, it seems to me that one can only thus designate a person who has charge of *civil* constructions, taking that word as opposed to *military*. But then that person would be an *ingénieur des ponts et chaussées*, if it were a question of public works, such as roads or waterways, or what one calls an *architect*, if it were a question of buildings for decoration or habitation, either public [an interesting concession of territory not all of his colleagues would have made] or private. You will object, perhaps, that there are individuals who are not *ingénieurs des ponts et chaussées* who concern themselves with public works, but, in accordance with the way such works are currently executed, such individuals, if I am not mistaken, are what one rightly refers to as *contractors, entrepreneurs*, or *concessionaires*. Perhaps these denominations do not appear honorable enough for these gentlemen, and they have thus taken the more exalted title of *civil engineer*. I say they *have taken*, because I do not think that the Government has accorded it to them. If such is the case, however, dare I ask, Monsieur le Directeur, that you consent to tell our readers under what conditions someone who aspires to this new title, imported from England, can obtain it? Must one enter the Ecole Polytechnique? I doubt it, because that school graduates *military* engineers, *ponts et chaussées* engineers, *ingénieurs des mines*, naval construction engineers, engineer-geographers, hydrographic engineers, officers of army and naval artillery, and finally some students who, having had the misfortune to fail at the beginning of their careers, did not succeed in entering any of the public services.

Well, in all that list of engineers, I see none designated as *civil* engineer, and I can believe that it is those students I talked about last who have taken the title:

because how can one suppose that the incapables are what the most capable only become after having received, in addition, during long years followed their graduation from the Polytechnique, a specialized instruction, and after having carried, during a more or less extended period, titles less exalted than that of *ingénieur*, such as student-engineer, aspirant, etc.

If these civil engineers do not come, as one must believe, from the Polytechnique, either they are born geniuses [*ils ont la science infuse*], or they have chosen to acquire their knowledge at another school where the instruction is undoubtedly more profound and extensive. However that may be, I think you would render real service to the readers of your journal by letting them know how, in France, one becomes a *civil engineer*.⁹⁹

The *Journal's* anonymous correspondent had thus, with no little condescending irony, presented the qualifications of the only kind of engineer he would accept: elite school training and a long apprenticeship at lower ranks. Nor did he fail to play the chord of nationalism by pointing out that the title had been "imported from England."

Immediately below the letter from Monsieur X, *ingénieur des ponts et chaussées*, appeared a reply from Monsieur Y, *ingénieur civil*, the length of which requires its summarizing. Monsieur Y pointed out first that public works and architecture hardly constituted all of *les travaux industriels*. New fields of activity had appeared which promised France prosperity; in these one could see the need for civil engineers in cotton, wool, linen, and hemp spinning mills, in weaving, in sawmills and pulp mills, in quarries, and even in agriculture (Could one deny the title of civil engineer to Mathieu de Dombale, director of the experimental farm at Roville?) Such economic activities had now been opened to everyone by the abolition of "corporations, guilds, and masterships"—this comment served perhaps as a veiled attack on the corporative structure of the Ponts et Chaussées. French governments since the Revolution had encouraged such individual initiatives by establishing a system of patents and import controls which "guaranteed ALL INDIVIDUALS" the right to the fruits of their inventions and by setting up new institutions for the promotion of *les arts industriels*, such as the Conservatoire des Arts et Métiers, the *écoles d'arts et métiers*, and the Société d'Encouragement pour l'Industrie Nationale. Certainly men engaged in the promotion of French industrial prosperity such as Jean-Antoine Chaptal, Mathieu Dombale, Isambard Brunel, Nicolas Clément, and Marc Séguin "could take the title of *ingénieur civil* without compromising themselves before society, the Government, or the Ecole Polytechnique." Nor could Monsieur Y accept Monsieur X's attempt to "throw disfavor" on the new title by referring to its English origins. Was it not the civil engineers of Great Britain who had built its roads, canals, and railroads, who introduced gas lighting and coke smelting, and who were the first to make industrial use of steam engines?

How would one decide who had the right in France to assume the new title? Certainly, Monsieur Y argued, the "capitalists and manufacturers who will employ these men" would watch closely to ensure their quality. In any case, the question of professional titles was rapidly changing: "the taking of *attributions libres*" was a practice "even younger than the representative government of which they are the consequence," and, in time, necessary clarifications would occur. The government might, indeed, play a role in assuring the benefits of the new freedom, but not by forcing all aspirants to take an examination. It might, instead, administer a test, including especially an evaluation of practical work accomplished, as a kind of "title of recommendation" in the event that the engineer "lacked patronage."

Monsieur Y was ready to admit that a certain minimal familiarity with mathematics, drawing, and, in certain cases, physics and chemistry would be necessary, but these subjects did not need to be learned at the Ecole Polytechnique: auditors at the School of Mines, students at the *écoles d'arts et métiers*, and many others could obtain this learning. What counted was having a sense of vocation. Monsieur Y suspected, moreover, that the Polytechnique's contribution to the civil engineering profession included more than just "incapables." There was a bit of *luxe* in the overly abstract mathematics taught at the school; however much one admired the learning of Monsieur Laplace and his disciples, it was hard to see how much advanced calculus one needed in engineering work. Could Monsieur X really deny the clear evidence that there were many capable Polytechniciens who, "preferring to plunge into some branch of private industry, had resigned their commissions upon graduation from the school" and that there were Polytechnicien officers in the state *corps* who, "badgered and mistreated by an unenlightened, severe, and nothing-less-than-paternalistic administration," had sought to offer their talents to private industry? Finally, with the anonymity of both parties eliminating the possibility of provoking a duel, Monsieur Y challenged Monsieur X to prove that he himself was not *incapable*.[100]

Despite Y's spirited defense, the first half of the century did not see the *ingénieur civil* definitively established as a recognized professional category. In 1837 a *Vocabulaire de la langue française* considered under *ingénieur* only Polytechniciens employed in the *corps* of the state.[101] In 1839 the former Saint-Simonian Léon Brothier, in a work presenting a general plan for social and educational reform, claimed that the title of *ingénieur civil* had become much abused, with all sorts of dubious individuals claiming the designation, the use of which he wished to see regulated by law, as were *avocat* and *médecin*.[102] In 1842 the first important French career guide, Edouard Charton's *Guide pour le choix d'un état*, complained that the title did "not yet have a precise or definitive designation." The denomination *ingénieur civil*, "not the exclusive property of anyone," was "in the public domain" and, "especially in recent years," had been occasionally "usurped by persons little worthy of the title of engineer." It was a "chancy career with vague functions."[103] As late as 1874 Emile Littré called *ingénieurs civils* all those engineers "who do not come from the Ecole Polytechnique or who work for private industry," thus blithely bestowing renegade status on those Polytechniciens who had traded in *corps* for capitalism.[104]

Such public definitions, however, constitute epiphenomena which provide only hints of underlying structural changes. Instead of pursuing philological investigations further, therefore, let us take a clue from Monsieur Y, who included in his list of educational institutions fostering the expansion of the French economy a school founded privately in the year he wrote, the Ecole Centrale des Arts and Manufactures. If, in examining the state's influence upon the engineering profession, I have suggested that the relationship between army engineering *corps* and Ponts et Chaussées *corps* was an imitative one, I hope also to have indicated that the influence was more complex than merely that of a template to its copy: Ponts rejected much that it saw as part of the army's ethos, and, especially under the Empire, it avoided what it saw as purely military assignments. The Ecole Centrale, explicitly established to train *ingénieurs civils* and captains of industry, also attempted to be selective in its imitation of the schooling and ideology of state-employed engineers. Although it gave theoretically informed surveys of the sciences to its first-year students, its curriculum rejected the advanced mathematics favored at this time by Polytechnique and Ponts et Chaussées.[105] Like the Ecole des Ponts et Chaussées, it permitted specialization by advanced students, but it sought to surpass that school in the practicality of its course instruction.[106] Oracular affirmations of the "unity of theory and practice" in its comprehensive *science industrielle* filled the Ecole Centrale's promotional literature and official pronouncements, but the value of theory was judged by the immediacy with which it served the cause of industrial utility.[107] In the context of the French association of theory with aristocracy—best reported by Alexis de Tocqueville—the Ecole Centrale's emphasis upon the theoretical aspects of its curriculum indicates that it purported to train a social elite, but that elite was also, unapologetically, an industrial elite.[108]

Equally as clearly as the formal curriculum, the Ecole Centrale's administrative routines and dominant values reveal the complexity of references to the state model. Like the Polytechnique in its early years and Ponts et Chaussées throughout the period, the Ecole Centrale formed its students into brigades, with elected *chefs* to act as intermediaries between students and administrators.[109] Like the Polytechnique, moreover, the responsibilities of these student leaders were gradually reduced, and the school came to rely more heavily upon a paid surveillance staff—although the Ecole Centrale's was proportionately much smaller. Both state and Centrale students wore uniforms, but only Polytechnique and Ponts et Chaussées students were subject to military forms of punishment.[110]

Perhaps the most significant difference between the lives of state and Centrale students, however, was the fact that Centrale was nonresidential: students boarded in *pensions* or with Parisian families approved by their parents. Published histories and records at the school thus reveal at Centrale only attenuated and sporadic forms of the *bizuthage* that played such an important part of the formation of the state students' esprit de corps. Although the Centrale's proprietors did not have the resources to construct or rent residences for their students, they were quick to make a virtue of this particular necessity. In an argument neatly complementary to the Polytechnique's insistence that its cloistering allowed its students to internalize better the collective values of the *corps*, the Ecole Centrale exalted the independence, self-reliance, and resourcefulness instilled by spending one's evenings and nights outside the walls. However distant from Paris the lone Ponts engineer might find himself, he remained encased in the succoring (and suffocating) toils of a semiautonomous bureaucracy. Centrale graduates could expect no such sturdy ropes offered to lift them up ambition's envisioned career: they had to find jobs where they could.[111]

On the other hand, partly to assure that external residence would not promote a vulnerability to the dangerous diversions of Parisian life, the directors of the Ecole Centrale gave the instillation of a work ethic no less high a priority than did the guiding spirits of the Corps des Ponts et Chaussées. Centrale's exercises, projects, problem sets, notebook-tending, note-reviewing, and, occasionally, even readings were "calculated and organized to avoid leaving the students a moment of idleness, to break them to work routines [*les rompre au travail*], to firm up their moral character, and to prepare them for the problems of practice and the difficulties of life."[112]

Yet the question of the sources of the Centrale's obsessiveness with the "industry" of its students is no less complex than it is important for understanding the stratifying consequences of engineers' schooling. It is doubtful that the severity of the work discipline was dictated only by worries about the *externat*, the imperatives of technological change ("Learning complex scientific and technical subjects just *is* hard"), or the needs of an attempt to close the gap with Britain ("We have to try harder because we're only Number Two"). Much attention has been paid to the way the working class was molded to a new life of labor in the early stages of industrialization: how it was forced to adopt new work rhythms, to develop new capacities of physical endurance, to accept the regimentations of the factory, the shop, and the work gang.[113] Although certain of the accompanying ideological pressures have been examined, especially political economy and English Methodism,[114] center stage has been occupied by the economic whip, the institutional routine, and *force majeure*. The entrepreneurial classes, on the other hand, are more often portrayed as disciplined by ideology: the Protestant ethic, the sense of being a cultural minority, the drive to overcome domination by a neighboring nation or city, or a belief in the inevitability of technological progress.[115] The work load at the Ecole Centrale suggests, however, that the institutional routines of such technical schools made them the factories of the bourgeoisie. True, a student who withdrew from the school rather than face another hour at the drafting board did not usually face starvation, but neither is it clear that dying of hunger was the alternative for every refractory proletarian.[116] In any case, just as the ideologies of sobriety and discipline in the British Industrial Revolution performed functions other than merely increasing productivity, so did productivity provide only a part of the motivation for the work discipline at the Ecole Centrale. More relevant to my concerns here was another motivation: ensuring the competitive advantage of the school's clientele.

In the first half of the nineteenth century technological knowledge had an accessibility which, though it certainly diminished as the century wore on, did not disappear as quickly as the arguments of Monsieur X (or, in America, advocates of university-based scientific engineering such as Cornell's Robert Thurston or RPI's B. Franklin Greene) suggested. His opponent, Monsieur Y, may not even have gone far enough in his reply: contemporary published sources contain numerous cases of achievement, including technological innovations, in which the principals appear to have had even less formal technical education than that represented by attendance at the Conservatoire's lectures, the *écoles d'arts et métiers*, or the instruction for external students at the Ecole des Mines.[117] If the cognitive acquisitions of a Centrale graduate did not guarantee his competitiveness, then, his capacity for sustained effort might fill the gap. The key to achieving or maintaining elite status may have been not *savoir* but *assiduité*, not *Wissenschaft* but *Sitzfleisch*.

In the eyes of the Ecole Centrale's staff, a well-enforced program of student tasks could succeed only if supplemented by the exclusion of politics from both curriculum and courtyard. In 1833 Theodore Olivier, the school's director of studies, received a letter from an Italian named Luchino Valeriani, who expressed the fear that his sovereign, the duke of Modena, would not look with favor upon the sending of Valeriani's son to politically troubled Paris. In reply Olivier listed in detail the various tasks assigned to students during the year, then declared that "as for politics, you know that one must not concern himself with such matters at the school; our statutes in this regard are quite severe. Order and economy: this is our religious dogma; work: this is our political dogma."[118] Although three members of the Corps des Ponts et Chaussées sat on the school's Council on Studies and at least two others taught there, this exclusion of politics cannot be attributed only to the diffusion of the Corps' own ethos of apoliticism: the Ecole Centrale clearly had its own reasons for such a stance. One of its more prominent administrators had a Carbonarist background, another had resigned from the army in 1830 because of his Legitimist sympathies, and in the biographies of other faculty members can be found allegiances distributed along all positions in between: the excision of politics ensured harmony in the staff. Besides, if disengagement from local politics helped maintain the autonomous bureaucratic power and unity of the Corps des Ponts et Chaussées, so the posture of disinterestedness allowed the Ecole Centrale to recruit its students from (and place its graduates with) Bonapartists, Orleanists, Republicans, and Bourbons, Bordeaux merchants pressing for freer trade, and textile manufacturers determined to maintain protectionism.[119]

Since it has been suggested above that an engineering education functioned as a device whereby higher strata maintained their standing in an increasingly industrial and bureaucratic age, a test for this suggestion lies in information about the Ecole Centrale students' social backgrounds. As Table 1.1 shows, two-thirds of the students were sons of the upper (*haute*) bourgeoisie (catagories A + B + C + E − G). Included in this category are 111 *propriétaires* (15.7 percent of the total), a category peculiar to the nineteenth century.[120] Those who used this title tended to be owners of substantial properties who moved in the same circles as high officials, doctors, lawyers, and other notables.[121] In the case of the Polytechniciens entering during this period, the research of Terry Shinn has found that the average net worth of a *propriétaire* family amounted to no less than 210,000 francs.[122] Even if Centrale *propriétaires* averaged only half this sum—and there is no reason to think that they differed in this way—they would still qualify clearly as *hauts bourgeois*. The other subcategories within the upper bourgeoisie include a good number of families from the noneconomic sectors: the upper ranks of the liberal professions (physicians, lawyers, and notaries), 9.9 percent, and high officials and military officers at the rank of major or above, 7.4 percent. The economic sector of this most privileged stratum sent the largest number of sons, however, including ninety-five bankers and large merchants (*négociants*), 13.4 percent of the total, and eighty-seven (12.3 percent) manufacturers and owners of industrial establishments. Scions of some of the greatest French metallurgical families, such as Ignace Léon Schneider and Léon Muel, appeared as students at the Ecole Centrale, as did Henry Boucart, whose father was an associate of the great textile firm of Schlumberger. Members of the Mulhouse business elite, in fact, had not yet surrendered all their sons to the liberal professions or the bureaucracy: the dossiers of Charles Dollfus, the son of Jean Dollfus, the leading figure in Mulhouse industry, and Jean-Jacques Heilmann, whose mother was Eugénie Koechlin, from a family as powerful as that of Dollfus, have been preserved in the Ecole's records. Tuition, after all, totaled 800 francs, to which must be added the cost of maintenance in Paris and the opportunity cost of earnings foregone during the years of preparation and attendance. For a substantial majority of those who sent their sons to the Ecole Centrale during the July Monarchy, François Guizot's famous declaration about the path of approved upward mobility—*enrichissez-vous par l'épargne et par le travail*—was a superfluous dictum. The fathers had already enriched themselves. Training their sons at the Ecole Centrale was a means to ensure that their wealth would make the best use of the new opportunities presented by French industrialization.

A comparison of the social origins of Centrale students with those of Polytechniciens reveals that the two schools had differing appeals for the various sectors of the French social elite. To be sure, the Polytechnique of the July Monarchy, with its thousand-franc tuition fee and its six-hundred-franc charge for room, board, and uniform, proved to be even less "popular" in its student intake than was Centrale: 79.5 percent of its students' fathers fell into the categories defined by Shinn as *rentiers* and *propriétaires*, liberal professions, high-ranking officials and military officers, and large merchants and industrialists, which roughly corresponds

Table 1.1
*Social Origins of Engineering Students
1830–1847 (percent)*

Father's Profession	Ecole Centrale (N = 707)	Ecole Polytechnique (N = ca. 2,300)[a]
A. Rentiers and *propriétaires*	20.4	36.8
B. Liberal professions, upper category[b]	9.9	15.5
C. High officials and military officers[c]	7.4	14.5
D. Engineers	1.3	
E. Large merchants and industrialists[d]	34.6	12.7
F. Large merchants, bankers	13.4	
G. Smaller merchants	4.2	
H. Manufacturers and owners of industrial establishments	12.3	
I. Middle functionaries, lower military officers	10.7	12.0
J. Petty functionaries, enlisted men	4.2	4.3
K. Primary schoolteachers	0.3	
L. Artisans and shopkeepers	9.5	4.0
M. Shopkeepers	1.4	
N. Artisans[e]	8.1	
O. Laborers, workers	0.3	
P. Peasants	1.7	0.2
Q. Domestic service	0.3	
R. Unclassifiable but known	1.0	0.0
	100.0	100.0

SOURCES: Terry Shinn, *L'Ecole Polytechnique, 1794–1914: Savoir scientifique et pouvoir sociale* (Paris, 1980), p. 185; student dossiers, Archives of the Ecole Centrale des Arts et Manufactures.

to the upper bourgeois category used above, whereas 72.3 percent of the Centrale fathers can be placed in these groups.[123] Only 4.2 percent of the Polytechniciens' fathers were artisans, shopkeepers, workers, peasants, or servants (the predominantly "popular" classes), as compared to 11.8 per cent for the case of Centrale. But it is the differences among the sectors which are most striking. As the table shows, large merchants and industrialists were nearly three times more strongly represented at Centrale, whereas the liberal professions and high-ranking servants of the state showed a clear preference for Polytechnique. *Rentiers* and *propriétaires*, prominent in the clientele of both schools, exceeded their Centrale proportion at Polytechnique by a margin of 80 percent. By contrast, shopkeepers, artisans, workers, and peasants were nearly three times as numerous at the July Monarchy Centrale. One suspects that the latter group, for whom a son at either school could mean the sacrifice of a sizable part of a laboriously earned and fairly recent fortune, had not yet acquired the taste for the state servant's status-honor that appealed so much to the comfortable *propriétaire*, lawyer, or colonel; they savored instead the more tangible rewards of private industry.[124]

In addition to its role in the transformation of a social elite into a technological elite, the Ecole Centrale, like the Polytechnique, shaped the structure of engineers' professional organizations. But it took some time for the version it sponsored to prevail. The acerbic Monsieur X had implied that the proper institutional framework for true engineers was a sort of pantheon sanctifying technological demiurges who had been formed by long, intensive, selective scientific training and even longer tempering in a bureaucratic *corps*. Through the pages of the *Journal du génie civil*, which resurfaced in 1846 after a disappearance of fifteen years, we can faintly but clearly perceive that still another vision existed. The *Journal* broached the matter in 1846 with an article titled "Necessity to Form in France a Society Bearing the Name Institution of Civil Engineers of France." The inspiration for many of the proposed statutes came from the Institu-

---

[a]Shinn gives no total, but an earlier study by Adéline Daumard gives a "known" total of 2,215 for the period 1831–47.
[b]Shinn does not distinguish between upper and lower categories, as suggested in Daumard's Code, but it is clear from his text that almost all his cases fall in the higher category. Lower categories for Centrale were grouped with I.
[c]Major and above.
[d]Includes manufacturers, entrepreneurs, and high-level managers.
[e]Includes *ouvriers spécialisés*.

tion of Civil Engineers, founded in England in 1818, but the arguments echoed the points made by Monsieur Y in 1829. Many of those not admitted to the Polytechnique—perhaps merely because they took examinations poorly or because no more places were available—clearly had the ability to become successful engineers, as their later performances testified. Other capable engineers who developed their sense of vocation late or whose abilities matured after they had passed the maximum age for Polytechnique entry never had the chance to try. The *Journal* then cited the case of an artillery sergeant, well over the age of thirty, who began studying privately after losing a leg: he had won the post of professor of mathematics at the artillery school at Vincennes, "defeating a large number of Polytechnique alumni and even professors at the Université de Paris in the competition for the post." Besides, the purely academic education of a state-employed engineer was no guarantee that he had the practical talents and character necessary for the tasks of civil engineering. In applications to the new Institution of Civil Engineers, then, "no candidate would be asked from what school he graduated." The proof of eligibility would lie in "authorship of printed or manuscript studies, distinguished inventions or discoveries, or the direction of important projects, public or private."[125]

The proposed institution was designed to become "a common center where all the civil engineers of France shall come to gain in strength [*se retremper*], regenerate themselves, and exchange old methods for new ones more appropriate to the needs of the age." But it was designed not only as a scientific and technological academy (*académie savante et d'application*); it was also to be a mutual aid society. Members, who would call each other by the title Comrade, would be required to come immediately to the aid of another member if an accident, fire, or other disaster occurred at a project on which he was employed; no fee could be offered or charged for such assistance. Members were also obliged to help unemployed and semiretired members find work and to look after their dependents.[126]

Certain other publications joined the *Journal du génie civil* in welcoming such an institution. The Anglophile *Journal des chemins de fer* rejoiced that "the profession of engineer would now cease to be a sort of monopoly reserved to the Elect of the Polytechnique who gain entry to the Ecole des Ponts et Chaussées." It would now be "open to all fortunes"; no one would ask if one had spent "3–4,000 francs a year" on his education, only "where are your projects?" Even that "subordinate group of engineers' assistants" in the Ponts et Chaussées administration, the *conducteurs des ponts et chaussées*, now "without hope of obtaining the title of *ingénieur*, whatever their abilities," would be eligible for membership.[127] An economic journal with more general interests, *L'Epoque*, also welcomed the fact that professional recognition as an engineer would now be possible for "students unlucky in examinations; soldiers who . . . acquired their knowledge by private study and in practice; workers [*ouvriers*] who raised themselves to the first rank of science by their industry and their inventions; graduates of the Polytechnique who renounced a state career; and, finally, men whose vocation sooner or later makes them engineers."[128]

The proposed institution seems actually to have been founded—at least, Volume 14 (1846) of the *Journal du génie civil* refers to a "provisional secretary," a M. Hageau, 6, rue Choiseul[129]—but I have as yet uncovered no evidence that anything more happened to it. The discussion of this apparently ephemeral institution does indicate, however, that the history of the French engineering profession in the first half of the nineteenth century no longer can confine itself to the activities of the state *corps* or the graduates of the Ecole Centrale. In 1846 the *Journal du génie civil* published the names of 1,898 French civil engineers, a list it claimed was only the "complement" to the "general list" of *ingénieurs civils* whose names, positions, and addresses were "already known." The editors stated that they had identified a total of 2,670 civil engineers, but they informed their readers that the list was still growing. Since we do not know the precise criteria for inclusion in the "general list," the "complement" serves mainly as an indicator of the variety of occupational specialties that could render their practitioners eligible for the title of civil engineer:

1. Former student at the Ecole Polytechnique, now *ingénieur civil* at _____
2. Former student at the Ecole Centrale, mechanical engineer (or: chemical engineer, construction engineer, metallurgical engineer)
3. District road superintendent
4. Departmental road superintendent
5. Chief surveyor
6. Military engineer (resigned, released, retired)
7. Construction engineer for gas works
8. Engineer of the Ponts et Chaussées (resigned or retired)
9. Engineer-mechanic
10. Subengineer and subdirector of a railroad
11. *Conducteur* des Ponts et Chaussées

According to the *Journal* the title could be claimed, moreover, by individuals with widely disparate social positions, from the Vicomte Decazes to a miner who had graduated from the middle-level mining school at Saint-Etienne.[130] If all those on the *Journal*'s lists had been admitted to the proposed institution—not a very likely possibility, it should be admitted—it would have been, I believe, the largest professional society in France, if not in the world.

When the civil engineering profession finally found an enduring organizational structure, however, a more exclusive pattern prevailed: it was a society that drew its members largely from the Ecole Centrale elite. The long delay in establishing a corporate identity for the graduates of Centrale is puzzling. At least two attempts to form such a society, and probably several others, were made during the July Monarchy. The very first class drew up a plan for a Union des Ingénieurs Civils et Industriels de l'Ecole Centrale, which was sent to all students and graduates in 1832. It referred to the "intellectual and moral influence" of a "society of civil engineers," which would help to "propagate enlightenment" throughout the country.[131] The plan found its way into the private papers of Olivier, as did correspondence indicating faculty opposition. Eugène Péclet, physicist and co-founder of the school, and two other professors argued that the membership requirements were not strict enough: only those who received the school's final *diplôme* should be considered civil engineers.[132] In 1840 both graduates of the school and students again tried to gain the approval of the school's directors for a Société Centrale des Ingénieurs Civils, but again the matter of standards was evoked. The Council on Studies would approve only a society of *diplômés;* they were also hostile to the proposal that non-Centraux be allowed to join.[133]

The papers of Jean-Baptiste Dumas, co-founder and professor of applied chemistry at Centrale, reveal that considerations other than a wish to preserve high membership standards played a role in delaying the establishment of civil engineering society. For example, in a "Plan of a Note for the Minister of Public Instruction" drawn up in 1852, Dumas showed that whatever affection he may have had for students as individuals, he feared what they might do as a group. The "Plan" was intended to be part of the co-founders' long campaign to convince the state to take over the school. Dumas's principal argument for such a takeover was that government stewardship assured a permanence and continuity to the school's activities that might otherwise be lost after the founders died. In explaining why he and his colleagues had not sought such assurance by forming an alumni association, which would then become the proprietor—as the Collège Sainte-Barbe had done—Dumas pointed out the "perils" of such an action:

If we had done so, our students would have been linked together in a veritable freemasonry, and who knows what that would have produced? . . . We have always believed that society would be placed in grave danger if such a lever were ever placed in the hands of an impassioned revolutionary. Such a fanatic could then give the word of command to the entire manufacturing population of the country at a moment of political and social crisis the occurrence of which one may still fear.[134]

At the beginning of his "Plan" Dumas had paid tribute to the "spirit of association" as the first of two elements that had "constituted the industrial regime of France," the other being the "nursery of civil engineers" provided by the Ecole Centrale. The "spirit of association" was also a favorite phrase in the lectures given by Prosper Enfantin and Saint-Amand Bazard during the years 1828–32 and later published as *The Doctrine of Saint-Simon: An Exposition*.[135] But whereas the Saint-Simonians would have welcomed the seizure of the state by engineers and industrialists[136]—some of them thought they had achieved this goal during the Second Empire—Dumas and his collaborators had no intention of preparing the ground for such political adventures. When it came to the organization of engineers, the spirit of association was best left without a body.

When revolution broke out in February 1848, those Centraux who had led the previous efforts to form a society sensed that the new political atmosphere had given them their chance. A committee composed largely of those who had led the attempts in 1840 chose a young engineer named Camille Laurens to negotiate with the school's directors.[137] Calculating, perhaps, that the immediate protection such an organized group might offer the school in the current political crisis was worth the risk of encouraging a freemasonry, the school's directors now agreed to lend their support to the project. On 4 March 1848 forty men met in the amphitheater of the Ecole Centrale to form the Société Centrale des Ingénieurs Civils. By the end of the year at least ninety-three more had joined.[138]

Although the Société was established partly to act as a scientific and technological academy in the manner of the ephemeral Institution, in its early years it spent most of its time attacking more urgent problems of the day. On all of these matters the Société's *ingénieurs civils* confronted as opponents the engineers of the Corps des Ponts et Chaussées, who were excluded from membership.[139] Emile Thomas, who had recruited Centraux to help him administer the National Workshops, and whose brother Léonce was among the founders of the Société, expressed most sharply the hostility between the two groups:

For many years the rivalry between the civil engineers and those of the governmental *corps* had approached a hatred characterized by hostile acts and well-deserved reproaches.

The difference, however, was that whereas the civil engineers were capable only of a certain acrimony, and of statements prejudiced by jealousy, the government engineers, because of their exalted sense of being a privileged corps, abuse their nearly magisterial position to turn down technical memoirs and undermine projects not drawn up by the members of their corps. Since they have the power to approve all engineering projects in which the State has an interest, they use this power needlessly to harm the material interests of entrepreneurs and the reputations of civil engineers.

Such, finally, are the most serious reproaches one can address to them, abuses inherent in the monopoly they exercise: the engineers of the Ponts et Chaussées stand accused of treating their subordinates, the *conducteurs*, with hauteur and harshness, as if they were cut from a different cloth [*pétris d'un autre limon*], and of nevertheless leaving to them all the cares of execution. They stand accused of working at a high price, because they are more attached to form than to solidity, and with an incredible slowness and attention to minute detail. Finally, they stand accused of eating at two troughs, that is, of receiving commissions from assignments given them by the State while at the same time using their position to monopolize all private projects, to the detriment of their less-favored confreres.[140]

In 1848 such internal squabbles within the profession had a larger significance. The National Workshops could work only if their current projects—chiefly shovel-work of dubious necessity—were dropped in favor of economically important activities that made better use of the workers' skills. On 6 May the Société addressed a petition to Armand Marrast, the mayor of Paris and a member of the Provisional Government, in which the members expressed their concern:

[We are] deeply convinced that there are projects which could be carried out in the public services, navigation, the railroad stations, the maintenance of roads, the construction of markets and distribution centers, the system for provisioning Paris, the railroads existing and to be built, the construction of workers' housing, etc. . . .

The Société formally requests that, to bring an end to a situation which the engineers of the State have let become aggravated without offering any solution, a commission be appointed which is composed of men independent of any esprit de corps and all hierarchical and administrative shackles.[141]

Even after the question of the National Workshops had been settled on the barricades, however, the Société pressed its attack upon the Ponts et Chaussées. Although the petition to Marrast had disparaged "hierarchical and administrative shackles," the Centraux nevertheless eagerly sought to wear some of those shackles themselves: their addresses to the national assemblies of the Second Republic sought legislation opening to *ingénieurs civils* access to administrative positions within the state services—the ministries of Public Works, Mines, Public Instruction, and other smaller units.[142] They also demanded that the state finance and facilitate a host of industrial and public works projects the plans for many of which lay moldering in the pigeonholes of the Ponts et Chaussées. Control of such expanded activities should pass to the rightful directors of such enterprises, the civil engineers. Finally, they suggested the establishment of a new industrial university, parallel to and independent of the existing state Université, with schools at all levels from elementary to higher, normal schools, faculties in the larger cities which would offer public lecture courses, and responsibility for apprenticeship training. Needless to say, the traditional classical subjects had no place in this system.[143] In addition to proposing such ambitious general projects, the civil engineers took more immediate steps to control popular education. When the Association Polytechnique, formed by Polytechniciens in 1830 to bring free instruction in various branches of "useful knowledge" to the common people, refused to admit Centrale graduates to its board of directors shortly after the outbreak of the 1848 Revolution, the *ingénieurs civils*, accompanied by science teachers from the secondary schools, formed a rival Association Philotechnique at a meeting in the Centrale amphitheater on 29 March 1848.[144] By the end of 1848 at least 110 Philotechnique members were offering evening courses on scientific and technical subjects.

With the goals outlined above, and the Corps des Ponts et Chaussées as its main opponent, a professional society of civil engineers was not likely to attempt to encompass the full diversity of individuals represented in the *Journal du génie civil*'s list of those worthy of the title *ingénieur civil*. In their struggle for jobs and projects, what the Centraux controlling the Société needed was a manipulatable, loyal combat organization, not a sprawling, latitudinarian *société savante*, or even a mutual aid society. Links forged in an elite training school were all but indispensable for maintaining the proper status, influence, and coordination. Whatever the fate of the Ecole Centrale itself—the takeover plans insisted on administrative and pedagogical autonomy—the Société Centrale des Ingénieurs Civils saw itself as forming a kind of counter-*corps*, dedicated to acquiring state positions as much as it was to moving its members ahead in private industry.

Other rivals of the Corps des Ponts et Chaussées expressed their wish to be formed into *corps* that copied even more closely the form that so effectively encased and empowered the Ponts engineers. Architects, for example, demanded to become a bureaucratic corporation within the state administration paralleling almost exactly the Ponts et Chaussées.[145] Like prisoners who incorporate the values, attitudes, and comportment of their guard even as they plan their escape, these would-be professionals in search of bureaucratic positions showed how fully they had been shaped by the French state as it had extended its influence through school and corps to profession and, ultimately, to the system of social stratification as a whole.

Conclusion

A classicist, expanding Université and an elitist, exclusionary Corps des Ponts et Chaussées thus served as magnetic poles in the state apparatus that realigned French society in subtly varied ways. The realignments discussed here all worked in the same direction—toward a narrower, less accessible engineering profession.

During the time it was being adopted as a formal entrance requirement by state bureaucracies and various professions, the *baccalauréat-ès-lettres* received ideological infusions that steadily increased its capacity as a repository of cultural capital. The right to membership in a social elite became associated with evidence of a personal encounter with the wisdom of Virgil or the sublimity of Cicero. As students in *lycées* and *collèges*, prospective engineers were less successful in resisting this cult of the classical than might have been expected in view of the power and comprehensiveness of the French scientific tradition in which they also participated. To be sure, the full measure of Latin betokened by the *baccalauréat* had at first been far less popular with engineering candidates than with other students. But arguments such as those of Villemain and the *Gazette spéciale* soon converged to establish the dominance of a *secondaire* ethos in which nonclassical studies were deemed a helot's fare: the *baccalauréat* provided the moral and cultural *sine qua non* for aspirants to "the high positions of social life," while also giving unsuccessful Polytechnique or Ecole Centrale candidates a credential that opened up alternative careers to such high positions. As the Polytechnique began to give special advantages to *bacheliers*, the expensive and increasingly demanding years of study needed to acquire the degree became a more and more essential part of an engineer's trousseau. For the non-*bachelier*, the bridge to the Polytechnique became increasingly narrow. Nor could the Ecole Centrale—which did nothing to encourage classical studies by its candidates—escape completely the influence of the *baccalauréat*. Like the Polytechnique, it recruited largely from students in the *secondaire* system; often the same individuals sought entry to both schools.

Our examination of the internal history of the Administration des Ponts et Chaussées between 1800 and 1850 has also revealed the extent to which the personnel, policies, and institutions of the French state reinforced a conservative pattern of social stratification. The predominant position of the Corps des Ingénieurs des Ponts et Chaussées within the engineering profession during the first half of the nineteenth century seemed to their opponents an irritating reminder that the Revolution had failed to sweep away all caste and corporate privilege. In fact, revolution and emperor had recast the Corps in a mold whose resilience has preserved it to this day. The Polytechnique of 1794 provided the semblance of meritocratic recruitment, Napoleonic decrees provided self-government within a strictly hierarchical structure, and both combined to create an institutional and ideological framework conducive to intensive professional socialization. As the *conducteurs* discovered, moreover, the expensive Polytechnique credential became an all-but-insurmountable barrier to advancement within the government sector of the engineering profession. No amount of administrative talent, technical prowess, or even political influence could compensate for its absence.

The history of the relationship between Ponts et Chaussées engineers and other engineering groups further reinforces the argument as to the importance of the state's role in social stratification. Monsieur X's article was only one particularly striking example of the state engineers' attempts to determine the pecking order within the profession by shaping the definition and status of its subspecialties. Surely in no other country did the title "civil engineer" become such a disputed designation. One can only wonder how many potential engineers responded to such attacks by choosing careers of less controversial legitimacy. Furthermore, the French state provided in the Ecole Polytechnique a partial model for the school that would train the largest number of private engineers, the Ecole Centrale des Arts et Manufactures. Whatever its differences from the older school, the Ecole Centrale became increasingly like the Polytechnique in its high cost, its pattern of recruiting largely from *enseignement secondaire*, its comprehensive curriculum, its distinguished scientific staff, and its dedication to training a relatively small elite through a long program of intensive, full-time study. The elitism of its graduates, moreover, helped to foster the rivalry with the Corps des Ponts et Chaussées that became such an important force in shaping the structure and ethos of the *ingénieurs civils*' professional organization.

It seems unlikely that the state-manipulated alignments, attitudes, and processes examined here can be reduced to mere second-order consequences of a "primary" or "underlying" pattern of class conflict. To be sure, a case could easily be made that during this period French society was dominated by alliances between various sectors of the upper bourgeoisie and the landed aristocracy. And it could further be claimed that certain state-initiated institutions or policies often served the interests of the dominant social classes. But international comparisons suggest that a broadly construed situation of class domination cannot provide a fully satisfying historical explanation. Class-struggle reductionism may contribute no more to our understanding of the particularities of social history than does hypostatizing the state.[146]

The various British elites, for example, wielded no less wealth, power, and cultural hegemony than their French counterparts, but nothing like the *baccalauréat* appeared in nineteenth-century Britain.[147] The Corps of Royal Engineers remained tiny and highly specialized, and its stratifying potential was further reduced by the fact that it operated far less in the home islands than in the empire.[148] In Britain, such permanently second-class professional citizens as the French *conducteurs* are difficult to locate. There, civil engineering remained a relatively open profession with a reputation as a channel for the upwardly mobile.[149] Engineering rivalries took a different form, with tensions (hardly as severe as in France) pitting civils against mechanicals, not elite Ponts against conglomerate *civils* as in France.[150] Finally, apprenticeship remained the most common form of training for English engineers. The engineering programs at Cambridge or London never achieved the strict control over the profession that was exercised in France by the Polytechnique or the Ecole Centrale and their graduates.[151] However much their vocation otherwise resembled that of their colleagues across the Channel, British engineers never felt the need to import the cultural and social barriers that by 1850 had sharply narrowed access to the French profession. Until an adequate and full-bodied history of the British engineering profession appears, we cannot fully appreciate the differences between the British and French situations. Nonetheless, the French evidence suffices to show that the *baccalauréat*, Corps, and elitist schools and professional organizations played a crucial role in shaping antagonisms and solidarities, vertical and horizontal, within the engineering profession. And it suggests how much responsibility the French state bears for the pattern of stratification in French society as a whole.

Notes

Two groups of scholars gave helpful criticisms of earlier versions of this essay: the members of the Friday seminar of the Shelby Cullom Davis Center for Historical Studies at Princeton University and the Technological Elites Study Group of the Massachusetts Institute of Technology. Others who have discussed the paper with me individually deserve special thanks: Lawrence Stone, Charles Gillispie, and Cecil O. Smith, Jr. I would also like to thank Pat Schafer and the other members of the Olin Library Interlibrary Loan Department for their energetic and imaginative assistance.

1. Adéline Daumard, "L'évolution des structures sociales en France à l'époque de l'industrialisation (1815–1914)," *Revue historique* 102 (1972):329–30. One of the rare studies of intermarriage patterns, by Jean-Pierre Chaline, "Les contrats de mariage à Rouen au XIXe siècle," *Revue d'histoire économique et sociale* 2 (1970):238–75, concludes that in the case of Rouen as early as 1886–87 the "era of parvenus and self-made men had ended." Rouen was a "social universe sclerotically stratified, where only the small category of shopkeepers kept open a narrowing gangplank of access between the popular classes and the *bonne bourgeoisie.*" A collaborative enterprise headed by Daumard is reported in *Les fortunes françaises au XIXe siècle* (Paris, 1977). It emphasizes the same lack of social success among workers and the "sentiment of frustration which is one of the distinctive traits of their condition in the epoch of liberal, financial, and industrial capitalism in the nineteenth century" (p. 177).
2. Jane Marceau, *Class and Status in France: Economic Change and Social Immobility, 1945–1975* (Oxford, 1977), p. 2.
3. Monique De Saint Martin, *Les fonctions sociales de l'enseignement scientifique* (Paris, 1971). Claude Grignon, *L'ordre des choses: Les fonctions sociales de l'enseignement technique* (Paris, 1971), argues that the technical schools also reproduce both the existing social hierarchy and the low rates of upward mobility.
4. This persistence seems to be a general phenomenon in all Western societies. Fritz Ringer, in his recent comparative study, *Education and Society in Modern Europe* (Bloomington, 1979), p. 261, observes that "greater inclusiveness [in education] was recommended both as an aid to the economy and as a democratic measure; it was expected to break down class barriers, to increase educational opportunities for lower-class students, and thus to encourage social mobility.... This expectation, of course, has been largely disap-

pointed. . . . We can see that wider access has led to no really satisfying improvements in the social distribution of educational opportunity."
5. Pierre Bourdieu and Jean-Claude Passeron, *Les héritiers* (Paris, 1964), and *La réproduction* (Paris, 1970). For a discussion of the impact of the former book see Suzanne Citron, "Enseignement secondaire et idéologie élitiste entre 1880 et 1914," *Le mouvement social* 96 (July–September 1976):82.
6. I do not claim that the profession became a closed caste, as did various occupations in the late Roman Empire or the *noblesse de robe* in the eighteenth century. Particularly in subspecialties such as mechanical engineering, a substantial degree of openness and upward mobility persisted. I argue rather that the three aspects examined here show a convergent pattern of narrowing.
7. The gropings of French Marxists toward an appreciation of the state's role are perceptively described by George Lichtheim in *Marxism in Modern France* (New York, 1964), pp. 112–50. Lichtheim does not make entirely clear, however, his own view of the degree to which the state has autonomous stratifying power. His statement about the "bureaucratic phenomenon" quoted above must be set against passages arguing that the stratifying power comes from the new power of the state in twentieth-century planned economies: "What is at stake in the end is control over the means of production." Nor does he give much attention to culture as a factor in stratification. Writing after Lichtheim, Ralph Miliband, *The State in Capitalist Society* (New York, 1969), is concerned largely with refuting bourgeois claims that the state is a class-neutral institution. Other Marxist writers such as Nicos Poulantzas, "The Problem of the Capitalist State," in Robin Blackburn, ed., *Ideology and Discontent* (New York, 1972), pp. 238–53, *Political Power and Social Classes* (London, 1973), and *Classes in Contemporary Capitalism* (London, 1975), argue that state structures and functions are not simply instruments of the dominant classes but are shaped by the particular form of the struggle between dominant and subordinate classes. Theda Skocpol, in discussing the "potential autonomy of the state" in her *States and Social Revolutions* (Cambridge, England, 1979), pp. 24–33, criticizes such "class-struggle reductionists" by asserting that "the state properly conceived is no mere arena in which socioeconomic struggles are fought out. It is, rather, a set of administrative, policing, and military organizations headed, and more or less well coordinated by, an executive authority." Rather than study the stratifying power of such a set of organizations, however, she goes on to describe clashes between these state organizations and the dominant classes within the context of a competitive international system. Ralf Dahrendorf, "Changes in the Class Structure of Western Europe since 1945," in Stephen Graubard, ed., *A New Europe?* (Boston, 1967), pp. 291–336, discusses the "division of labor of power" as a source of stratification, but he refers to all large organizations and does not deal with the state as a special case. Ezra N. Suleiman, *Elites in French Society* (Princeton, 1978), pp. 17–56, discusses "state-created elites," but he deals with a somewhat limited set of connections between state insti-

tutions and elite formation. None of these authors, moreover, gives more than passing attention to the role of culture in social stratification. Eric Nordlinger, *On the Autonomy of the Democratic State* (Cambridge, Mass., 1981), argues that because "autonomy" necessarily refers to the correspondence between a social entity's preferences and its actions, avoiding "Hegelian implications (substantive and metaphysical)" when referring to the state's preferences requires a definition of the state that makes individuals central. "Only individuals have preferences and engage in actions that make for their realization" (p. 9). He thus proposes a definition of the state as "all those individuals who occupy offices that authorize them, and them alone, to make and apply decisions that are binding upon any and all segments of society" (p. 11). Yet offices themselves carry prescribed modes of behavior, expectations, and cultural traditions that limit and shape individual officeholders' preferences. Autonomous stratifying power as discussed here can also work through relations of imitation or of emulation that do not always embody explicit statements of preference by public officials. For the purposes of this study, then, a definition of the state that draws upon both Nordlinger and Skocpol is most useful: the State as individuals who as public officials interact with social roles embedded in a set of administrative, policing and military organizations headed, and more or less well coordinated by, an executive authority.

8. The largely mathematical *baccalauréat-ès-sciences* was usually awarded after the *lettres* and had a certain importance only for medical students and prospective science teachers.
9. Official decrees and ordinances relating to the *baccalauréat* are collected in Jean-Baptiste Piobetta, *Le baccalauréat de l'enseignement secondaire* (Paris, 1937), pp. 335–1020. The collection of documents published in *Recueil de lois et règlemens concernant l'instruction publique depuis l'édit de Nantes de Henri IV, en 1598, jusqu'à ce jour*, 5 vols. (Paris, 1828), is more complete because it contains speeches, "expositions of motive," and other items which Piobetta did not include.
10. Piobetta, *Baccalauréat*, p. 24.
11. Ibid., pp. 337, 32.
12. See the decrees collected in ibid., pp. 352–63.
13. Ibid., pp. 380–81.
14. Ibid., p. 31.
15. Antoine Cournot, *Des institutions de l'instruction publiques en France* (Paris, 1864), p. 358.
16. Piobetta, *Baccalauréat*, p. 32.
17. The circular of 1810 is printed in ibid., p. 343; for those of 1808 and 1820, see ibid., pp. 336, 352.
18. Ibid., p. 31.
19. Antoine Prost, *L'enseignement en France, 1800–1967* (Paris, 1968), p. 27, apparently unaware of the earlier ruling, in fact treats it as new.

20. Piobetta, *Baccalauréat*, p. 31.
21. See *Recueil des lois*, 4:8–9, 47.
22. The decrees relating to libraries and the book trade were printed in Ambroise Rendu, *Code universitaire* (Paris, 1835), p. 118.
23. The *écoles centrales* were the relatively independent secondary schools set up under the Directory. On the situation in medicine see Charles Coury, *L'enseignement de la médecine en France des origines à nos jours* (Paris, 1968), pp. 5, 111–25, and Jacques Léonard, *La vie quotidienne du province au XIXe siècle* (Paris, 1977), pp. 13–51. For measures to reconstruct the legal profession, such as the reestablishment of the *barreau* in 1803, see Felix Ponteil, *Les institutions de la France de 1814 à 1870* (Paris, 1965), pp. 41–47.
24. *Recueil des lois*, 4:333–34.
25. Rendu, *Code universitaire*, p. 115.
26. Saint-Marc Girardin, *De l'instruction intermédiaire et de ses rapports avec l'instruction secondaire* (Paris, 1847), p. 16.
27. *Recueil des lois*, 5:9, 390; emphasis added. The key drafting role here may have belonged to the minister of the interior, the comte de Siméon. In the interpretation of Paul Meuriot, *Le baccalauréat* (Nancy, 1919), p. 5, this ordinance "gave the *baccalauréat* a primordial social importance."
28. Rendu, *Code universitaire*, p. 112.
29. *Moniteur universel*, 11 March 1841, pp. 613–14.
30. Frédéric Bastiat, *Baccalauréat et socialisme* (Paris, 1850), p. 6.
31. See the table in Piobetta, *Baccalauréat*, p. 304.
32. See R. P. DeDainville, "Effectifs des collèges et scolarité aux XVIIe et XVIIIe siècles dans le nord-est de la France," *Population* 10 (1955):477–78.
33. This general argument is made with reference to the entire nineteenth century by Edmond Goblot, *La barrière et le niveau* (Paris, 1925).
34. Fritz Ringer discusses similar claims to superiority made by the German educated strata in *The Decline of the German Mandarins* (Cambridge, Mass., 1969), pp. 14–127.
35. Raymond Oberlé, *L'enseignement à Mulhouse de 1798 à 1870* (Paris, 1961), pp. 164, 166, 187.
36. See the table in *Gazette spéciale de l'instruction publique*, 2 June 1842, p. 90.
37. Terry Shinn, *L'Ecole Polytechnique, 1794–1914: Savoir scientifique et pouvoir social* (Paris, 1980), p. 27.
38. *Gazette spéciale de l'instruction publique*, 2 June 1842, pp. 90–91. And see Lenore O'Boyle, "The Problem of an Excess of Educated Men in Western Europe, 1800–1850," *Journal of Modern History* 42 (December 1970):471–95.
39. *Gazette spéciale de l'instruction publique*, 27 January 1842, pp. 14–15.
40. An interesting comparison here is with the "magic" of the Edwardian public schoolboy described by Rupert Wilkinson, *Gentlemanly Power* (New York, 1961).
41. *Gazette spéciale de l'instruction publique*, 17 February 1842.
42. The campaign was led by the Ministry of Public Instruction, Abel Ville-

main, and Victor Cousin, philosopher, power broker in the Université, and the chief ideologue of the Trinity of the Good, the True, and the Beautiful as the objects of *secondaire* culture.
43. *Le National*, 18 March 1842.
44. *Gazette spéciale de l'instruction publique*, 24 March 1842.
45. Bobin's pamphlet was first published as articles in *L'écho du monde savant*, February 1842.
46. The ideology of meritocratic recruitment can be found in an early statement in A. Fourcy, *Histoire de l'Ecole Polytechnique* (1828).
47. A. Bobin, *Questions importantes concernant les jeunes gens que l'on destine à l'Ecole Polytechnique* (Paris, 1842), pp. 13–15, 24, 26, 29.
48. Bobin remains an obscure figure. He was not a Polytechnicien himself. In a pamphlet entitled *Plan complet d'organisation et d'administration du travail et des travailleurs* written in March 1848, Bobin described himself as "a former socialist, decorated in the July Revolution, French citizen, and a member of several clubs." On the cover he placed a quotation from Saint-Simon: "The Golden Age that a blind tradition placed in the past lies before us."
49. Chamber of Deputies, session of 1 April 1843, reported in *Le National*, 2 April 1843.
50. The entire debate of 26 May 1842 was reported in *Le National*, 27 May 1842.
51. The point at which half the students were *bacheliers-ès-lettres* may have been reached as early as 1843. P. F. DuBois made this claim, in any case, during debate on 1 April 1843 occasioned by a petition of heads of private secondary students against the degree requirement (reported in *Le National*, 2 April 1843).
52. Shinn, *L'Ecole Polytechnique*, p. 51. The *baccalauréat-ès-sciences*, which demanded little extra work of the students in the Polytechnique preparatory classes, became a requirement in 1855. This change nevertheless betokened a further extension of the Université into the Polytechnique's domain. See the *Moniteur universel*, 17 April 1855.
53. Based on an analysis of the types of *baccalauréat* presented for admission, 1909–11. One of the four classes of *baccalauréat*, "Sciences-Langues ·Vivantes," involved no Latin (Archives of the Ecole Centrale des Arts et Manufactures [hereafter A. ECAM].
54. The social origins and hitherto-unappreciated success in engineering of the *arts et métiers* students are described in C. Rod Day, "The Making of Mechanical Engineers in France: The Ecoles d'Arts et Métiers, 1803–1914," *French Historical Studies* 10 (Spring 1978):439–60.
55. Finally, in 1917 the Société des Ingénieurs Civils, after a debate including most major figures in French engineering, recommended the Latin *baccalauréat* option. See Société des Ingénieurs Civils, *L'enseignement technique supérieur devant la Société des Ingénieurs Civils* (Paris, 1917), p. 308.
56. Georges Bourgin, *Fragments d'une enquête économique du Ministre Rolland auprès des ingénieurs des ponts et chaussées* (Besançon, 1942), pp. 18–40, 100–106.

57. The fate of the military engineers is described in A. Blanchard, "Les ci-devant ingénieurs du roi," *Revue internationale d'histoire militaire* 30 (1970):97–108.
58. J. Couderc, *Essai sur l'administration et le corps royal des ponts et chaussées* (Paris, 1829), pp. 50–51, lists the names of those who went with Napoleon.
59. Jean Petot, *Histoire de l'administration des ponts et chaussées* (Paris, 1958), p. 425.
60. They might have met even earlier in the Polytechnique-preparatory sections in *lycées* or (as they were known under the two monarchies) *collèges royaux*.
61. The higher the student's rank, the greater his ability to choose which *service* he would join. In this same period only the Corps of Mining Engineers was more select: 100 percent of its entrants ranked in the top ten at Polytechnique. By contrast, only 2 percent of the military engineers ranked that high; 61 percent of the Polytechniciens entering that *service* ranked below fiftieth in their graduating class (Shinn, *L'Ecole Polytechnique*, p. 186).
62. Petot, *Histoire*, p. 428.
63. After 1831 the Corps' journal, the *Annales des Ponts et Chaussées*, in listing each student's assignment, officially introduced him to the other members of the Corps.
64. J. R. Delaistre, *Encyclopédie de l'ingénieur* (Paris, 1812), and Couderc, *Essai*, p. 8.
65. Cf. Burton Bledstein, *The Culture of Professionalism* (New York, 1976), pp. 288–90, and passim.
66. Maurice Jeannin, "Du traitement des ingénieurs des ponts et chaussées," *Journal de génie civil* 5 (1829): 153–77; Paul Gerbod, *La condition universitaire en France au XIXe siècle* (Paris, 1966), p. 29. Prefects earned 15–50,000 francs per year, teachers in a primary school in a medium-sized town no more than 1,000 francs.
67. His pension depended upon length of service, and its amount was based on an averaging of his last three years of service.
68. The reports are filed in Archives Nationales (hereafter AN) F14/11459–11510.
69. Minutes of the "Comité" of the Conseil Général des Ponts et Chaussées, 2 March 1857, AN F14/15490.
70. Petot, *Histoire*, pp. 153, 182.
71. Jean Bernard Tarbé de Vauxclairs, *Dictionnaire des travaux publics* (Paris, 1835), 310–11. I have not yet discovered a case in which a bride-to-be was rejected by the Corps.
72. *Pièces relatives au corps avant et après la Révolution*, Ecole des Ponts et Chaussées Archives, Paris, p. 661.
73. *Décret impérial portant organisation du corps des ingénieurs des ponts et chaussées*, 7 fructidor An XII, Title V, Art. 22.
74. See Francis Tarbé de Saint-Hardouin, *Notices biographiques sur les ingénieurs des ponts et chaussées* (Paris, 1884), p. 92ff.
75. The most celebrated test of such rules, established with some difficulty over

a period of thirty years, was the case of the engineer Charles Alfred Oppermann, who was expelled from the Corps when he established himself as an architectural publisher ("Comité" of Conseil Général des Ponts et Chaussées, December 1856, AN F14/15490).

76. Fernand Cavenne, *Du corps des ponts et chaussées et des conseils généraux* (Mâcon, 1871).
77. The minutes of the Conseil Général's "Comité," the Corps' highest disciplinary body, make clear that "bringing dishonor to the Corps" was the ultimate phrase of condemnation (AN F14/15490).
78. *Décret impérial*, 7 fructidor An XII, Title IX, art. 47–48, 52.
79. A. MM. *les membres de la Chambre des Députés*, 18 January 1840, p. 2.
80. Prefect to Ministre Conseiller d'Etat, 15 March 1833, AN F14/11070.
81. Henri-Charles Emmery, *Notice abrégée sur l'histoire et l'organisation et l'utilité sociale du corps des ponts et chaussées* (Paris, 1839), p. 22.
82. Ibid., p. 7.
83. A. MM. *les membres de la Chambre des Députés*, pp. 2–3.
84. Le citoyen Stourm, *Rapport fait au nom de la commission des travaux publics, sur le project de loi relatif à des changements dans l'organisation du corps des conducteurs des ponts et chaussées et dans le mode de recrutement des ingénieurs* (Paris, 1849), p. 16.
85. Alphonse Léon, *De la condition des employés subalternes des ponts et chaussées et des moyens de l'améliorer* (Paris, 1840), pp. 1–3.
86. *Réponse à l'écrit de M. Léon . . . sur la condition des conducteurs des ponts et chaussées* (Paris, 1840), p. 1.
87. See the file "Surveillance des agents subalternes," AN F14/11070.
88. Stourm, *Rapport*, 13–15; Citoyens Detours, Mie, Pietre, et Delbetz, *Proposition relative aux emplois des ingénieurs des ponts et chaussées*, 24 August 1848.
89. Assemblée Nationale, *Proposition tendant à apporter des modifications au mode de recrutement des ingénieurs des ponts et chaussées par MM. Charras et Latrade* (Paris, 1849).
90. During the 1840s, Cantagrel was an editor, *gérant*, and contributor for the Fourierist newspaper *La démocratie pacifique*. His views on the reform of the Corps des Ponts et Chaussées were summed up in *De l'organisation des travaux publics et de la réforme des ponts-et-chaussées* (Paris, 1847), also the most valuable source for the history of the *conducteurs*' campaign to open up the Corps in the last decade of the July Monarchy.
91. A good example of Dupin's position can be found in his speech to the National Assembly published as *Défense des corps des ponts et chaussées et de l'Ecole Polytechnique* (Paris, 1850).
92. See John M. Merriman, *The Agony of the Republic: The Repression of the Left in Revolutionary France* (New Haven, 1978).
93. Adolphe Robert et al., *Dictionnaire des parlementaires français*, 3 vols. (Paris, 1891), 1:573–74.
94. C.-P. Marielle, *Répertoire de l'Ecole Impériale Polytechnique* (Paris, 1855), p. 42.

95. Details of the implementation of the law can be found in *Rapport de la commission chargée de préparer un projet de règlement d'administration publique pour l'exécution de la loi du 30 novembre 1850 concernant de mode de recrutement du corps des ingénieurs des ponts et chaussées* (Paris, April 1851), and the *Rapport supplémentaire* of June 1851.
96. In Britain the word engineer, unqualified by the adjective "civil," means just about anyone who works with machines.
97. Anatole Mallet, "La Société des Ingénieurs Civils de France de 1848 à 1896," Société des Ingénieurs Civils de France, *Annuaire de 1911* (Paris, 1911), pp. 20–21.
98. 1828–31, 1846–47; numbered continuously despite the fifteen-year gap. The journal was probably the personal creation of its *directeur de l'administration*, Alexandre Corréard, whose brother Charles was a graduate of the Polytechnique. Despite the wide range of professions in the intended readership, all but one of the thirty-three men listed as collaborators were either engineers, *savants*, or architects.
99. *Journal de génie civil* 4 (1829):143–44.
100. Ibid., pp. 144–49.
101. Cited in Terry Shinn, "Des Corps de l'Etat au secteur industriel: Genèse de la profession d'ingénieur, 1750–1920," *Revue française de sociologie* 19 (1978): 40.
102. Léon Brothier, *Du parti social* (Paris, 1839), p. 116.
103. Edouard Charton, *Guide pour le choix d'un état* (Paris, 1842), pp. 314–15. The article in Charton's volume was probably written by the Ponts engineer Léon Lalanne listed as collaborator on the cover.
104. Emile Littré, *Dictionnaire de la langue française*, 7 vols. (Paris, 1874), 4:983.
105. The richest source of information about any aspect of instruction at the Ecole des Ponts et Chaussées at this time is the discussion of mechanics and structural analysis in Claude L.-M. Navier, *Résumé des leçons données à l'Ecole des Ponts et Chaussées sur l'application de la mécanique à l'établissement des constructions et des machines* (Paris, 1864). This third edition includes a 307-page history of mechanics by Navier's colleague, Barré de Saint-Venant, as well as a biographical notice on Navier by Prony, the school's director.
106. See the letter by Auguste Perdonnet to the *Journal des chemins de fer* 44 (4 February 1843):378, in which he pointed out that until 1843 the Ecole des Ponts et Chaussées had no course dealing with locomotives, hence "no course in which one could seriously consider the question of the design of railroads."
107. See, e.g., *Prospectus de l'Ecole Centrale des Arts et Manufactures* (1834), p. 2. This is discussed further in John H. Weiss, *The Making of Technological Man: The Social Origins of French Engineering Education* (Cambridge, Mass., 1982).
108. Alexis de Tocqueville, *Democracy in America*, 2 vols. (New York, 1945), 2:45–47.
109. Registre de l'Ecole, 18 March 1830, A. ECAM.

110. "Rapport à présenter à Monsieur le Ministre" (unpublished history of the Ecole Centrale), p. 3–1, Dumas Papers, Archives of the Académie des Sciences.
111. A good short statement of the Ecole Centrale engineer's self-reliant self-image can be found in an address by the school's most illustrious graduate, Gustave Eiffel, *Discours prononcé à la distribution des prix de Ste-Barbe* (Paris, 1886).
112. "Rapport à présenter," p. 6–8.
113. For example, in Lewis Mumford, *Technics and Civilization* (New York, 1974), pp. 151–211, Sidney Pollard, *The Genesis of Modern Management* (Baltimore, 1962), pp. 189–243, and E. P. Thompson, "Time, Work-Discipline, and Industrial Capitalism," *Past and Present* 38 (December 1967):56–97.
114. As in E. P. Thompson, *The Making of the English Working Class* (New York, 1963), pp. 350–400, and Reinhard Bendix, *Work and Authority in Industry* (New York, 1963), pp. 46–85.
115. Bendix, *Work and Authority*, pp. 99–116; Max Weber, *The Protestant Ethic and the Spirit of Capitalism* (New York, 1958), pp. 155–84; David Landes, *The Unbound Prometheus* (New York, 1968); David McClelland, *The Achieving Society* (New York, 1961), pp. 46–57, 145–49, 336–90.
116. We can only guess at how a student at Centrale was affected when he left in rebellion or fatigue or was dismissed as a poor student: such men seem to leave memoirs even less often than successful engineers. Nor do they begin strike movements and thus appear collectively in historical documents. What is most bitterly paralyzing about scholastic failure is that it seems a completely individual failure.
117. One of the best sources for such cases is the *Bulletin de la Société d'Encouragement pour l'Industrie nationale*.
118. Dossier Roberto Valeriani, A. ECAM.
119. The divisions between various milieux on the question of protectionism are outlined in Bertrand Gille, *Recherches sur la formation de la grande entreprise capitaliste (1815–1848)* (Paris, 1959).
120. Adéline Daumard, "Une référence pour l'étude des sociétés urbaines en France aux XVIIIe et XIXe siècles: Project de code socio-professionel," *Revue d'histoire moderne et contemporaine* 10 (July–September 1963):200, notes the absence of this designation in the eighteenth century and its disappearance in the twentieth. The groupings of categories into classes such as "upper bourgeoisie," "popular classes," and so forth given below are also based on Daumard's suggestions.
121. Georges Dupeux, *La société française, 1789–1970* (Paris, 1972), p. 131.
122. Shinn, *L'Ecole Polytechnique*, p. 66.
123. Ibid., pp. 49–50, 187. Shinn does not distinguish between large merchants (often wholesalers) and smaller merchants.
124. Adéline Daumard, "Les élèves de l'Ecole Polytechnique de 1815 à 1848," *Rev. d'hist. mod. et contemp.* 10 (1958):229, also concludes that artisans and

shopkeepers considered the military and functionary posts available to Polytechniciens to be "badly remunerated."

125. "Note sur la nécessité de former en France une société portant la dénomination Institut des Ingénieurs Civil de France," *Journal du génie civil* 13 (1846):479–81.
126. Ibid., p. 485; ibid. 14 (1846):150–51.
127. *Journal des chemins de fer* 298 (15 August 1846):695–96.
128. *L'Epoque* 509 (10 August 1846).
129. *Journal du génie civil* 14 (1846):144.
130. Ibid., pp. 166–210.
131. "Rapport à présenter," p. 4–4.
132. Ibid. Cf. Francis Pothier, *Histoire de l'Ecole Centrale des Arts et Manufactures* (Paris, 1887), pp. 105–6.
133. Henri Mouchelet, *Notice historique sur l'Ecole Centrale* (Paris, 1913), p. 21.
134. "Projet de note pour Monsieur le Ministre," Dumas Papers, Archives of the Académie des Sciences.
135. *The Doctrine of Saint-Simon: An Exposition*, trans. George Iggers (New York, 1972), pp. 69, 72, and passim.
136. And so would Saint-Simon himself. See Frank Manuel, *The New World of Henri Saint-Simon* (Cambridge, 1959), p. 282.
137. Mouchelet, *Notice historique*, p. 22.
138. These are probably minimum figures, counting only the numbers officially admitted rather than the total number who took part in meetings.
139. *Compte-Rendu des séances de la Société des Ingénieurs Civils*, March–May 1848, p. 6 (hereafter *Compte Rendu*).
140. Emile Thomas, *Histoire des Ateliers Nationaux* (Paris, 1848), pp. 42–43.
141. *Compte-Rendu*, March–May 1848, pp. 11–12.
142. *Observations presentées au Comité des Travaux Publics de l'Assemblée Nationale par la Société des Ingénieurs Civils sur le projet de décret relatif au mode de recrutement du Corps des Ponts et Chaussées*, October 1848, p. 46.
143. The plan is "Enclosure H" in *Compte Rendu*, March–May 1848.
144. Association Polytechnique, *Distribution des prix* (1862), p. 10.
145. "De la nécessité de réformer l'Académie et les écoles d'architecture pour les reconstituer sur de nouvelles bases," *Journal du génie civil* 4 (1829): 117–29; Maurice Jeanin, "Des Ponts et Chaussées et des batimens civils," ibid. 5 (1829):539–57; M. Chapuy, "Réflexions sur quelques parties de l'organisation du service des travaux publics," ibid. 9 (1830):208–12; C. Reynaud, "Mémoire sur l'organisation à donner au corps des architectes," ibid. 10 (1831): 288–306; "Lettre au directeur du Journal du génie civil par un architecte du gouvernement," ibid. 11 (1846):62–68. The rivalry between engineers and architects is discussed at length in Helene Lipstadt, *Architecte et ingénieur dans la presse* (Paris, 1981).
146. See note 7, above.
147. The examinations that did begin to appear after midcentury seem to have

gone in the opposite direction, away from claims to "general culture" and toward specialization. See D. S. C. Cardwell, *The Organization of Science in England* (London, 1957), pp. 114–18.
148. Whitworth Porter, *History of the Corps of Royal Engineers*, Vol. 1 (London, 1889), reports that the Corps had 115 members in 1804.
149. George S. Emmerson, *Engineering Education: A Social History* (London, 1973), pp. 91–131. Emmerson also points out that the Institution of Civil Engineers was established in 1818 as a "less exclusive society" than the Smeatonians, which more nearly resembled a social club than a professional organization.
150. W. J. Reader, *Professional Men* (London, 1966), p. 70.
151. Emmerson, *Engineering Education*, pp. 66–77; T. J. N. Hilken, *Engineering at Cambridge University* (Cambridge, England, 1967), pp. 26–27.

2
ROBERT FOX

Science, the University, and the State in Nineteenth-Century France

During the nineteenth century, the place of the academic scientist in French society was transformed. In the first three decades of the century, he was still the privileged member of a small, powerful elite. He would almost certainly be close to the leaders not only of his discipline but also of the nation's cultural life generally, as a protégé of one of the great patrons (Georges Cuvier or Pierre Simon de Laplace, for example), as a fellow member of the Institut de France, or as a colleague in one of the major Parisian institutions of research or higher education. By the same token, since a dominant position in the intellectual community depended on an ability to exploit the opportunities afforded by the state's

---

A note on currency and terminology:
Currency: In making comparisons with other currencies, the following exchange rates can be assumed:

German Empire	mark	worth	1.2 francs
Great Britain	pound sterling	worth	25 francs
United States	dollar	worth	5.4 francs

"Universitaire": The term *universitaire* is used here in its conventional sense, to describe anyone who held an academic post in the Université [Royale, Impériale] de France, whether in the secondary sector of *lycées* and *collèges communaux* or in the faculties. The *universitaires* that I consider, however, were almost invariably engaged in higher education.

"Academy": I have adopted the convention of using "Academy" (with a capital A) in referring to national or provincial learned academies. I use "academy" for the administrative regions (sixteen of them for most of the nineteenth century) into which France was divided for educational purposes.

educational system, he would almost invariably have some connection with those who wielded political power as well. He belonged, in short, to the circle of *notables*[1]—a circle whose elevated cultural values were little different from those that had characterized *notables* in the Old Regime, whose *locus operandi* was Paris, and whose coherence was secured by strong personal ties based on family, friendship, and indebtedness for past favors.

By the beginning of the twentieth century, however, the scientist in academic life was part of a much larger community, with its numerical strength located firmly in the hugely expanded network of faculties of science and medicine scattered throughout the country (see Tables 2.1 and 2.2). If he felt himself to be a member of an elite, it was an elite that had become so capacious and impersonal that the gratification it bestowed was negligible. As a teacher in a faculty, he would have followed a well-defined career pattern: he would hold a doctorate and, at least in mathematics or physics, would probably be a graduate of the Ecole Normale Supérieure as well.[2] Moreover, whatever his discipline, he would have owed his position less to the enterprise of a patron than to his formal qualifications and a record in teaching and research which commended him to the minister of public instruction. In a minority of cases (that of Marcellin Berthelot, for example), political activity or service as a senior government adviser might have taken him to a position of eminence in public life. But more probably he would have to be content with a reputation that extended no further than his own institution and a small circle of fellow specialists in his field.

What had occurred is simply described. From being the visible, if somewhat mysterious, representatives of an exclusive clerisy of the learned, academic scientists had moved, for a mixture of good and ill, toward a position of near-anonymity in the eyes of even the well-educated general public. In its broad outline, the change will appear familiar to students of the professionalization of science and scholarship. As recent accounts have shown, by the later nineteenth century German classical philologists and British geologists had won their long struggle to define the intellectual boundaries and the essential principles of their disciplines and to win an important place for them in the *cursus* of university studies.[3] Forms of training were regularized, the number of posts for the products of that training had been greatly increased, and to an unprecedented degree it was now thought proper for qualified experts to address their arcane discourse to one another, regardless of their intelligibility to the layman.

The essential similarity of the conditions of academic life which came

Table 2.1.
Scientific Posts in Higher Education
(Including Advanced Technical and Medical Education) and Research*

Year	Major research institutions[a]	Paris			Provinces			Major scientific grandes écoles[c]	"Free" faculties of science and medicine[d]
		Faculty of Science	Faculty of Medicine	School of Pharmacy	Faculties of Science	Faculties of Medicine	Schools of Pharmacy[b]		
1827	28 (18)	18 (6)	25 (23)	6 (8)	28	31 (23)[e]	6 (4)	35 (11)	—
1852	30 (25)	18 (6)	26 (23)	9 (3)	63	30 (24)[e]	10 (4)	37 (10)	—
1877	33 (29)	19 (3)	28 (27)	9 (4)	98	54 (37)[f]	10 (1)	43 (23)	8 (Paris) 26 (Provinces)
1902	35 (35)	25 (35)[g]	35 (44)[g]	10 (17)[g]	129 (144)[g]	98 (106)[g]	11 (13)[g]	67 (55)	7 (Paris) 58 (Provinces)

SOURCES: For 1827: *Almanach royal, pour l'an MDCCCXXVII* (Paris, 1827); for 1852, 1877, and 1902: The appropriate volumes of the *Annuaire de l'instruction publique*.

*All figures indicate the number of posts. I have not attempted to take account of *cumul*, the effect of which would have been negligible for the provinces and small even for Paris (though see note g). The main figures given indicate the number of senior academic posts of a rank comparable with that of a chairholder in a faculty, a *maître de conférences* at the Ecole Normale Supérieure, or an astronomer at the Paris Observatory. The figures in parenthesis indicate the number of additional posts at a more junior level, such as those of *aide-astronome* at the Observatory or *agrégé* in a faculty of medicine. Posts in technical schools below the level of the *grandes écoles* and in the secondary schools of medicine have been ignored. The locations and dates of foundation of the various institutions considered are summarized in

Table 1 of Robert Fox and George Weisz, "The Institutional Basis of French Science in the Nineteenth Century," in Fox and Weisz, eds., *The Organization of Science and Technology in France, 1808–1914* (Cambridge, 1980).

[a]Includes the Collège de France (scientific and medical chairs only), the Muséum d'Histoire Naturelle, and the Paris Observatory. For 1877 and 1902, provincial observatories and the Observatoire d'Astronomie Physique at Meudon have been included.

[b]The relevant schools are those of Montpellier and Strasbourg, with Nancy (where a school of pharmacy and a faculty of medicine were created after the Franco-Prussian War) replacing Strasbourg for 1877 and 1902.

[c]Ecole Polytechnique, Ecole des Ponts et Chaussées, Ecole des Mines, and the scientific section of the Ecole Normale Supérieure.

[d]The "free" faculties were established in the wake of the state's abandonment of its monopoly of higher education in 1875. By 1877, there were eight chairs in the Faculté libre des sciences in Paris, which formed part of the Université (later Institut) Catholique de Paris. The 26 provincial chairs were in the Faculté libre des sciences and the "free" schools of medicine and pharmacy at Lille. By 1902, the system had been extended by the creation of "free" faculties of science at Angers and Lyons; by this date also, the School of Medicine and Pharmacy at Lille had assumed the rank of a faculty.

[e]The only faculties of medicine in the provinces before the Third Republic were those at Montpellier and Strasbourg. On the later foundations, see note f. The faculty at Strasbourg was moved to Nancy after the Franco-Prussian war (see note b, above).

[f]The medical faculties at Bordeaux, Lille, Lyons, and Toulouse, all founded under the Third Republic, were "mixed" faculties of medicine and pharmacy. At all of them, some teaching in pharmacy was offered, but they functioned effectively as medical schools and have been treated as such for the purposes of this table.

[g]A significant proportion of the junior posts that existed in the faculties by 1902 were held on a part-time basis. Hence the figures in parenthesis are slightly misleading, especially for the medical faculties.

Table 2.2.

*The Proportions of Chairs in Faculties of Science in Paris and the Provinces**

Year	Percentage		Number of chairs		
	Provinces	Paris	Provinces	Paris	Total
1827	61	39	28	18	46
1852	78	22	63	18	81
1877	84	16	98	19	117
1902	84	16	129	25	154

SOURCES: As for the relevant parts of Table 2.1.
*Only the full chairs are counted.

to prevail in Germany and Britain, as in France, by 1914 is striking. For the historian, it is also a snare. As the work of both Susan Cannon and Roy Porter has made clear, it is all too easy falsely to equate professionalization with excellence and progress.[4] I share the misgivings of these scholars, and toward the end of this essay I discuss the grave problems of French science just before World War I, many of which arose from the pursuit of professional autonomy. Still more misleadingly, our familiarity with the endpoint of the academic institutionalization of science in the nineteenth century can give the process an air of inevitability and obscure the diversity of the conditions that governed the course, even the very meaning, of professionalization in different disciplines and in different countries. For this reason, I make no apology for the particularist cast of my essay. I believe that the expansion of France's national university system and the consequent engagement of a growing proportion of academic scientists in what was effectively a unified state corps of *universitaires* determined in crucial respects what they conceived to be the best interests of their profession.[5] Their main problem, in fact, was that of reconciling ideals rooted in notions of the freedom and universality of science with the reality that they were servants of the state.

I have chosen to trace the developing perception of this problem in a roughly chronological fashion, taking the incompatibility between the intellectual and the bureaucratic conceptions of the *savant* as a central recurring theme. This choice of theme is particularly appropriate for a study of French academic life, since the incompatibility to which I refer was far more obtrusive in the centralized Université de France than it was in the diffuse university structures of Germany and Britain, and it was obtrusive from a very early stage. By the 1820s, it was already becoming clear that the appointed guardians of learned culture in France were no longer the men of superior intellect as had been the case earlier in the century; even Laplace and Cuvier could not fail to realize that their personal authority, founded above all on their scientific achievements, was weakening.[6] During the July Monarchy of 1830–48, as the system of higher education grew in size and complexity and as bureaucratization advanced, so the difficulty of exercising personal control mounted. In these years, as I show in the following section, the authority of the Ministry of Public Instruction became more assertive, and the professors of the Université assumed, increasingly, the role of obedient functionaries. Some who had known the old order bitterly lamented the change, but generally the creation of new openings in academic life and the regularization of career patterns were regarded as appropriate in an age of bourgeois ascendancy.

In the second section, I discuss the gathering reaction to this trend during the Second Empire. From the time of Louis-Napoleon's coup d'etat in December 1851 until 1863, *universitaires* found themselves serving two ministers of public instruction—Hippolye Fortoul and Gustave Rouland—for whom political expediency carried far greater weight than the interests of learning or the professional aspirations of their employees. A heightened sense of grievance in the academic profession was only to be expected, though there is evidence that the condemnation of Fortoul and Rouland among *universitaires* was not as widespread as many later historians would have us believe. The small circle of ministerial advisers who implemented the bureaucratic conception of learned culture and worked to bolster the loyalty of the rank and file in the faculties and *lycées* saw no reason to seek change. And even professors in the provinces, where salaries were lowest and conditions of work were particularly discouraging, seemed generally reluctant to complain about their allotted role. As the political character of the Second Empire changed and the authoritarianism of Fortoul and Rouland gave way to the circumspect liberalism of Victor Duruy (1863–69), however, a program of reform to which most members of the academic profession could adhere was developed.

As I show in the third section, scientists were prominent in both the agitation during the Second Empire and the major reconstruction of France's system of higher education which began in the late 1870s under the Third Republic. Scientists felt, even more keenly than their colleagues in the humanities, the loss of the high status which the community of *savants* had enjoyed in the early years of the century. For them, the remedy was simple. They set out to exploit the special skills that distinguished them from other men of learning. They argued that the contributions they made, whether to theoretical knowledge or to the economy and society at large, should be ones that arose from their high calling as creative men of science. Hence the emphasis the scientific reformers placed on the need to improve laboratory facilities, to develop specialized journals and societies, and, most important, to secure new patrons and a more serious public to replace the cultivated dilettantes to whom professors in the faculties of science had traditionally ministered. Although, as I argue, the scientists' quest for new patrons and a new public in the worlds of industry and municipal and departmental administration proved, in the long run, to be intellectually damaging, it succeeded in one essential respect. By the beginning of this century, state control had been greatly reduced. Academic scientists were no longer the pawns of government policy.

It would be satisfying if this study could be used to endorse or to topple some revered model of professionalization. But I find it hard to do either—and not only because of the irreverence with which models in this field have come to be regarded. The fact that most of the professional men I consider were at once men of learning without clients in the normal sense of the word[7] and the salaried servants of a single state administration makes the case an odd one. Moreover, I begin my account in the early nineteenth century when, thanks to the decrees of Napoleon I, the profession of the university scientist was, at least in principle, established. My subject, therefore, is not so much the creation of a profession as its painful and fitful evolution in response to its own expansion, changing ministerial policy, and the appearance, in the last decades of the century, of a market for scientific knowledge in industry, where none had existed before.

Science and the Academic Role to ca. 1850

During the years of revolutionary and Napoleonic rule, the eighteenth-century trend toward the proliferation of science-based careers was consolidated. The system of specialized schools for the training of technical experts was maintained and developed, with survivors of the Old Regime, such as the Ecole des Ponts et Chaussées, the Ecole des Mines, the Ecole Vétérinaire at Alfort, and schools of medicine and pharmacy being joined by the glitteringly successful Ecole Polytechnique (1794) and a reorganized Ecole de l'Artillerie et du Génie at Metz (1802). The traditions of the Old Regime were also perpetuated in the field of scientific research: existing institutions such as the Collège de France, the Jardin du Roi (now refurbished as the Muséum National d'Histoire Naturelle), and the Paris Observatory all continued to provide employment for *savants* who were free to devote their time to the advancement and, to a lesser extent, the diffusion of scientific knowledge. Here too there was modest expansion of the system, notably with the creation of the Bureau des Longitudes in 1795.

Such growth as there was in the vocational schools and the research institutions did not, however, fundamentally alter the structure of the scientific community or the personal character of the allegiances that bound scientific novices to their benefactors. It merely gave the patrons a somewhat greater scope in their search for openings for their protégés. Laplace quickly seized on the new opportunities afforded by the Bureau des Longitudes, placing first Jean-Baptiste Biot, then François Arago, and finally Denis Poisson in modest positions in the Bureau between 1806 and 1808.[8]

In view of this pattern of expansion within an essentially unchanged institutional structure, I am entirely convinced by a recent argument that the quarter of a century separating the Revolution from the fall of Napoleon should not be seen as decisive in the emergence of the profession of the academic scientist in France.[9] In 1815 the quality of advanced scientific education, in particular for mathematicians and physical scientists at the Ecole Polytechnique, was certainly better than it had been at the end of the Old Regime, and the number of posts that permitted the pursuit of science without immediate regard to its applications had increased. But the openings still remained too few and too subject to the vagaries of personal patronage for any young man realistically to identify scientific research and teaching as his chosen career.[10]

Nevertheless, it was in this period that the foundations for a new and more impersonal pattern of career-making that developed under the July Monarchy were laid. The foundations were outlined in a series of Napoleonic decrees, in particular those of 17 March 1808 and 16 February 1810,[11] which established the Université Impériale de France as an administrative structure embracing not only the faculties of science, letters, law, medicine, and Catholic and Protestant theology but also the associated network of *lycées*, municipal colleges (*collèges communaux*), and a variety of lesser schools. An explicit purpose of the decrees was to create a precise career structure that would allow "learning" and "good conduct" to be rewarded by access to the highest positions in the Université.[12] To this end, the decrees meticulously prescribed the order in which posts could be held and the qualifications that were necessary for every appointment. Chairholders in the faculties were to hold the new degree of doctorate, as were the most senior teachers of mathematics and literature in the *lycées;* the *agrégation* (a form of competitive examination which Napoleon revived after its sporadic use in the eighteenth century) was established as at least one way to a permanent chair in a *lycée;* and there was an elaborate hierarchy of lesser posts for which the lower qualifications of *licence* and *baccalauréat* were required.[13]

Despite the profusion of detail, the decrees of 1808-10 came close to being stillborn. By the end of 1815, only fifteen doctorates had been awarded in the sciences,[14] the first examinations for the *agrégation* had yet to be held, and the number of candidates entering the science section of the Ecole Normale—the specialized school established to provide training for the academic profession—averaged only eight a year from 1810 (when the first students were admitted[15]) until the end of the Empire.[16] Such was the provisional nature of the Université that dispensations from the formal regulations governing the careers of *universitaires* were the norm rather than the exceptions they were originally intended to be. Of ninety chairholders in the faculties of science in 1813, for example, not one held the *doctorat-ès-sciences.*[17]

An obvious explanation for this halting start, which was equally apparent in the faculties of letters, was the lack of any clearly defined roles that these faculties could, in practice, fulfill. In the faculties of law and medicine, which soon began to function in the manner of vocational *grandes écoles*, there was no such problem, and both types of institution attracted substantial student enrollments. But who were the clients for the esoteric intellectual wares of the professors of chemistry, French literature, or classical languages? Aspirants to the only university qualification in science or letters that was prized at all, the *baccalauréat*, were taught in the *lycées*, whereas candidates for the higher qualifications were pitifully few in number and they normally prepared themselves by private study, without ever setting foot in a faculty before the day of their examination.

The lack of serious students in the faculties of science and letters was a cause of vexation to the professors and of extreme vulnerability for their institutions. It made effective resistance virtually impossible when, in

January 1816, at a time of financial stringency, the restored Bourbon administration decided to close three of the ten faculties of science which had been set up by that date in French territory (out of a total of twenty-six that were planned) and seventeen of the faculties of letters (leaving only six).[18] The discarded faculties, it was justly observed, had not attracted enough students to justify their cost and so, on straightforwardly utilitarian grounds, had to be declared a failure.[19]

Despite the closures and the attacks of those who, like H. F. Robert de Lamennais,[20] wanted to do away with the Université as a vestige of the Napoleonic past and a threat to religion, morality, and the social order, the system of faculties survived. Moreover, it survived largely in the form conceived by Napoleon, though it was only in 1822 that it finally lost the "provisional" status it had received in 1815 and only then that a grand master was placed once again at the head of the system, after nearly seven years during which the minister of the interior had governed the Université through a small and generally biddable Commission (later Conseil) de l'Instruction Publique.[21] Both before and after this reorganization, compromises were unavoidable if the partisans of the Université were to achieve their essential objective of demonstrating the compatibility of a state monopoly of secondary and higher education with a Catholic monarchy. As president of the Commission de l'Instruction Publique from 1815 to 1819, the liberal Pierre-Paul Royer-Collard had had no alternative but to condone some clerical infiltration in the *collèges royaux* (the Bourbon successors of the *lycées*), and in the 1820s clericalization continued to counter the Napoleonic ideal of a Université that would be part of the national administration while enjoying a high degree of intellectual and professional autonomy. Purges of liberal *universitaires*[22] and the closure of the Ecole Normale from 1822 to 1826 show how political and religious considerations colored educational policy in this period. Yet the fact remains that in 1822 the formal administrative structure of the Université was salvaged and, if only in principle, its independent, secular character was reaffirmed. Even the six years for which the reactionary bishop of Hermepolis, Denis de Frayssinous, served as grand master (1822–28) did nothing to change this state of affairs.

Once the provisional phase in the history of the Université was past, the regulations of 1808 and 1810 concerning careers and qualifications began to be observed, imperfectly yet to a degree that had never been achieved even under Napoleon. In 1821, the first *concours* for the *agrégation* were held, and it was stipulated that from 1 January 1822 new appointments to chairs in the *collèges royaux* would be made exclusively from *agrégés*.[23] In the faculties, by contrast, the formal conditions governing posts were enforced far more slowly. Of fourteen men who were appointed to chairs in the faculties of science between 1821 and 1829, only three held the *doctorat-ès-sciences*, and it was not until the 1830s that the qualification became normal for professors, though throughout the July Monarchy about a quarter of all chairs still went to candidates who had no doctorate (see Table 2.3).

Table 2.3

The Educational Backgrounds of Professors Appointed to Faculties of Science, 1820–1869*

Decade	Number of appointments	Number holding *doctorat-ès-sciences*	Number of *agrégés*	Former pupils of Ecole Normale	Former pupils of Ecole Polytechnique
1820–29	14	3	0	1	3
1830–39	38	25	4	7	4
1840–49	35	27	9	8	7
1850–59	53	48	24	22	4
1860–69	31	31	13	12	3

SOURCES: *Doctorat-ès-sciences:* Maire, *Catalogue des thèses de sciences; Agrégation:* For the period up to 1850, the list in the *Annuaire de l'instruction publique* for 1851, pp. 283–96, for later years, the annual lists in subsequent issues of the same publication; Ecole Normale: *L'Ecole Normale (1810–1883);* Ecole Polytechnique: B. Charles-Philippe Marielle, *Répertoire de l'Ecole Polytechnique, ou renseignements sur les élèves qui ont fait partie de l'institution depuis l'époque de sa création en 1794 jusqu'en 1853 inclusivement* (Paris, 1855), and Marc-Alexis-Paul Leprieur, *Répertoire de l'Ecole Impériale Polytechnique ou renseignements sur les élèves qui ont fait partie de l'institution depuis l'année 1854 jusqu'à l'année 1863 inclusivement* (Paris, 1867). Information on the identity of professors and the dates of their appointments is taken chiefly from the annual *Almanach impérial* [*royal*] (for the period before 1851) and the *Annuaire de l'instruction publique* (for those appointed from 1851).

*The qualifications concerned are those held by professors at the time of their first appointment to a chair in a faculty of science. Appointments to junior posts, for example as *chargés de cours* or as *suppléants*, are ignored.

Since pupils were no more abundant in the faculties of science and letters after 1815 than they had been during the Empire, the return of the Bourbons brought little change in the lifestyle of professors. Their only essential function remained, as it had been from the start, the conduct of state examinations, in particular the *baccalauréat*. Their duty was, first and foremost, that of a public official, with the professor appearing as the guardian of the means of access to the learned professions and to academic careers.[24] The work was tedious, and although the bourgeois families of the Restoration and the July Monarchy were only too glad to enjoy the legitimation of their rising power which the *baccalauréat* bestowed, it gave professors very little of the status that might have accrued to them if they had actually prepared the candidates they tested. But the bouts of activity were, mercifully, few and brief. Typically, as at Caen in the 1840s, there would be three ten-day sessions a year, at Easter and in August and November, and there might, in addition, be short tours of duty to smaller centers in the region; in all, between fifty and a hundred candidates might be examined each year in the sciences.[25] Although the case of Caen was fairly normal, the level of activity could vary significantly according to the region. At Grenoble, for instance, there were only 111 successful candidates for the *baccalauréat-ès-sciences* in the forty-one years between 1811 and 1852, a figure which, even allowing for failures, implies a negligible burden on professors.[26]

In addition to examining, professors were formally required to teach. By the university statutes of 1810, chairholders in the provincial faculties were to offer courses for nine months of the year, giving three lectures per week, each of one hour and a half, while their colleagues in Paris gave two lectures a week over eight months.[27] Again the burden was hardly excessive, and it became less so in 1841: then, by a ministerial decree of Abel Villemain, the Parisian load of two weekly lectures became the norm for all faculties.[28] Of course, the load could always be made to appear heavy by virtue of *cumul*, the characteristically French practice of accumulating posts. Pierre Dulong in 1828 stated that he was being "killed" by the burden of teaching in the chairs that he held at both the Sorbonne and the Ecole Polytechnique.[29] But Dulong's was a self-inflicted predicament peculiar to those with power and access to the opportunities of the capital.

For most professors, the greatest problem was not so much the amount of teaching as the level at which lectures had to be pitched if an audience of any sort was to be mustered. In the absence of pupils working for specific examinations, there was no choice but to turn to a nonacademic public in search not of qualifications but of personal improvement or diversion. The choice was not necessarily an ignoble one. Indeed, there was a hallowed French belief that intelligibility was an indispensable quality of the true *savant*. When François I established the Collège Royal (later the Collège de France) in 1530, it was decreed that professors should give free public lectures; and at the Jardin du Roi there was a similar dual commitment to the diffusion as well as to the advancement of knowledge. During the Bourbon Restoration, the tradition had gained renewed strength, with the great *savants* and *érudits* of the capital setting a style which the emerging professoriate in the provinces naturally sought to emulate.[30] The undisputed "stars" of the 1820s had been in history, literature, and philosophy: François Guizot, Villemain, and Victor Cousin. But in the sciences, Biot, Louis-Jacques Thenard, Joseph-Louis Gay-Lussac, Cuvier, and Charles Dupin were capable of drawing audiences of several hundred; and the tradition was sustained with undiminished brilliance during the July Monarchy by Jean-Baptiste Dumas and, most notably, by François Arago's immensely popular lectures at the Paris Observatory.[31] These lectures, which disgusted the purists for their triviality, so enthralled polite society that even the royalist duchesse de Duras overcame her dislike of Arago's republican views to attend.[32] It is clear that the most successful performers, far from resenting their public role, reveled in *haute vulgarisation*. They saw the calling as lofty and invigorating, with rewards that were well worth working for. The grander their vision of the universe and the nobler their delivery, the greater was the reputation awaiting them, as the case of Cuvier shows. Using a text which he had largely committed to memory and making the most of a magnificently versatile voice, he indulged in every rhetorical device. Contempories observed that his variations of pace and tone, even the way he raised his head to receive applause, would have done credit to a tragedian.[33]

In the provinces, the public for polite science was smaller and less well informed than in Paris, and it was less easily won. The mathematician and philosopher Antoine-Augustin Cournot complained that the attendance at his mathematical lectures in the newly opened Faculty of Science at Lyons in 1834–35 quickly dwindled to about ten[34] (though, by provincial standards and for a series of specialized lectures on differential calculus, this would suggest an unusual drawing power on Cournot's part). In other provincial faculties, similar complaints abounded. At Caen a recurring difficulty was the bourgeois custom of leaving the town at the beginning of the *belle saison*.[35] This practice seems, year after year, to have reduced initially promising audiences to a derisory level. And even when a significant audience could be assembled, as was possible at certain times of the year, there was always the problem that it contained few serious students. As the dean and professor of chemistry, Pierre-Boniface Thierry, observed in 1840, the audiences in his faculty were composed largely of "amateurs ou gens du monde" who were totally uninterested in the more forbidding aspects of science.[36]

The remedy, advocated in vain by Thierry and by deans throughout France, was to give the faculties an educational function that would attract young people and direct their energies to worthwhile objectives. It was stated that as a matter of self-interest the middle classes should offer this wholesome alternative to their sons in order to protect them from the lures of dissipation, politics, and what Thierry described as "a so-called literature devoid of reason, taste, propriety, and integrity."[37] The appeal to self-interest was also apparent in Thierry's insistence that the qualifications of the Université provided the best possible justification for the superior status of the bourgeoisie. At a time when bourgeois families were ready to grasp any way of consolidating their new-found power, the argument was compelling; but so long as qualifications could be obtained without attending courses in the faculties, it did little to enhance enrollments. The means to that particular end which Thierry proposed—that instruction in the basic sciences for medical students should become the responsibility of the faculties of science rather than of the faculties of medicine[38]—was not adopted until 1893, when the certificat d'études physiques, chimiques et naturelles was introduced.[39]

At least in the provinces, communicating with a public that changed from one lecture to the next and valued science primarily as superior entertainment was an activity fraught with tribulations, and the need to cater for such a public came eventually (though, I would argue, slowly) to seem incompatible with the high professional status to which professors in the faculties aspired. The zoologist and anthropologist J. L. Armand de Quatrefages de Bréau was one professor who seems to have found his sojourns in provincial faculties a dispiriting experience. As an assistant in the Faculty of Medicine at Strasbourg (1830–32) and then as a *suppléant* in chemistry and professor of zoology in the Faculty of Science at Toulouse (1835–40), he complained of isolation from his disciplinary peers, a low salary (about 4,000 francs a year as a professor), and a local administration that regarded research as a self-indulgent frippery.[40] It was no surprise to Quatrefages that the great majority of newly appointed chairholders in the provincial faculties of science sank quickly into "disgraceful idleness."[41] Quatrefages's solution was to resign his chair in Toulouse and to take the road to Paris, where he lived for the next ten years without an academic post. A similar solution was adopted shortly afterward by Auguste Laurent, whose complaints as professor of chemistry in the Faculty of Science at Bordeaux from 1839 to 1845 were virtually identical to Quatrefages's. "I am dying of boredom here," he wrote to his friend Charles Gerhardt in June 1845. "I don't want to stay any longer. Whatever the cost, I must leave, even if I had to make do with a job at 2500 francs in Paris."[42] Some two months later, desperation brought him finally to the capital, where he pursued an unsatisfactory career on the margins of academic chemistry until his death in 1853.

It would be absurd to dismiss these complaints as insignificant. Clearly, disquiet among scientific *universitaires* was becoming more common during the 1830s and 1840s. Yet we should beware of assuming that at the end of the July Monarchy the academic profession was seething with discontent. In fact, at the midcentury, the majority of professors in the faculties of science throughout France, faced with precisely the same problems as confronted Thierry at Caen, Quatrefages at Toulouse, and Laurent at Bordeaux, seem to have accommodated to the limitations of their audiences and even to have exploited opportunities to appear as officially appointed cultural leaders or to earn modest fees by offering advice on technical matters. The professors of Bordeaux were particularly successful in this respect. Under the guidance of Jérémie-Joseph-Benoît Abria, who was professor of physics from 1838 to 1886 and dean from 1845 to 1886, they developed a tradition of public lecturing which avoided the snare of triviality. Of course, there were concessions: Abria's first task on his appointment to Bordeaux was to purchase apparatus for use in lecture demonstrations rather than in research.[43] But skillful husbandry and a municipal council that valued the faculty's contribution to the cultural life of the city ensured that there were funds left over to support the research of professors. Abria published fifty papers, most of them experimental contributions, in his long career in the faculty.[44] And he was by no means the only heavy producer among the six professors who held chairs in the Bordeaux faculty in 1850. Alexandre Baudrimont, who was professor of chemistry from 1848 until his death in 1880, published 125 papers in that period; Victor-Amédée Lebesgue, as professor of pure mathematics from 1838 to 1858, published 68 papers in his twenty years in the faculty; and there was a comparable degree of activity in the natural history sciences, in which Victor Raulin (professor of botany, mineralogy, and geology from 1846 to 1876 and professor of botany from 1876 to 1885) and Pierre-François-Aman Bazin (professor of zoology from 1839 to 1865) were both prolific, with 92 and 29 papers respectively. The professor of astronomy and rational mechanics, Constant Rollier (1841–58), who published nothing but his doctoral thesis, was the odd man out.

So, despite the running sore of low salaries and the requests for funds with which certain faculties bombarded the Ministry of Public Instruction, it would appear that the academic scientists who held posts in the faculties of science about 1850 were more contented with their lot, more active in their research, and better integrated with their local communities than has commonly been supposed. The publication records and the average length of service of the six Bordeaux professors I have mentioned (thirty years) do not suggest intellectual lethargy or profound dissatisfaction. Even Baudrimont, who had grounds for believing that his views on molecular structure were not taken seriously by the Parisian "establishment," overcame his early restlessness and settled contentedly into the life of the faculty.[45] The true malcontents were a small minority whose importance, I believe, has been exaggerated and whose voice became significant only from the 1850s.

But the continued readiness of most *universitaires* to conform to the traditional conception of the academic role cannot conceal the fact that the July Monarchy had marked a turning point for their profession. Both the nature and the status of the scientific community had undergone a fundamental change. As early as the 1830s, Biot perceived what was afoot, and he roundly deplored the assimilation of science to the state bureaucracy.[46] The effect had been to demean the *savant* and to make him neglect his high intellectual calling in order to pursue a variety of unworthy public duties. The criticism is all the more revealing since it came from someone who had never been averse to *haute vulgarisation*. But Biot became increasingly aware that the character of scientific debate was being debased by its constant exposure to an untutored mass audience of intellectual voyeurs. The admission of the general public to the meetings of the Académie des Sciences was typical of trends that had been in progress since the 1820s. As a result of this innovation, speakers were more likely to worry about their oratorical style than about the elucidation of difficult points; and there was always the danger that members would be reluctant to air unformed ideas for fear of ridicule in a press that was (as Biot rightly observed) avid for academic gossip and receptive to shallow brilliance.[47] The protests of Cuvier, as one of the permanent secretaries of the Académie from 1803 to 1832, had been in vain,[48] and the process had continued for a quarter of a century after his death. Writing in 1858, Biot observed:

[The Académie] has become a kind of free clearing-house for announcements, open indiscriminately to anyone and attended by a captive audience. As a result of this invasion by outsiders, scientific discussions among the members of the Académie have become rare and hard to conduct since all too often they are fired by feelings of personal animosity or by a desire to gain the attention of the crowd of onlookers, rather than by a true love of science or by any feeling of a need to exchange information.[49]

To some extent, Biot's testy reaction can be interpreted as that of a scientist whose standing with his peers and hopes of emerging as a great patron in his own right had suffered from the bitter assaults on the reputation of his mentor Laplace[50] and from his own adherence to the abandoned corpuscular theory of light. But it was also the response of an elder who had witnessed the descent of science into the marketplace, its expansion into a profession open to men of mediocre talents, and its growing dependence on an administration that cared little for the intellect and, in the sacred name of democracy, was unwilling to give men of learning the independence which Biot believed was due to them. Biot's ideal was a small, close-knit community of *savants* that would be free to engage in disinterested inquiry, always ready to address the lay public from on high but never its servant. He had expounded the ideal as a young man in his late twenties in 1803, when he argued that science could flourish only when its practitioners were placed above the vagaries of politics, economic need, and popular taste;[51] he retained it undimmed until his death in 1862.

Despite some reticence in his published statements, Biot was evidently in no doubt about the identity of those who were responsible for the change. The troubles of the Académie began when the ailing Joseph Fourier became one of the two permanent secretaries in 1822,[52] but more culpable by far (the implication was clear, though the name was never mentioned) was Biot's old rival (and Cuvier's), Arago. It was Arago, as permanent secretary from 1830 to 1853, who had made the ruminations of academicians instantly accessible not merely to the throngs in the public gallery, whom he welcomed, but also to anyone who cared to read the Académie's *Comptes rendus*, a weekly publication which he launched 1835. "Vulgarity" was a word that came readily to Biot's mind as he wrote of the meetings of the Académie,[53] and it was a word that others were quick to use in endorsing his perception of the ills of the French scientific community in the 1830s and 1840s. In this respect, the similarity between Biot's analysis and that of the mathematician Guglielmo Libri is particularly striking. In a violent and lengthy rebuke in the *Revue des deux mondes* in 1840, Libri made public the resentment which he had felt for some years as a member of the Académie des Sciences.[54] The new openness of the Académie had served to undermine the public's esteem for the *savant*, to turn academic elections into political events, and to divert science in the direction of the trivial and the useful at the expense of the elevated universalism which the more abstruse theoretical disciplines and mathematics helped to cultivate. For Libri, as for Biot, the chief culprit—"the wizard who has had the power to effect this great transformation"[55]—was Arago, a parvenu showman whose political interests persistently overrode those of the learned community which he so imperfectly represented.

But Biot and Libri were fighting against a tide in full spate. Not only did the leading scientific "performers" of the midcentury have a conception of academic life that was totally at odds with Biot's, but also the education of the new generation of *savants*, in particular that offered by the Ecole Normale, rewarded precisely the rhetorical skills that bore fruit in the public lecture. The *agrégation*, which gave access, via the *lycées*, to many careers in the faculties, especially in mathematics and physics,[56] was a test of verbal and intellectual dexterity and breadth in learning. Oral tests, including the delivery of a lecture on a subject announced only a few hours in advance, were decisive in determining the ranking of *agrégés*, so that glibness and the mastery of an immense body of received truths were the qualities that brought academic success. To some extent, this disregard for depth and originality was counteracted by the doctoral research that a growing proportion of aspirants to chairs undertook, usually in their late twenties while they held a teaching post in a *lycée* (see Table 2.3). But the effect of the doctorate was slight, for doctoral theses were almost invariably perfunctory affairs, written with little supervision and of striking brevity. Before 1850, for example, 63 percent of all theses in science were of less than forty pages.[57]

The dominant style of scientific life which emerged under the July Monarchy was further reinforced by the Ministry of Public Instruction, which controlled the entire *cursus* of academic career-making. From the time public instruction definitively became a separate ministerial responsibility under Guizot in 1832,[58] ministers encouraged the notion that professors should not shut themselves away in ivory towers. Chairholders, especially those in the provinces, were to involve themselves in their communities: they were to join local Academies and collaborate in research projects with the cultural elites of their region.[59] As a result, the man of learning came to be regarded as an official of the state in much the same way as a prefect or a judge. Hence he was sent to his post with a mission that was ostensibly routine but in reality was redolent with ideology. By appearing as the visible representatives of a benign administration, *universitaires* were fostering a sense of indebtedness that would bind the provincial bourgeoisie to Paris, help to reconcile regional *notables* to the regime (whether Orleanist, from 1830 to 1848, or Bonapartist, in the 1850s and 1860s), and further the quest for a unified national culture in which central government would assume the dominant place once occupied by the landed nobility and the Church.

As interpreted by a sensitive minister, this ideal was not necessarily damaging to the interests of learning. Guizot's achievements as a patron of historical scholarship in the 1830s bear witness to this.[60] But during the Second Empire, when political considerations loomed particularly large, the intellectual role of the professoriate was seriously at risk. Now, obedience to central authority on the one hand and the ability to establish good relations with the local community on the other were the only qualities that really mattered. As Fortoul put it in a ministerial circular in 1858, provincial *universitaires* should be ready to abandon the novelties and grand generalizations that might be appropriate to specialized teaching within their faculty. Instead, they should seek to imbibe the "spirit" of their region, and (most revealingly) should never forget the obligations imposed on them by their role as functionaries.[61]

By the same token, even the great *savants* of the capital came to be regarded primarily as ornaments, symbols of France's greatness. If they were supreme among the scientists of the world, as Fortoul contentiously maintained in August 1852, they owed their supremacy not so much to their superior intellect as to their being French. Their most valuable asset was their language:

Does our language not seem peculiarly well suited to the cultivation of science? With its clarity, sincerity, and lively yet logical character (which quickly and invariably gives primacy to the processes of thought rather than to those of observation), is it not destined to be not merely the most natural tool for science but also the most useful of guides? Are not its beauties, which foster both truth and reason, the most appropriate vestments in which science could be clothed?[62]

The statement is a telling one. In asserting that the public face of science mattered far more than its content, Fortoul was justifying the bureaucratic conception of academic life which had steadily gained ground since 1830. On the eve of the declaration of Napoleon III's Empire, the trends of the previous twenty years were being recognized explicitly. The *savant* was a servant, not a leader, of society.

The Roots of Reform in the Second Empire

It was to be expected that any organized form of protest within the academic profession would come first from the Université, in particular from the Faculties of Science, Letters, and Medicine. For, despite the reticence which most of them had shown before 1850, professors in these institutions had always had grounds for concern about their status and conditions of employment. By the midcentury, they were all too familiar with the desultory functioning of most faculties and with the superior position of both the *grandes écoles* and (a source of constant irritation in the medical faculties) the major teaching hospitals.[63] There was also no mistaking the fact that their profession had assumed a lowly rank in the hierarchy of occupations, and they knew, to their cost, that lowly status had its inevitable corollary in poor salaries. An income of between 4,500 and 7,000 francs, which was normal for chairholders in the provincial faculties in the 1850s and 1860s, made it hard for them to fulfill the expectations of the minister of public instruction.[64] How could they mix easily with the men they were supposed to regard as their social peers when established lawyers and senior government officials might easily earn between 15,000 and 20,000 francs? In circumstances of such blatant financial inferiority, the rank of even a modest local *notable* was beyond their expectations.

The only professors whose income rose significantly above the paltry norm were the leading Parisians. By the middle of the century, incomes comparable with those of Laplace and Claude-Louis Berthollet, which probably exceeded 100,000 francs a year in 1814,[65] were inconceivable. But a major *savant* in Paris might still earn between 10,000 and 60,000 francs, depending on his ability to manipulate the system of *cumul*.[66] In this respect, the disparity between center and periphery was glaring, and it was a major source of weakness in the academic profession. As Quatrefages de Bréau, Charles Gerhardt, and many other critics observed amid the egalitarian euphoria that followed the February revolution of 1848, *cumul* seriously reduced mobility and helped to maintain the superior position of professors in Paris with respect to their colleagues in the provinces.[67]

The gulf that separated the interests of Parisians and provincials helps to account for the comparative quiescence of *universitaires* during the Bourbon Restoration and the July Monarchy: the leaders and the rank and file of the academic profession simply had no sense of a common occupational identity. A strong patron in the capital might, if pressed, exert his influence in favor of a provincial professor, as Thenard agreed to do in 1834 to improve the conditions of work for the naturalist Alfred Moquin-Tandon of the Faculty of Science at Toulouse.[68] But Moquin-Tandon's plea was that of a desperate, neglected individual to a remote and essentially indifferent master with political power. The exchange does not suggest in any way that the two men saw themselves as pursuing the same profession, and Moquin-Tandon was certainly not acting in the interests either of his discipline nationally or even of his faculty. A personal favor was being requested and a personal favor was duly granted.

It was in the 1850s, during the "authoritarian" phase of the Second Empire, that the dissatisfaction that had hitherto been voiced in a piecemeal, uncoordinated fashion began to develop into a feeling of shared injustice. The main catalyst in this change was the Ministry of Public Instruction, in which, as ministers between 1851 and 1863, Hippolyte Fortoul (1851–56) and Gustave Rouland (1856–63) pursued a relentless policy of centralization and purification. A typical measure was the curtailing of the power of the Conseil de l'Instruction Publique. Since its establishment as the Napoleonic Conseil de l'Université Impériale in 1808, this important body had managed to temper the ascendancy of political considerations, especially in the matter of appointments, and it had acted (in the way Napoleon I had intended) to ensure some measure of corporate autonomy for the Université and its employees. Already, in the 1840s, the comte de Salvandy had allowed the autonomy, which his predecessors Guizot and Cousin had jealously protected, to be somewhat eroded.[69] But, from the time of the clerically inspired Falloux Law in March 1850, the process gathered a new and sinister momentum.[70] The representation of the clergy and of legal and political figures (many of them hostile to the Université) was enhanced to such an extent that the Conseil (like the councils of the individual academies) ceased in any way to speak for the academic profession; its function became that of a watchdog guarding the interests of society as a whole.[71] Under Fortoul, worse was to come, as power passed inexorably from the Conseil to the minister and his appointed representatives, in particular to his eight general inspectors of higher education (three of them for the sciences[72]) and his national network of compliant rectors.[73] The consequence was to make *universitaires* directly answerable to the ministry and further to reduce their capacity for independent action.

Fortoul's motives are clear enough. The move to greater centralization was his way of strengthening the secular institutions of the Bonapartist regime at a time when they were under the critical scrutiny of both the bourgeoisie and the Church. With the troubles of 1848 an all too vivid memory and with such Catholics as the comte de Montalembert and the bishop of Orléans, Félix Dupanloup, seeking to present the Church as the only sure bastion against social disorder, it was an unavoidable priority, for Fortoul, to allay public anxiety, in particular about the subversive opponents of Catholicism who were thought to have been working uncontrollably in the Université since the 1830s.[74] These same motives were equally evident in other innovations of the early 1850s: Fortoul's major reform of the *agrégation* and the associated program of *bifurcation*.[75] The thrust of these measures, which made five years' service in teaching a prerequisite for aspirants to the title of *agrégé* and reduced the number of *agrégations* from six (including Fortoul's special *bête-noire*, the *agrégation* in philosophy) to two (in science and letters), was to stress the pedagogical functions of *agrégés* at the expense of their intellectual aspirations. In Fortoul's words: "The measures that are proposed will serve to fashion modest teachers, rather than orators more adept at delving into dangerous and unsolvable problems than at conveying practical knowledge."[76] It was intended that the new provisions would remove the temptation for professors to resort to an empty theatrical performance or, worse still, to secure attention by "an appeal to the passions." Instead, the lessons of *agrégés* who went on to posts in the *lycées* were to be "dogmatic and purely elementary."

By parading discipline, self-effacement, and moral rectitude as virtues of overriding importance in *universitaires*, Fortoul hoped to counter the attractions of the independent Catholic colleges, which were beginning to proliferate and to attract middle-class support in the wake of the state's abandonment of its monopoly of secondary education by the Falloux Law. In the battle for bourgeois minds, the faculties too had their part to play, as the Catholic hierarchy proceeded to divert more of its energies to higher education and to its campaign for the right to establish its own system of universities. Given Fortoul's priorities, it is not surprising that the Ecole Normale Supérieure, of which he had spoken with derision some ten years earlier, was handled with particular harshness.[77] In accordance with the new system of *agrégations*, speculative studies were deemed inappropriate for *normaliens*, and both philosophy and modern history gave way to an even greater emphasis on the classical languages.[78]

The provocation was considerable to a profession struggling to maintain the last vestiges of a more dignified, independent style of learned culture. This was especially so as Fortoul's measures came hard on the heels of a purge of the faculties and *lycées* in which the moderate republican Jules Simon lost his post at the Sorbonne for publicly protesting against the coup d'etat of December 1851 and in which many other *universitaires* either resigned or suffered a similar fate for refusing to take an oath of allegiance to Louis-Napoleon.[79] Even those who did acquiesce seldom came easily to their decision: the doubts that racked the literary critic and *voltairien* Francisque Sarcey, who held a junior post in the *lycée* at Chaumont, are a case in point.[80]

The unprecedented meticulousness of ministerial supervision after 1851 is abundantly clear both from published sources and from the confidential reports which deans were required to submit to their rectors and which rectors in turn passed on to the ministry. Less than a week after the establishment of the Empire in December 1852, Fortoul found time to write a detailed letter to the rector of the academy of the Gironde observing that the professor of history, Joseph-François Rabanis, should be reprimanded for two assertions in the outline for his forthcoming lecture course: he should be informed that Roman law was not used by all the Germanic peoples of Gaul and that to suggest (as Rabanis evidently had done) that modern notions of human dignity were introduced by the pagans of northern Europe rather than by Christians was to betray "a false appraisal of the evidence."[81] Such misdemeanors were normally dealt with discreetly, and it was rare for a rebuke to become public. In this respect, the case of Victor de Laprade, professor of French literature in the Faculty of Letters at Lyons, is unusual. The notorious case in which Laprade lost his post for a satirical poem, "Les muses d'état," in December 1861, however, serves as a useful reminder that the control of academic life was as close under Rouland as it had been under Fortoul and that piety alone (Laprade was a Catholic and a Legitimist) was no protection for someone who voiced open opposition to the Empire.[82]

The evidence of forced intellectual and political conformity and the resentment that this caused between 1851 and 1863 is, as I have indicated, plentiful. Yet even in this period of repression, the patchy nature of the resentment is beyond question. At one pole, there was a network of young, liberally minded philosophers, recent graduates of the Ecole Normale Supérieure, who did feel keenly aggrieved; many of them turned from academic life to other pursuits, notably journalism.[83] But there were also those, including many resolutely secular *universitaires*, who saw no need for such a refuge and who actively supported Fortoul and Rouland. They recognized the advantages that might accrue to them from a policy whose aim was to enhance, not diminish, the public reputation of the faculties. It is no coincidence that these sympathizers were often scientists. For, in certain respects, the policies of Fortoul actually favored their disciplines. This was true, for example, of the notion of *bifurcation* and the establishment of the *baccalauréat* in science as an alternative rather than a sequel to the *baccalauréat-ès-lettres*.[84] By obliging pupils to opt for either the sciences or the humanities at the age of fourteen, Fortoul encouraged earlier specialization in the *lycées* and gave aspiring scientists the opportunity of reducing the time they devoted to classical studies—a change which Urbain Le Verrier and Dumas seem, understandably, to have welcomed. In view of the unhappy fate of philosophy and modern history under Fortoul, it is inconceivable that this could have happened if the sciences he particularly favored—the sciences of observation and mathematics—had not been seen as ideologically sound. In his eyes, such pursuits as natural history, astronomy, and experimental physics and chemistry appeared as "solid" as the study of the texts and artifacts of classical antiquity or the records of a provincial diocese, and they were supported accordingly.

Of the scientists who benefited from this conception of the anodyne nature of at least certain sciences, the most prominent, until the very end of the Second Empire, was the astronomer Le Verrier. He had all the qualities that the imperial regime looked for. In addition to a burning ambition, he was an orthodox Catholic, he was politically reliable (as a declared supporter of the Empire), and he possessed a reputation that far transcended the narrow world of technical astronomy. When Arago died in 1853, there could have been no better choice as the new director of the Paris Observatory than the immortal and exceedingly visible discoverer of Neptune. That Le Verrier thereupon inaugurated fifteen years of unparalleled wretchedness for the younger members of the Observatory's staff and seriously impaired the scientific reputation of the institution was a matter of little consequence in the Ministry of Public Instruction.[85] His subordinates' complaints about his maladministration, the stormy resignation of Camille Flammarion in 1862, and a saga of capricious dismissals all went unheeded until, in the more liberal political climate of 1870, he was finally removed from the directorship, following a ministerial inquiry.

Clearly it was because of, and not despite, imperial educational policy that Le Verrier prospered. And the same could be said of Dumas, the physicist Victor Regnault, the naturalists Henri Milne Edwards, Adolphe Brongniart, and Emile Blanchard, and several others who took advisory posts as scientists under direct ministerial patronage. By accepting such patronage, usually bestowed in the form of an influential position on the revitalized Comité des Travaux Historiques or as a general inspector of higher education,[86] these men were endorsing the official view that to live the life of the *savant* was to engage in a public act as an obedient servant of the Empire. To the extent that they were intended, as an essential part of that act, to stand prominently at the head of the world of learning in France, their position bore some resemblance to that of the great patrons of the early nineteenth century. But the resemblance was superficial. For even the leading men of French science under Fortoul and Rouland had neither the freedom of action nor the financial means and independence that had allowed the patrons of the age of Laplace and Cuvier not merely to advance or impede the prospects of younger men (that was still possible in the Second Empire) but to make or break academic careers and to dictate, unchecked, the course of entire disciplines. Even as determined an autocrat as Le Verrier had to act within bounds set by the Ministry of Public Instruction, and even he was eventually brought to heel.

Although the ministerial takeover impaired both the morale and the intellectual performance of large sections of the learned community, it did not lead to total inactivity. Far from it. But the research that was promoted, chiefly through the Comité des Travaux Historiques, was conceived almost invariably as a way of advancing the political objectives of the ministry. If such prizes as the unity of France and the good opinion of the bourgeoisie were to be won, it followed that the work of *savants* and *érudits* should be uncontroversial and, when possible, patriotic. The best possible example was set by the emperor himself, as he sought diligently (and, as it turned out, perceptively) to identify the site of the Gallic city of Alésia, where Caesar's victory over Vercingetorix had sealed the fate of the Gauls.[87] Precisely the same chauvinist tone was upheld by one of the most prominent figures on the Comité, Désiré Nisard, for whom the detached, rule-bound style of the seventeenth century represented the ideal in French literature.[88] And it appeared just as clearly in the renewed vigor with which the publication of documents concerning French history was pursued, and in an attempt, launched in 1853, to obtain a complete record of the nation's folk poetry and songs.[89] Even more blatantly nationalistic was a new biennial prize of 20,000 francs, which Rouland established in 1861, for the contribution to knowledge that would render the greatest honor or service to France. But perhaps the most ambitious new departure was the costly program of research that Rouland inaugurated under the auspices of the Comité des Travaux Historiques in 1858, which was intended to yield an exhaustive, multivolume description of the topography, archaeology, and natural history of the whole country. In the sciences, the scheme came to nothing: the *Description scientifique*, which was to describe the flora, fauna, geology, and meteorology of each department, was quickly abandoned as impracticable and ill-conceived. But, thanks largely to the efforts of self-taught devotees in the regions, the *Dictionnaire topographique* and *Répertoire archéologique* came to at least partial fruition, as did another patriotic venture launched at the same time, the *Dictionnaire archéologique de la Gaule*.[90]

The favor that Fortoul and Rouland showed to the Comité des Travaux Historiques was wholly in keeping with the policies of the *Empire autoritaire* of the 1850s. It reflected a determination to court the vast and hugely productive army of independent *savants* and *érudits* who had experienced some inevitable marginalization as the system of faculties had expanded in the 1830s and 1840s. Both Fortoul and Rouland insisted that these private scholars, no less than *universitaires*, should be eligible for official patronage and encouragement. In this way, as they knew, they would bind the educated bourgeois elites to the imperial regime while at the same time curbing any exaggerated intellectual pretensions on the part of professors in the faculties. The more the boundary between devotee and professional was obscured, the less appropriate such pretensions would become. And that, plainly, was seen as a desirable objective.

There could be no mistaking the fact that relations within the French world of learning were being drastically and deliberately altered. In all they did, Fortoul and Rouland were intent on pressing their claims to exclusive authority in intellectual matters and hence on challenging the existing holders of that authority both inside and outside the official institutions. Among those who felt moved to resist, general political opposition to the Empire became inextricably bound up with a stubborn defense of the autonomy of the learned community. This attitude is well illustrated by the response of the Académie Française, which emerged as a focus for opposition both to the ministry and to the emperor. The elections of the Legitimist lawyer Antoine Berryer and a succession of known opponents of the Empire, including Dupanloup, Antoine Silvestre de Sacy, and the duc de Broglie, were all seen as famous victories; and there were similar episodes in the Académie des Sciences Morales et Politiques (which elected the Orleanist Odilon Barrot despite Fortoul's clandestine machinations) and the Académie des Inscriptions et Belles-Lettres (in which Fortoul's election, embarrassingly, was secured only at the second attempt in 1855).[91]

Equal resentment was felt by the leaders of independent science and scholarship, most of them in the provinces, who had directed the cultural life of their diverse regions since the great days of the provincial academies in the eighteenth century. The main spokesman for their cause was the Norman naturalist, musician, and antiquarian, Arcisse de Caumont. Since the 1830s, Caumont had been engaged in a determined campaign against the centralization of French intellectual life. In his eyes, the Ministry of Public Instruction's promises of help with publication and the offers of expert guidance by the Comité des Travaux Historiques were siren calls to which a deaf ear should be turned. Private scholars who accepted assistance would have no choice, in return, but to recognize the ministry as their patron and to defer to the expanding official bureaucracy of learning in the faculties—a bureaucracy of which Caumont was intensely suspicious. As I have argued elsewhere, the sheer scale of government patronage offered a sore temptation to provincial *savants* and *érudits* who aspired to national recognition, and, to Caumont's disgust, many of those whose allegiance he sought duly succumbed, to the point of participating in the publishing ventures of the Comité des Travaux Historiques and accepting the prizes offered to independent scholars by the ministry.[92] In response, Caumont could offer a capacious purse (secured by a profitable marriage) and a resolve fired by a studiously concealed Legitimism, an unquenchable zeal for decentralization, and a nostalgia for social hierarchies based on birth, privilege, and property. It is a mark of Caumont's extraordinary pertinacity that the institutions he created at the beginning of his campaign in the 1830s—the Congrès Scientifiques and Congrès Archéologiques (both peripatetic bodies modeled on the British Association for the Advancement of Science) and the Institut des Provinces (his provincial counterpart to the Institut de France)—were still in existence at the time of his death in 1873. But, with the exception of the Congrès Archéologiques (which have survived to this day, albeit with few vestiges of independence), Caumont's sturdy provincialism had virtually no lasting effect on the world of learning in France.

The rhetoric of intellectual freedom loomed equally large in yet another, far more effective form of opposition to the territorial aspirations of the ministry. This opposition came from a vociferous minority within the corps of *universitaires* itself and was of a very different cast from that mounted by Caumont and the remnants of the landed Catholic nobility who backed his campaign. Its aim, like Caumont's, was to loosen the shackles of government, but its method was to strengthen the faculties and give them the independence and intellectual vigor they so palpably lacked. The political tinge of the opposition was distinctly liberal; its concern was not to extend clerical influences in education (as it was for Caumont) but to diminish them; and its social base lay not among private scholars but in the swelling ranks of younger men in the earlier stages of university careers.[93] Above all, it was an opposition committed to the ideals of free inquiry and research and hostile to the ministerial notion of the Université as a learned bureaucracy.

Although in the 1850s it would be extravagant to see this response as a unified reform movement, the signs of changing priorities among at least some *universitaires* are unmistakable. One such sign was a new dissatisfaction with the parochialism that had plagued French scientific life for a quarter of a century and had already drawn a pungent comment from Sir John Herschel. In a letter to Edward Sabine in 1843, Herschel wrote (with reference to his plan for an international program of meteorological and magnetic observations):

It is not only in want of observational cooperation that French science is insulating itself. I see or fancy I see a kind of moody self-concentration and withdrawal from contact with the science of all other nations—a sort of *ignoring* of what is done *out of France* which it is not pleasing to contemplate. This has been going on for many years. Perhaps I am wrong. I hope so.[94]

In fact, Herschel was not wrong. At the time of the restoration in 1814, French scientists had been as zealous as any of their compatriots for a renewal of contact with Britain, but the enthusiasm soon waned. There is clear evidence that, from the 1820s, the French withdrew from major areas of international collaboration in science.[95] It is significant, in this respect, that when Arago attended the meeting of the British Association for the Advancement of Science at Edinburgh in 1834, he was received with an excitement appropriate to an exceedingly rare event.[96] Still more important, in the long term, was the indifference displayed during the July Monarchy toward Germany. In this period, the scientists of France showed little of the interest in developments across the Rhine that was evident in the humanities and the arts.[97] With Alexander von Humboldt back in Berlin and appearing only intermittently in Paris, science had no equivalent of Edgar Quinet and his fellow contributors to the *Revue des deux mondes* to convey the scientific dimension of Germany's intellectual revival.

So at a time, before 1848, when German scholarship was beginning to make its mark on the historical writing of Jules Michelet or, in philology, on the young Ernest Renan, science remained largely unaffected. But in science, as in politics, the events of 1848–52 seem to have marked a watershed. By the early 1850s, a few French scientists were beginning to air publicly opinions identical to Herschel's. The charge of parochialism was clearly implied, for example, in the introduction, in the main French journal for the physical sciences (the *Annales de chimie et de physique*), of regular translations of papers that had been published abroad. It was in this series, begun in 1852 and still going strong in the 1870s, that the major papers by Rudolf Clausius, James Prescott Joule, and William Thomson (the future Lord Kelvin), among many others, first became well known in France. The translations were the work of the organic chemist Adolphe Wurtz and the physicist Emile Verdet, both Protestants from distant provinces (Alsace and Provence respectively), and both academics dedicated to combating the insularity of French science.[98] By their work for the *Annales*, they were asserting unmistakably that academic life should be a life of criticism and innovation, dedicated to the universality of knowledge. According to their unspoken ideals, the proper public for the *savant* was the dispersed international community of disciplinary peers rather than the *grand public* gathered in a comfortable amphitheater or a minister in search of political advantage or administrative efficiency.

From the start, the two pillars of the reformers' case were the need to cultivate independent research in accordance with the state of the discipline and the opening of French intellectual life to foreign audiences and influences, in particular to the influences of Germany. The case was one that easily transcended disciplinary boundaries. The interests of the scientific reformers were seen as being no different from those of Renan and a network of young, liberally minded scholars in the humanities. These nonscientific allies included Gabriel Monod (in history), Michel Bréal (in linguistics), and Karl Hillebrand (in modern European literature), all of whom had experienced the excitement of German university life at first hand.[99] The extent of the common cause is displayed very clearly in the balanced analysis of the shortcomings of the French university system which Hillebrand wrote in 1868 from his perspective as professor of foreign literature in the Faculty of Letters at Douai.[100] Scientists were not alone in their admiration for the prosperous and largely autonomous universities of Germany and the "scientific spirit" which they nurtured.

A fortnightly journal, the *Revue germanique*, encapsulated the intellectual breadth and the liberalism and internationalism of the early reform movement.[101] Founded in 1858 by two bilingual Alsatian liberals, Charles Dollfus and Auguste Nefftzer, it combined scientific, literary, and philosophical interests and quickly became a powerful instrument in the awakening of France to the achievements of the German cultural tradition. As a mark of its modernity, it pursued a policy of giving prominence not only to the "old" Germany of romanticism and metaphysics but more particularly to experimental science, archaeology, and biblical and historical scholarship. Since German science by this time included the materialism of Jacob Moleschott, Ludwig Büchner, and Carl Vogt, there were those who found the message of the *Revue* loathsome. Bonapartists and conventional Catholics saw articles on these subjects as a demonstration of the evils that would accrue from unbridled criticism and the intrusion of alien philosophies. The argument of Dollfus and Nefftzer in favor of the breaking down of national barriers, and their assertion that solidarity among nations was a mark of the highest civilization,[102] made conspicuously little impression on the rank chauvinism of the conservative supporters of Napoleon III.

The association between liberal politics and the professional aspirations of those who admired the German style of university life is striking. Openness to foreign influences, in particular, became a mark of opposition to the Empire. In this respect, the traditions of the *Revue germanique* were soon reinforced by other periodicals, notably the *Revue des cours scientifiques de la France et de l'étranger*. The *Revue* was launched in 1863 by Germer Baillière, a publisher who consistently espoused the cause of academic reform. Under its first editor, Odysse-Barot, the friend of Emile de Girardin and a future *communard*, and then under two prominent liberal journalists, Emile Alglave and Eugène Yung, it gave weekly publicity to the work of the most creative scientists both in France and abroad, while leaving its readers in no doubt concerning the growing marginality of French *savants* in the international world of science. A similar point was made for the humanities in a companion publication, the *Revue des cours littéraires*, which came from the same publishing house and appeared under the same editorship.[103]

It cannot be stressed too strongly just how far the new emphasis on criticism and the international character of learning departed from the official policy of the 1850s and early 1860s. It implied a distancing of the chairholders in the faculties both from the administration in Paris and from the lay public, which they had traditionally been appointed to serve. It also implied contempt for research of the kind encouraged by Fortoul and Rouland. Their grand patriotic enterprises were despised both for their accessible, uncontentious character and for the high degree of involvement on the part of self-taught enthusiasts. As the reformers knew very well, the really important goals of higher professional standing and greater autonomy were not going to be achieved by supervising scholarly activity that was at once superficial and of no interest to the learned community outside France.

Similar considerations dictated the cool response of reforming *universitaires* to the annual congresses of delegates from the nation's learned societies begun by Rouland in 1861.[104] At these glittering occasions in the Sorbonne, the "States General of study and learning," as Rouland called them,[105] met for four or five days each autumn to witness prizes and unctuous praise being bestowed by the leading figures on the Comité des Travaux Historiques: Dumas, Henri Milne Edwards, Emile Blanchard, and Le Verrier in the sciences, Nisard and Amédée Thierry in the humanities. The labors that won approval did so, typically, for their thoroughness, seldom for their depth or novelty. Ritual was paramount; hierarchies were fulsomely reinforced; bourgeois self-esteem was bolstered; and, most provocatively in the eyes of the reformers, the gulf that separated the academic elite of Paris from their peers in the provinces was blithely obscured. In principle, of course, Parisian and provincial professors were engaged in the same profession. But Milne Edwards's arrogant dismissal of complaints emanating from the provinces at the first congress in 1861 showed how illusory this unity was: "I often hear young professors in the Université bemoaning what they call their banishment to the provinces, and ascribing the inactivity of which they are sometimes guilty to the difficulties of isolation. But these are false notions which it is important to eradicate."[106] To such embittered campaigners as Félix Pouchet and Victor Meunier—both of whom recognized the obstacles to serious intellectual production in the provinces—such lofty disregard for their problems was an affront. As Meunier observed, it was all too predictable that the delights of provincial life should be extolled by those who, under no circumstances, would consider accepting a post outside the capital.[107]

It is customary to see the arrival of Victor Duruy at the Ministry of Public Instruction in 1863 as the dawn of a new age in the history of the academic profession in France. In some respects, this was the case, though it is not clear how much the improving morale of the profession after that date owed to Duruy himself and how much it owed to the general liberalization of Napoleon's regime. Duruy, at all events, was in every respect a man of the liberal Empire of the 1860s. His unexpected appointment (over the heads of the more obvious candidates, Nisard and Le Verrier) owed everything to his personal friendship with the emperor,[108] and his presence, as an agnostic, at the head of the educational system aggravated the steady deterioration of Napoleon III's relations with the Church following his capricious intervention in Italian affairs in 1858–59.

It was evident to friend and critic alike that Duruy had little in common with his two predecessors. As a historian, he was convinced of the virtues of German scholarship. And, as a *universitaire*,[109] he had suffered from the oppressive policies of the 1850s. In 1853 he had entered the ranks of liberal heroes when his doctoral thesis provoked a much-publicized confrontation with his examiner, Nisard, who improperly interpreted Duruy's judgment of Caesar as an implied statement of support for Napoleon I and the French imperial dynasty.[110] Hence it was no surprise, but a source of delight to the reformers, that Duruy showed himself ready to foster the links with the wider world of critical research which the traditionalists had always spurned. In a way that would have been unthinkable ten years earlier, a major inquiry into the state of French higher education was undertaken,[111] employees of the Université were sent to study teaching practices and research in Germany, Switzerland, Belgium, Italy, and Britain,[112] and in 1868 Duruy had his greatest triumph when he established the Ecole Pratique des Hautes Etudes to promote both scientific and humanistic research.

Although Duruy's desire to help the reformers is beyond question, his achievements on their behalf were modest. Even the Ecole Pratique was no more than a federation of existing research facilities; it led to the establishment of some new posts (chiefly research assistantships) and of several specialized journals, but it was poorly financed and did little to improve the lot of anyone who lacked connections with the Parisian academic elite.[113] The greatest obstacle was conservative opposition, both inside and outside Parliament, to the notion of the uncontrolled, researching professor. Ultramontane clergy, piqued by the growing antagonism between the Church of Rome and the Empire, saw no reason why the faculties, with their traditions of free-thinking and secularism, should be strengthened. And no traditionalist, clerical or lay, could see any virtue in the provision of funds to allow a *savant* to shrug off his various public functions simply to retreat to his laboratory or library and thereby to advance materialism and pantheism. The fruits of that form of liberty were there for all to see in the mounting vogue for Hegel (a trend particularly deplored by Dupanloup), in Félix Pouchet's speculations on spontaneous generation (so effectively combated by the Catholic Louis Pasteur between 1859 and 1864[114]), and in Renan's hateful *Vie de Jésus* (1863). And that was to say nothing of the continuing student unrest, especially at the Faculty of Medicine in Paris, which professors seemed unable, in some cases unwilling, to suppress.

Conservative fears on all these grounds were expressed with increasing stridency during the six years during which Duruy served as minister.

The fears tended to be conflated with general attacks on liberalism in all its forms, with the faculties being identified as nests of republicans, positivists, and deviants in religion, ranging from members of the Orthodox Church (Auguste Axenfeld), Protestants (Paul Broca), and Jews (Germain Sée) to professed materialists (for example, the disciple of Auguste Comte and Emile Littré, Charles Robin). Naturally, the most virulent attacks came from the leaders of the Catholic clergy, now more determined than ever to secure the freedom of higher education. In their rhetoric, Duruy was portrayed as an unworthy guardian of the minds and morality of the young; he was a man whose religious skepticism smacked strongly of positivism and the friend of an emperor whose allegiance to the Church of Rome was itself in doubt. Opposition to Duruy came to a head with the appearance of a petition (with some two thousand signatures), which was presented to the Senate in June 1867 by a leading Catholic journalist, Léopold Giraud.[115] In drawing attention to the "baneful doctrines" of materialism being propagated in the faculties, the petition left no doubt that the chief culprits were certain professors in the Faculty of Medicine in Paris. As a result, it was these professors—Robin in particular—who took the brunt of the onslaught from the ultramontane cardinal archbishop of Rouen, Boisnormand de Bonnechose, when the petition was debated by the Senate a year later.

Amid the clerically inspired furore that followed the Giraud petition, it was all too easy for Duruy to be branded as the champion both of the Université (which he was, resolutely) and of the pernicious philosophy it was said to be promoting. In fact, this was a travesty of Duruy's position. For although one of his first acts as minister was to reestablish the *agrégation* in philosophy (as part of a dismantling of Fortoul's *bifurcation*), he always insisted that he did not condone the views of the extreme freethinkers. His caution was not simply a matter of expediency. Duruy was a moderate: modern-minded and a critic of the secular authority of the Church but in no sense a radical either in politics or in philosophy. Hence if we are to understand the limited character of his achievements in the cause of educational reform, we have to take account not only of the external constraints on his actions but also of his own streak of conservatism, which made the preservation of order the highest of his priorities. His determination to control the world of learning in France was quite as firm as Fortoul's or Rouland's, and his discipline was no less strict.[116] He saw to it that five students who attended the radical International Congress of Students at Liège in 1865 were punished by the Conseil de l'Instruction Publique.[117] And when Robin was charged with purveying materialist doctrines in a lecture at the Faculty of Medicine in 1866,

Duruy issued a prompt rebuke: Robin's job was to teach physiology, not metaphysics.[118] Likewise, in March 1868, the approval of a doctoral thesis that denied free will, the distinction between man and beast, and moral responsibility was withdrawn by Duruy's personal decree, and the professor who had accepted it was reprimanded.[119]

Duruy's determination to steer a prudent middle course was apparent in every aspect of his policy. It is entirely in keeping with his approach that at the same time as he worked to improve research facilities and raise the status of the creator of knowledge, he also reinforced the traditional function of the *savant* as a performer. In 1864, he took steps to revive the practice of public lecturing, which had flagged though it had never died under the strict censorship of Fortoul and Rouland. Duruy reminded his rectors that authorization to give public lectures for adults could be granted to anyone, whether or not he was employed by the Université. *Universitaires* had a special role and expertise, however, and they were to be particularly encouraged, though control was to be strict.[120] Duruy stressed that all titles would have to be approved by him in advance. Moreover, he would sanction only subjects of a scientific or literary nature that fulfilled his twofold objective of providing useful and morally improving information for the *classes laborieuses* and what he termed "an elegant and beneficial diversion" for the *classes élevées*.[121] In pursuit of this objective, the discussion of political and religious matters, however obliquely it might be cast, would be forbidden, and permission would be granted only to speakers who gave evidence of "maturity, experience, and ability,"[122] a euphemism that had the intended effect of excluding all those who were not ideologically acceptable. In practice, the scrutiny of applications and of the lectures that were actually given was every bit as careful as Duruy promised it would be. National and departmental archives are littered with correspondence concerning the soundness of potential lecturers, and it was not unusual for permission to be refused, sometimes to the accompaniment of a major public outcry.[123] Yet the policy was markedly more liberal than it could conceivably have been under Fortoul and Rouland, and the lectures were, by any standards, a success, even if those who attended were socially very restricted. Occasionally lectures were given free of charge, but a fee of about three francs for a lecture, often with a concessionary rate for a family ticket, was more normal. Even such a modest financial barrier helped to secure the tone of the audience—a consideration of great importance for Duruy.[124]

Of course, ministerial encouragement alone would not have sustained the new vogue, and the lectures depended heavily on the willing cooperation of both *universitaires* and private citizens and on private as well as public initiative. Among the private enterprises that flourished in response to Duruy's call, one of the earliest was that of a circle centered on Emile Deschanel, a former professor of Greek, who had lost his posts at the Ecole Normale Supérieure and the Lycée Louis-le-Grand in 1850 and been exiled after the coup d'etat of December 1851. The lectures mounted by this circle, first in the rue de la Paix and later in the boulevard des Capucines, were still a major society event on the eve of the Franco-Prussian war.[125] But outstanding among the private patrons of lectures was the Jewish German banker Louis-Raphaël Bischoffsheim, who placed a newly built theater in the rue Scribe at the disposal of a lecture society when it was not in use for musical events. It was here, in the subterranean "cave à Bischoffsheim," that the society's secretary, the liberal journalist Eugène Yung, organized the most successful of all the Parisian lecture halls of the 1860s. From 1866 to 1869, on three evenings a week, he offered lectures on science, medicine, literature, the arts, travel, and history to packed audiences of teachers, students, and both men and women of the *beau monde*.[126]

As a patron, Duruy himself was not to be outshone. Indeed, he became something of a pacesetter when, in March 1864, he began the weekly "Soirées scientifiques et littéraires" at the Sorbonne. At these semiofficial lectures, the forum was reserved for *universitaires* and the professoriate of the *grandes écoles* and the national research institutions. The presentation was somewhat more academic than in the rue de la Paix and the rue Scribe, but the receptions were no less rapturous. At the first lecture, given by Jules Jamin, the professor of physics at the Sorbonne and the Ecole Polytechnique, two thousand people squeezed into the great *amphithéâtre des lettres*, leaving three or four thousand more clamoring for entry outside.[127] The crowd was so great that Duruy himself could not get into the hall until after the lecture had started, and Jamin was interrupted by salvoes of applause as he moved eloquently from one startling demonstration to another, to expound the three states of matter. Predictably, Victor Meunier, the most acerbic of all critics of imperial science, viewed the exercise with wry amusement, though by the end of the first series of lectures even he had to acknowledge their success: in his words, what had once been a mere fad had become a need.[128]

The element of *immobilisme* that characterized the policies of Duruy was enough to ensure that the indignation of the reformers continued to grow. Despite his obvious sympathy for the Université and for reform, Duruy was not exempt from criticism. Resentment against the intellectual censorship which, even under Duruy, prevented men of the stature of Jules Simon, Saint-Marc-Girardin, and Edouard Laboulaye from giving public lectures slipped easily into resentment not only against the imperial regime but also against those who served it.[129] As Duruy knew well, this politicization of the reform movement was a divisive and potentially unhelpful development. His ideal had always been an academic community that would secure the higher status due to it by presenting a united front in the face of the clerical challenge. But if Duruy was to back the aspirations of the community while retaining the bourgeois support on which the Empire depended, the Université could not afford to appear as a threat to morality and the order of society. So at one moment Duruy had to be seen to have acted firmly to allay fears about Robin's materialism, while at another, in 1867, he had to intervene to remove the very Catholic Pasteur from his post as administrator and director of scientific studies at the Ecole Normale Supérieure, following student unrest precipitated by Pasteur's authoritarianism.[130] The task was particularly delicate because the Bonapartist Pasteur, no less than the republican Robin, was a champion of the new breed of researching professor which Duruy wanted to introduce. In fact, in his ten years at the Ecole Normale, Pasteur had contributed significantly to reform by his efforts to establish a distinctive career-pattern for young *normalien* scientists aspiring to a post in higher, as opposed to secondary, education. Thanks to Pasteur, it became easier, though by no means normal, for such men to substitute a junior research appointment at the Ecole Normale for the traditional debilitating spell in a *lycée*.[131]

In all he did, Duruy had the support of the emperor to set against the conservative opposition in Parliament.[132] But eventually even that support was withdrawn in July 1869, when Napoleon sacrificed his old friend in his quest for a rapprochement with the Church. With Duruy's dismissal, the Université was abandoned once again to the whims of an unfriendly administration, which showed its mettle some months later by peremptorily closing the medical faculty in Paris in response to a politically motivated student disturbance.[133] To outraged liberals such as Jules Ferry, the implication was clear: even the modest degree of intellectual and administrative independence which the academic profession had secured since 1863 was in jeopardy.[134]

A New Public for Science: The Industrial Constituency

By the late 1860s, the clamor of the reformers had assumed an unprecedented intensity and coherence. One essential condition for this change was the growing sense of corporate identity among teachers in the faculties. They were not only more numerous than they had been twenty years before (by a factor of about one-third in the faculties of science), but they were also far more likely to have shared common experiences and aspirations in their education and early careers. For the sciences, Table 2.3 makes the point clearly. Among those who held scientific chairs at the end of the Empire, a career pattern that included attendance at a major *lycée*, three years at the Ecole Normale Supérieure, followed by success in the *agrégation* and roughly ten years' service in secondary education (during which a doctoral thesis would have been written) was common; the exceptions tended to be found in the comparatively marginal disciplines of natural history and geology, for which an early background in medicine was more usual.

Another new element that served to direct the reform movement was the continuing rise of the German universities as centers of research. The style of German university life was now the standard to be emulated, with the inevitable result that calls for a strengthening of the performance of the Université in research became increasingly strident. A study of German medical education by Paul Lorain,[135] a submission which Pasteur made privately to the emperor in 1868,[136] and Adolphe Wurtz's magisterial description of the lavishly endowed German university laboratories[137] all bore the unmistakable implication that France had culpably neglected creative science. Even a series of works commissioned by Duruy as a way of glorifying the intellectual achievements of France at the time of the Universal Exhibition in Paris in 1867[138] contained signs of discontent. In his report on the state of French physiology, for example, Claude Bernard referred enviously to the facilities of the German universities, contrasting them with the material impediments which he and, before him, François Magendie had encountered at the Collège de France.[139] No less significantly for a study of professionalization, he argued for the need to separate his discipline from the lesser pursuit of natural history, "les sciences naturelles," in which fieldwork and simple observation were all-important.[140] For Bernard, physiology was, or should be, a laboratory science of great complexity. It required a rigorous training that placed it beyond the reach of the enthusiast and so severed the bond that had made such self-taught provincial natural historians and geologists as Léon Dufour, Henri Lecoq, and Jacques Boucher de Perthes important auxiliaries in the work of the Parisian masters.[141]

As Duruy knew better than anyone, legitimation of these various demands for better conditions and higher professional status was far from easy. The plain fact was that cases vaguely couched in terms of national prestige or the long-term material benefits that might accrue if scientists were given their head (the argument of Pasteur[142]) were not likely to win public approval at a time when the Church was inveighing against materialism and free thought and when the needs of the state for technical manpower seemed to be amply satisfied by the *grandes écoles*. Hence the reformers looked in vain to a minister whose goodwill toward the Université was beyond question but whose room for maneuver, amid overwhelming political and clerical pressures, was negligible.

The most obvious remedy was for the academic profession as a whole to secure a new role that would commend it to government and laymen alike. Academics, in short, needed a public that would appreciate them for their ability to train, innovate, or render expert advice, rather than to entertain and administer state examinations. For scholars in the humanities, utilitarian arguments along these lines tended to lack conviction, and it was only very late in the century that historians and social scientists persuaded republican politicians of their special capacity to instill an appropriate form of moral and civic virtue.[143] But in the sciences, such arguments were more easily made, and they became steadily more potent as new opportunities in science-based industry extended the market for technical knowledge and trained manpower. Of course, a rhetoric of industrial utility had the great disadvantage of driving a wedge between the useful and the purely scholarly. The conflict between disciplines on this count was unmistakable, though it was treated with such discretion that it rarely became overt. From the time of its foundation in 1878, the Société pour l'Etude des Questions d'Enseignement Supérieur countered the conflict by bringing together advocates of reform in both the sciences and the humanities; through its influential journal, the *Revue internationale de l'enseignement*, it did much to sustain the disciplinary unity that had characterized the nascent reform movement in the Second Empire.[144] But by the 1870s the tide was flowing against unity, and thereafter the interests of scientists in academic life diverged ever more markedly from those of their peers in the faculties of letters.[145] Crocodile tears might be shed, but, for professors in the faculties of science, disunity was a small price to pay for rewards that soon proved irresistibly lucrative.

At the beginning of the Second Empire, there had been few regions in which the industrial alternative to state patronage was realistic. But the department of the Nord, with its textile and chemical industries, was a notable exception; and it was there, in Lille, that some of the earliest attempts to establish the bond between academic and industrial science were made in the newly established Faculty of Science.[146] As the first dean and professor of chemistry, from 1854 to 1857, the ever-enterprising Pasteur set the pace, but he had willing colleagues and successors who maintained the lectures on industrial matters which he initiated and produced a stream of learned publications on applied science. There were similar successes, too, at another new science faculty of the 1850s, in Nancy. Here, Alexandre Godron, as dean and professor of natural history, argued for a total reorientation of the function of the nation's faculties of science. Their aim should no longer be simply to produce "educated men"; they should provide France with those practically trained "useful citizens" who would advance the industries of their various regions.[147] By 1855, his colleague Hervé Faye, the professor of pure and applied mathematics, could envisage the emergence, on the periphery of the faculty, of an informal faculty of industry.[148] And that is effectively what happened. By the end of the Second Empire, the professors of Nancy collaborated with representatives of the world of industry and commerce to offer a remarkable program of evening lectures on the applications of both the physical and the biological sciences.

In Paris, the association with industry aroused distinctly less interest. To all appearances, the lack of serious commitment that killed Dumas's plan for industrially oriented courses and a new *licence* and doctorate in *sciences pratiques* at the Sorbonne at the end of the July Monarchy lingered on.[149] It could scarcely have been otherwise, for there was little reason why the official elite of French science, basking in ministerial favor, should have chosen, at this stage, to abandon its traditional roles. Yet even in Paris there were a few dissenters as early as the 1850s. Wurtz, not yet in the Académie des Sciences and with no standing in the ministry, was one of the first Parisians to exploit the new industrial market.

The context that Wurtz chose was the Société Chimique de Paris. The society, founded in 1857 as a modest discussion group by three young laboratory assistants, was taken over in 1858 by a circle of academic reformers, headed by Wurtz, who used it as a vehicle for uniting all those with a serious interest in chemistry.[150] The bond between members was emphatically competence in the discipline, irrespective of the particular branch of the subject which interested them, irrespective of the school in which they were trained, and irrespective of the public service or industry in which they were employed. Within a decade, the success of the Société Chimique had amply vindicated the decision to break with the traditional resort of discontented *universitaires*. Instead of addressing yet more pleas to the minister, Wurtz and his associates had gone out to secure a new public for chemical expertise. The fruits of their enterprise were evident by the late 1860s in a membership of almost three hundred, an annual income of about 8,000 francs, and a journal of pure and applied chemistry that contained over a thousand pages a year.[151]

But it was only after the Franco-Prussian war of 1870 that the new alliance between academic science and utility was consolidated and only then that it spread from chemistry to other disciplines. The conditions that followed the defeat at Sedan could hardly have been more favorable to the reform movement. The widespread conviction that France had been betrayed by the Empire and its institutions led easily to a clamor for change. The crisis was so keenly felt that even some senior members of the scientific establishment expressed their concern. Witness the momentous meeting of the Académie des Sciences on 6 March 1871 at which member after member rose to deplore the state of science in France.[152] Such public criticism from within the Académie was unheard-of, but most of the complaints had been voiced in other contexts for some years: the parsimony of government support, overcentralization, and excessive bureaucracy. One other complaint, which had been felt throughout the Second Empire without being fully articulated, was that the Académie had ceased to represent what the critics conceived to be the true interests of the scientific community. The charge undoubtedly had substance. For not only had the membership of the Académie aged somewhat since the Bourbon Restoration,[153] it had also done nothing to prevent the control of science from passing from scientists into the hands of ministerial officials.

It was clearly the Académie's failure to resist the bureaucratization of science that caused the greatest resentment, if we are to judge by the debate of 6 March. Academicians had stood idly by as French science had become an arm of the state and, as a result, declined relative to that of Germany. In the words of the chemist Henri Sainte-Claire Deville, who initiated the debate, successive administrations since the Revolution all had their share of blame:

The cause lies in the regime that has crushed us for the last eighty years. It is a regime which makes men of science subject to politicians and administrators, and which entrusts the business of science—its dissemination, teaching, and application—to bodies and departments in which competence and hence the desire for progress are lacking.[154]

As it happened, Sainte-Claire Deville's criticism of the incubus of government control had little effect. With the Commune only days away, the committee of inquiry which the Académie appointed never met, and the institution resumed its position as the increasingly unrepresentative oligarchy at the head of France's men of science. From 1866 to 1913, in a period when the number of practicing scientists in academic and industrial life grew hugely, the Académie underwent neither expansion (from its membership of sixty-six) nor structural change.

Outside the Académie, however, the determination to break with the traditional hierarchies and to fashion a new community that would embrace representatives of the academic, manufacturing, and public service sectors gained strength from the sense of crisis. This was clear from the accelerating growth of the Société Chimique[155] and, even more so, from the history of the Société Française de Physique, which emerged in 1873 from a private discussion group that Pierre-Auguste Bertin had held for some years in his physics laboratory at the Ecole Normale Supérieure.[156] From the start, the academic exclusiveness of Bertin's circle was abandoned (though not without a revealing protest from Bertin himself),[157] and the society set out to court trained, practicing physicists, regardless of where they were employed. The policy of openness achieved its objectives. By 1875, membership stood at 235; ten years later it was 720; and between 1885 and 1910, it increased still further to 1,558. By 1910, the Société Française de Physique was easily the biggest and most prosperous of the national societies devoted to a single scientific discipline.[158]

The price the Société Française de Physique paid for its success was not negligible. If the society was to embrace *polytechniciens* working in the state telegraphic service, *normaliens* teaching in *lycées*, and graduates of the Ecole Centrale des Arts et Manufactures and other technical schools employed in the electrical industry, it could not afford to be too esoteric. As a result, there was a tendency, especially before 1900, for the meetings to be dominated by the gadgetry of physics and for advanced theory to be neglected. In 1876, the elderly physicist Jean-Antoine Quet, as president of the society, found Marcel Brillouin's interest in the kinetic theory of gases absurd;[159] and meetings were regularly devoted to demonstrations of apparatus, while such discussion as there was betrayed a conspicuous disregard for the theories of thermodynamics and electromagnetism being developed in the universities of Germany and Britain. It is a telling reflection on the society and the long legacy of French isolation in science that as late as 1880, no less a figure than the professor of physics at the Sorbonne, Paul Desains, expressed amazement on hearing of Gustav Kirchhoff's two laws concerning electrical circuits, although the laws had been published in the *Annalen der Physik* thirty-five years earlier.[160] To some extent, the society's orientation might be regarded as a natural perpetuation of the tradition of precise measurement in French experimental physics—a tradition in which Victor Regnault and Hippolyte Fizeau (the society's first president) had excelled. But before his tragically early death in 1866, Emile Verdet had given French physicists, in particular his pupils at the Ecole Normale Supérieure, a well-publicized vision of an alternative, more theoretical approach in his work on optics, electromagnetism, and thermodynamics. And at least one journal, Charles d'Almeida's *Journal de physique théorique et appliquée*, kept this tradition alive in the Third Republic.[161] Hence I am inclined to see the rather pedestrian empiricism that is apparent in the publications and lectures of the Société Française de Physique as resulting not merely from French unresponsiveness to new departures in physics but at least equally from the desire to secure the wider audience of nonacademic physicists to whose professional lives abstruse theory was irrelevant.

The history of the Société Française de Physique illustrates at once the rich opportunities that were available to science under the Republic and the compromises that had to be made in pursuit of the all-important new alliance between academics and the category of what Nathan Reingold has called "practitioners" of science.[162] Suddenly the forging of that alliance became a dominant priority for academic scientists, rather than the concern of a minority of reformers. In the eyes of the majority, a demonstration of the economic worth of science was a way of securing the public and private support that scientists needed if they were to raise their status and increase the pace of the research to which they now attached such great importance; it was a new means to a familiar end. The old ideal of a privileged aristocracy of *savants* paid by the state to pursue timeless truths was quickly laid aside. It was done with few signs of regret, for the experience of the previous forty years had shown how the pursuit of that ideal had led to the integration of science in the bureaucracy of government and to a profession subservient to administrators concerned only with the diffusion and examination of received truths. The new ideal was a very different one, which conflated rather indistinctly the innovating role and utility of the scientist and the congruence of science with the objectives of a Republic wedded to modernity.

Of the several new institutions that promoted this ideal after 1870, the most prominent by far was the Association Française pour l'Avancement de Sciences. It is significant that the Association was founded in 1872 in the immediate aftermath of the war and the Commune. As its name suggests, it was modeled on the British Association for the Advancement of Science, then just over forty years old.¹⁶³ Like the British Association, it met for a week or more each year in a different provincial town and preached incessantly the principle of decentralization. In this way it sought to enlarge the boundaries of the community of scientists by demonstrating that competence was not the preserve of a clique of Parisian academicians, nor even of those who held posts in the Université. Yet, in the manner of the liberal reformers of the Second Empire, it also vehemently asserted that science was no field for the dilettante: hence its decision to follow the British Association in organizing its work around specialized sections. If science was to win the prize of a special status among the learned disciplines, democratization could not be extended beyond the bounds of the competent. That sort of inclusiveness had long been a main source of the weakness of the French scientific community, and it was seen, understandably, as contrary to the proper objectives of the Association.

It is not surprising that most of those who had advocated reform in the 1850s and 1860s emerged as the Association's leaders. Wurtz, unquestionably, was the chief inspiration, and Claude Bernard was appointed president for the inaugural meeting at Bordeaux (though illness prevented him from attending). Prominent positions were also taken by Charles Combes, the railway engineer and director of the Ecole des Mines, and Quatrefages, both of whom had spoken vehemently at the Académie on 6 March 1871.¹⁶⁴ Other leaders included Paul Broca, whose attempts to promote the study of anthropology in France had aroused the suspicions of Rouland,¹⁶⁵ and Le Verrier's colleague and bête-noire of long standing, Charles Delaunay. Policies no less than personalities reflected the modernizing, reforming thrust of the Association. Quite blatantly, the "new men" at the head of the Association set out to conquer nationally the very public which the professoriate of a handful of industrial towns had been courting locally since the 1850s, the public of commerce and industry. Prominent on the first council, and the Association's most important private benefactor, was the Alsatian Jewish banker Adolphe Seligman d'Eichtahl. And among corporate benefactors, by far the most generous were the four national railway companies, each of which made initial donations of 2,500 francs.

The main theme in the Association's rhetoric was Saint-Simonian utility allied to the patriotism of a defeated nation. Its motto, "Par la science pour la patrie," was well chosen in the France of the early 1870s. For if, as observers as diverse as Sainte-Claire Deville, Pasteur, Emile Zola, Gustave Flaubert, and Renan maintained,¹⁶⁶ Prussia owed her military supremacy to the excellence of German science and to the "scientific

Science, the University, and the State

spirit" that pervaded German life, it followed that France's hopes of gaining revenge on the aggressor depended on the reinvigoration of her scientific effort. The contribution scientists were yearning to make in the cause of national revival was made abundantly clear in Quatrefages's presidential address to the Bordeaux meeting in 1872:

Now more than ever, the greatness of states cannot be measured simply by their extent or the number of their inhabitants; the struggle between them does not take place on the field of battle alone. Now more than ever, the realm of the intellect and the world of science also have their battles, their victories, and their laurels. As we await the future, it is there that we must first seek revenge.

The scientific worker is therefore also a soldier.[167]

Throughout its early years, the Association proclaimed the clear and simple message that science was central to the material and intellectual well-being of the nation. Science was a uniquely powerful form of knowledge; it was noble, beneficent, and morally pure, the antithesis of the feckless hedonism of the Second Empire. In Wurtz's words:

Science is . . . one of the mainsprings of modern civilization . . . it elevates and strengthens the mind and, at the same time, it bestows on society the additional benefit of highly useful discoveries. Through its applications, it has changed the face of the world.[168]

It was part and parcel of such rhetoric that science could no longer be seen either as a threat to morality and good order or as a self-indulgent cultural frippery comparable with archaeology and belles-lettres; certainly, it could no longer be left in the hands of a small circle of otherworldly *savants* subject to the whims of the Ministry of Public Instruction. The Republic, it was argued, needed science if it was to emerge from the travail of discord and recrimination and efface the nation's humiliation. Accordingly, from the time they began laying their plans in August 1871, at the height of national disorientation, the founders of the Association missed no opportunity to win favor with the new republican regime. It was no accident that the first two meetings were held in towns, Bordeaux and Lyons, where hostility to the Empire had been particularly marked and where republicans in local government were only too glad to play the role of modern-minded patrons. It was no coincidence, either, that positivists, Jews, and Protestants were prominent among the Association's leaders. These men, who had formed the backbone of the liberal opposition under the Empire, were presented in the 1870s as the symbols of a new, secular enlightenment.

Despite their unmistakable republican sympathies, the leaders of the Association steered a politically prudent course aimed above all at reconciliation. They tempered their secularism by an occasional inaugural mass and a determination to win over those supporters of the Empire who were willing to come to terms with the Republic. The remnants of Arcisse de Caumont's circle, irredeemably associated with the landed aristocracy and the Catholic Church and with a conception of science as an avocation, were never reconciled to the Association. And though Pasteur, Dumas, and a number of other scientists who had actively sympathized with the Empire gave at least lukewarm support, there were many thoroughgoing conservatives, including Le Verrier and Henri Milne Edwards, who distanced themselves from the Association and the political order which, at least by clear implication, it was endorsing.[169]

But residual nostalgia for the Empire faded rapidly during the 1870s and 1880s. Most *universitaires*, especially those in the sciences, readily endorsed the Republic in return for the favor it showed to them and their institutions. Likewise, most of the industrial scientists who eventually formed the largest single group within the Association had no reason to regret the passing of the old regime. For they were very much men of the new age, the representatives of a profession that had barely existed before the war and became prominent only after the Republic was firmly secured in the late 1870s, by elections first to the Chamber of Deputies and then to the Senate. It was only then that the chemical and electrical industries emerged as major employers of superior scientific manpower. And it was only then that the educational system expanded to meet the demand, with the creation of such institutions as the Ecole Municipale de Physique et de Chimie Industrielles (founded in Paris in 1882), the Ecole Supérieure d'Electricité (also in Paris, founded in 1894), and the network of well over a score of technical institutes in the faculties of science, to which I refer below.[170]

In a somewhat fortuitous way, therefore, the modernization of French industry in the 1880s created the conditions in which the Association could prosper and achieve most of the objectives it had conceived in the very different circumstances of 1872. And prosper it did. Membership rose from about two thousand in the mid-1870s to more than three thousand in 1880, and it reached a peak of over four thousand in the 1890s. The growth in the Association's funds was even more spectacular. On the eve of World War I, its capital was not far short of 2 million francs and it was distributing about 40,000 francs a year in support of research (a sum comparable with the grants for research administered by the Académie des Sciences).[171]

Membership and income do not tell the whole story, however, and in one respect at least the Association had failed. It had not bridged the gulf between the scientific community as a whole and the Académie. It was rare for more than half a dozen academicians to be present at a meeting of the Association, and even when the annual meeting was held, exceptionally, in Paris in 1900 (to mark another Universal Exhibition), only seven members of the Académie bothered to attend. The obvious explanation for this indifference lies in what most academicians must have seen as the subversive thrust of the Association's policy. The implied aim of the Association, after all, was that of the liberal reformers during the Empire: to subvert the traditional notion of science as a state service whose fortunes were dictated principally by the needs of government, whether for technical expertise, academic certification, national prestige, or the satisfaction of bourgeois tastes in one form or another. Also, by asserting its independence of the state, its commitment to decentralization, and its opposition to the deferential relationship that bound the scientists of the periphery to those at the center, the Association threatened the very hierarchies from which the Parisian elite derived its power.

It cannot be stressed too strongly that the various ideals I have outlined were not peculiar to the Société Française de Physique and the Association Française pour l'Avancement des Sciences. Other national societies were striving, at about the same time, for a more egalitarian ordering of the scientific community.[172] And both the Société de Physique and the Association flourished to the extent that they promoted and drew strength from a utilitarian ideology that came to prevail in the scientific community as a whole in the last thirty years of the nineteenth century. Similar success stories could be told of the Société Internationale des Electriciens (founded in 1883 to promote research and education in applied electricity), a dozen or so "industrial" societies in the provinces,[173] scores of industrial schools (most of them under the control of the Ministry of Commerce),[174] and a spate of new journals catering for the industrial market.[175]

Most academic scientists, especially those in the expanding provincial faculties of science, were glad to adopt the new emphasis, casting aside the detachment traditionally associated with the title of *savant* and lessening their commitment to the main role the state still envisaged for them in the 1870s and 1880s—that of training teachers.[176] Courses in applied science became more common, and the trend was reinforced from the 1890s by the establishment of a network of technical institutes attached to any science faculty that could find local sponsors to pay salaries and build laboratories.[177] It is probable that in these institutes academic standards were low and that lecturers performed at an intellectual level no higher than their predecessors had done in the heyday of the public lecture. But the students who attended were (so far as we can tell) serious and regular, they were numerous (at least in the more vigorous faculties[178]), and, to the extent that the institutes were not directly funded by the state, those who taught in them could regard themselves as masters of their own destiny.

Virtually everyone, it seemed, was content with what had happened. The Ministry of Public Instruction saw the alternative means of funding as a welcome step in its program of administrative decentralization. It had the added merit of promising some easing of the financial burden on the ministry, though, as Terry Shinn has shown, the opportunity of reducing government expenditure on the university system was not properly seized until after 1900.[179] (To an unprecedented degree thereafter, universities were left to their own devices, with financial consequences that I discuss below.) From a different perspective, professors in the faculties could congratulate themselves on having at last conquered a substantial public in whose eyes their scientific competence mattered far more than their eloquence or bureaucratic efficiency. Confident of their special status in the learned community and of their capacity to survive competition with other disciplines, they warmly applauded the moves toward the autonomy of universities between the late 1870s and 1896.[180] For them as for most academics, René Goblet's granting of "civil status" to the faculties in 1885 (a decision that gave the faculties the right to raise whatever funds they could, independently of the state) and Louis Liard's establishment of sixteen self-governing universities in 1896 were professional triumphs. They were triumphs, too, for the lay communities of the university towns. Civic pride and economic need could be satisfied at the same time by the raising of local funds for building and equipment. The most common pattern was for the municipality and the ministry to assume a roughly equal burden, though in several cases the state's contribution was very much the smaller of the two. The point is illustrated by the collaboration leading to the construction and fitting out of the new buildings for the Faculties of Science and Letters at Bordeaux: of 2,615,436 francs that were spent on this project between 1880 and 1894, less than an eighth (300,000 francs) came from the state, the rest being donated by the city.[181]

In view of the material benefits that flowed in the last twenty years of the century, it was natural that university teachers should seek to make common cause with municipal and, as appropriate, manufacturing or commercial elites. From the 1870s, in response to the ravages of phylloxera and mildew, the scientists of the Faculty of Science at Bordeaux were able to emerge as the saviors of the region's economy. Alexis Millardet, a botanist with a special interest in hybridization and the importation of American vines, and Ulysse Gayon, a chemist of the Pasteur school, were duly rewarded with statues in the town's Jardin publique. In many towns, the bonds between universities and their local communities were further strengthened by the involvement of academics in political life, usually in support of strongly republican administrations. The presence on local or departmental councils of such men as Liard (Bordeaux), Ernest Bichat (Nancy), and Edouard Herriot (Lyons) clearly did a great deal to ease the flow of money to the institutions that employed them.[182]

It has been estimated that between 1885 and 1900 industry, private donors, and departmental and municipal authorities contributed more than 30 million francs (roughly three-quarters) of the sum spent on the construction and refitting of provincial science faculties.[183] It was patronage on a generous scale. Yet it is not clear that the new system of financing was the unmixed blessing that it appeared to be at the time. One obvious problem was the disparity between the economies of the various regions. This disparity was reflected in the very different levels of local funding which allowed the incomes and recruitment of the science faculties of the Sorbonne, Nancy, Lyons, Bordeaux, Lille, Toulouse, and (late in the day) Grenoble to grow spectacularly in the quarter of a century after 1885, whereas the faculties in the smaller, less industrial towns of Besançon, Caen, Clermont, and Poitiers were relatively deprived. The evidence in Tables 2.4 and 2.5 makes the point plainly, as do the contrasting experiences of the universities of Grenoble and Clermont in a typical year, 1907. For both universities, the year had been marked by what each regarded as a major financial coup.[184] But while Grenoble rejoiced in Casimir Brenier's gift of a vast and extremely valuable site for the rehousing of the Institut Electro-technique and in the town's donation of a working electrical power station, the president of the Council of the University of Clermont had to be thankful for 65,000 francs from the municipal council of Clermont toward the cost of refurbishing the risibly inadequate premises of the Faculty of Science. As Table 2.4 shows, success bred success. Students flocked to the splendid facilities of Grenoble in ever-increasing numbers, while Clermont, for all its attempts at refurbishment, became a backwater in science and technology. The huge and growing inequalities between the half dozen or so thriving provincial universities and the rest

Table 2.4.

Students Enrolled in Universities and Faculties of Science in 1898 and 1913

	1898		1913	
	University	Faculty of Science	University	Faculty of Science
Aix-Marseille	849	157	1,012	247
Besançon	197	75	271	91
Bordeaux	2,144	224	2,548	316
Caen	598	47	643	95
Clermont	257	86	268	111
Dijon	604	89	1,034	108
Grenoble	476	77[a]	1,475	502[a]
Lille	1,354	208	1,405	284
Lyons	2,335	321	2,774	376
Montpellier	1,496	225	2,155[b]	310[b]
Nancy	1,001	223	2,287	945
Paris	12,047	1,273	17,556	1,793
Poitiers	764	106	1,431	136
Rennes	1,063	167	1,597	322
Toulouse	1,885	219	2,685[b]	857
Algiers	(763)[c]	(47)[c]	606	135
Total	27,833	3,544	39,747	6,628

SOURCES: "Rapports des conseils des universités pour l'année scolaire 1897–1898," in *Enquêtes et documents relatifs à l'enseignement supérieur* 71 (1899), and "Rapports des conseils des universités pour l'année scolaire 1912–1913," ibid. 108 (1914). The figures given here can be compared with those for 1876, 1890, and 1914 given in Table 2 of Robert Fox and George Weisz, "The Institutional Basis of French Science in the Nineteenth Century," in Fox and Weisz, eds., *The Organization of Science and Technology in France, 1808–1914* (Cambridge, 1980), p. 12; also with those for 1890, 1900, 1910, and 1913 in Table 3 of Harry W. Paul, "Apollo Courts the Vulcans: The Applied Science Institutes in Nineteenth-Century French Science Faculties," ibid., p. 160. A comparison shows that the figures for the different faculties vary slightly with the sources used. This is especially noticeable, in my case, for

Science, the University, and the State   115

were blatant. In a quite brutal way, they vindicated the opinion of most of the leading educational administrators of the Third Republic—Paul Bert, René Goblet, Léon Bourgeois, and Liard among them—who had argued that the ideal number of universities was far smaller than the sixteen that were actually founded in 1896.

Such experiences underlined the precariousness of the new course on which the French universities were embarked. However parsimonious and uncomprehending central government had been in the past, it was now clear that local patrons too could be capricious. Town councils tended to be interested in providing ostentatious showpieces rather than facilities for private research. Municipal lectures, a grandiose *séance de rentrée*, or ornate buildings could all too easily have a higher claim than a well-equipped laboratory, and there was nothing to stop municipal support from being withdrawn altogether, as happened once at Besançon.[185] Industrialists, for their part, had different priorities. They wanted technically competent operatives, rather than *savants*, so that their donations (like student enrollments) tended to be directed not to the faculties as a whole but to specific technical courses and to the specialized institutes, such as those for applied chemistry at Lille, Toulouse, Nancy, and Lyons, for electrical technology at Toulouse and Grenoble, for winemaking at Dijon, and so on.[186] And with industry, as with the departmental and town councils, there was the constant problem of changes in policy, which seem to have led, between 1909 and 1914, to a sudden and significant reduction in the size of industrial contributions to the faculties of science.[187] Hence there were good reasons why not only scholars in the

---

1913. For this year, the data in the *Annuaire statistique de la France* do not tally with those in the university reports that I have used. But the differences are insignificant for my purposes. On the contribution to the total figures for certain faculties made by enrollments in the technical institutes, see note a to this table and note 178 of the text.

[a]The expansion of the Faculty of Science at Grenoble between 1898 and 1913 is particularly striking. It was almost entirely the result of the growth of the Institut Polytechnique (comprising the Institut Electro-technique Brenier and the Ecole Française de Papeterie and some associated laboratories and factories), which accounted for 356 of the 502 students in the Faculty of Science in 1913.

[b]Figures for these cases are lacking in the main sources that I have used. They are taken instead from the relevant volume of the *Annuaire statistique de la France*.

[c]In 1898, Algiers had an Ecole préparatoire à l'enseignement supérieur des sciences et des lettres (founded in 1880) as well as a school of law and a secondary school of medicine and pharmacy. The 47 students counted are those studying science in the Ecole préparatoire. A full Faculty of Science was not established until 1909.

Table 2.5.

The Income of Universities in 1898

University	Income (in francs)
Aix-Marseille	461,330
Besançon	213,492
Bordeaux	1,128,284
Caen	402,037
Clermont	201,430
Dijon	404,668
Grenoble	389,130
Lille	936,006
Lyons	1,310,601
Montpellier	984,702
Nancy	1,016,877
Paris	5,005,812
Poitiers	355,861
Rennes	410,108
Toulouse	639,669

SOURCE: "La situation financière et scolaire de nos universités en 1898," *Revue internationale de l'enseignement* 37 (1899): 424–26.

humanities but also some scientists expressed concern about the preoccupation of the faculties with the training and certification of middle-level technical employees at the expense of "pure" research. It was perhaps not immediately obvious that the intellectual interests of science had been impaired rather than advanced by the attempt to serve the local economy and community. But the point could not be missed that when Ernest Solvay and Brenier made their donations, worth several hundred thousand francs, to (respectively) the Institut Chimique at Nancy and the Institut Electro-technique at Grenoble, and when Basil Zaharoff showed even greater generosity in financing a chair of aerodynamics in Paris, they were not playing the patrons of learning for its own sake.[188]

Yet another constraint, which affected professors in all disciplines, arose from the tiresome fact that the new benefactors had to be won and pandered to, with the result that by the 1890s *universitaires* found themselves obliged to appear once again before nonacademic audiences. Their aim was not to entertain and elevate, as it had been in the July Monarchy and the Second Empire, but to "sell" their universities to the industrial or commercial bourgeoisie of the region and to local councils and their electorates. The "selling" might be done by mounting series of lectures directed at the *grand public*, as happened at Besançon in 1906 (amid signs of desperation on the part of the university authorities).[189] But more typically the context in which universities wooed their new patrons was that of the *sociétés des amis*—essentially university supporters' clubs—which were set up in most of the larger university towns to provide funds for all aspects of university life, including the support of needy students. By bringing together academic, manufacturing, and commercial interests, these societies were important agents in the integration of academics with the lay public that increasingly supported them. In return for approval and modest financial aid from a society, professors would lecture or write semilearned papers for the society's publication. The intellectual concessions were less flagrant than they would have been in faculty lectures half a century earlier: a professor would be more likely to present a digest of his research than an introduction to a very general area of science. But there still were concessions. It could even be argued, in fact, that one tyranny—that of the ministry—had been replaced by another—that of the local *industriels* and politicians. The work of the *savant* in university life was still determined, in some degree, by a public, outside his profession, whose interests and priorities were often at odds with his own.

Once the euphoria of 1896 was behind them, professors in the faculties were left to count the cost of university autonomy. Elementary teaching in the technical institutes, in which professors took a leading role, and public relations exercises of one kind or another were, perforce, an increasingly obtrusive part of academic life. They consumed time and energy that might otherwise have been devoted to research, and they were a constant reminder that administrative and financial independence brought with it the threat of intellectual thralldom. Research programs and teaching came to be dominated by considerations of immediate utility, and the size of enrollments became a constant obsession, especially as the prospect of war with Germany loomed and university students gradually lost the partial dispensations with regard to military service which they had enjoyed earlier in the Third Republic.[190] Also there is some evidence that, as an all too predictable consequence of the concern with relevance, the pace of scientific publishing in the faculties dropped significantly between 1901 and 1914, after a quarter of a century in which it had risen hearteningly.[191]

There was obvious nostalgia (and a wealth of personal experience) in Marcellin Berthellot's sketch of the worldly existence of the *savant* in 1905:

> Perhaps he would prefer to remain shut up in his laboratory and to devote all his time to his favorite studies. But he is not permitted to confine himself in this way. . . . He is sought out, and his services are requested. Often they are even urgently solicited in the name of the public interest, in the most diverse spheres: particular applications in industry or national defense, public education, or even general politics.[192]

Over the next twenty years, nostalgia hardened to the unpalatable certainty that, in the name of academic expansion and in the pursuit of utility, the intellectual role of the *savant* had been grievously impaired. For the mathematician Emile Picard, writing in 1912, the process was one of the penalties of democracy, which inevitably favored the applications of science at the expense of science itself.[193] His remedy—like that of Charles Richet, a physiologist and Nobel prize winner whose career had begun in the high days of reform about 1880[194]—was to recreate the opportunities for disinterested research. Both men, in fact, were arguing for the creation of a new scientific aristocracy of researchers whose duties would exempt them from the multiple diversions of normal university life. Of course, even Picard and Richet could not deny that in some ways the role of the professional academic had actually been narrowed: notably in the transfer of much (though by no means all) of the task of popularization to a new breed of scientific writers and journalists such as Jean-Henri Fabre and Camille Flammarion.[195] But by the eve of World War I, it was plain that the vacuum was all too readily filled with other commitments in teaching and administration that impeded research.

Conclusion

By 1914, academic scientists had every reason to look back with mixed feelings on what had occurred in the previous hundred years. The more nostalgic might pine for the undisputed "golden age" in the first three decades of the nineteenth century, when French science had derived strength from its very lack of professionalism. Then, those who crossed Laplace or Cuvier had known all too well the drawbacks of a system of personal authority, especially because the community was small and alternative patrons were few. But there had been ample consolation in the independence of the great patrons, which had meant that the pursuit of the most elevated forms of science had never required legitimation. From about 1830, by contrast, the expansion and associated formalization of the academic profession had led to a weakening of personal bonds and a growing subjection of science to whatever was conceived in the Ministry of Public Instruction to be the public interest. Now, bureaucratic incomprehension, rather than the unfriendly whim of a patron, was the greatest threat. And that threat, by the 1860s, had become the unpleasant reality that led Wurtz and the other reformers to seek to break the shackles of state control by redrawing the boundaries of what constituted the scientific community and its public.

The fact that French scientists about the time of World War I appeared almost as unhappy with the state of science as they had been half a century earlier suggests that, for all the excitement of the 1880s and 1890s, the academic reform movement had yielded little benefit. This is not to say, of course, that none of the reformers' aspirations had been realized. Many of them had. Hence Jules Ferry, in 1880, could preen himself with some justice on his success in bestowing on *universitaires* a high degree of professional autonomy. He had eliminated clerical and other nonacademic interests from the Conseil de l'Instruction Publique and, by ensuring that the Conseil was elected by the members of the profession it controlled, he had gone at least some way toward transforming the Université from the administration which, according to him, it had been since the 1850s, into a body that he proudly described as "living" and "free."[196] Yet, as I have argued, the change—though a step along the road of self-regulation—was no panacea. Science was not free. In the first place, there were still alien pipers who called the tune. And it was also soon apparent that one set of debilitating political prejudices had merely replaced another. Thus against the zoologist Raphaël Blanchard's recollection of the Second Empire as a deplorable period in which the administration awarded chairs to political allies whose merit lay not in their scientific work but in their loyalty to the Emperor,[197] we have to set the evidence of no less a prejudice, on the part of senior republican academics, against the Catholic geologist Albert de Lapparent and, most conspicuously, Pierre Duhem.[198]

Among other unrighted wrongs were the continuing practice of *cumul*, which remained a source of grievance in the 1920s,[199] and, most strikingly, the gulf that continued to separate Parisians from provincials, despite the efforts of the Association Française pour l'Avancement des Sciences and the national disciplinary societies. On the one hand, there was the mass of the scientific community, greatly increased in size and constantly called upon to make its own difficult way in the quest for funds. On the other, there was the Parisian elite, still small, still centered on the Académie and the major institutions of the capital, and as close as ever to the Ministry of Public Instruction—to its obvious advantage, not least in the matter of salaries.[200] The Parisians, in fact, benefited hugely from the young Republic's determination to outshine the Germans and to proclaim the modernity and secularism of the regime. If the proper culture of a republic was scientific, as such administrators as the positivistic Ferry and René Goblet believed, it was only just that special favor and protection should be offered to its leading scientists. The snag for those outside Paris was that, despite the Republic's rhetoric of decentralization, "leading scientists" usually meant the senior Parisians who had a ready entrée to the ministry and no intention of sacrificing their traditional privileges or of making more than a modest concession to the vulgar demands of utility. The fruits of this special status are still to be seen in the spacious buildings of the "new Sorbonne," built at a cost of 32 million francs between 1885 and 1901, half of the sum being contributed by the state.[201] It is not surprising that those who belonged to the scientific elite of Paris, with few exceptions, rallied to the Republic and endorsed its scientism, secure in the knowledge that the hierarchy that set them apart from, and above, their peers in the provinces would be preserved.

There is, needless to say, great irony in all this. The quest for institutional and financial autonomy and the deliberate pursuit of specialization were natural responses to the centralization, parochialism, and intellectual superficiality of the Second Empire. Predictably, as I have tried to show, the moves were powerfully reinforced after 1870 by the reaction against anything that smacked of the vestiges of imperial rule. But in the end, the inherent tensions of the academic scientist's predicament—his need for both freedom in his research and a wider public of nonscientists which could guarantee him that freedom—were cruelly exposed. For as scientists courted and conquered the new industrial constituency in which most of them saw their salvation, they abandoned any hope of the insulation from ill-informed scrutiny which only government patronage, however changeable it might be, was capable, at least in principle, of giving. In view of the longstanding neglect of the facilities for research and the consequent need for a huge investment at a time when the Third Republic was suffering from both economic hardship and debilitating political strife, it is admittedly hard to see what other strategy could have been pursued. Moreover, in the 1880s especially, the rhetoric of utility and service, allied to the quest for greater autonomy, did yield some rich material rewards. Yet I believe that the alliance with industry and local commercial and political interests set French science on a course that eventually inhibited its intellectual achievement. Only a far more detailed analysis will show precisely how the different regions of France and the different sciences were affected, though I think it virtually certain that physical scientists in the provinces suffered most. The continued strength of French mathematics and the prosperity of the Institut Pasteur are both compatible with this conclusion.

The tale, then, is a cautionary one. It points to the difficulties of scientific research under the two very different forms of support that were available, first in the July Monarchy and early Second Empire and then in the thirty years or so before World War I. With regard to the earlier of these periods, it is customary to speak of a decline of French science. But the term is equally applicable, I believe, to the early years of this century. That, at all events, was the view of many French scientists at the time. For they perceived, clearly and through unhappy personal experience, the blighted harvest that had been yielded by what we should now call advancing professionalization.

Notes

This essay grew from work begun while I was a Visiting Fellow in the Davis Center in the fall semester of 1978. It has benefited since then from research in France and Britain made possible by the generous financial support of the Royal Society of London, the Small Grants Research Fund of the British Academy, and the Senate Research Fund of the University of Lancaster. In recent work on the third section of the paper, I have drawn on funds granted by the joint committee of the Science and Engineering Research Council and the Social Science Research Council for a study of the relations between scientific education and industrial performance in modern Europe.

I am grateful to Dorinda Outram for her critical reading of an early draft of the paper and to Hans Aarsleff and J. B. Morrell for help on specific points.
1. The definition of a *notable* is notoriously difficult. Wealth, occupation, and family connections could all contribute to the *considération* by society that was essential to the rank. For a brief discussion of the problem, see André-

1. Jean Tudesq, *Les grands notables en France (1840–1849): Etude historique d'une psychologie sociale*, 2 vols. (Paris, 1964), 1:7–14. Although Tudesq's book is chiefly concerned with the 1840s, his comments on the *notabilités intellectuelles* (1:456–74) are of obvious relevance to my discussion.
2. On the changes in the career-patterns and qualifications of scientists holding posts in the Université de France during the nineteenth century, see Victor Karady, "Educational Qualifications and University Careers in Science in Nineteenth-Century France," in Robert Fox and George Weisz, eds., *The Organization of Science and Technology in France, 1808–1914* (Cambridge, 1980), pp. 95–124. See also the evidence summarized in Table 2.3 of this essay.
3. Anthony T. Grafton, "*Polyhistor* into *Philologe*: Notes on the Transformation of German Classical Scholarship, 1750–1850," *History of Universities* 3 (1983), in press, and Roy Porter, "Gentlemen and Geology: The Emergence of a Scientific Career, 1660–1920," *Historical Journal* 21 (1978): 809–36.
4. Susan Faye Cannon, *Science in Culture: The Early Victorian Period* (New York, 1978), pp. 141–51, and Porter, "Gentlemen and Geology," pp. 829–36.
5. The bearing of diverse national contexts on the general trend toward the growing prominence of universities in nineteenth-century intellectual life is very evident in Edward Shils's suggestive analysis of the American case, "The Order of Learning in the United States from 1865 to 1920: The Ascendancy of the Universities," *Minerva* 16 (1978): 159–95. On the term *universitaire*, see my preliminary note on currency and terminology.
6. See Robert Fox, "The Rise and Fall of Laplacian Physics," *Historical Studies in the Physical Sciences* 4 (1974): 89–136, esp. 109–27, and Dorinda Outram's forthcoming biography of Georges Cuvier, to be published in 1984 by Manchester University Press.
7. Some implications of the lack of a "lay" public for scientific research are explored in Edward Shils, "The Profession of Science," *Advancement of Science* 24 (1967–68): 469–80, esp. 472–74.
8. Maurice Crosland, *The Society of Arcueil: A View of French Science at the Time of Napoleon I* (London, 1967), pp. 212–13.
9. Dorinda Outram, "Politics and Vocation: French Science, 1793–1830," *British Journal for the History of Science* 13 (1980): 27–43.
10. The haphazard nature of career-making in science about 1800 is brought out well, with regard to Biot, in Eugene Frankel, "Career-Making in Post-Revolutionary France: The Case of Jean-Baptiste Biot," *British Journal for the History of Science* 11 (1978): 36–48. As Frankel observes (p. 37), of a brilliant generation of early graduates, Joseph-Louis Gay-Lussac, Poisson, Arago, and Biot were fortunate enough to secure patrons soon after graduation, whereas Etienne Malus and Augustin Fresnel, with no one to make an academic career for them, drifted into government service and were very nearly lost to science.
11. The decrees are reproduced in Alfred de Beauchamp, *Recueil des lois et règlements sur l'enseignement supérieur*, 7 vols. (Paris, 1880–1915), 1:171–88 and

249–61, and in *Recueil de lois et règlements concernant l'instruction publique, depuis l'édit de Henri IV, en 1598, jusqu'à ce jour*, 8 vols. (Paris, 1814–28), 4:1–30, and 5:125–49.

12. See, for example, paragraph 30 of the decree of 17 March 1808: "Après la première formation de l'Université impériale, l'ordre des rangs sera suivi dans la nomination des fonctionnaires et nul ne pourra êtra appelé à une place qu'après avoir passé par les places inférieures. Les emplois formeront ainsi une carrière qui présentera, au savoir et à la bonne conduite, l'espérance d'aspirer aux premiers rangs de l'Université impériale" (Beauchamp, *Recueil des lois*, 1:176; and *Recueil de lois*, 4:8).

13. The theses presented for the degree of *docteur-ès-sciences* are listed in Albert Maire, *Catalogue des thèses de sciences soutenues en France de 1810 à 1890* (Paris, 1892). For the history of the *agrégation*, see Charles Jourdain, *Rapport sur l'organisation et les progrès de l'instruction publique* (Paris, 1867), pp. 87–104. On the *baccalauréat*, see Paul Meuriot, *Le baccalauréat, son évolution historique et statistique, des origines (1808) à nos jours* (Nancy, 1910).

14. Twenty-three doctorates in letters had been awarded in the same period. See Albert Maire, *Répertoire alphabétique des thèses de doctorat ès lettres des universités françaises, 1810–1900* (Paris, 1903), p. 169.

15. The Ecole Normale had functioned briefly in 1795, but it was effectively recreated by the decree of 17 March 1808 and opened to students in 1810.

16. The student population of the Ecole Normale can be studied easily through the lists in *L'Ecole Normale (1810–1883): Notice historique, liste des élèves par promotions, travaux littéraires et scientifiques* (Paris, 1884). By the Second Empire, a class of about fifteen was normal in science, enrollments in the letters section being consistently higher.

17. The figure of ninety is deceptively high because forty-three of the professors held chairs in parts of the empire outside France. For the identity of chair-holders before 1851, I have relied chiefly on the annual *Almanach impériale [royale]*.

18. The science faculties of Besançon, Lyons, and Metz were closed, leaving faculties in Paris, Caen, Dijon, Grenoble, Montpellier, Strasbourg, and Toulouse. The surviving faculties of letters were those in Paris, Besançon, Caen, Dijon, Strasbourg, and Toulouse. No town outside Paris had a full complement of faculties of all five types. The closest approximations were at Strasbourg, where there were faculties of science, letters, law, and medicine (completed in 1818 by the addition of a faculty of Protestant theology), and Toulouse, where there were faculties of science, letters, law, and theology, but only a secondary school of medicine.

19. See the decree of the Commission de l'Instruction Publique (31 October 1815) and the royal ordinance (18 January 1816), in Beauchamp, *Recueil des lois*, 1:387–88 and 402, and in *Recueil de lois*, 6:58–60, 101–2.

    The history of the Université between 1814 and 1822 is described in detail in Jean Poirier, "L'Université provisoire," *Revue d'histoire moderne* 1

(1926): 241–79, and 2 (1927): 3–35, 261–306. For a more general account, see Louis Liard, *L'enseignement supérieur en France, 1789–1889 [1893]*, 2 vols. (Paris, 1888–94), 2:125–77. Volume 2 of Liard's work is still an indispensable source on all aspects of French higher education in the nineteenth century, despite Liard's partiality as a champion of reform under the Third Republic. I have not thought it necessary to provide detailed references for standard information given by Liard.

20. [H.F. Robert de Lamennais], *De l'Université impérialé* (Paris, 1814); also in *Oeuvres complètes de Lamennais*, new ed., 10 vols. (Paris, 1843–44), 5:359–75.
21. The small size of the commission (five members, raised to seven in 1820) and the fact that its members were appointed by the minister of the interior ensured close government control. The relevant regulations (15 August 1815 and 1 November 1820) are in Beauchamp, *Recueil des lois*, 1:386, 452–54, and in *Recueil de lois*, 6:27–30, 7:1–5.
22. Paul Gerbod, "Les épurations dans l'enseignement public de la Restauration à la Quatrième République (1815–1946)," in Gerbod et al., *Les épurations administratives. XIXe et XXe siècles* (Geneva, 1977), pp. 81–98, esp. 90.
23. See *Recueil de lois*, 7:42–48. An earlier regulation (24 August 1810) which had prescribed that a similar procedure should come into effect from 1 January 1815 had never been observed; see ibid., 5:226–34.
24. The attraction of the *baccalauréat*, from its inception, lay in its role as a qualifying examination for the professional careers over which the French bourgeoisie quickly established a monopoly. Although the detailed regulations changed a good deal, the *baccalauréat-ès-lettres* was generally required for entry to the faculties, government administration, and the *grandes écoles*. For entry to the faculties of science and medicine and the technical state services, the *baccalauréat-ès-sciences* was required as well.

It is clear that changing professional requirements, especially in law, medicine, and the technical *corps d'état*, had an immediate effect on the demand for the *baccalauréat* and hence, indirectly, on the functions of professors in the faculties. In the 1850s, for example, the number of *baccalauréats-ès-lettres* awarded fell markedly as a result of Fortoul's decision that the qualification would no longer be a prerequisite for the admission to the *baccalauréat-ès-sciences* (see note 75 below). From 1858, the number of *baccalauréats-ès-lettres* rose again, following a ministerial decision that all medical students would have to possess the qualification, as well as the *baccalauréat-ès-sciences*. The relevant evidence is in Meuriot, *Le baccalauréat*.
25. Albert de Saint-Germain, "Recherches sur l'histoire de la Faculté des Sciences de Caen de 1809 à 1850," *Mémoires de l'Académie Nationale des Sciences, Arts et Belles-Lettres de Caen* (1891), 42–104, esp. 65–68.
26. Jean Collet, "Centenaire de la Faculté des Sciences de Grenoble," *Revue internationale de l'enseignement* 63 (1912): 401–13, esp. 404.
27. Beauchamp, *Recueil des lois*, 1:205, 253, and *Recueil de lois*, 5:125, 133.
28. Beauchamp, *Recueil des lois*, 1:903–4.

29. Dulong to Berzelius, 8 August 1828, in H. G. Söderbaum, ed., *Jac. Berzelius Bref*, 14 vols. (Uppsala, 1912–32), 4:74. The volume contains a good deal of evidence of the physical and financial strain under which Dulong labored in the 1820s.
30. On the rhetorical style of French intellectual life during the Bourbon Restoration, see Robert Fox, "Scientific Enterprise and the Patronage of Research in France, 1800–70," *Minerva* 11 (1973): 442–73, esp. 452–58.
31. For some typical eulogies of the scientific lecturers of the Restoration and July Monarchy, see Charles-François-Marie de Rémusat, *Mémoires de ma vie*, ed. Charles H. Pouthas, 3 vols. (Paris, 1958–60), 1:241–44; Pierre Flourens, *Analyse des travaux de Georges Cuvier* (Paris, 1841), pp. 1–70, esp. 53–56; Dominique-François-Jean Arago, *Astronomie populaire*, ed. J. A. Barral, 4 vols. (Paris, 1854–57), 1:1–2.
32. Abel-François Villemain, *Souvenirs contemporains d'histoire et de littérature*, 2 vols. (Paris, 1854–55), 1:467–68. But it was Cuvier's lectures at the Muséum d'Histoire Naturelle and the Collège de France that the duchesse de Duras preferred and Cuvier's presence which she especially prized at her salon. For a critical view of Arago's lectures, which he delivered at the Observatory from 1813 to 1846, see [Guglielmo B.T.I. Libri], "Lettres à un Américain sur l'état des sciences en France. I. L'Institut," *Revue des deux mondes*, 4th ser., 21 (1840): 789–818, esp. 808–9. According to Libri, Arago's sole aim was to attract a large audience; the lectures were nothing more than "a kind of supplement to the *Spectacle de la Nature* by the Abbé Pluche."
33. Isidore Bourdon, *Illustres médecins et naturalistes des temps modernes* (Paris, 1844), pp. 116–18. Cf. the eulogy of Cuvier as a lecturer in Flourens, *Analyse des travaux de Cuvier*. I am grateful to Dorinda Outram for drawing my attention to the work by Bourdon.
34. Antoine-Augustin Cournot, *Souvenirs (1760–1860)*, ed. E. P. Bottinelli (Paris, 1913), p. 156.
35. See the letter from the dean of the Faculty of Science at Caen, Pierre-Boniface Thierry, to the rector of the academy of Caen, 6 January 1840, in *Bulletin de l'instruction publique et des sociétés savantes de l'académie de Caen* 1 (1840–41): 130–42, esp. 134.
36. Ibid. The enrollments for the year 1829–30 in the Faculty of Science at Caen illustrate the problem very clearly. In that year, there was only one formally registered student, but ninety *auditeurs* followed courses, with varying degrees of seriousness. See de Saint-Germain, "Recherches sur l'histoire de la Faculté des Sciences de Caen," p. 71.
37. Thierry, letter of 6 January 1840 (cited in note 35), p. 134.
38. Ibid., p. 136. Cf. the similar plea in Thierry's report on his faculty at the *rentrée solennelle* of the Caen academy, 8 November 1841, *Bulletin de l'instruction publique et des sociétés savantes de l'académie de Caen* 2e année, vol. 1 (1841–42): 99–108, esp. 105.
39. The certificat, or PCN as it was usually called, was awarded by the faculties

of science at the end of a one-year course in general science. Successful students then proceeded to a faculty of medicine to begin their medical studies.

40. J. L. Armand de Quatrefages de Bréau, "De l'enseignement scientifique en France," *Revue des deux mondes*, 18ᵉ année, n.s., 22 (1848): 489–507, esp. 498–501. In 1833 Quatrefages left Strasbourg to practice as a physician in Toulouse. Until he left Toulouse for Paris in 1840, he maintained his practice, while serving successively as *suppléant* to the professor of chemistry, Jean-Pierre-Thomas Boisgiraud (1835–39) and as professor of zoology (1839–40). There is evidence that Quatrefages's discontent in Toulouse owed something also to his failure to be appointed director of the town's Jardin des Plantes even though the post seems to have been promised to him. On this and other aspects of his life, see Georges Hervé and L. de Quatrefages, "Armand de Quatrefages de Bréau, médecin, zoologiste, anthropologiste (1810–1892)," *Bulletin de la Société Française d'Histoire de la Médecine* 20 (1926): 309–30 (esp. p. 320); 21 (1927): 17–35, 200–231.
41. Quatrefages, "De l'enseignement scientifique," p. 498.
42. Laurent to Gerhardt, 12 June 1845, quoted in Edouard Grimaux and Charles Gerhardt, *Charles Gerhardt: Sa vie, son oeuvre, sa correspondance, 1816–1856* (Paris, 1900), p. 96. Despite his dissatisfaction, Laurent published almost a hundred papers in his six years at Bordeaux. As I indicate in the next paragraph, a serious commitment to research and publication was by no means unusual among the scientific professoriate of Bordeaux, which suggests that Laurent may have exaggerated not only the impediments to his own work but also the extent of his isolation from active colleagues.

Gerhardt's sense of deprivation as professor of chemistry in the Faculty of Science at Montpellier was no less strong than Laurent's. On 2 December 1856, for example, Gerhardt prepared a report to the minister of public instruction in which he urgently requested funds and facilities to allow him to undertake serious laboratory teaching, as opposed to lecturing to a transient audience of amateurs. See *Correspondance de Charles Gerhardt*, ed. Marc Tiffeneau (Paris, 1918), pp. 348–50. From 1848, Gerhardt worked with Laurent in Paris while on leave, on half pay, from Montpellier; in 1851 he finally resigned his post to found a private laboratory in Paris.
43. Georges Rayet, "Histoire de la Faculté des Sciences de Bordeaux (1838–1894)," *Actes de l'Académie Nationale des Sciences, Belles-Lettres et Arts de Bordeaux*, 3d ser., 59ᵉ année (1897): 5–369 esp. 90–91. The city of Bordeaux allocated 20,000 francs for the initial equipping of the laboratory.
44. The evidence on publications that follows is taken from Rayet, "Histoire de la Faculté des Sciences de Bordeaux," pp. 155–363.
45. Laurent-Léopold Micé, "Discours d'ouverture de la séance publique du 19 mai 1881," *Actes de l'Académie Nationale des Sciences, Belles-Lettres et Arts de Bordeaux*, 3d ser., 42ᵉ année (1880): 729–66, esp. 753.
46. See Biot's two contributions to the *Journal des savants* for February 1837 and

November 1842, reproduced in Jean-Baptiste Biot, *Mélanges scientifiques et littéraires*, 3 vols. (Paris, 1858), 2: 257–92.

47. The practice of including regular reports on the meetings of the Académie des Sciences in literary and general periodicals seems to have begun in the *Revue encyclopédique* and *Le globe* in the 1820s. A new generation of semipopular journals of science adopted the practice after 1830; see, for example, *L'institut*, which began publication in 1833. Thereafter it was increasingly in such journals as this and the abbé Moigno's *Cosmos* and *Les mondes* (see note 195, below) that the reading public followed the doings of academicians. The changing pattern suggests a gradual withdrawal of science from the realm of general literate culture.
48. For Biot, one of Cuvier's greatest merits was his appreciation of the "dignity" of science. See Biot, *Mélanges scientifiques*, 2:271.
49. Ibid., p. 292. The comment appears in a note added to the reprinted version of the articles from the *Journal des savants*.
50. On the decline of the influence of Laplace and his school, see Fox, "Rise and Fall of Laplacian Physics," pp. 109–27.
51. This is the thrust of Biot's *Essai sur l'histoire générale des sciences pendant la Révolution française* (Paris, 1803).
52. Biot, *Mélanges scientifiques*, 2:275–82.
53. See ibid., p. 292: "[The Academy] has lost in independence, what it has gained in vulgarity."
54. The first of Libri's unsigned "Lettres à un Américain" is cited in note 32, above. The second appeared in the *Revue des deux mondes*, 4th ser., 22 (1840): 532–54. The third, a warm tribute to the recently deceased Poisson (ibid., 23 [1840]: 410–37), was written in a similar spirit of protest, Poisson's reputation as a physicist having suffered badly during the regime of Arago.
55. Libri, "Lettres à un Américain. I," p. 797.
56. As late as the 1850s, the great majority of professors appointed to a first chair in a faculty of science had taught in a *lycée*. From the late 1860s, it became more usual to avoid service in a *lycée* altogether and to begin an academic career by holding a junior research post. The transition is displayed very clearly in Craig Zwerling's analysis of the careers of *normalien* "scientists" (i.e., graduates of the Ecole Normale who went on to publish at least three scientific articles). Of those *normalien* scientists who entered the Ecole Normale between 1830 and 1839, 94 percent proceeded, on leaving the Ecole, to an appointment in a *lycée;* for those who entered between 1857 and 1867, the proportion was only 28 percent. See Table 3 of Zwerling, "The Emergence of the Ecole Normale Supérieure as a Centre of Scientific Education in the Nineteenth Century," in Fox and Weisz, eds., *Organization of Science*, pp. 31–60, esp. 43. In considering these figures, it should be borne in mind that a *normalien* going on to a career in a faculty of science would typically obtain his first chair between twelve and fifteen years after entering the Ecole Normale. As a result, the effect of the changes which Zwerling

describes on the scientific professoriate of the faculties was still slight even by 1870.
57. Karady, "Educational Qualifications and University Careers," p. 111n.
58. The reorganization of 1832 gave the Université a new prominence in the affairs of state by making education the exclusive concern of a minister for virtually the first time. A move in this direction had been made in 1824, when education had come under the control of the new Ministry of Ecclesiastical Affairs and Public Instruction (after being one of the many concerns of the Ministry of the Interior). In February 1828, Public Instruction (under Henri de Vatimesnil) had been separated from Ecclesiastical Affairs, but the combined ministry was restored in August 1829.
59. Virtually all ministers of public instruction, from Guizot to Duruy, struggled to bring together *universitaires* and private scholars. There is abundant evidence of this effort in the ministerial circulars and other documents in volume 2 of Xavier Charmes, *Le Comité des Travaux Historiques et Scientifiques (Histoire et documents)*, 3 vols. (Paris, 1886).
60. For Guizot's version of the ideal, see his *Mémoires pour servir à l'histoire de mon temps*, 8 vols. (Paris, 1858–67), 3:146–84. In 1834, while Guizot was minister of public instruction, the forerunner of the Comité des Travaux Historiques et Scientifiques was founded. Guizot's patronage was particularly effective in the publication of documents concerning the history of France.
61. Fortoul, "Circulaire . . . concernant la réorganisation du Comité des Travaux Historiques et des Sociétés Savantes," in Charmes, *Comité des Travaux Historiques*, 2:189.
62. Speech of 12 August 1852; see "Concours général des lycées et collèges de Paris et de Versailles," *Journal général de l'instruction publique* 21 (1852): 417–19, esp. 418.
63. Throughout the nineteenth century, the Ecole Polytechnique was attacked for the theoretical cast of its curriculum and for the privileges its graduates enjoyed, notably in securing appointments in the most prestigious of the various state corps of engineers. Criticism of the Polytechnique and the associated *écoles d'application* and corps became particularly severe in the aftermath of the 1848 Revolution. In November 1850, for example, the Assemblée Nationale debated a proposal (from the republican deputies Jean-Baptiste-Adolphe Charras and Louis Chassaignac de Latrade) for the opening of at least some places as *ingénieurs des ponts et chaussées* to candidates from the ranks of the academically far less well qualified *conducteurs des ponts et chaussées*. In speeches to the Assembly on 19 and 20 November 1850, Charles Dupin and Urbain le Verrier argued for the preservation of the graduates' virtual monopoly on these posts, but in the vote that followed, they were heavily defeated. The debate is recorded in *Le moniteur universel*, no. 324 (20 November 1850), pp. 3297–3307, and no. 325 (21 November 1850), pp. 3309–15.

For a contemporary attack on the curriculum of the Ecole Polytechnique, see Théodore Olivier, "Monge et l'Ecole Polytechnique," *Revue scientifique et industrielle . . . du docteur Quesneville*, 3d ser., 7 (1850): 64–68. Olivier had already made a similar case in favor of a more practical curriculum in a paper written in July 1847; see "De l'Ecole Polytechnique," in Olivier, *Mémoires de géométrie descriptive* (Paris, 1851), pp. iii–xxiii.

On the problems of the medical faculties, see George Weisz, "Reform and Conflict in French Medical Education, 1870–1914," in Fox and Weisz, eds., *Organization of Science*, pp. 61–94, esp. 63 and 66–68.

64. Throughout the Second Empire, the basic professorial salary in a provincial faculty of science or letters was 4,000 francs; in theology and law, it was 3,000 francs. The *éventuel*, a supplement financed by examination fees, brought the salaries in science, letters, and law up to the levels I indicate, while in theology there was virtually no *éventuel*. In medicine, salaries were distinctly higher: in 1865, the professorial salary in the Montpellier faculty was 6,815 francs, that at Strasbourg 6,001 francs. In Paris in 1865, professors in the Faculty of Science earned a total of 11,443 francs, a little less than professors in letters (12,500 francs). See *Ministère de l'instruction publique: Statistique de l'enseignement supérieur, 1865–1868* (Paris, 1868), pp. 342–43.

65. Fox, "Rise and Fall of Laplacian Physics," p. 135n.

66. The income of Gay-Lussac, which was about 60,000 francs in the 1840s, was exceptional; most of it came from his appointment as technical adviser to the Mint (see note 67, below). According to Thenard, a successful *cumulard* in this period might earn 13,000 or 14,000 francs, though his own income was around 30,000 francs for a few years in the early 1830s. See Maurice Crosland, *Gay-Lussac: Scientist and Bourgeois* (Cambridge, 1978), pp. 228–34, and Paul Thenard, *Un grand Français: Le chimiste Thenard* (Dijon, 1950), pp. 206–9.

67. Quatrefages de Bréau, "L'enseignement scientifique," pp. 501–2, and Grimaux and Gerhardt, *Charles Gerhardt*, pp. 173, 178–81. Gerhardt's protest was conducted with the paleontologist Gérard-Paul Deshayes and others in the context of the ephemeral Société pour le Progrès des Sciences et la Réforme des Institutions Scientifiques. This society submitted a petition against *cumul* to the National Assembly in the spring of 1848; see *Pétition contre le cumul présentée à l'Assemblée Nationale par la Société pour le Progrès des Sciences et la Réforme des Institutions Scientifiques* (Paris, [1848]). The petition's analysis of the incomes of leading scientists is of great interest, though it has to be read with caution. No salary rivaled that of Gay-Lussac, said to be 62,300 francs (including an estimated 50,000 francs earned as "essayeur chimiste" at the Mint).

68. Alfred Moquin-Tandon, *Un naturaliste à Paris sous Louis-Philippe: Journal de voyage inédit (1834)*, ed. Marcel Roland (Paris, 1944), pp. 168–69.

69. Louis Trenard, *Salvandy en son temps, 1795–1836* (Lille, 1968), pp. 705–25.

70. The most important measure in the Falloux Law (15 March 1850) was the abandonment of the state's monopoly in secondary education. In a substan-

tial concession to conservative Catholics and the *bien-pensant* bourgeoisie, it was decreed that anyone holding the *baccalauréat* could establish an institution of secondary education. Although the state's monopoly of higher education was preserved, the law seriously undermined the secular character of the Université. Clericalization was further facilitated by the reorganization of the educational administration referred to in note 71, below.

71. Reorganization of the Conseil and of the councils of the academies of the Université was an important provision of the Falloux Law; see *Bulletin administratif de l'instruction publique*, 1 (1850): 57–80, and Beauchamp, *Recueil des lois*, 2:85–106. The law also raised the number of academies to eighty-six, one for each department, each headed by a rector. This move, which intentionally allowed local clerical influence in education to increase, was reversed by Fortoul in 1854. In a major reform (14 June 1854) aimed at recovering ministerial control, Fortoul reduced the number of academies (and hence of rectors) to sixteen; see *Bulletin administratif de l'instruction publique* 5 (1854): 163–66, and Beauchamp, *Recueil des lois*, 2:316–23, esp. 316.

72. For most of the Second Empire, the three were Urbain Le Verrier, Jean-Baptiste Dumas (replaced in 1867 by Antoine-Jérôme Balard), and Adolphe Brongniart. Their closeness to the minister and to the imperial regime and their strong identification with Paris prevented them from ever appearing as truly representative of academic scientists throughout France as a whole.

73. The erosion of the independent authority of the Conseil is brought out well in Jourdain, *Rapport*, pp. 1–13, and in *Ministère de l'instruction publique: Statistique de l'enseignement supérieur. Enseignements, examens, grades, recettes et dépenses, en 1876* (Paris, 1878), pp. 13–36.

74. It was in the 1830s that the secular eclecticism of Victor Cousin became established as the approved philosophy of the Université. Louis Veuillot was only the most celebrated of many Catholic writers who, as a result, attacked the Université for its impiety. The virtual withdrawal of philosophy from the Université under Fortoul and Rouland served to diminish Catholic criticism, but the cautious reintroduction of the subject under Duruy (1863–69) stimulated a renewed attack. By the 1860s, the main targets were the materialist doctrines of Littré and his circle. See Paul Gerbod, "L'Université et la philosophie de 1789 à nos jours," in *Comité des Travaux Historiques et Scientifiques: Actes du 95ᵉ Congrès National des Sociétés Savantes (Reims, 1970). Section d'Histoire Moderne et Contemporaine. Tome 1, Histoire de l'enseignement de 1610 à nos jours* (Paris, 1974), pp. 237–330.

75. Fortoul's restructuring of the *agrégation* was effected by article 7 of the decree of 10 April 1852; see *Bulletin administratif de l'instruction publique* 3 (1852): 59–63, esp. 60–61. See also Jourdain, *Rapport*, pp. 93–96, and Paul Gerbod, *La condition universitaire en France au XIXᵉ siècle* (Paris, 1965), pp. 313–15.

The restructuring was part of the broader system of *bifurcation*, which forced pupils in secondary education to make a simple choice between science and letters about the age of fourteen. The effect was that the *baccalauréat-ès-sciences* became an alternative of equal status to the *baccalauréat-ès-lettres*.

A similar division was effected at the level of the *licence*, as well as for the *agrégation*. Since the program of study in science at each of these levels was undifferentiated, specialization in a particular branch of science was hindered, though (as I observe later in this section) *bifurcation* helped specialization in another sense by removing the necessity for pupils to obtain the *baccalauréat-ès-lettres* before going on to the *baccalauréat-ès-sciences*.

76. This quotation and the others in this paragraph are from Hippolyte Fortoul, "Nouveau plan d'études pour les lycées et les facultés," 10 April 1852, *Bulletin administratif de l'instruction publique* 3 (1852): 53–58, and Beauchamp, *Recueil des lois*, 2:216–19.
77. See Fortoul's disparaging comment in a letter to Edgar Quinet, referring to *normaliens* "who haven't an idea in their heads and are crammed with texts, facts, and futile arguments." The letter, dating from the summer of 1840, is quoted in Paul Raphael and Maurice Gontard, *Un ministre de l'instruction publique sous l'empire autoritaire: Hippolyte Fortoul, 1851–1856* (Paris, 1975), p. 26. Fortoul himself had pursued a career in the Université, serving as a professor in the faculties of letters at Toulouse and Aix in the 1840s. But he had not been through the Ecole Normale.
78. Paul Dupuy, "L'Ecole Normale (1810–1883)," *Revue internationale de l'enseignement* 6 (1883): 888–918, 937–55, 1057–75, esp. 1058–66. Dupuy's history also appears as a "Notice historique" in *L'Ecole Normale (1810–1883)*, pp. 1–79.
79. On the urge, which affected both *lycées* and the institutions of research and higher education, see Gerbod, *La condition universitaire*, pp. 296–304; also Félix Hémon, *Bersot et ses amis* (Paris, 1911), pp. 100–109. Among scientists who either resigned or were dismissed were Auguste-François Chomel of the Faculty of Medicine in Paris and the physicist Claude Pouillet of the Conservatoire des Arts et Métiers.
80. Francisque Sarcey, *Souvenirs de jeunesse* (Paris, 1885), pp. 197–98.
81. Fortoul to the rector of the academy of the Gironde, 8 December 1852, in Archives Départementales de la Gironde, Fonds du Rectorat, T 107.
82. On Laprade's dismissal, see Edmond Biré, *Victor de Laprade: Sa vie et ses oeuvres* (Paris, [1886]), pp. 229–51. "Les muses d'état" satirized the regimented centralization of "official" literary life under Napoleon III. The chief butt of the satire was Charles-Augustin Sainte-Beuve, at the time an ardent Bonapartist, who was portrayed as a whipper-in of the nation's writers, chastising any who fell out of line. There was justification for this view in the private memorandum of March 1856 in which Sainte-Beuve urged the emperor to give official encouragement to men of letters outside the faculties and learned academies; his ideal was to "coordinate . . . literature with the whole network of institutions of the Empire." Sainte-Beuve cited bohemianism and the quest for cheap notoriety as the consequences of a lack of official recognition. See "Note de M. Sainte-Beuve au sujet des encouragements à donner aux gens de lettres," in *Papiers et correspondance de la famille impériale*, 2 vols. (Paris, 1870–72), 2:257–62.

83. Eugène Véron was typical of the numerous graduates of the Ecole Normale Supérieure with republican sympathies who resigned their posts on the declaration of the Empire. His criticism of the educational policies of the 1850s and early 1860s is conveyed clearly in his article, "De l'enseignement supérieur en France," *Revue des cours littéraires de la France et de l'étranger* 2 (1865): 401–4, 435–37, 449–52 (see esp. pp. 450–52).
84. The *bifurcation* in secondary education was effected by the decree of 10 April 1852 cited in note 75, above. It is significant that Fortoul appointed two of his scientific advisers, Le Verrier and Dumas, as the chief spokesmen on the measure both in the Conseil de l'Instruction Publique and in the more specialized committee appointed to reorganize the *baccalauréat*. An exploration of the implications of the *bifurcation* for science appears in Nicole Hulin, "A propos de l'enseignement scientifique: Une réforme de l'enseignement secondaire sous le Second Empire, la 'bifurcation' (1852–1864)," *Revue d'histoire des sciences* 35 (1982): 219–45.
85. On Le Verrier's autocratic rule at the Observatory, see Camille Flammarion, *Mémoires biographiques et philosophiques d'un astronome* (Paris, 1911), pp. 508–23; Désiré Nisard, *Souvenirs et notes biographiques*, 2 vols. (Paris, 1888), 2:277–78; and Victor Meunier, *Scènes et types du monde savant* (Paris, 1889), pp. 79–81.
86. On the history of the Comité, see Charmes, *Le Comité des Travaux Historiques*, esp. 1:i–ccxxvi. The attempts of Fortoul and Rouland to use the Comité in their quest for the control of learning are discussed in Robert Fox, "The *Savant* Confronts His Peers: Scientific Societies in France, 1815–1914," in Fox and Weisz, eds., *Organization of Science*, pp. 241–82, esp. 263–65.
87. For Napoleon III's identification of Alésia with the Mont Auxois at Alise-Sainte-Reine (Côte d'Or), see his *Histoire de Jules César*, 2 vols. and Atlas (Paris, 1865–66), 2:299–300, 555–61, and Atlas, plates 25–28. The case was based on the literary evidence of Caesar's *Commentarii* and on excavations at the site, which the emperor initiated and largely financed.
88. For an exposition of his views, see Désiré Nisard, *Histoire de la littérature française*, 4 vols. (Paris, 1844–61), esp. vols. 2 and 3.
89. For the administrative documents concerning these and the other ventures mentioned in this paragraph, see Charmes, *Le Comité des Travaux Historiques*, 2:153–55, 157–60, 162–64, 171–79. Ministerial patronage of the publication of French historical documents had begun in 1834, under Guizot (see note 60, above). By 1848, 67 volumes had been published; by 1874, the figure had risen to 258. See *Rapport à M. le ministre de l'instruction publique et des cultes sur la situation des travaux historiques au 1er janvier 1849* (Paris, [1849]), and *Rapports au ministre sur la collection des documents inédits de l'histoire de France sur les actes du Comité des Travaux Historiques* (Paris, 1874), p. 29. A thorough study based on the voluminous archives of the Comité is Marie-Elizabeth Antoine, "Un service pionnier au XIXe siècle: Le Bureau des Travaux Historiques d'après ses papiers aux Archives Nationales," published as part 10

(1977) of the *Bulletin de la Section d'Histoire Moderne et Contemporaine (depuis 1610)*, published by the Comité des Travaux Historiques et Scientifiques.
90. Interest in the history of the Gauls was almost invariably a mark of a strong nationalistic sentiment. This is evident in the Commission de Topographie des Gaules, launched by a decree of Napoleon III on 17 July 1858 "to study the geography, history, and archaeology of the nation up to the accession of Charlemagne." During the Second Empire, the commission produced a series of magnificent maps of Gaul and began work on the *Dictionnaire archéologique de la Gaule*, which was eventually completed in successive parts comprising two large volumes between 1875 and 1923. See Salomon Reinach, "La Commission de Topographie et le Dictionnaire Archéologique de la Gaule," *Revue archéologique*, 5th ser., 2 (1915): 209–27.
91. Fortoul's battles with the various Academies composing the Institut de France are well described in Raphael and Gontard, *Un ministre de l'instruction publique*, pp. 283–96. On election to the Académie des Inscriptions, Fortoul proceeded to add to his unpopularity by introducing a number of measures which extended the influence of the Ministry of Public Instruction in the Académie's affairs, notably in the award of its prizes. See René Dussaud, *La nouvelle Académie des Inscriptions et Belles-Lettres*, 2 vols. (Paris, 1946–47), 1:243.
92. Fox, "The *Savant* Confronts His Peers," pp. 258–65, and "Learning, Politics, and Polite Culture in Provincial France: The *Sociétés Savantes* in the Nineteenth Century," *Historical Reflections/Réflexions historiques* 7 (1980): 542–64, esp. 550–52. The latter volume of *Historical Reflections/Réflexions historiques* was also published, with identical pagination, as Donald N. Baker and Patrick J. Harrigan, eds., *The Making of Frenchmen: Current Directions in the History of Education in France, 1679–1979* (Waterloo, Ontario, 1980).
93. For a study of the reform movement in the Université in this period and the early Third Republic, see George Weisz, "Le corps professoral de l'enseignement supérieur et l'idéologie de la réforme universitaire en France, 1860–1885," *Revue française de sociologie* 18 (1977): 201–32.
94. Herschel to Sabine, 4 August 1843, BJ3/26 in Correspondence and Papers of Sir Edward Sabine, Public Record Office, London. I am grateful to J. B. Morrell for drawing my attention to this letter.
95. See the comments on the growing French indifference to the study of geomagnetism in John Cawood, "Terrestrial Magnetism and the Development of International Collaboration in the Early Nineteenth Century," *Annals of Science* 34 (1977): 551–87, esp. 585–87.
96. Jack Morrell and Arnold Thackray, *Gentlemen of Science: Early Years of the British Association for the Advancement of Science* (Oxford, 1981), p. 375. French visitors to British Association meetings were never numerous, and they became less so in the 1840s than they had been in the 1830s.
97. The continuing tradition of French interest in German literature, philosophy, and art from the time of Madame de Staël to that of Quinet and Renan is described well in Jean-Marie Carré, *Les écrivains français et le mirage alle-*

mand, 1800–1940 (Paris, 1947), pp. 3–105. For more detailed studies, see André Monchoux, *L'Allemagne devant les lettres françaises de 1814 à 1835* (Toulouse, 1953), and Louis Reynaud, *L'influence allemande en France au XVIIIe et au XIXe siècle* (Paris, 1922), pp. 145–258.

98. Although Wurtz and Verdet were by no means academic novices, they had only recently obtained senior appointments: Wurtz as Dumas's successor in the chair of organic chemistry and pharmacy at the Faculty of Medicine in Paris, Verdet as *maître de conférences* (i.e., professor) in physics at the Ecole Normale Supérieure.

99. Monod had attended George Waitz's medieval seminar at Göttingen in 1868; see Gabriel Monod, *Portraits et souvenirs* (Paris, 1897), pp. 99–115. On Bréal, who studied with Bopp and Weber at Berlin in the late 1850s, see Salomon Reinach, "Michel Bréal," *Revue archéologique*, 5th ser., 3 (1916): 138–50. Hillebrand was born in Giessen and studied law at the Universities of Giessen and Heidelberg before fleeing to France after the revolutionary troubles of 1848; see *La grande encyclopédie*, ed. Marcellin Berthelot et al., 31 vols. (Paris, [1887–1902]), 20:81.

100. Karl Hillebrand, *De la réforme de l'enseignement supérieur* (Paris, 1868), published as a book after its earlier appearance in the *Revue moderne* 45 (1868): 194–220; 46 (1868): 589–610; and 47 (1868): 282–98.

101. On the history of this journal, which became the *Revue moderne* in 1865 and ceased publication in 1869, see Georges Pariset, "Le Revue Germanique de Dollfus et Nefftzer d'après la correspondance des deux directeurs communiquée par M. Charles Dollfus et Mme Heim-Nefftzer," *Revue germanique* 1 (1905): 617–40, and 2 (1906): 28–62. The *Revue germanique* in which Pariset wrote was a distant descendant of the journal edited by Dollfus and Nefftzer.

102. Charles Dollfus and Auguste Nefftzer, "De l'esprit français et de l'esprit allemand," *Revue germanique* 1 (1858): 1–20, esp. 1.

103. On the history of these journals, see Jacques Lux, *Histoire de deux revues françaises: La Revue bleue et la Revue scientifique 1863–1911* (Paris, 1910). The main function of the journals was originally to publish lectures given at French institutions, in particular the Sorbonne, but foreign contributions became increasingly numerous. In 1871, the *Revue des cours scientifiques* (also known as the *Revue rose*) was renamed the *Revue scientifique*, and the *Revue des cours littéraires (Revue bleue)* became the *Revue politique et littéraire*. Germer Baillière was a publisher with liberal sympathies and an unusually adventurous policy (shown in his support for Littré and other positivists of the period and in the series of books by Taine, Janet, and others composing the "Bibliothèque de Philosophie Contemporaine"). As a municipal councillor in Paris, Baillière was involved in the establishment of the Ecole Municipale de Physique et de Chimie Industrielles in 1882; see Terry Shinn, "Des sciences industrielles aux sciences fondamentales: La mutation de l'Ecole Supérieure de Physique et de Chimie (1882–1970)," *Revue française de sociologie* 22 (1981): 167–82, esp. 169.

104. For complementary reports on the opening meeting, see *Revue des sociétés savantes*, 2d ser., 6 (1861): 393–487, and *Revue des sociétés savantes: Sciences mathématiques, physiques et naturelles* 1 (1862): 1–143. Reports on the subsequent meetings were carried in the *Revue*, a journal which Fortoul had launched in 1854 as part of his campaign to direct the voluntarist world of learning. (The series devoted to science began in 1862.) The Congrès des Sociétés Savantes are still held as one of the main activities of the Comité des Travaux Historiques et Scientifiques.
105. The phrase appears in the account of the first distribution of prizes, by Rouland, on 25 November 1861. See *Revue des sociétés savantes*, 2d ser., 6 (1861): 438 and *Revue des sociétés savantes . . . Sciences* 1 (1862): 1.
106. Henri Milne Edwards, "Discours sur les progrès des sciences dans les départements pendant la dernière période décennale," *Revue des sociétés savantes*, 2d ser., 6 (1861): 446–61, esp. 446–47, and *Revue des sociétés savantes . . . Sciences* 1 (1862): 8–23, esp. 8–9.
107. Victor Meunier, *La science et les savants en 1865: Deuxième année, deuxième semestre* (Paris, 1866), p. 39. The comment was made in the context of a scathing criticism of Emile Blanchard's patronizing eulogy of the naturalist Léon Dufour, who spent nearly all his life as a doctor at Saint-Sever in the Landes.

    Interestingly and significantly, this volume of *La science et les savants* was fulsomely dedicated to Félix Pouchet, whom Meunier supported against Pasteur in his struggle to vindicate his theory of spontaneous generation; see ibid., pp. 264–313. Pouchet shared Meunier's astringent views on the attitudes of Parisian *savants* toward work done in the provinces. See, for example, Pouchet's letter to Meunier, quoted in Meunier, *Scènes et types du monde savant*, pp. 60–61. In the letter, Pouchet objects indignantly to the implication, contained in Milne Edwards's address to the 1863 congress, that the intellectual shortcomings of the provincial faculties were chiefly the fault of their professors. The passage that offended Pouchet is presumably in the first paragraph of Milne Edwards, "Rapport sur les travaux scientifiques présentés au Comité en 1862," *Revue des sociétés savantes*, 3d ser., 1 (1863): 573–92, esp. 573, and *Revue des sociétés savantes . . . Sciences* 3 (1863): 185–204, esp. 185.
108. The unexpectedness of the appointment is brought out well in Duruy's own account. See Victor Duruy, *Notes et souvenirs (1811–1894)*, 2 vols. (Paris, 1901), 1:171–95, which makes it clear that the friendship between Napoleon III and Duruy grew from Duruy's involvement as an adviser on the emperor's *Histoire de Jules César*.
109. After graduating from the Ecole Normale in 1833, Duruy served for many years as professor of history in major Parisian *collèges* (Henri IV and Saint-Louis) and was eventually appointed *maître de conférences* at the Ecole Normale (1861) and general inspector of secondary education (1862).
110. For two perspectives on this episode, see Ernest Lavisse, *Un ministre: Victor Duruy* (Paris, 1895), pp. 26–27, and Nisard, *Souvenirs*, 1:87–98.

111. The fruits of Duruy's investigations appeared as the very impressive *Statistique de l'enseignement supérieur, 1865–1868*.
112. See, for example, Jean-Magloire Baudoüin, *Rapport sur l'état actuel de l'enseignement spécial et de l'enseignement primaire en Belgique, en Allemagne et en Suisse* (Paris, 1865); Jacques Demogeot and Henry Montucci, *De l'enseignement secondaire en Angleterre et en Ecosse: Rapport adressé à son Exc. M. le ministre de l'instruction publique* (Paris, 1868); Charles-Adolphe Wurtz, *Les hautes études pratiques dans les universités allemandes* (Paris, 1870).
113. For the official documents concerning the Ecole and a review of its first ten years, see *Statistique de l'enseignement supérieur, 1865–1868*, pp. 711–33, and *Statistique de l'enseignement supérieur, 1876*, pp. 707–28. By 1878, only five out of thirty-four approved laboratories for scientific research were outside Paris.
114. John Farley and Gerald L. Geison, "Science, Politics and Spontaneous Generation in Nineteenth-Century France: The Pasteur-Pouchet Debate," *Bulletin of the History of Medicine* 48 (1974): 161–98.
115. On the Giraud petition and the subsequent debate in the Senate, see *L'enseignement supérieur devant le Sénat* (Paris, 1868), and Robert Fox, "Positivisti, liberi pensatori e la riforma della scienza francese nel Secondo Impero," in Antonio Santucci, ed., *Scienza e filosofia nella cultura positivistica* (Milan, 1982), pp. 171–92.
116. Unlike Fortoul and Rouland, Duruy was an enthusiastic advocate of the freedom of higher education but on terms that would limit the power of the Church and ensure a dominant role for his own administration. It was particularly important for Duruy that the state should retain the exclusive right to award academic qualifications, though not necessarily that of preparing candidates for the qualifications. See Duruy, *Notes et souvenirs*, 2:1–75.
117. Ibid., 1:360.
118. Ibid.
119. *L'enseignement supérieur devant le Sénat*, pp. 49–52.
120. Duruy, "Circulaire engageant les professeurs de facultés à faire des cours publics dans les villes de leur ressort [1 October 1864]," in *Circulaires et instructions officielles relatives à l'instruction publique*, 12 vols. (Paris, 1863–1902), 6:176–79.
121. Duruy to the rector of the academy of Montpellier, 6 April 1864, ibid., pp. 100–101, esp. 101.
122. Duruy, "Instruction aux recteurs sur les cours publics libres [23 January 1865]," ibid., pp. 201–6, esp. 203.
123. Reaction to the banning of several lectures that were to have been given at the headquarters of the Société d'Encouragement pour l'Industrie Nationale in 1865 was typically indignant. See Charles Louandre, "Les conférences libres" and other related material, *Journal général de l'instruction publique*, 34 (1865): 60–64.
124. The nature of the audience was quite different from that for the *cours d'adultes*, which were launched at about the same time chiefly to provide rudimentary

instruction in reading and writing. On these lectures, which were attended in the late 1860s by nearly eight hundred thousand people a year, see the Ministry of Public Instruction's annual *Statistique des cours d'adultes* for 1866–67 and 1867–68.

125. Emile Deschanel, *Les conférences à Paris et en France* (Paris, 1870).
126. For a vivid account of these lectures, written by one of the most successful speakers, see Francisque Sarcey, *Souvenirs d'âge mûr* (Paris, 1892), pp. 24–58. Bischoffsheim's oddly constructed theater was to become the Athénée-Comique.
127. Victor Meunier, "Inauguration des conférences de la Sorbonne; leçon de M. J. Jamin," in Meunier, *La science et les savants en 1864* (Paris, 1865), pp. 242–57.
128. Meunier, "Les conférences de la Sorbonne," in Meunier, *La science et les savants en 1865*, pp. 270–83, esp. 280.

For an impression of the range of lectures that was available, see the list of more than two hundred series (nearly two-thirds of them in Paris) that were authorized for the winter of 1864–65, in *Bulletin administratif du ministère de l'instruction publique*, n.s., 2 (1864): 623–30. By 1865–66, more than a thousand such series were offered, most of them in the provinces and including roughly a fifth on science or applied science; see *Statistique de l'enseignement supérieur, 1865–1868*, pp. 704–5.

129. Sarcey, *Souvenirs d'âge mûr*, p. 43.
130. For a view of the events of 1867 which, characteristically, presents Pasteur in the most favorable possible light, see René Vallery Radot, *La vie de Pasteur* (Paris, 1900), pp. 193–202. A fuller and more measured account, which also explores the roles of Sainte-Beuve (as a recent convert to liberalism, much admired by the students) and the unpopular director of the Ecole, Nisard, is in Jean Thomas, *Sainte-Beuve et l'Ecole Normale, 1834–1867* (Paris, 1936), pp. 149–202.
131. Zwerling, "Emergence of the Ecole Normale Supérieure," pp. 36–50. The improvement of laboratory facilities at the Ecole and the launching of the *Annales scientifiques de l'Ecole Normale Supérieure* (a journal intended primarily for the research of former *normaliens*) in 1864 were both important elements in Pasteur's strategy.
132. There is much evidence that the emperor was genuinely concerned for the welfare of science and scholarship and that he personally financed a good deal of activity. In 1869, for example, he provided funds for a geological field trip for Edmond Hébert's students at the Ecole Pratique des Hautes Etudes; see *Journal général de l'instruction publique*, 39 (1869): 225–26. See also note 87, above, on his support for the excavations at Alise-Sainte-Reine.
133. The disturbance occurred at a lecture by Auguste-Ambroise Tardieu, the professor of forensic medicine, shortly after Tardieu had been involved as an expert witness in the acquittal of Prince Pierre Bonaparte on a charge of murdering the radical journalist Victor Noir.

134. Ferry's indignant address to the Chamber of Deputies (12 April 1870) is reproduced in Paul Robiquet, ed., *Discours et opinions de Jules Ferry*, 7 vols., (Paris, 1893–98), 1:305–10.
135. Paul Lorain, *De la réforme des études médicales par les laboratoires* (Paris, 1868).
136. The submission, entitled "Suppression du cumul de l'enseignement des sciences physiques et naturelles," was written in March 1868. It was a sequel to a pamphlet, *Le budget de la science*, which Pasteur had published in January 1868. The accounts of the penury of French scientists in *Le budget de la science* had so shocked the emperor that he had summoned Pasteur, Henri Milne Edwards, Claude Bernard, and Henri Sainte-Claire Deville to a meeting at the Tuileries. In response to the emperor's request that each of the four should outline his grievances in writing Pasteur prepared "Suppression du cumul." Poor laboratories, *cumul* (which diverted able men from research), the weakness of the provincial faculties, and the shortage of junior research posts were all cited as causes of what Pasteur saw as the incipient decadence of pure science in France. The document, which was not intended for publication, is reproduced in *Louis Pasteur: Pour l'avenir de la science*, Preface by Jacques Nicolle (Paris, 1947), pp. 39–60.
137. Wurtz, *Les hautes études pratiques*.
138. The series, which covered virtually all the academic disciplines and ran to twenty-nine volumes before it was interrupted in 1870, bore the title "Recueil des rapports sur les progrès des lettres et des sciences en France." The selection of the authors clearly betrays the hand of Duruy, especially the choice of Charles Delaunay rather than Le Verrier to write the volume on astronomy. The titles, including some that were planned but never published, are listed in Victor Duruy, *L'administration de l'instruction publique de 1863 à 1869* (Paris, [1870]), pp. 882–83.
139. Claude Bernard, *Rapport sur les progrès et la marche de la physiologie générale en France* (Paris, 1867), pp. 143–49, 234–37.
140. Ibid., pp. 139–43, 229–35.
141. See ibid., pp. 146–47, 235–36, for Bernard's insistence on the need to establish forms of training and a regular career structure in physiology.
142. The argument is clearly implied in Pasteur, *Le budget de la science*, see esp. p. 4.
143. William R. Keylor, *Academy and Community: The Foundation of the French Historical Profession* (Cambridge, Mass., 1975), esp. pp. 90–100; George Weisz, "L'idéologie républicaine et les sciences sociales: Les durkheimiens et la chaire d'histoire d'économie sociale à la Sorbonne," *Revue française de sociologie* 20 (1979): 83–112. For an example of the cases that were made by scholars in the humanities, see Louis Liard, *Universités et facultés* (Paris, 1890), pp. 151–66, in which Liard develops his notion of universities as "écoles d'esprit public" capable of fashioning the "soul" of a nation.
144. On the early history of the society, see François Picavet, "La Société d'Enseignement Supérieur (1878–1903)," *Revue internationale de l'enseignement* 45 (1903): 479–512.

145. The concern of one of the most ardent reformers in the humanities, Michel Bréal, is a clear symptom of the diverging interests of *universitaires* in the last two decades of the century. As a member of the Conseil de l'Instruction Publique between 1880 and 1896 and afterward, Bréal repeatedly expressed his concern about the declining position of the classical languages and the growing preoccupation with utility in secondary education. See Reinach, "Michel Bréal," pp. 146–47, and S. Delesalle, "Michel Bréal: Philologie, instruction et pouvoir," *Langages*, IIe année, no. 45 (1977): 67–83, esp. 68–70. I am grateful to Hans Aarsleff for drawing my attention to these sources.
146. Harry W. Paul, "Apollo Courts the Vulcans: The Applied Science Institutes in Nineteenth-Century French Science Faculties," in Fox and Weisz, eds., Organization of Science, pp. 155–81, esp. 156–58, and Denise Wrotnowska, *Pasteur professeur et doyen de la Faculté des Sciences de Lille (1854–1857)* (Paris, 1975), pp. 55–56, 63–67, 70–75.
147. See the extract from a speech by Godron in Ernest Bichat, "L'enseignement des sciences appliquées à la Faculté des Sciences de Nancy," *Revue internationale de l'enseignement* 35 (1898): 299–307, esp. 299.
148. Ibid., p. 300.
149. The plan Dumas presented, in his capacity as dean of the Faculty of Science at the Sorbonne, is expounded in a pamphlet, *Rapports adressés à M. le ministre de l'instruction publique* (Paris, [1846]), pp. 9–11. The development of industrial studies formed part of a broader scheme aimed at securing funds for a much-needed program of rebuilding at the Sorbonne and for the encouragement of research in general. Documents in carton 18 of the Dumas papers in the archives of the Académie des Sciences show that the proposal aroused objections both inside and outside the Sorbonne. Although the minister, Salvandy, was sympathetic, the view that industrial studies were not properly the concern of the Sorbonne prevailed, and any interest there may have been succumbed to the upheavals of 1848 and Salvandy's consequent departure from the ministry.

    For evidence of Dumas's simultaneous advocacy of a more practical orientation in the work of the *collèges royaux* and other schools, see his report (on behalf of a five-man committee) published in 1847 as *Rapport sur l'enseignement scientifique dans les collèges, les écoles intermédiaires et les écoles primaires*.
150. On Wurtz's strategy within the Société Chimique, see Fox, "The *Savant* Confronts His Peers," pp. 269–72.
151. Even more rapid expansion occurred after 1880, as the openings for industrial chemists multiplied. In a quarter of a century beginning in 1880, the membership of four hundred rose to over a thousand, the annual turnover increased to almost 50,000 francs, and the society's *Bulletin* for the year came regularly to contain more than three thousand pages.
152. *Comptes rendus hebdomadaires des séances de l'Académie des Sciences* 71 (1871): 237–39, 261–69.
153. The evidence of this slight but unmistakable aging can be found in Alfred

Kastler, "Evolution de l'âge moyen des membres de l'Académie des Sciences depuis la fondation de l'Académie," *Comptes rendus hebdomadaires des séances de l'Académie des Sciences* 276, ser. A and B, no. 7 (12 February 1973): 65–66.

154. *Comptes rendus de l'Académie des Sciences* 71 (1871): 238.
155. See note 151.
156. Marcel Brillouin, "Les débuts de la Société Française de Physique," *Livre du cinquantenaire de la Société Française de Physique* (Paris, 1925), pp. 5–18. The society's *Bulletin des séances* also provides much information about the society, in particular concerning membership and income.
157. Brillouin, "Les débuts de la Société Française de Physique," pp. 8–9.
158. Cf. the membership of the Société Chimique de France, which stood at 1,124 in 1910, and the figures for other societies noted in Table 2 of Fox, "The *Savant* Confronts His Peers," p. 275. One national disciplinary society that might broadly be described as scientific and had a larger membership than the Société Française de Physique was the Société de Géographie with more than 2,200 members in 1910. The figure of 2,200, however, was certainly swollen by members who subscribed to obtain the society's attractive popular journal, *La géographie*.
159. Brillouin, "Les débuts de la Société Française de Physique," p. 16. Quet (1810–84) had followed the classic older style of academic career. He entered the Ecole Normale at the age of nineteen and, after succeeding in the *agrégation*, had served in a number of *lycées* before becoming rector of the academies of Besançon and then Grenoble. His final post was as inspector general of scientific secondary education.
160. Ibid.
161. On d'Almeida's editorship of this journal, see Edmond Bouty, "Notice sur la vie et les travaux de J.-Ch. d'Almeida," *Journal de physique théorique et appliquée* 9 (1880): 425–34, esp. 428–30. For most of his academic career, d'Almeida taught physics at the lycée Henri IV in Paris.
162. Nathan Reingold, "Definitions and Speculations: The Professionalization of Science in America in the Nineteenth Century," in Alexandra Oleson and Sanborn C. Brown, eds., *The Pursuit of Knowledge in the Early American Republic: American Scientific and Learned Societies from Colonial Times to the Civil War* (Baltimore 1976), pp. 33–69, esp. 46–50.
163. The early history of the Association is best studied through the annual *Comptes-rendus* of its meetings. On its origins, see Alfred Cornu, "Histoire de l'Association Française," in *Association Française pour l'Avancement des Sciences: Comptes-rendus de la 1re session 1872, Bordeaux* (Paris, 1873), pp. 44–49. A brief general history is *Association Française pour l'Avancement des Sciences: Notice historique publiée à l'occasion du centenaire de la création de l'Association (1872–1972)* (Paris, 1972).
164. *Comptes rendus de l'Académie des Sciences* 72 (1871): 268–69. Combes acted as president of the provisional council of the Association until his death in January 1872. He was replaced by Bernard, though, with Bernard indisposed, Quatrefages presided at the Bordeaux meeting.

165. Léonce Manouvrier, "La Société d'Anthropologie de Paris depuis sa fondation 1859–1909," *Revue internationale de l'enseignement* 60 (1910): 234–51.
166. Sainte-Claire Deville, in *Comptes rendus de l'Académie des Sciences* 71 (1871): 238; Louis Pasteur, "Pourquoi la France n'a pas trouvé d'hommes supérieurs au moment du péril," first published in the Lyons newspaper, *Salut public*, and then reprinted in the *Revue scientifique* 1 (1871–72): 73–77; Emile Zola, "Lettre à la jeunesse" (1879), in *Le roman expérimental*, 2d ed. (Paris, 1880), pp. 57–105, esp. 97; Gustave Flaubert, letters to George Sand, 8 September [1871] and 4 or 5 October 1871, in *Oeuvres complètes de Gustave Flaubert*, 16 vols. (Paris: Club de l'Honnête Homme, 1971–75), vol. 15, *Correspondance, 1871–1877*, pp. 40 and 44. Renan identified German "science" as the source of Prussia's strength well before 1870; see Renan, *Questions contemporaines* (Paris, 1868), p. vii, in which he states that the victor at Sadowa in 1866 had been "la science germanique." The theme reappears frequently in Renan's analysis of France's ills after 1870; see his *La réforme intellectuelle et morale* (Paris, 1871), esp. p. 95.
167. Quatrefages de Bréau, "La science et la patrie," in *Association Française, Comptes-rendus, 1872*, pp. 36–41, esp. 38.
168. From Wurtz's address to the first general assembly of the Association, held in Paris on 22 April 1872; see *Association Française pour l'Avancement des Sciences: Documents et informations diverses*, no. 1 (20 July 1872), pp. 6–7.
169. It is notable that plans to merge the Association with the Association Scientifique de France, a national society which Le Verrier had founded in 1864, came to nothing until 1886, nine years after Le Verrier's death. Even before the inaugural meeting at Bordeaux, the Association Française had sought a union, and provisional statutes for an organization that would embrace the Association Scientifique had been agreed upon by July 1872; see *Association Française, Documents et informations diverses*, no. 1, pp. 4–5. Henri Milne Edwards, who succeeded Le Verrier as president of the Association Scientifique in 1877, was more sympathetic to a merger, but it was only after he too had died that the two associations were combined.
170. On the establishment of industrial engineering as a profession of high standing between 1880 and 1914 and on some of the institutions that aided its rise, see Terry Shinn, "From 'Corps' to 'Profession': The Emergence and Definition of Industrial Engineering in Modern France," in Fox and Weisz, eds., *Organization of Science*, pp. 183–208, and Shinn, "Des sciences industrielles aux sciences fondamentales."
171. On the funds administered by the Association and the Académie des Sciences at this time, see Fox, "The *Savant* Confronts His Peers," p. 274, and Elisabeth Crawford, "The Prize System of the Academy of Sciences, 1850–1914," in Fox and Weisz, eds., *Organization of Science*, pp. 283–307.
172. For a study of the objectives and strategy of another new society of the 1870s, the Société Zoologique de France (founded in 1876), see Robert Fox, "La Société Zoologique de France: Ses origines et ses premières années," *Bulletin de la Société Zoologique de France* 101 (1976): 799–812.

173. Fox, "The *Savant* Confronts His Peers," pp. 256–57.
174. The schools and their diverse administrative structures are described in C. R. Day, "Education for the Industrial World: Technical Education and Modern Instruction in France under the Third Republic, 1870–1914," in Fox and Weisz, eds., *Organization of Science*, pp. 127–53, and Day, "The Making of Mechanical Engineers in France: The *écoles d'arts et métiers*, 1803–1914," *French Historical Studies* 10 (1978): 439–60. Day's work on the institutions under the Ministry of Commerce serves as an important reminder that by no means all education in nineteenth-century France was controlled by the Ministry of Public Instruction.
175. The electrical industry was particularly well served by such publications as *L'électricité* (founded in 1876), *La lumière électrique* (1879), *L'électricien* (1881), the *Revue internationale de l'électricité et de ses applications* (1885), and *L'industrie électrique* (1892).
176. In the early Third Republic, the champions of the Université in the Ministry of Public Instruction still believed that the faculties of science and letters could best be strengthened by being involved in the preparation of teachers for the *lycées* and municipal *collèges*. It was to this end that, beginning in 1877, the ministry established a system of scholarships to allow full-time study for the *licence* or the *agrégation* in the faculties of science or letters. By the mid-1880s, there were 350 scholarships for candidates for the *licence*, 200 for those working for the *agrégation*.

    For evidence of the academic cast of these early attempts at reform, see Albert Dumont, "Notes sur l'enseignement supérieur en France," *Revue internationale de l'enseignement* 8 (1884): 193–234, esp. 227–28.
177. On these institutes, see George Weisz, "The French Universities and Education for the New Professions, 1885–1914: An Episode in French University Reform," *Minerva* 17 (1979): 98–128, and Paul, "Apollo Courts the Vulcans."
178. By the time of World War I, the largest and most prosperous of the provincial faculties were clearly those with strong technical institutes. At Grenoble, for example, 356 of the 502 students in the Faculty of Science in 1913 (see Table 2.4, note a) were in the Institut Polytechnique, while of the 857 students in the Faculty of Science at Toulouse, 422 were in the Institut Electro-technique, and 77 were in the Institut de Chimie. The proportion may well have been even higher in the largest of the provincial faculties, at Nancy, though no precise figures are available. These larger faculties also led the way (with Montpellier) in attracting foreign students, 434 of the 945 students at Nancy coming from outside France.
179. Terry Shinn, "The French Science Faculty System, 1808–1914: Institutional Change and Research Potential in Mathematics and the Physical Sciences," *Historical Studies in the Physical Sciences* 10 (1979): 271–332, esp. 304–6 and 315–19.

180. These moves can be traced most conveniently through the documents reproduced in volumes 16 (1885) and 68 (1897) of the series of *Enquêtes et documents relatifs à l'enseignement supérieur*, 124 vols. (Paris, 1883–1929).
181. Rayet, "Histoire de la Faculté des Sciences de Bordeaux," p. 55.
182. According to Weisz, "The French Universities and Education for the New Professions," p. 104, Bichat was instrumental in securing donations totaling half a million francs from the municipal council of Nancy and the departmental council of Meurthe-et-Moselle, on both of which he sat. Bichat was the founder of the very successful Institut Chimique, which was attached to the science faculty at Nancy. For a vivid impression of the vigorous development of industrial studies at Nancy in the late nineteenth century and of the close relations between the science faculty and the local authorities and industrialists of the region, see Bichat, "L'enseignement des sciences appliquées."
183. Shinn, "French Science Faculty System," pp. 311–12.
184. The evidence that I cite appears in the annual reports on these two universities, in *Enquêtes et documents* 95 (1908): 136–56 (on Grenoble in 1906–7); 97 (1909): 149–84 (on Grenoble in 1907–8), and 100–131, esp. 101 (on Clermont in 1907–8). In the report on Clermont, the president of the University's Council, Alfred Coville, did not conceal his sense of frustration in dealing with the town council. The 65,000 francs were granted only after repeated requests, and Coville clearly doubted whether the improvements would ever be effected. In fact, they were completed, though not until just before World War I.
185. Eugène Fournier, "L'Université de Besançon," *Revue internationale de l'enseignement* 67 (1914): 457–63, esp. 461. Fournier reported that in April 1913 the departmental council of the Doubs had restored its annual grant of 10,000 francs after withdrawing it in the previous year. Fournier's report makes very plain the acute financial problems of most of the smaller faculties just before World War I.
186. The success of the Institut d'Oenologie at Dijon and the work of Millardet and Gayon on diseases of the vine, to which I refer above, show that agriculture as well as manufacturing industry could provide a favorable economic context for the development of technical interests in the faculties of science. However, the financial rewards and the associated enrollments were smaller than for the industrially related activities on which my argument chiefly rests.
187. Shinn, "French Science Faculty System," p. 318.
188. On these and other benefactors of applied science, many of whom made donations of a similar order, see Weisz, "French Universities and Education for the New Professions," p. 109, and Paul, "Apollo Courts the Vulcans," pp. 163–64.
189. "Rapports des Conseils des universités pour l'année scolaire 1906–1907," in

Enquêtes et documents 95 (1908): 76–77. The reporter for Besançon, Edouard Droz (a professor in the Faculty of Letters), stresses the conspicuous lack of local support for the university.

190. The main source of concern in the faculties was the law of 7 August 1913, which made three years of active military service compulsory for all males and drastically reduced the possibility of exemptions or postponements on educational grounds. By the law of 27 July 1872, teachers in institutions controlled by the Ministry of Public Instruction were exempt from military service, and anyone holding the *baccalauréat* was required to serve for only one instead of the normal five years. Although effecting some modifications, the new legislation of 1889 still accorded special privileges to employees of the Ministry of Public Instruction, but the concessions began to be undermined by the law of 21 March 1905. The various measures are recorded fully in Beauchamp, *Recueil des lois*, 2:822–24; 5:7–9, 35–49; 6:695–97; and 7:622–25.

    Concern about the effect of the new law of 1913 is evident in the reports on the Universities of Bordeaux and Lille, in *Revue internationale de l'enseignement* 68 (1914): 47, 120–21. The concern is all the more understandable since in several faculties enrollments were beginning to fall after reaching a peak, in most cases, about 1911. An air of mounting crisis among *universitaires* is unmistakable.

191. Shinn, "French Science Faculty System," pp. 315–26, 328–29.
192. Marcellin Berthelot, *Science et philosophie* (Paris, 1905), pp. i–ii.
193. Emile Picard, "La science et la recherche scientifique," *Revue scientifique* 50e année, part 2 (1912):577–81, esp. 581.
194. Charles Richet, *Le savant* (Paris, 1923), pp. 123–27.
195. The process by which popular scientific writing passed from the hands of academic scientists was lengthy. Although the wide readership for the writings of Henri Poincaré shows that the process was still far from complete in the early years of this century, it was during the Second Empire that the specialist in popularization began to dominate the field. Then the abbé Moigno emerged as a particularly distinguished scientific writer. The weekly journals which he edited from 1852 to 1881—*Cosmos* (1852–63) and its successor, *Les mondes* (from 1863)—combined the straightforward diffusion of scientific knowledge with trenchant comment on the contemporary world of French science.

    From the midcentury, the practice of simply publishing the lectures of leading *savants* began to die out. Illustrations of this earlier *genre*, which was especially popular during the July Monarchy and which reinforced the vogue for public lecturing, can be found in the twice-weekly *Echo du monde savant* (founded in 1836) and Arago's *Leçons d'astronomie professées à l'Observatoire Royal*, five editions of which were published between 1835 and 1849.

    By the later nineteenth century, scientific *universitaires* who wished to address a public beyond that of their disciplinary peers tended to write textbooks or specialized monographs of the kind published in Félix Alcan's "Bibliothèque scientifique internationale." See H. W. Paul, "The Role and Reception of the Monograph in Nineteenth-Century French Science," in A. J. Meadows, ed., *Development of Science Publishing in Europe* (Amsterdam, 1980), pp. 123–48.

196. The description appears in Ferry's inaugural address to the reorganized Conseil Supérieur de l'Instruction Publique (31 May 1880); see *Discours et opinions de Ferry*, 3:504–8, esp. 505. The limitations of Ferry's reform are apparent in his insistence that the Conseil was and should remain answerable to the Conseil d'Etat.

197. Raphaël Blanchard, *Les universités allemandes* (Paris, 1883), p. 118.

198. On the opposition to Duhem's advancement from Bordeaux to Paris, which was sustained by Liard and, most vehemently, by Marcellin Berthelot, see Hélène Pierre-Duhem, *Un savant français: Pierre Duhem* (Paris, 1936), esp. pp. 95–157. The case of Lapparent is less clear, but the fact that in 1879 he was obliged to abandon his part-time position as a state mining engineer if he wished to retain his chair of geology and mineralogy at the Institut Catholique de Paris has been interpreted as a hostile act on the part of the republican regime; see Emmanuel de Margerie, "Albert de Lapparent," *Annales de géographie* 17 (1908): 344–47, esp. 346, and Charles Barrois, "Albert de Lapparent et sa carrière scientifique," *Revue des questions scientifiques*, 3d ser., 16 (1909): 9–44, esp. 18–19.

199. Henri Maillart, *L'enseignement supérieur: Enquête sur la situation de l'enseignement supérieur scientifique et de l'enseignement supérieur technique* (Paris, 1925), pp. 92–97.

200. For a comment on the disparity between salaries in the provinces and in Paris, see Romain Moniez, "La décentralisation intellectuelle et le budget de l'enseignement supérieur," *Revue internationale de l'enseignement* 37 (1899): 507–13, esp. 509. In the provincial universities, professorial salaries ranged from 6,000 to 11,000 francs; in Paris, from 12,000 to 15,000 francs. A comparison between these figures and those cited in note 64 above suggests that the disparity was as great in 1899 as it had been during the Second Empire.

201. Louis Liard, *L'Université de Paris: La vieille université—la nouvelle université—la nouvelle Sorbonne* (Paris, 1909), pp. 98–99. The city of Paris provided the rest of the cost of the new Sorbonne. It is revealing to compare the sum of 32 million francs mentioned here with the 40 million francs which, as I indicate in the previous section, seem to have been spent on new buildings for all fourteen provincial science faculties between 1885 and 1900. Even the four best-endowed faculties (Lyons, Bordeaux, Nancy, and Lille) received only 20 million francs between them. See Shinn, "French Science Faculty System," pp. 311–12.

PART TWO
Surgeons, Physicians, and Psychiatrists

3

TOBY GELFAND

A "Monarchical Profession" in the Old Regime: Surgeons, Ordinary Practitioners, and Medical Professionalization in Eighteenth-Century France

Modern concepts of professionalization emphasize the formation of a fairly homogeneous elite, which establishes authority over a given occupation by virtue of acquired knowledge and consequent expertise. Uniform standards of training and certification reinforce the collegial nature of modern professions and foster a high degree of competence, autonomy, and social prestige.[1]

Modern medicine provides a striking example of such professional unification. To be sure, continued stratification within the medical profession results in considerable socioeconomic disparities between the extremes. But members of the profession now share a common fundamental education consisting of relatively standardized knowledge and institutional experience. Building on this common basis, the various specialists are linked with one another and with general practitioners. Such modern professional structure emerged in France in the wake of the Revolution at the end of the eighteenth century—before the advent of recognizably modern medical science and well before medical men could make a convincing case for therapeutic efficacy.[2]

This essay builds on the premise that medical professionalization, as it occurred in revolutionary France, was the result of an abrupt and definitive break with the past rather than an evolutionary process. This position is familiar enough, but it is often presented in a misleadingly general way (as in the work of Michel Foucault, for whom the emergence of a modern medical profession is part and parcel of the shift from a "classical" to a "modern" episteme). Much of the sociological literature simply denies the existence of any viable medical profession anywhere before the end of the nineteenth century.[3] To the extent that historians have resisted either of these simplistic judgments, they have done so by focusing on the "professional" credentials of the medical elite in early modern Europe as represented by those who held degrees conferred by medical faculties of the universities. In practice, however, this approach has tended to confirm the notion that early modern medicine lacked the attributes of a genuine profession as measured against its modern counterpart and by the same criteria, including competence, authority, monopoly over practice, and so forth.[4] In other words, the existing literature—historical as well as sociological—tends to deny the existence of a legitimate medical profession before the French Revolution.

I shall argue here that there was in fact a group of medical practitioners in eighteenth-century France which can be considered a profession in the sense of an organized occupational group with broad demand for its services. It was, however, organized along very different lines from the modern medical profession. It consisted not of university-educated medical doctors but of "ordinary practitioners," those called in eighteenth-century France "surgeons" or barber-surgeons and, in other places and times, apothecaries, apothecary-surgeons, *wundarzt*, feldshers, and sometimes even "doctors."[5] I shall further argue that these "ordinary practitioners" did not "evolve" into a modern profession but were replaced by a new sort of practitioner who underwent a profoundly different training and occupied a very different sociocultural space. It is in this more specific sense that the French Revolution marks an abrupt break in the history of medical professionalization—not in the sense that a legitimate medical profession emerged then and there for the first time but rather that one form of legitimate profession was replaced by a dramatically different one.

To make this case, I shall first outline a general scheme for the medical profession constituted by ordinary practitioners. With some qualification, this model could probably be applied to other groups of healers elsewhere and at other times, but the focus here will be on eighteenth-century French surgeons. I have chosen this group not only because it fits my model so well, nor even because the sources are particularly rich, but mainly because of the widely acknowledged importance of France in the historical transformation of the medical profession. If a case can be made

The Surgical Profession in the Old Regime 151

that these surgeons constituted a legitimate but nonmodern profession, our conception of professions will have been enriched by the historical exercise. At the same time, it should be possible to address the question why early modern France provided such congenial soil for the emergence of this profession. And, finally, the modern transformation of the medical professional structure can then be situated in the perspective of what it changed from instead of simply what it changed toward. This analysis may permit a better formulation of the nature and causes of that transformation.

Ordinary Practitioners: A Model

My model of the profession of ordinary practitioners includes the following features: (1) legal status as members of an occupational group, typically a guild or corporation such as apothecaries or barber-surgeons; (2) substantial numerical strength with levels of density approaching one practitioner per thousand inhabitants; (3) wide geographic distribution extending into rural villages; (4) low to modest social origins, status, and aspiration, roughly comparable to those of skilled artisans; (5) initial training by apprenticeship (a private contractual arrangement binding the master and the apprentice's family) and subsequent training by further private arrangements as opposed to such public settings as schools and hospitals; (6) versatility of practice, embracing various aspects of internal medicine, surgery, pharmacy, and other activities related to bodily care but not considered part of medicine today (barber's work, other grooming and cosmetic attention, baths, massage, and the like) but no one or all of which functions need be pursued as a full-time occupation; (7) a group identity, independent training structures, and a degree of *de facto* autonomy, despite nominal subordination to medical faculties—in effect, an independent corps of practitioners in potential competition and conflict with nominal superiors; and (8) a relatively equalitarian relationship with clients or patients, in which the latter have considerable discretionary powers.

This last feature, as we shall see, is particularly significant and deserves elaboration. In premodern medicine, patients not only had a choice of practitioner and whether to comply with his advice; they also played an active role in determining the conditions and even the content of the medical task. At higher social levels, this relationship may be described as a patronage system in which a wealthy patron retained a personal doctor for his health needs just as he might hire an artist for aesthetic projects. The patron fixed goals and made decisions based on his own understanding of the matters at hand and the technical suggestions of his professional adviser.[6] At the lower end of the social scale, for instance a peasant seeking out a country barber-surgeon for a phlebotomy, the power relationships are analogous, though the problem may be much simpler than that which prompted the aristocrat to consult his physician. In the final analysis, the practitioner-patient relationship in both cases was shaped by the patient's wishes and values. In both instances, too, one could say that the patient sought a practitioner who would share his point of view. Thus a social fit between practitioner and patient takes on particular importance: a matching process occurred between extraordinary physicians and extraordinary clients, on the one hand, and between ordinary practitioners and ordinary patients on the other.

An Application of the Model: Barber-Surgeons in Eighteenth-Century France

Let us now test this model systematically against the historical experience of barber-surgeons in eighteenth-century France. Taking each feature of the model seriatim, let us see whether or how far it is valid and whether or how much it contributes to our understanding.

(1) Legal status.

Barber-surgeons enjoyed recognized legal status as members of *communautés*, professional societies constituted along the lines of guilds and possessing statutory codes. Beginning in the 1720s, royal legislation established a common framework for surgical *communautés* throughout the kingdom. The king's personal or *premier* surgeon presided over this network, delegating his authority to local lieutenants in each *communauté*.[7]

Surgical *communautés* had control over the licensing of ordinary practitioners. Each *communauté* conferred degrees of "master" in surgery and

The Surgical Profession in the Old Regime

other certificates within a specific geographical region over which it had jurisdiction, normally corresponding to juridical subdivisions, the royal *bailliage* or *sénéchausée*. The *communauté* conducted examinations according to its statutes and was responsible for the regulation of practice in the region. The statutes defined three levels of master surgeon according to type of examination sustained and fees paid, the lowest level being the village barber-surgeon, who took a single three-hour examination on surgical "principles": bloodletting, abscesses, wounds, and medicaments.[8]

The village master barber-surgeon was thus a legal practitioner distinct from many other categories of "irregular" ordinary healers—military and naval doctors trespassing into civilian practice, veterinarians, occasional healers drawn from the ranks of artisans and peasants as well as charitably inclined nobles and their wives, members of clerical healing orders such as the brothers of the Charité hospitals, the Augustine nursing sisters of the Hotels-Dieu, parish curés, empirics, charlatans, magical healers, witches, and so on.[9]

At times, the dividing line between the ordinary practitioner received by a *communauté* and these other denizens of the Old Regime medical landscape was blurred. Thus, surgical *communautés* also examined and certified midwives, bonesetters, dentists, hernia experts, and oculists; they permitted widows of deceased masters to rent out to nonmasters the "privilege" to practice legally without the usual examination. Finally, there were "students"—apprentices and journeymen—who might wait many years before taking their qualifying examinations, if they ever did. All these persons might and presumably often did evade the *communauté*'s licensing mechanism and invade its exclusive jurisdiction over practice. But in principle, they belonged to a legally constituted hierarchy of ordinary practitioners. Together with the master barber-surgeons, their numbers were vast.[10]

(2) Numerical Strength and Population Density.

Eighteenth-century commentators guessed that there were as many as thirty to forty thousand barber-surgeons in the kingdom, which would mean well in excess of 1 per 1,000 inhabitants.[11] Using medical surveys from the 1780s, Jean-Pierre Goubert has found somewhat lower densities in six northern *généralités* of France (ranging from 6.82 per 10,000 [Amiens] to 1.76 per 10,000 [Rennes]).[12] These official medical surveys may have failed to count many barber-wigmakers and other marginal types who nonetheless formed part of the extended surgical network subject to the king's *premier* surgeon. Moreover, as Goubert's results indicate, there was probably considerable variation in the density of medical practitioners from one region to another. Certain regions of the southwest of the kingdom, for instance, appear to have had a much more extensive implantation of country surgeons than the northern *généralités*. Languedoc, the French Basque country, and the dioceses of Toulouse, Bordeaux, and probably Auch en Gascogne all had surgical densities of the order of one per thousand if we can trust contemporary counts of surgeons and of population.[13] Even though the data lack precision, the general pattern of the numerical strength of ordinary practitioners is clear.

In comparison with barber-surgeons, the number of medical doctors was minuscule. The six northern *généralités* contained fewer than 500 physicians (fewer than 1 per 10,000 inhabitants) or 1 physician for 4.8 surgeons; the diocese of Toulouse (not including the city) had 101 surgeons, 134 midwives, and only 8 physicians serving a population of about 80,000.[14]

(3) Geographic Distribution.

If the small towns and countryside of eighteenth-century France tended to be "medical deserts" as far as physicians were concerned, barber-surgeons did not neglect small population centers. Among more than two hundred villages in the countryside around Toulouse (see Figure 3.1), one-quarter had resident surgeons; and of the settlements lacking surgeons, virtually all were within one *lieu* (about four kilometers) of a practitioner, an easy walk for the surgeon.[15] The tendency of surgeons to be distributed widely throughout an overwhelmingly rural population was remarked by the lieutenant of the *communauté* at Saint-Gaudens (Haute Garonne) in 1790: "One can easily count one surgeon in each *bourg* or hamlet, and there are even quite small villages with as many as three."[16] Tours had 19 surgeons in town and more than 100 scattered through the region; St. Pierre le Moutier (Nièvre) (population less than two thousand) counted about 120 surgeons in smaller places in its region.[17] Between 1766 and 1789, the *communauté* at Auch conferred the mastership upon more than 200 surgeons, of whom about 70 percent sustained the single examination for village practice (the remainder, except for 5 who qualified for Auch, a town of six thousand inhabitants, practiced in small towns in the surrounding diocese).[18]

Of the nearly four hundred surgical communities in the kingdom during the second half of the eighteenth century, almost half were located in towns with fewer than four thousand inhabitants.[19] The surgical profes-

The Surgical Profession in the Old Regime

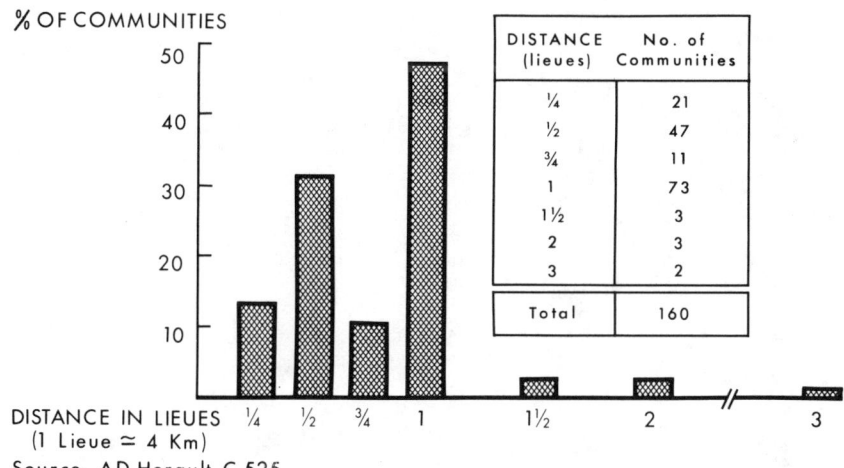

FIGURE 3.1. Distance to nearest surgeon for places lacking medical practitioners, Diocese of Toulouse, 1783.

In the diocese of Toulouse, 218 villages responded to the survey. Only about 30 had populations of 1,000 or greater. One or more resident surgeons were reported by 58 villages, as compared to 7 settlements reporting physicians. (SOURCE: "Etat du nombre des médecins, chirurgiens, et sage-femmes qui sont dans les communautés du département de Toulouse (1783)," AD Herault C 525, Archives départmentales Herault)

sional network thus extended down to a much finer level than the other two major medical corporations of the Old Regime, the physicians and the apothecaries (see Figure 3.2). Its diffusion was probably comparable to that of ordinary craft guilds, but these latter did not have the degree of central organization that the surgeons developed in the eighteenth century.

(4) Social Origins and Status.

The ordinary practitioners in the barber-surgeons' communities came from humble social origins. It could hardly have been otherwise in an early modern society in which the bourgeoisie composed less than 10

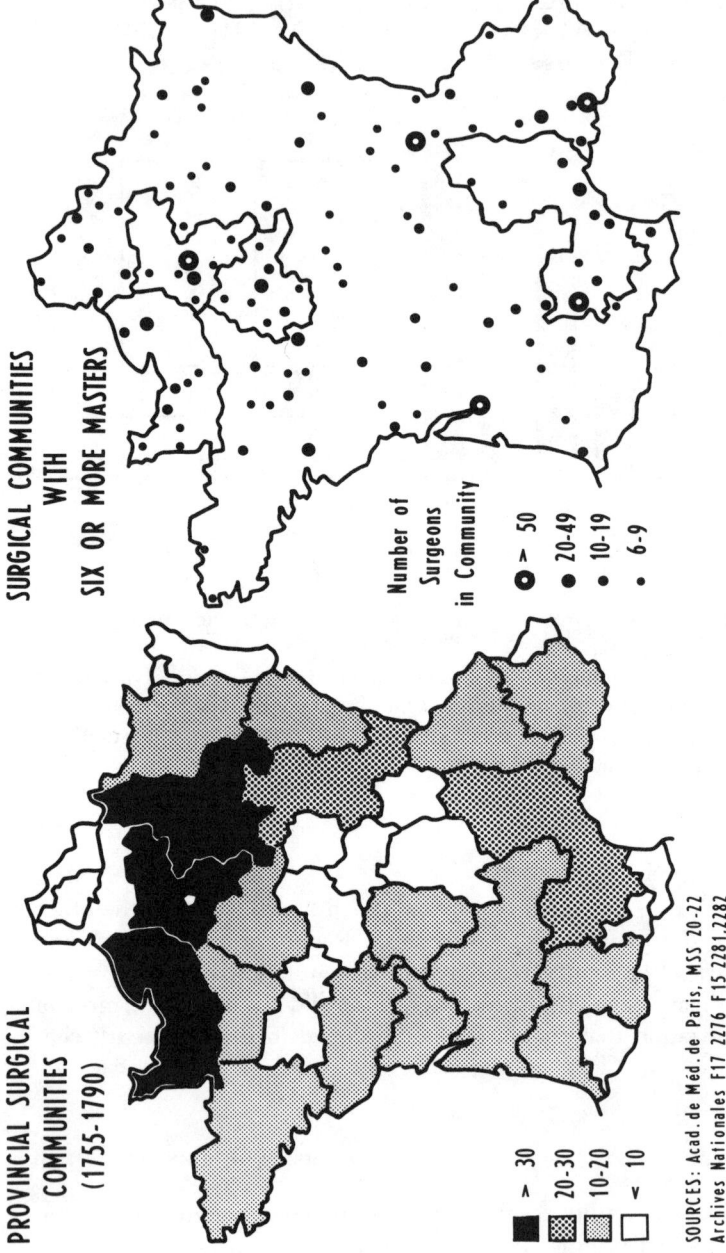

FIGURE 3.2. Surgical communities in eighteenth-century France.
More than 100 surgical communities counted 6 or more masters and could grant licenses to practitioners in their surrounding regions. By comparison, there were 40 faculties and/or colleges of medicine and even fewer guilds of apothecaries with 6 or more members. (SOURCES: Académie de Médecine de Paris, MSS 20–22; Archives Nationales F17 2276 F15 2281, 2282)

percent of the population.[20] A considerable body of prescriptive evidence—legal codes, financial and social privileges, and the like—indicates that physicians, both as individuals and in their corporate identity with the university, fell within the ranks of this privileged bourgeoisie. Surgical communities, on the other hand, were classed with *arts et métiers*, or "mechanical" professions. From about the middle of the eighteenth century, the upper-level surgeons increasingly protested the inclusion of their art among the "vile" occupations, a linkage they attributed to the conjunction between barbers' and surgeons' work.[21]

It is difficult, however, to get systematic empirical evidence on the family origins of ordinary practitioners. If one seeks to determine fathers' occupations and is fortunate enough to find such information, one then encounters the problem that a substantial proportion of ordinary practitioners were sons and often grandsons of ordinary practitioners. This pattern suggests a traditional artisanal occupation with little upward social mobility, but it remains difficult to locate barber-surgeons in relation to other craftsmen. Among the master barber-surgeons from the diocese of Auch en Gascogne whom I am currently studying, at least one-third were sons of surgeons (only four other fathers' occupations have been found so far—two merchants, one tailor, and one brewer[22]). Significantly, in one instance of middle-class professional background—a son and brother of notaries who apprenticed to a village barber-surgeon in the mid-seventeenth century—the contract explained that the young man was in dire circumstances, having lost both parents and wishing "to take up some trade in order to eke out a living."[23]

It seems safe to conclude that barber-surgeons came from the common people. In a predominantly peasant society, ordinary practitioners probably resembled their clients, like the surgeon in Diderot's *Jacques le Fataliste*, whom the author describes as an *espèce de paysan*.[24] The Paris surgical elite recognized that the bond between their humble colleagues and patients of similarly modest status constituted one of the strengths of the profession and a distinct marketplace advantage over doctors of medicine. A memoir dated 1749 in behalf of Louis XV's *premier* surgeon, Germain Pichaut de La Martinière, remarked that the common people (*le menu peuple*) were accustomed to surgeons. Even the surgeon's garb struck the poor person as familiar, whereas the physician's grander attire intimidated him. More pragmatically, common folk frequented surgeons because their work often disposed them to accidents requiring surgical care.[25] Similar styles of work and life thus linked ordinary practitioners with other manual workers who constituted their clientele.

(5) Training and Careers.

After completion of a contractual apprenticeship, a legal requirement for surgeons until 1772, the further training of ordinary practitioners was also on an apprenticeship basis arranged between private individuals; recipients came away with testimonials certifying satisfactory completion of the terms of service. The particular setting might be continued service as a journeyman under a master in private practice, or military or naval service, or hospital experience, but the pattern was basically the same. Masters evaluated apprentices according to moral and social criteria as summarized in the expression *vie et moeurs*. Diligence, attention to duty, obedience, devotion, fidelity, reliability, and other virtues counted more than merit, intelligence, talent, or skill, the latter qualities seldom receiving mention in the master's certificates.[26] Even the surgical colleges or schools, which began to supersede apprenticeship for theoretical instruction in eighteenth-century Paris and in major provincial centers, did not make an evaluation of ability in cognitive matters; they too issued certificates of attendance rather than grades. Surgical schools did not have admission requirements or the power to grant degrees or licenses to practice.[27]

Licensing remained a regional matter under the control of the local *communautés*. If we take Auch en Gascogne once again as typical of a surgical *communauté*, virtually all who became master surgeons were natives of the diocese, and more than one-half qualified for practice in the same village or town in which they had been born. Often, hometown practice meant a return to home rather than a failure to leave one's birthplace, for ordinary practitioners displayed remarkable geographical mobility. Like other artisans, barber-surgeons evidently participated in elaborate *tours de France* lasting many years and usually including a period in Paris.[28] At Auch (where about 30 percent of the masters had studied at Paris), the age of reception to the mastership tended to be advanced, averaging nearly forty years, and varied greatly. About as many became masters in their fifties as in their twenties.[29]

(6) Practice.

The ordinary practitioner engaged in all varieties of medical activity as well as other kinds of work no longer recognized as part of medicine. In eighteenth-century France, cutting hair and trimming beards remained central to the livelihood of ordinary practitioners, especially during the long and mobile period before they became masters, if they ever did.[30] Pharmacy and the treatment of internal ailments, though legally prohibited to barber-surgeons, also entered into their practice in a major way. This is not to claim that barber-surgeons had the training, knowledge, or therapeutic skills to deal with medical problems as adequately as physicians of the time; contemporaries, especially those concerned with medical reform, loudly and perhaps somewhat hastily condemned ordinary practitioners as incompetent and dangerous. Even a lieutenant of a surgical *communauté* complained that most country practitioners knew only how to shave and bleed.[31] But those affiliated with surgical communities must have had a broad market for their services or they would not have survived in such numbers. That they, rather than medical doctors, served as ordinary practitioners was obviously the case in most villages and towns of eighteenth-century France, where, as we have seen, physicians were absent or very few.

The same pattern obtained in the major cities. At Paris, a leading physician of the medical faculty admitted that the sick consulted first with surgeons, and surgeons themselves noted that "the *fauxbourgs* of Paris, refuges of the poor citizenry, contain more people than a good many major cities of the kingdom; yet no physicians live in the *fauxbourgs*."[32] The conclusion appeared obvious: "[The surgeon] will always be the physician for the poor."[33] At Lyons, France's second city, a doctor of medicine estimated that surgeons (of whom there were about one hundred compared with thirty physicians) pocketed 90 percent of the revenues from general medical practice. He said that this sort of "medical anarchy" reigned throughout France, in cities as in the countryside.[34]

(7) Relationship with Physicians.

Eighteenth-century surgeons thus constituted an organized group of ordinary practitioners separate and distinct from the doctors of medicine. The geographical, economic, social, and cultural distance between the two groups led to de facto autonomy for ordinary practitioners, an autonomy partially recognized in law by an independent corporative structure. Despite a formal hierarchy favoring physicians, interaction between the two medical corps was normally slight. In cities, however, where doctors and surgeons lived and practiced in proximity and where their prospective clientele might overlap, there was increased potential for competition and conflict.

My model of the ordinary practitioner in eighteenth-century France

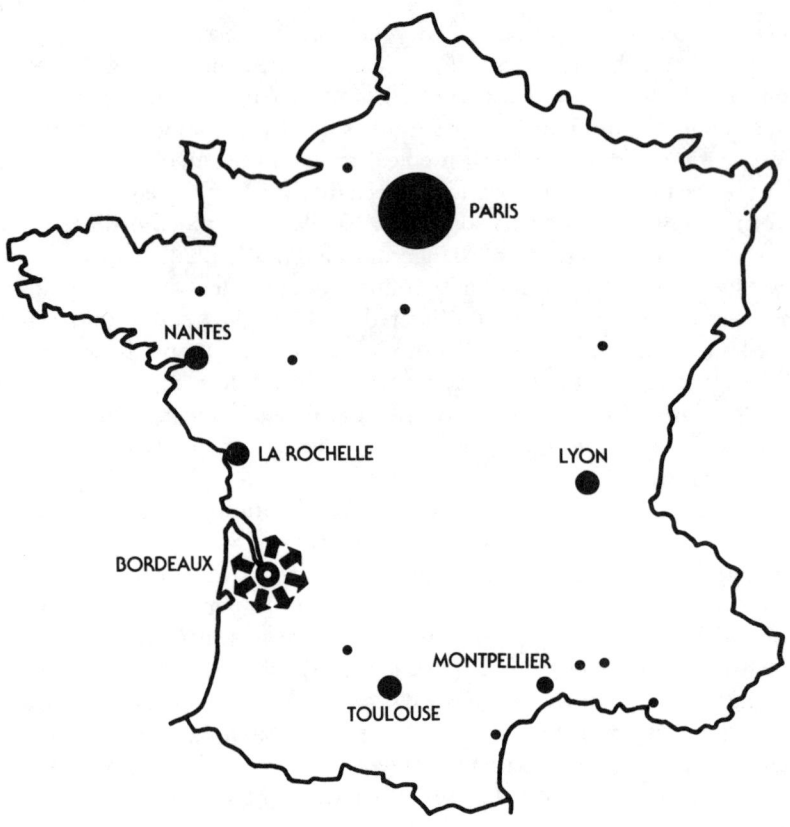

FIGURE 3.3. Main stopping places in *tour de France* of surgeons received as masters at Bordeaux, 1693–1700, based on twenty-eight cases, of which eighteen mentioned Paris. SOURCE: (AD Gironde 6E 24). See n. 28.

has thus far been presented in static terms in order to draw attention to certain structural and fairly stable elements. But in fact, the surgical profession experienced considerable change during this period. This dynamic process cannot be followed in detail here, but a few generalizations will help place the last two elements of the model of the ordinary practitioner (relationship to physicians and relationship to patients) in a historical context.[35]

During the late seventeenth and early eighteenth centuries, an elite

The Surgical Profession in the Old Regime

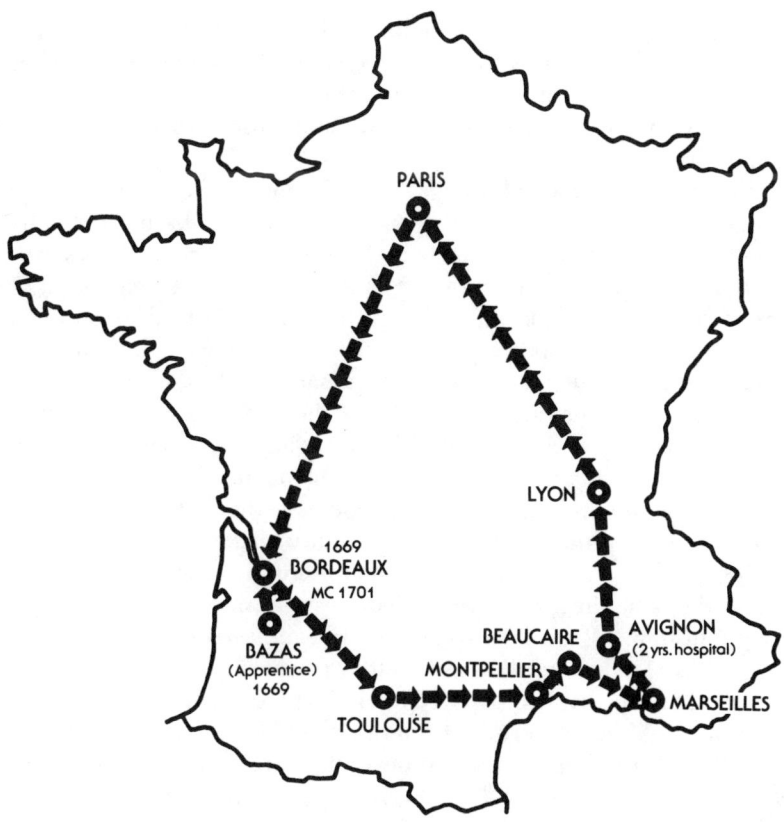

FIGURE 3.4. A case example of a journeyman surgeon's travels for thirty-two years: Jean Lavieu who apprenticed in 1669 and was received as master surgeon in 1701 for a *bourg* in the Bordeaux region. Arrows indicate towns in order of mention. The application states that Lavieu also worked in other towns.

group of Paris surgeons led by the king's *premier* surgeon cultivated a special relationship with the French crown. By means of royal patronage and legislation in their behalf, they modified the organization of local surgical communities so that instead of being isolated units, the communities became an interconnected if somewhat loosely unified professional network. An important step was the establishment in 1723 of lieutenants of the king's *premier* surgeon in each community. The Paris leadership imposed on this structure new institutions in the form of a school (1724) and an academy (1731), both of which were royal foundations, national in scope and centralized at Paris. A concerted effort was undertaken to define and achieve higher educational standards and loftier social and intellectual aspirations.

This campaign implied changes in professional relationships with physicians on one hand, and with the vast rank and file of barber-surgeons on the other. Events reached a climax in April 1743, when the Paris surgeons secured a royal declaration requiring a university arts degree for all Paris master surgeons and forbidding them to work as barber-surgeons. The declaration of 1743 appeared to split elite surgeons from ordinary practitioners and, ultimately, this did indeed happen. At the time, however, the new law demonstrated the power of the Paris leadership to improve the image of surgery as an occupation without surrendering its authority over ordinary practitioners throughout the kingdom.

By the 1740s, it was becoming evident to the enlightened public as well as to an alarmed Paris medical faculty that the surgical elite was making good its claims to professional authority over ordinary practitioners. At the same time, the scientific authority of surgery was bolstered by the publication of the first volume of the *Mémoires* of the Academy of Surgery in March 1743. Both, of course, were domains in which medical doctors traditionally had asserted their own prerogatives and claims to superiority. Although physicians' interests tended to be confined to symbolic control, this supremacy had never been seriously challenged. Now, as if to add insult to injury, the Paris surgeons openly rejected symbolic deference to the medical faculty, refusing oaths of homage and financial tributes. In 1743, the surgeons suspended receptions to the mastership rather than have medical doctors continue to preside over examination of candidates.

The mounting intraprofessional tensions boiled over into open warfare. Legal memoirs, public letters, anonymous pamphlets, broadsides, and other literary genre were the weapons with which one side did battle with the other. [36] Known collectively as *contestations* because of the legal contest over the 1743 declaration at issue, the public debate between physicians and surgeons raged from 1743 until midcentury, when the crown intervened with compromise legislation effectively resolving the dispute in the surgeons' favor.

The *contestations* brought into the open latent competition, indeed hostility, between physicians and surgeons, not simply or necessarily as individual practitioners but as rival corporations. The group representing

The Surgical Profession in the Old Regime

ordinary practitioners prevailed in a legal confrontation with the officially recognized medical elite. That surgeons rather than physicians took care of ordinary medical practice and ought to do so had been an underlying theme in the surgeons' polemic with the medical faculty:

> This custom [of surgeons working as ordinary practitioners] is so simple, so natural, and so invariably established by necessity, that one could not possibly conceive of another more appropriate to the condition [*l'état*] of the patients and which would assure them with such certainty the minor aid that they receive.[37]

Victory in the *contestations* appeared to vindicate the surgeons' account of the ordinary practitioner's role and to justify their normative conclusion that medical practice ought to be left in his hands: "The natural order is so clearly manifested in this practice that humanity should respect it, maintain it, and promote it by all necessary means."[38]

François Quesnay (1694–1774), the author of the anonymous essay of 1748 whose Enlightenment rhetoric is quoted above, was the surgeons' chief spokesman in the *contestations*. A clever *accoucheur* and surgeon, professor of therapy at the surgical school, and secretary of the Academy of Surgery, Quesnay became physician to Louis XV's mistress, Mme de Pompadour, and founder of the physiocrat school of political economy. In 1748, at the height of the *contestations* and at a turning point in his own career away from medicine, Quesnay offered his brilliant intellect and polemical skills one last time to the surgical professional cause he had served for twenty years. His *Examen impartial des contestations des médecins et des chirurgiens, considérées par rapport à l'intérêt public* brought out in bold relief the special importance of the last feature of my model of the ordinary practitioner—his relationship to his patient.

(8) Relationship with Patients.

According to Quesnay, it was of little import from a medical point of view whether physicians or surgeons treated most patients.[39] For ordinary patients typically needed only a "simple and perhaps the best" medical care: "bloodletting, *tisanne*, a few purgatives, and very few other remedies."[40] What did matter was that the patient be free to choose his surgeon or physician or both. Neither medical corps should be allowed to have the power (*le pouvoir des médecins et des chirurgiens*) to infringe upon the patient's rights (*les droits des malades*).[41]

According to Quesnay, patients in most cases chose surgeons for the following reasons: (1) technical: competence to carry out phlebotomy, the central therapeutic act in medicine (it was axiomatic for Quesnay that he who controlled phlebotomy would control ordinary practice[42]); (2) economic: surgeons cost less than physicians and charged only for their services and materials, not for consultations and advice[43]; and (3) social and cultural: surgeons were more accessible and had better rapport with ordinary patients. In caricaturing their rivals as ignorant artisans, physicians drew attention to this social fit between surgeons and lowly patients. Surgeons, a physician noted, loved to meet domestic servants in noble households, for these "lackeys" were their "old comrades": "they drink together, shake each other's hand, and slap one another on the back in a friendly way."[44]

If these considerations made surgeons the "natural" healers of the poor, Quesnay continued, ultimate power rested with the patient: "The patient alone has the absolute right to decide [on treatment] or to determine as he sees fit after having taken their [the doctor's and surgeon's] advice."[45] Wealthy patients could avail themselves of the luxury of consulting both a physician and a surgeon, but this was clearly out of the question for "nearly all men not well off," for the "poor citizens burdened with the painstaking work of society."[46] Quesnay's discussion reflected an ancient tradition going back to Hippocratic medicine in which the medical man's role was that of adviser, not arbiter or judge: "He gives advice, counsel, prescriptions, not orders or commands."[47] The patient remained the best judge of his ailment as well as the life circumstances that contributed to it and would govern its management.[48]

In any case, except for the occasional charitable gesture, which by definition did not involve fees, the doctor of medicine seldom dealt with patients of the lower social orders. He served his social equals or superiors. It would not do for such a practitioner to go beyond gentle recommendations to a patient who was at the same time a patron and who usually had a good understanding of theoretical medical knowledge himself. These basic intellectual and social conditions of medical practice had not changed substantially over the course of the eighteenth century.[49] In the doctor-patient relationship, ultimate authority belonged to the latter.

Quesnay's analysis, of course, despite his disingenuous claim of impartiality, was also a shrewd tactic in the surgeons' struggle for legal equality with physicians. If a physician prescribed a phlebotomy for a medical condition but both the patient and the surgeon-phlebotomist disagreed with this choice of therapy, Quesnay declared that the surgeon was justified in refusing to perform bloodletting. Because the patient, not the physician, controlled the medical transaction, the physician should not control the surgeon either: "The physician does not have the right to order the execution of what he advises, nor to decide the fate of patients according to his ideas." The analogy of the physician as architect and the surgeon as mason, a favorite metaphor of physicians, broke down because the patient was not a block of wood but rather the "master" of the task at hand.[50] Both parties were in principle subordinate to the patient they sought to serve.

In such a situation, competition for patients, prestige, and knowledge was no accident. Competition followed as a necessary and even desirable structural feature of medical practice. Let the guilds compete in open and healthy rivalry (*émulation*), declared Quesnay.[51] Let the most suitable practitioners prevail, as determined by their patients—anticipating in this special case his later general doctrine of economic liberalism, freedom of trade, and the famous physiocratic maxim, *laissez faire—laissez passer*.[52]

Eighteenth-Century French Surgeons as a Monarchical Profession

A historical perspective requires that one resist the temptation to impose modern patterns of occupational organization on eighteenth-century France—a preindustrial society in which vast political authority ostensibly derived from the royal administration and in which power flowed through the tortuous channels of the monarchical bureaucracy as well as through the informal network described by Norbert Elias as the *société de cour* at Versailles.[53]

In the preceding account of surgeons and barber-surgeons, I have offered an example of an occupation that was a product of the Old Regime and disappeared with it at the end of the eighteenth century. During a relatively brief period corresponding to the Regency and the early decades of the reign of Louis XV, surgeons enjoyed a series of successes culminating at midcentury with their recognition as an essentially autonomous group of medical practitioners. Contemporaries spoke of a "revolution" within the occupation that involved sweeping institutional, social, and—to a lesser extent—technical changes.[54] Had they come somewhat later in time, these changes might have been subsumed under our current conceptions of professionalization.

But, as we have seen, eighteenth-century French surgery did not fit the pattern of a modern collegial profession in Terence Johnson's sense of a homogeneous community of practitioners and peers. Nor did surgeons resemble the learned professions of their period as embodied in the university faculties of theology, law, and medicine. On the contrary, surgeons owed whatever strength they had in the marketplace to an extraordinary group heterogeneity that permitted a similarly broad range of clients.

To be sure, a semblance of collegiality did arise in the form of the Academy of Surgery. Here, intellectual criteria outweighed traditional social distinctions, and—as in eighteenth-century academies in general—seniority by age or social rank yielded to merit.[55] Yet the Academy of Surgery was but one façade of an otherwise hierarchical profession, and it too ultimately fell under the rule of the king's *premier* surgeon, its permanent president. At most, the Academy introduced a new element of collegiality into a more traditional occupational framework.

For the surgeons, as for other groups, this traditional framework certainly included "patronage" and "mediative" occupational control described by Johnson.[56] Indeed, the surgical elite in Paris and other urban centers was even more dependent on aristocratic patronage than the university-based professions.[57] At the same time, however, the surgeons drew institutional support and a sense of their legitimacy from a third party or mediator between themselves and their clients. This third party was the royal state. In this respect, surgeons lacked the autonomy of a modern collegial or even an Old Regime university-based profession.

Perhaps, therefore, eighteenth-century French surgery could best be designated a "monarchical profession" as a way of indicating the extent to which its organization depended upon and reflected the royal state. The king's *premier* surgeon played a pivotal role, using his position of intimate access to the sovereign at Versailles to obtain royal patronage and legislation for his profession. His network of lieutenants, held together by reciprocal bonds of offices bought and sold, recalled the mixture of feudal, financial, and bureaucratic arrangements upon which the centralized monarchy was built. In both instances, enormous geographical, social, and cultural diversity became integrated into a common framework. Extending the parallel, one might liken the pyramidical social structure of the surgical profession—with a relatively few elite surgeons serving the *notables* and vast numbers of ordinary village practitioners—to that of early modern France itself.

In any case, the role of the ordinary practitioner in providing medical services in early modern Europe has been neglected by sociologists as well as by those historians who fail to emphasize the critical differences between physicians and other categories of professional healers, including particularly the barber-surgeons on whom this essay focuses. Thus Eliot Freidson has argued that medicine remained a "learned" as opposed to a "consulting" profession until the late nineteenth century, by which he means that physicians had slight demand for their services because their clientele consisted of only the few patients who could pay their fees and chose to do so.[58] In support of this argument, attention is drawn to the very low proportion of physicians in the population of early modern European cities and their virtual absence in the countryside.[59] From such considerations, it is inferred that the vast majority of sick people seldom if ever consulted professional healers. Self-medication failing, the argument continues, they must have had recourse to "charlatans," midwives, cunning men, and white witches; that is, to people totally cut off from the medical profession.[60]

The neatness of the above line of reasoning is somewhat disturbed by the relatively high proportion of medical doctors Carlo Cipolla has found in Italian Renaissance cities.[61] But this situation appears to have been exceptional and was clearly not the case in the rest of Europe. A far more serious objection arises from the abundance of surgeons and, in particular, from the rich implantation of professional communities we have observed across eighteenth-century France. It is difficult to account for the existence of this network unless one allows that its members had a clientele. That country surgeons were consulted for services no longer considered relevant to health but then believed to be cognate (such as the barber's performance of bodily care and grooming) or even directly therapeutic (such as bloodletting) should not ipso facto disqualify them as professional healers. To do so would be anachronistic and would ignore the economic and social realities of the healing transaction in the early modern setting.

The eighteenth-century French surgeons provide an example of a professional structure that was socially inclusive and comprehensive rather than exclusive and elitist in the manner of modern professions. It allowed for much wider diversity in standards for entry and certification and in practical competence. Without attempting to quantify the volume of medical practice among lower levels of the professional spectrum, it seems virtually certain that sick people in the eighteenth century did consult these practitioners to a greater extent than has been recognized by scholars, who have tended to emphasize magical and folk healing. It seems more plausible to suggest that both categories of healers—professional surgeons and folk practitioners—were consulted in parallel. Moreover, many of those designated as "charlatans" or empirics may well have been journeymen who, for various reasons, never qualified for even the lowest category of surgical mastership. These practitioners, along with midwives, may be better understood as marginal professionals rather than as folk healers—at least in regard to their training and legal status, though in practice the boundary between the empirical and the magical was often indistinct.[62]

The professional success of surgery in eighteenth-century France depended upon an ability to balance the traditional hierarchical occupational structure with a new and dynamic collegial element. Surgeons made the collegial-*cum*-hierarchical model work. Their leader, the king's *premier* surgeon, was acutely aware that the source of his profession's power lay in this combination. He held what seems in retrospect to be a nearly schizoid posture, being at once "permanent president of the Academy of Surgery" and "chief of barbers and wigmakers" throughout the kingdom. The *premier* surgeon imposed a monarchical style of professional control when he, like the French monarchy, sought to reconcile Enlightenment science and ideology (embodied in the Academy) with a complex hierarchy of social status, financial privilege, and career prospects characteristic of the occupation as a whole. As long as the two meshed effectively (and definite stresses appeared after midcentury), they formed a potent combination.

Despite its profound differences from modern professions, there seems no good reason to disqualify the multilayered structure I have described for eighteenth-century French surgery as a historically valid profession. As a corrective to the assumption that a profession must be a prestigious occupation, one need only recall that the traditional meaning of the term referred to humble pursuits. The *Oxford English Dictionary* cites "haberdasher, taylor, sadler, barber, waterman" as "professional" categories in usage in 1616; the *Dictionnaire de l'Académie Française* (1694) makes reference to "an exhausting and oppressive profession" and "folks of every sort of profession." The word "profession" when not otherwise qualified typically had this vulgar connotation rather than that of a liberal or learned pursuit.[63] Only in the nineteenth century did the notion of a profession as superior to a trade or handicraft become well established.

Eighteenth-century French commentators clearly thought of professions as hierarchies between different occupations and also within the same occupation. And they liked to think that such a continuous chain structure—reminiscent of contemporary political, social, and biological conceits—facilitated upward mobility or at least assuaged aspirations for such. Thus the *Encyclopédie* article "profession" called for intergenerational progress up an occupational stepladder from "basses ou deshonnetes" to "honnetes" to "glorieuses" professions.[64] Within the framework of this great chain of professions, each link had a purpose and a legitimacy. Even when movement up the ladder did not exist, each rung still had a proper and legitimate place, however modest and far removed from other branches of the same profession.[65] Such a system stressed social harmony, reconciliation with one's lot, and acceptance of the status quo.

Occupations that managed to combine marked internal diversity with a sense of professional coherence and unity might be expected to be successful in a society that had similar attributes and values. During the middle decades of the eighteenth century, at least, French surgery represented one such profession well adapted to its cultural setting.

From "Ordinary Practitioners" to "General Practitioners": The Shift from Premodern to Modern Professional Structures

It should be clear by now that there are sharp structural differences between the eighteenth-century French surgeons and the modern medical profession. Insofar as they constituted a legitimate but premodern profession of "ordinary practitioners," the eighteenth-century surgeons had no direct successors. Their position as a distinct and legally recognized profession of healers, enjoying de facto autonomy from physicians, has no fully comparable modern counterpart. Beginning in the nineteenth century, many of their functions were assumed by "general practitioners," who were increasingly likely to hold M.D. degrees and who, in any case, belonged de jure and often de facto to the same profession as consultants or elite physicians. Until perhaps the end of World War II, such general practitioners in France (and presumably in other European countries as well) never attained a density in the general population or a relative numerical strength to match that of the eighteenth-century barber-surgeons. The nineteenth-century French health officer [*officier de santé*], an intermediate form between barber-surgeons and modern general practitioners, makes an interesting comparison in this respect. At their most numerous, the officers of health comprised no more than about half of the French medical corps; their density in the population on a national basis in 1845–47 was just over 2 per 10,000, and in no region except Corsica did they approach levels of 1 per 1,000 inhabitants. From the mid-nineteenth century on, their numbers declined sharply until their abolition in 1893—at which point, only about 2,000 survived, representing less than 10 percent of the official medical corps.[66]

By the 1880s, in fact, the number of legally recognized medical practitioners in general had also declined dramatically in France. In 1886, their population density fell as low as 3.3 per 10,000—a decisive reduction from early nineteenth-century figures (for example, 5.7 per 10,000 in 1844)[67] and a drastic decline by comparison with the multilayered professional structure of the Old Regime. This "demedicalization" of France was parallelled by a sharp decline in medical densities in Great Britain between midcentury and the 1880s.[68] Elsewhere in Europe, too, the gradual elimination of such ordinary practitioners as the barber-surgeons led to low "doctor"-to-population ratios by the late nineteenth century—for example, 3.3 per 10,000 in Germany by 1885 and 3.1 per 10,000 in Austria by 1889. Only in the last decade of the century did the increase in legal medical practitioners begin to outstrip that of population in the countries of Continental Europe.[69]

In Canada, and more especially in the United States, medical densities remained much higher than in European countries. In his famous *Report* of 1910, Abraham Flexner drew attention to this situation and emphasized how much it owed to the legions of marginal practitioners with medical degrees (in effect, ordinary practitioners), who were then actively competing in the American market for medical services.[70] Between 1870 and 1930, however, the American medical profession grew at a slower rate than the general population and five times slower than professional occupations as a whole. After reaching a peak of 17 "doctors" per 10,000 persons in 1900, the American profession dropped to 13 per 10,000 in 1930.[71] It would thus seem that the modern medical profession in different countries at different times, in different ways, and perhaps for different reasons has gone through a comparable stage of eliminating "ordinary practitioners."

In nineteenth-century France, the emergent "general practitioners" tended to be located in large towns and cities—a trend that accelerated there and in other Western countries in the twentieth century.[72] This trend emphasizes the extent to which eighteenth-century village barber-surgeons had no legitimate successors. However humble their social origins and status, "general practitioners" were generally much more solidly middle class than the artisan barber-surgeons or other "ordinary practitioners" they replaced.[73] Moreover, the training of the new general prac-

The Surgical Profession in the Old Regime 171

titioners normally took place in schools, thus ensuring minimum selection for and standardization of education. Finally, and most important, the nineteenth-century medical elite gained control over educational institutions and examining and licensing of general practitioners (as well as of such paramedicals as the French officers of health)—though the precise scenario, timing, and degree of government involvement varied from one country to another.[74]

It is, perhaps obviously, more difficult to detect any fundamental change in the relationship between medical practitioner and patient. The new "general practitioners" continued to serve essentially as advisers to patients whom they cultivated with tact if no longer with deference. Yet the need for social compatibility between "physician" and patient became less compelling as public respect for medical knowledge and authority increased. The perceived scientific and social status of medicine as a profession became more pertinent to patients than did the social status of individual practitioners. In France (and, it seems, in England too), medicine's elevated professional prestige preceded a substantial scientific basis in achievement such as the germ theory of disease.[75] Honoré de Balzac's *médecin de campagne* evoked the new status of a general practitioner to whom society was willing to grant authority. As medicine increasingly became a middle- or upper-middle-class occupation (and thus had a more homogeneous membership), medical men were able to provide services to a broader, more hetereogeneous spectrum of society, thus conforming to one of the characteristics of a "collegial" profession as described by Terence Johnson.[76]

Conclusion

If the above analysis is at all accurate, we are left with a discontinuity in the history of medical professionalization. A modern profession did not simply evolve gradually from eighteenth-century precedents; ordinary practitioners—barber-surgeons, apothecaries, feldshers, and the like—were not precursors in any meaningful sense of modern general practitioners. On the contrary, ordinary practitioners declined and became extinct and were replaced by general practitioners. Unlike such "new" technical professions as engineering, modern medicine emerged not primarily by direct expansion but by a process of reducing, purifying, and standardizing its ranks. This process required a severe winnowing of ordinary practitioners. On this view, the general practitioner is as modern a figure as the specialist against whom he is defined.[77]

What brought about this transformation in professional structure? Some causes were as general, complex, and interwoven as demographic expansion and population migration from village to town and city, the rise of well-to-do urban middle classes, and the beginnings of industrial capitalism.[78] All these forces acted to create demand for and a supply of professional medical men who tended to be middle class in their origins, outlooks, and clientele. Medicine, perhaps more than other professions, could claim to respond to the material needs and to embody the secular values of nineteenth-century bourgeois society. Furthermore, the role of government with respect to professions changed. Older patterns of monarchical patronage declined. Increasingly powerful central governments attempted (first on an ideological level and later by legislation) to counter regional distinctions by establishing uniform national standards in sensitive areas of social policy, including health needs and medical education.[79]

Factors operating within medicine are equally familiar and even more difficult to separate from one another. The profession's capture of hospitals and their conversion into instruments for research and teaching gave medicine a kind of territory it had never had before (except perhaps in the military setting)—a specific, controlled environment as a workplace. Poor patients, once viewed as clients by ordinary practitioners or as souls deserving charity by the Church, became clinical material while alive and subjects for anatomical study after death. They were admitted and treated under conditions set by the profession instead of by themselves or secular authorities. This transformation, as it first occurred in revolutionary and early nineteenth-century Paris, has been documented by Michel Foucault and Erwin Ackerknecht, each in his own way.[80] Nevertheless, both authors agree on the time, place, and historic significance of the medicalization of hospitals.

I have maintained elsewhere and suggested here that professional unification helped bring about a modern medical profession.[81] Specifically, the unification of medicine and surgery and the formation of unified training institutions marked a decisive shift from earlier patterns. It meant the end of an autonomous surgical profession and, more important, of its multilayered structure. Educational unification provided a basis for the recruitment and production of highly and uniformly trained medical practitioners.[82] By placing administrative power firmly in the hands of a

The Surgical Profession in the Old Regime 173

professional elite (with influential connections in society or directly with government), unification made it possible to impose standards and reduce intraprofessional competition. An achievement of the Revolution in France, this medical unification gradually emerged in England during the middle decades of the nineteenth century and still later in North America.

The rapid growth of esoteric, increasingly technical aspects of medicine no longer accessible to laymen, not even to the best educated, also contributed to professional transformation. Among these aspects were emerging medical sciences, the first of which was pathological anatomy; specialization; methodological innovations (in particular, the application of statistics to public health, pathology, and therapy); and a host of new instruments and diagnostic techniques such as the stethoscope for mediate auscultation. Noticeably absent, however, was an objective increase in therapeutic efficacy. On the contrary, medical men displayed increasing skepticism about the usefulness of traditional remedies, given the state of medical knowledge. One object of this skepticism was the time-honored panacea of bloodletting, which began to come under question at Paris in the 1830s.[83] Phlebotomy, of course, continued to be practiced until much later in the century, well after a modern medical profession had emerged. But in the absence of a detailed comparative study of the two phenomena, it is tempting to speculate that the decline of bloodletting hastened that of the ordinary practitioner who, as we have seen, relied on this procedure as his basic stock in trade.

One way to assess the impact of this bewildering array of novelties on professional transformation is to return to the analysis of power.[84] In place of the traditional arrangement in which power rested with the patient rather than the ordinary practitioner, the modern medical profession acquired three forms of power: power in society as expressed by career opportunities, high prestige, social authority, and political influence; power over its own profession as expressed by elite control and values, institutional unity, and high standards of entry and training; and power over patients.

One has only to consider the modern hospital interaction, epitomized by a surgical operation, to comprehend the extent of the transformation in this third category of power. In the early nineteenth century—before anesthesia, before the aseptic operating room and the impressive symbolic as well as biological sterility of the surgeon's white gown, mask, and rubber gloves—a radical transformation in power had taken place. Baron Guillaume Dupuytren, the Napoleon of surgery, who dominated and sometimes brutalized unfortunate charity patients on his wards at the

Hotel-Dieu of Paris during the first third of the nineteenth century, may have been flagrant and excessive, but with his virtues and faults, he personified a new image of heroic physician.[85]

Hospital medical men, as a group, and the profession they led made good their claims to power over patients. More often and more subtly expressed than the direct brutality of a Dupuytren was the physician's calm and confident assertion that he knew the patient's illness more accurately and intimately than did the patient himself.[86] Invoking their newly acquired knowledge and techniques, physicians dislodged patients from the privileged position they had held with respect to their own bodies and ailments. This dominant role assumed by physicians represented considerably more than a dramatic increase in medical knowledge and technology; it was also, and more importantly, a reversal in power relationships whereby physicians acquired the power to impose their professional definitions of disease. Ordinary practitioners had never aspired to or dreamed of such power. In this sense, the decline of the ordinary practitioner and the rise of a modern profession were different but complementary aspects of the same transformation.

Notes

Earlier versions of this paper were presented at the Davis Center for Historical Studies on 8 December 1978 and at a symposium of the Calgary Institute for the Humanities on 21 May 1980; see *Doctors, Patients, and Society: Power and Authority in Medical Care*, ed. Martin S. Staum and Donald E. Larsen (Waterloo, Ontario, 1981), pp. 105–29.

1. Useful formulations of profession in these terms are in Terence J. Johnson, *Professions and Power* (London, 1972), and Magali Sarafatti Larson, *The Rise of Professionalism: A Sociological Analysis* (Berkeley and Los Angeles, 1977). For a conventional list of the characteristics of modern professions, see E. Greenwood, "Attributes of a Profession," *Social Work* 2 (July 1957):44–55.
2. Toby Gelfand, *Professionalizing Modern Medicine: Paris Surgeons and Medical Science and Institutions in the Eighteenth Century* (Westport, Conn., 1980), pp. 156–60, 170–71, 189–92.
3. Michel Foucault, *Naissance de la clinique: Une archéologie du regard médical*, 2d ed. (Paris, 1972); Eliot Freidson, *Profession of Medicine: A Study of the Sociology of Applied Knowledge* (New York, 1970), p. 12.
4. Vern L. Bullough, *The Development of Medicine as a Profession* (Basel, 1966), esp. pp. 93–111.
5. For the designation "doctors" in reference to ordinary practitioners lacking medical degrees, see Eric H. Christianson, "The Emergence of Medical Communities in Massachusetts, 1700–1794: The Demographic Factors," *Bulletin*

of the History of Medicine 54 (1980):64. In general, apothecaries and apothecary-surgeons predominated in Great Britain and barber-surgeons were ordinary practitioners throughout western Europe. In German-speaking lands and Russia, the latter were known as *wundarzt* and feldshers.

6. See Johnson, *Professions and Power*, pp. 63–74; N. D. Jewson, "Medical Knowledge and the Patronage System in 18th Century England," *Sociology* 8 (1974): 369–85; Catherine W. Zerner, "The New Professionalism in the Renaissance," in *The Architect*, ed. S. Kostof (New York, 1977), pp. 124–28.

7. For detailed description of the surgical *communautés*, see Toby Gelfand, "Medical Professionals and Charlatans: *The Comité de Salubrité enquête* of 1790–91," *Histoire sociale–Social History* 11 (1978):62–97, and Gelfand, "Deux cultures, une profession: Les chirurgiens Français au XVIIIe siècle," *Revue d'histoire moderne et contemporaine* 27 (1980):468–84.

8. *Statuts et règlements généraux pour les maîtres en chirurgie des provinces du royaume* (1730), 5th ed. (Paris, 1772), pp. 45–46.

9. Gelfand, "Medical Professionals and Charlatans," pp. 81–86; Jacques Léonard, "Religieuses et médecins au XIXe siècle," *Annales ESC* 32 (1977):887–907.

10. Perhaps the largest category of all were the "students," most of whom did not succeed to the mastership in surgery. Some idea of their numbers in Paris during the second half of the eighteenth century can be had from the registration lists of the College of Surgery. See Gelfand, "Deux cultures, une profession." The size of this group, amounting to several thousand in Paris at any given time, and its intermediary status between "irregular" and master surgeon indicates the problem of attempting a sharp distinction between "regular" and "irregular" practitioners in the Old Regime.

11. C. P. Luynes, *Mémoires sur la cour de Louis XV: 1735–1768*, ed. L. Dussieux and E. Soulie, 17 vols. (Paris, 1860–65), 1:143; François Chaussier, *Mémoire sur quelques abus dans la constitution des corps et collèges de chirurgie* (Dijon, 1789), pp. 29, 32–33.

12. Jean-Pierre Goubert, "The Extent of Medical Practice in France around 1780," *Journal of Social History* 10 (1977):410–27.

13. Mireille Laget, "La naissance aux siècles classiques," *Annales ESC* 32 (1977): 980–84; Pierre L. Thillaud, *Les maladies et la médecine en pays basque nord à la fin de l'ancien régime* (Geneva, 1983), pp. 115–19; "Etat du nombre des médecins, chirurgiens, et sage-femmes qui sont dans les communautés du département de Toulouse (1783)," AD Herault C 525; Philippe Loupès, "L'assistance paroissiale aux pauvres malades dans le diocèse de Bordeaux au XVIIIe siècle," *Annales du Midi* 84 (1972):47; Archives départmentales Gers E 304, "Registre des recipiendaires pour la maîtrise en l'art de chirurgie de la communauté d'Auch."

14. "Etat du nombre des médecine."

15. Ibid.

16. Archives Nationales (Paris), F 17 2276, doss. 2, pièce 277. In the diocese of Bordeaux (mid-eighteenth century), 45 percent of the rural parishes had at

least one surgeon and 10 percent had between three and five (Loupès, "L'assistance paroissiale," p. 47).
17. Gelfand, "Medical Professionals and Charlatans," p. 95.
18. "Registre des recipiendaires."
19. Ibid., p. 97.
20. Pierre Goubert, *L'ancien régime 1: La société* (Paris, 1969), pp. 164–209.
21. [François Quesnay], *Recherches critiques et historiques sur l'origine, sur les divers états et sur les progrès de la chirurgie en France* (Paris, 1744), pp. 317–19, 340–49; Jean Verdier, *La jurisprudence de la médecine en France*, 2 vols. (Alencon, 1763), 2:14–19. See also Toby Gelfand, "From Guild to Profession: The Surgeons of France in the 18th Century," *Texas Reports on Biology and Medicine* 32 (1974): 121–34.
22. AD Gers, série 5E (registres paroissiales). In a series of nineteen apprenticeship contracts involving Toulouse master surgeons between 1738 and 1772, the following occupations of apprentices' fathers are given: master wigmaker, turner, printer, town official, bourgeois, royal official, painter, messenger, two surgeons, and four *habitants* (AD Haute Garonne, E1152, 1153). Fifty-three applications for reception by surgeons for the Bordeaux region between 1693 and 1706 mentioned fourteen fathers' occupations, of which twelve were surgeons, one a wine merchant, and one a cloth merchant (AD Gironde, 6E 24).
23. Gabriel Laplagne-Barris, "Un contrat d'apprentissage de chirurgien barbier au XVIIe siècle à Montesquieu," *Bulletin de la Société Archéologique, Historique, Littéraire et Scientifique du Gers* 80 (1979):494–96.
24. Denis Diderot, *Oeuvres romanesques*, ed. Henri Bénac (Paris, 1962), p. 496.
25. *Mémoire présenté au roy par son premier chirurgien* (Paris, 1749), pp. 38–39.
26. "Registre des recipiendaires."
27. Gelfand, "Deux cultures, une profession."
28. "Registre des recipiendaires." Information on the surgical *tour de France* is particularly rich from the fifty-four applicants to the mastership from the Bordeaux region. Virtually all claimed to have "parcouru les bonnes villes" during periods lasting on the average nearly eighteen years. Of the twenty-eight candidates who mentioned towns by name, eighteen had visited Paris. Other stopping places were Lyons (seven mentions), Nantes (six), Toulouse (six), La Rochelle (five), and Montpellier (three) (AD Gironde, 6E 24). See Figures 3.3 and 3.4.
29. "Registre des recipiendaires." The pattern was similar at Bordeaux; see AD Gironde, 6E 24.
30. Gelfand, "Deux cultures, une profession."
31. Gelfand, "Medical Professionals and Charlatans," esp. pp. 74–75.
32. *Mémoire présenté au roy*, p. 37; E.-C. Bourru, *Discours pronouncé aux écoles de médecine* (Paris, 1780), p. 20. Another spokesman for the surgeons claimed that common working people living in the center of Paris (domestic servants, journeymen, and other artisans of limited means) likewise could not "hope" for care from physicians [François Quesnay], *Examen impartial des contestations*

des médecins et des chirurgiens, considérées par rapport à l'intérêt public (Paris, 1748), p. 73.
33. *Mémorie présenté au roy*, p. 39.
34. Jean-Emmanuel Gilibert, *L'anarchie médicinale ou la médecine considérée comme nuisible à la société*, 3 vols. (Neufchâtel, 1772), 1:357.
35. The following discussion is based on my *Professionalizing Modern Medicine*, esp. chap. 4.
36. Alphonse Pauly, *Bibliographie des sciences médicales* (London, 1954), pp. 677–94, lists 102 printed items under the heading "Contestations relatives à la Déclaration du Roi du 23 avril 1743."
37. [Quesnay], *Examen impartial des contestations*, p. 75.
38. Ibid.
39. Ibid., pp. 52–53, 58–59.
40. Ibid., p. 71.
41. Ibid., p. 52.
42. Ibid., pp. 84–85, 122–23: "Medical practice among the common people revolves around the performance of bloodletting." Quesnay pointed out as well that bloodletting had crucial economic importance for surgical training and for the mobility and sustenance of young surgeons:

Now the main reason why masters take in students is to have assistants for doing bloodletting, assistants who get lodging and nourishment. They seek to recover these expenses by means of the profits from bloodletting. . . . Bloodletting makes it possible for surgical students to come from all the provinces of the country to Paris for instruction under the direction of masters of the art and at the schools of surgery, because bloodletting makes them useful to these masters, and they can support themselves at Paris until they are able to set up practice.

43. Ibid., pp. 66, 71–72. "Surgeons do bloodletting for a modest price; the rest of the consultation costs nothing, so that poor patients receive free care insofar as medical services are concerned."
44. *Le médecin véridique à l'avocat curieux* (La Haye, 1747), p. 40.
45. [Quesnay], *Examen impartial des contestations*, p. 98.
46. Ibid., pp. 63, 72, 75–76.
47. Ibid., p. 140. For the doctor-patient relationship in Greek antiquity, see *Ancient Medicine: Selected Papers of Ludwig Edelstein*, ed. Owsei and C. Lilian Temkin (Baltimore, 1967), esp. "Hippocratic Prognosis," pp. 87–110, and "The Relation of Ancient Philosophy to Medicine," pp. 349–66.
48. See William Coleman, "Health and Hygiene in the Encyclopédie: A Medical Doctrine for the Bourgeoisie," *Journal of the History of Medicine* 29 (1974): 399–421, esp. 402–6, in which the individual's primary responsibility for his own health is discussed in the context of the ancient doctrines of the "non-naturals" (environmental factors) and the healing power of nature. Coleman describes the physician's role as "that of pedagogue and advocate."
49. Ibid., Jewson, "Medical Knowledge and the Patronage System."
50. [Quesnay], *Examen impartial des contestations*, pp. 145–49, 138–41. "Only they [patients] have the right to give orders to the surgeon."

51. Ibid., p. 80. "Rivalry between two corps equally capable to cultivate knowledge of the healing art assured the citizens of superior men in medicine and surgery." See also pp. 52–53.
52. The medical sources of Quesnay's concept of economic liberalism remain to be explored. For a recent general discussion see Elisabeth Fox-Genovese, *The Origins of Physiocracy: Economic Revolution and Social Order in Eighteenth-Century France* (Ithaca, N.Y., 1976).
53. On the notion of monarchical profession, see my *Professionalizing Modern Medicine*, pp. 6–14. Norbert Elias, *La société de cour*, trans. P. Kamnitzer (Paris, 1974).
54. Antoine Louis, "Eloge de Ledran" (1771), p. 164; Louis, "Eloge de La Martinière" (1784), pp. 299–300, in *Eloges lus dans les séances publiques de l'Académie Royale de Chirurgie de 1750 à 1792*, ed. E. F. Dubois (Paris, 1859); M.-J.-A. Condorcet, "Eloge de M. Bordenave," *Histoire de l'Académie Royale des Sciences, 1782* (Paris, 1785), pp. 78–79; Jean Goulin, "Chirurgie," *Encyclopédie Méthodique: Médecine*, 8 vols. (Paris, 1792), 4:815.
55. Pierre Huard, *L'Académie Royale de Chirurgie* (Paris, 1966). A study of this Academy in the perspective of the sociology of knowledge remains to be written. Daniel Roche, *Le siècle des lumières en province, Académies et académiciens provinciaux, 1680–1789*, 2 vols. (Paris, 1978), a magisterial synthesis of academic culture in eighteenth-century France, deals only tangentially with Paris institutions and not at all with the surgical academy.
56. Johnson, *Professions and Power*, pp. 46, 65–86.
57. See G. Chaussinand-Nogaret, "Nobles médecins et médecins de cour au XVIIIe siècle," *Annales ESC* 32 (1977): 851–57. During the period 1724–60, eleven surgeons were ennobled as compared with five physicians. Antoine Louis makes frequent reference to the dependence of surgeons upon aristocratic patronage (*Eloges lus*, pp. 178–79, 184–85, 396–97, 407–9).
58. Freidson, *Profession of Medicine*, pp. 16–22.
59. Carlo Cipolla, *Public Health and the Medical Profession in the Renaissance* (Cambridge, 1976), p. 82; George Clark, *A History of the Royal College of Physicians of London*, 2 vols. (Oxford, 1964), 2:736–39; Goubert, "Extent of Medical Practice," pp. 420–23.
60. Keith Thomas, *Religion and the Decline of Magic* (New York, 1971), pp. 10–13, 177ff.
61. Cipolla, *Public Health and the Medical Profession*, pp. 79–86.
62. Françoise Loux, "Recours convergents à la médecine officielle et à la médecine parallèle de soins aux enfants en France (XIXe–XXe siècles)," paper read at International Colloquium, West Berlin, September 1978. For suggestive evidence that many "charlatans" had in fact studied at the Paris College of Surgery, see Gelfand, "Deux cultures, une profession."
63. "Becoming a priest or a military officer, choosing a career in justice or finance, is known as taking on a position. The other occupations, those most useful, content themselves with the degrading label of profession or trade" (Dangeul, 1754), quoted in Elias, *La société de cour*, p. 34.

64. *Encyclopédie*, 17 vols. (Paris, 1765), 13:426. The marquis d'Argenson, *Les loisirs d'un ministre*, 3 vols. (Liège, 1787), 1:12–13, considered the dreams of a young man to rise to the top of his profession, "one of the illusions that lift the soul and fill the mind with great and beautiful notions." D'Argenson noted the example of the surgical professional hierarchy.
65. Turgot conceived of merchants as forming such a professional chain: "Between the petty saleswoman, who spreads out herbs at the marketplace, and the shipping merchant whose transactions extend as far as the Indies and America, the profession is divided into infinite branches; that is to say, ranks" (quoted in J.-C. Perrot, "Rapports sociaux et villes au XVIIIe siècle," in *Ordres et Classes*, Colloque d'Histoire Sociale 2e Saint Cloud, France, 1967 [Paris, 1973], p. 145).
66. Jacques Léonard, *La vie quotidienne du médecin du province au XIXe siècle* (Paris, 1977), pp. 166–70; George Sussman, "The Glut of Doctors in Mid-Nineteenth Century France," *Comparative Studies in Society and History* 19 (1977):287–304.
67. Léonard, *La vie quotidienne du médecin*, pp. 47–51, 173–76.
68. Abraham Flexner, *Medical Education in Europe* (New York, 1912), p. 29; W. J. Reader, *Professional Men: The Rise of the Professional Classes in Nineteenth-Century England* (London, 1966), pp. 208–11. During the decade 1851–61, the medical profession (physicians and surgeons) decreased by 18 percent while the population of England and Wales increased by 12 percent. For the period 1841–81, the figures were −14 percent and +63.2 percent respectively.
69. Flexner, *Medical Education*, pp. 16–31. Matthew Ramsey informs me that Prussia did not undergo a demedicalization during the second half of the nineteenth century, and he cites Claudia Huerkamp, "Ärzte und Professionalisierung in Deutschland: Überlegungen zum Wandel des Arztberufs im 19. Jahrhundert," *Geschichte und Gesellschaft* 3 (1980):371.
70. Abraham Flexner, *Medical Education in the United States and Canada: A Report to the Carnegie Foundation for the Advancement of Teaching* (New York, 1910), pp. 14–19; Jacques Bernier, "Les praticiens de la santé au Québec, 1871–1921: Quelques données statistiques," *Recherches sociographiques* 20 (1979): 41–58.
71. H. Dewey Anderson and Percy E. Davidson, *Occupational Trends in the United States* (Stanford, 1940), pp. 494–97, 534–40.
72. Léonard, *La vie quotidienne du médecin*, pp. 8–9; Flexner, *Medical Education in the United States and Canada*, pp. 14–18.
73. Léonard, *La vie quotidienne du médecin*, esp. pp. 13–51; M. Jeanne Peterson, *The Medical Profession in Mid-Victorian London* (Berkeley and Los Angeles, 1978), esp. pp. 194–204.
74. Peterson, *Medical Profession*, pp. 37, 88–89, 241–43; George Weisz, "The Politics of Medical Professionalization in France, 1845–1848," *Journal of Social History* 10 (1977): 3–30, esp. 4.
75. Léonard, *La vie quotidienne du médecin*, pp. 252–54; Peterson, *Medical Profession*, pp. 3–4.

76. Johnson, *Professions and Power*, pp. 51–54.
77. Ivan Waddington, "General Practitioners and Consultants in Early Nineteenth-Century England: The Sociology of Intra-Professional Conflict," in *Health Care and Popular Medicine in Nineteenth-Century England: Essays in the Social History of Medicine*, ed. John Woodward and David Richards (New York, 1977), pp. 164–68, notes the modernity of the nineteenth-century general practitioner. I have discussed specialization from this perspective in "The Origins of a Modern Concept of Medical Specialization: John Morgan's *Discourse* of 1765," *Bulletin of the History of Medicine* 50 (1976):511–35.
78. Larson, *Rise of Professionalism*, presents a compelling analysis in terms of the "great transformation" to industrial capitalism. The expression is Karl Polanyi's, as discussed in ibid., esp. pp. 2, 9, 76–80.
79. Elias, *La société du cour*; Michel de Certeau, Dominique Julia, and Jacques Revel, *Une politique de la langue: La Révolution française et les patois: L'enquête de Grégoire* (Paris, 1975).
80. Foucault, *Naissance de la clinique*; Erwin H. Ackerknecht, *Medicine at the Paris Hospital, 1794–1848* (Baltimore, 1967). See also Ivan Waddington, "The Role of the Hospital in the Development of Modern Medicine: A Sociological Analysis," *Sociology* 7 (1973):211–25.
81. Gelfand, *Professionalizing Modern Medicine*.
82. Larson, *Rise of Professionalism*, p. 31.
83. Ackerknecht, *Medicine at the Paris Hospital*, esp. pp. 129–38.
84. Johnson, *Professions and Power*; N. D. Jewson, "The Disappearance of the Sick Man from Medical Cosmology, 1770–1870," *Sociology* 10 (1976):225–44.
85. *The Parisian Education of An American Surgeon: Letters of Jonathan Mason Warren (1832–1835)*, ed. Russell M. Jones (Philadelphia, 1978), pp. 108, 189. With private patients, however, Dupuytren was "another man." Other leading clinicians exhibited similar, if less extreme, behavior toward ward patients (ibid., pp. 116–229).
86. See Georges Canguilhem, *Le normal et le pathologique*, 2d ed. (Paris, 1972), pp. 50–51. Canguilhem cites the example of patients' mistaken references of pain to immediately underlying organs as in "kidney pain." Modern clinicians, he concludes, are led "to consider the firsthand experience of a patient with his disease as irrelevant, indeed even as systematically falsifying the objective pathological fact."

4
JAN GOLDSTEIN

"Moral Contagion": A Professional Ideology of Medicine and Psychiatry in Eighteenth- and Nineteenth-Century France

When in October 1885 young Sigmund Freud arrived in Paris to study with the renowned psychiatric *maître* Jean Martin Charcot, a deeply unsettling general election had just taken place. The Third French Republic, based on democratic suffrage from the outset but dominated by its enemies for the first nine years of its existence, had been "conquered by the republicans" only in 1879. Now, just when the republican consolidation of power seemed a fait accompli and ministerial stability was becoming habitual, a substantial proportion of the voters had unexpectedly withdrawn their support.[1] With a divided Chamber of Deputies, the Republic returned to its precarious condition; and in less than a year, General Georges Boulanger, the "man on horseback" with a charismatic martial air and a notoriously vague political program, would draw large, malcontented crowds into the streets—a scenario that seemed to presage a Bonapartist-style coup. Freud, of course, had come to Paris on a scientific pilgrimage, but the agitated political mood in the French capital in the closing months of 1885 could not escape his notice. "I am," he wrote to the sister of his fiancée in December, "under the full impact of Paris. . . . The city and its inhabitants strike me as uncanny. . . . I hear them yelling 'A la lanterne' and 'A bas' this man and that. . . . They are people given to psychical epidemics, historical mass convulsions."[2]

Freud's choice of words here may seem wryly fanciful or laden with national character stereotypes, but it was certainly also touched by the spirit of the times. The conceptualization of social phenomena as "psychi-

181

cal epidemics," or, more usually, mental or moral contagion, was becoming a commonplace in fin-de-siècle France. Already in 1884, Gabriel Tarde declared that it was not reciprocal economic services or juridical constraints but "imitative contagion" that held society together. In 1895, in what was to become a best-selling work of scientific vulgarization, Gustave Le Bon pronounced his era "the era of crowds" and provided a rambling description of the crowd mentality, which included among its components the eradication of the individuality and sense of moral responsibility of the crowd's members and the establishment of psychological homogeneity through "contagion." "In a crowd," stated Le Bon flatly, "every sentiment and act is contagious." And Emile Durkheim devoted a chapter of his *Suicide* (1897) to a discussion of whether "moral contagions" could appreciably influence the suicide rate.[3]

The vogue of the term "moral contagion" can be connected to the efflorescence of collective psychology at the fin de siècle and in the years preceding World War I, an intellectual trend that has attracted a good deal of scholarly attention.[4] This collective psychology was not simply equivalent to the theory of moral contagion, but the latter was one of its significant building blocks. In light of this relationship, three general points can be made about the use of the term "moral contagion" in the intellectual discourse of the period, roughly, 1880–1914.

First, it had a markedly antidemocratic animus. Linguistic usage itself hints at this. The images conjured up by the mention of "contagion" are highly charged: the word is fraught with connotations of pollution, danger, and uncontrollable disorder. That some form of contagion should be attributed to groups of people as a simple and inevitable consequence of their social interaction seems to express a distrust in mass participation, an utter lack of that faith in collective good judgment that characterizes the democrat. In fact, the historical record shows that crowd psychology was formulated in response to and as a critique of the extension of political democracy. Just as Freud's comments on "psychical epidemics" were elicited by his encounter with what he saw as the caprices and disconcerting noisiness of parliamentary democracy in France, so it was the Boulanger Affair, which provided Le Bon with his prime example of the individual surrender of moral responsibility to the sweeping "contagion" of the crowd.[5]

Second, "moral contagion" played a pivotal role not only in the foundation of the new science of collective psychology but also in the foundation of other new sciences of man—for example, criminology and, especially, sociology. It was at the crux of the famous debate between Durkheim and Tarde over whether the data of sociology were *sui generis*, irreducible

"Moral Contagion" and Psychiatry

to any other order of fact, or whether they were "intermental" and governed by the laws of individual psychology.[6] Thus Durkheim's main reason for exploring moral contagion in *Suicide* was precisely to discard that "intermental" phenomenon from his sociological consideration of his subject on the grounds not of its nonexistence but of its failure to "contribute to the unequal tendencies in different societies to self-destruction." In other words, moral contagion could not, for Durkheim, furnish a genuinely sociological explanation of anything. With this in mind, Durkheim offered his own subtle modification of the existing terminology:

It would perhaps be interesting . . . to distinguish moral *epidemics* from moral *contagions;* these two words used carelessly for one another actually denote two very different sorts of things. An epidemic is a social fact produced by social causes; contagion consists only in more or less repeated repercussions of individual phenomena.[7]

This second general point is related to the first. Durkheim's distaste for Tarde's "intermental" sociology was, on one very fundamental level, intellectual—a desire to found sociology on autonomous bases and a commitment in this regard to the philosophy of science of his former teacher at the Ecole Normale Supérieure, Emile Boutroux.[8] But the distaste had a political aspect as well: Durkheim's allegiance to the Third Republic made him shrink from the antidemocratic bias of the collective psychology of his contemporaries.

The third point concerns the relationship of the theory of moral contagion to the fin-de-siècle "discovery of the unconscious." The process of moral contagion was depicted not only as involuntary but also as occurring beneath the level of conscious awareness. It was linked to the notions of the hypnotic state and to the absolute obedience of the hypnotized subject to the suggestions of the hypnotist, notions popularized in France from the 1880s on by both Charcot's Parisian Salpêtrière school and Hippolyte Bernheim's Nancy school of psychiatry. It was also linked to other altered or twilight states of consciousness, those of the dreamer and the sleepwalker. Thus Le Bon: "When defining crowds we said that one of their general characteristics was an excessive suggestibility, and we have shown to what an extent suggestions are contagious in every human agglomeration." "A crowd [is] perpetually hovering on the borderland of unconsciousness. . . . The individual forming part of a psychological crowd . . . is no longer conscious of his acts. . . . His case [is like that of] the hypnotized subject. . . . Under the influence of suggestion, he will undertake the accomplishment of certain acts with irresistible impetuosity." And Tarde's terse and dramatic summary of his argument: "Society is imitation, and imitation is a kind of somnambulism." It was a fitting extension of this aspect of the vogue of moral contagion that Freud, long after becoming the great systematizer of the workings of the unconscious, used the crowd psychology of Le Bon, including its notion of contagion, as the jumping-off point for his own psychoanalytic essay on social cohesion, *Group Psychology and the Analysis of the Ego* (1929). And it was prescient that, in his prepsychoanalytic 1885 letter, Freud described the Parisians' proclivity for "psychical epidemics" as "uncanny," for he would later identify the experience of "uncanniness" with the emergence of a "hidden familiar thing" from repressed unconsciousness.[9]

I have begun this essay with a discussion of moral contagion at the fin de siècle in order to establish firmly the nature and significance of the theory at that historical juncture. But my primary purpose will be to explore the generally unrecognized antecedents of this "heyday" of moral contagion, to sketch the prehistory of French collective psychology. These antecedents are to be found in eighteenth-century medicine and, in the first half of the nineteenth century, in the emergent medical specialty of psychiatry. Whether the late nineteenth-century crowd psychologists were aware of their antecedents is unclear: Durkheim scrupulously footnoted the early nineteenth-century psychiatric literature in *Suicide*, indicating an impressive acquaintance with it,[10] but no such attributions are given by Le Bon or Tarde. Modern scholars have been, in this matter, less historically minded than Durkheim, treating moral contagion theory as a creation de novo of the latter nineteenth century.[11] My inquiry here has a dual purpose. The first, already adumbrated in this introduction, is the very traditional one of the discipline of the history of ideas: to trace what Arthur O. Lovejoy would call a "unit-idea"—in this case, moral contagion—over time, observing both its persistence and its vicissitudes. The second, and the more challenging, derives from the approach of the social history of ideas: to situate the idea, in its medical and psychiatric forms, within its social context, to see how it functioned as a professional ideology which both reflected the self-definition of a rising professional corps and fostered the professional goals of that corps.

Implicit in this second purpose is a particular conception of professionalization. Professions have often been depicted as coming into being when there is a body of highly specialized "esoteric" knowledge at hand and those schooled in it seek to acquire a monopoly over its exercise and application. The body of knowledge is, in this view, a prerequisite for the process of professionalization and essentially separate from it. The conception proposed here denies this compartmentalization. It suggests that at least for certain professions—and especially new professions, such as early nineteenth-century psychiatry, with still fluid bodies of knowledge and unclearly defined rules of investigative procedure—the body of knowledge will evolve, in part, as a function of the process of professionalization. Certain theories will be accentuated or deemphasized, certain lines of argument pursued or allowed to lapse, in response to professional exigencies and the need to achieve public recognition. A theory that develops in this context is a "professional ideology." In contending that moral contagion was one such professional ideology, my discussion will be more general and schematic for the eighteenth century and more detailed and specific for the early nineteenth century.

The Eighteenth-Century "Vocabulary" of Moral Contagion

An account of the early history of moral contagion theory takes on, of necessity, an almost anecdotal character: the theory was developed not through systematic investigation or abstract speculation but in the course of the contemporary interpretation and subsequent reinterpretation of a series of events which came to be regarded as salient and exemplary instances of the phenomenon. Some of these events appeared in the medical literature with such regularity that allusion to them became a medical tradition, a formulaic rehearsal of verities. These prototypal events are the affair of the Jansenist convulsionaries in Paris in the 1720s and 1730s; an outbreak of convulsions in a Haarlem orphanage, treated and reported by the great eighteenth-century Dutch physician Hermann Boerhaave; the vogue of the mesmerist *baquets* in Paris in the 1780s; and an event from ancient history which became a justificatory touchstone for eighteenth- and early nineteenth-century medical men—a wave of suicides among the women of Miletus, as described in Plutarch's *Moralia*. A first approach to the problems of this essay must be, then, to master the "vocabulary" of early moral contagion theory—that is, to set forth the basic narrative of each of these four events and the medical glosses given to them.

The affair of the convulsionaries was one of the most conspicuous aspects of the period of heated ecclesiastical politics in France that followed upon the promulgation of the papal bull Unigenitus (1713). The bull, which condemned the major tenets of Jansenism as heretical, was intended to deal the final blow to a Jansenist movement already weakened by the destruction of Port-Royal; but it had the opposite effect, galvanizing the remnants of the sect into an obdurate and vocal resistance. In the midst of the controversy, the death in 1727 of François de Pâris, a revered Jansenist deacon, and his burial in the cemetery of Saint-Médard on the rue Mouffetard (in a poor and overcrowded *faubourg* of Paris populated primarily by artisans) transformed that spot into a sacred one, the locus of a new cult of defiant Jansenist enthusiasts. The adherents were seized by convulsions, frenzied paroxysms, screams, and swoons so uncontrollable and violent that their associates placed mattresses and cushions around the gravesite to prevent injuries. Initially, only those who touched the deacon's tomb were convulsed; later, the geographical range widened, so that individuals throughout the cemetery, in the church, in nearby houses, and even in the streets were affected.

For the participants, these convulsions were an intensely religious experience, an evidence of the Holy Spirit working within them through the intercession of Monsieur de Pâris. For the French government, the cult, which rapidly outgrew its neighborhood character and began to draw people from all over the capital and even from elsewhere in France, was both a nuisance and, insofar as the issue of Jansenism was intimately connected to the delicate Gallican Church-state balance that was part of the underpinnings of political authority in the Old Regime, a potentially dangerous public disorder. In 1732, the Saint-Médard cemetery was closed by royal ordinance. Undaunted, the adherents of the cult transferred their activities to private conventicles, where what was now called the *oeuvre des convulsions* was cultivated as the highest manifestation of religiosity. Again the government stepped in, first with sporadic police harassment and then, in 1733, with a royal decree prohibiting all convulsionary activity.[12]

The convulsions thus had two fundamentally different meanings for the faithful of the sect and for the royal government; they had yet a third meaning for Dr. Philippe Hecquet. A physician of the highest stature, Hecquet had been elected dean of the Faculty of Medicine of Paris in 1722; he was also of Jansenist persuasion and had served as physician at Port-Royal for five years.[13]

Hecquet shocked the Jansenist camp (and the distress he felt at his iconoclasm is apparent in the manuscripts found after his death in which he repeatedly attempted to clarify his position and soothe his coreligionists) by asserting unequivocally in a brochure published in 1733 that the

Saint-Médard convulsions were "the effects of pure nature, or of an evident Naturalism" and, as such, fell "precisely within the competence of Medicine." Hecquet's mode of conceptualizing this "naturalism"—his depiction of the human organism as composed primarily of nerves, whose chief attribute was their elasticity and contractility and which were also hollow threads filled with an "aerial fluid," likewise elastic, capable of expansion and compression, so that the equilibrium between these two variables, one solid and the other fluid, was easily upset, the disequilibrium constituting a spasm or convulsion—need not concern us in detail here. More relevant is his "naturalist" mode of explaining why the convulsions of Saint-Médard were a group phenomenon of ever-increasing proportions, for here Hecquet invoked the model of the "epidemic" and of "contagion" and thus became the first formulator of the theory of moral contagion.[14]

The contagion of convulsions, Hecquet argued, was analogous to sexual attraction or, as he called it, "the so natural contagion between the two sexes." There was a continual abundant emanation of corpuscles escaping in the form of vapor through the pores of the skin of each individual, creating an "atmosphere" around each. These corpuscles were "affixed with the seal" of that individual's body, carrying all of its distinctive properties. When two individuals were in proximity, their surrounding "atmospheres" mingled, and they breathed in each other's corpuscles through the lungs. Viewing this process from the male perspective (and a parallel argument could easily be made for the female experience), Hecquet noted that the corpuscles of a young girl, bearing "the dispositions proper to the gentle sweetness [*douceur*] of her sex," transmitted into the body of the man "inclinations to gentle sweetness" and that his nerves softened correspondingly so as to approach the physiological condition of female nerves. "His heart and his imagination" were then aroused "in a girlish manner."[15] Thus attraction between men and women did not merely draw and bind together opposites; if worked by a sympathetic identification of one sex with the other, a mutual imitation and "contagion" of their gender characteristics, which rendered them more alike than before. Similarly, the corpuscular emanations of a convulsionary bore the imprint of that particular neurological state and were prone to replicate it in any individual who inhaled the convulsionary's "atmosphere": whence the contagious nature of the convulsions in the cemetery on the rue Mouffetard and the ever-widening circles of contagion that radiated out from that central point. Hecquet's model of the contagion of psychological states (love) or psychomotor disturbances (convulsions) was thus a materialist one, as he himself insisted: it was "founded on things that are hardly the less material for being subtle and hidden from the senses."[16]

In replying to a critic of his 1733 brochure, Hecquet brought into the discussion a second term from our basic "vocabulary"—Plutarch's episode of the Miletian women—offering it as proof of his assertion that an abnormal nervous condition could be transmitted by contagion. Here is Hecquet's version of Plutarch:

You have a celebrated and very palpable [example] in the Miletian women described by Plutarch who, afflicted with a mental malady [*maladie d'esprit*]—it was hysterical vapors—communicated from one to another the mad furor of hanging themselves. The contagion of these disturbed imaginations overtaking, like an epidemic, the entire country . . . , the Miletians found no better remedy than to strike the imaginations of these female citizens with another passion. . . . That was modesty. . . . To accomplish this, the wise Magistrates published an ordinance throughout the land that all girls found hung would, after their death, be exposed entirely nude, the rope around their neck, to the eyes of everyone. This was for those girls an imagining of the future . . . so powerful that from that time on, no one hung herself.[17]

This rendition is essentially correct, but it includes some strategic embellishment. Apart from offering no explicit diagnosis of the malady, Plutarch presented as the hypothesis widely held at the time that the Miletian girls had lost their reason and become suicidal because of a malign pestilence in the air. That is, he gave a good Hippocratic explanation of an epidemic. Ironically, then, the social dimension so critical to the modern theory of moral contagion—the transmission from a contaminated individual to a healthy one (as Hecquet put it, "communicated *from one to another* the mad furor")—was totally absent from the ancient source and, with scant respect for textual accuracy, had to be attributed to it.

The third event is of a more circumscribed nature than the others. Boerhaave recounts in his *Praelectiones academicae de morbis nervorum* (1761) that "by menacing to apply a hot iron . . . I once cured the entire orphanage of Haarlem" of a convulsive nervous disease. Boerhaave's nephew supplies more detail. A girl belonging to the institution had been seized with convulsions after being subjected to a severe fright; within a few days, all the children living there were affected. Boerhaave regarded the convulsions as a "simulated epilepsy" (because all the remedies for bona fide epilepsy had been tried and found unavailing) and thus, displaying to the assembled children a stove filled with glowing coals and, atop them, iron pokers, he improvised his "menace."[18]

The fourth event is another affair of *convulsionnaires*,[19] though *convulsionnaires* devoid of religious aspiration or self-definition, who were instead the patients of mesmerists. Franz Anton Mesmer had arrived in Paris from Vienna in 1778, claiming to have discovered nothing less than the magnetic fluid that filled the entire universe and formed the connecting medium between men, the earth, and the celestial bodies. The amount and distribution of this fluid within the individual organism were, he held, responsible for its health or sickness; and by provoking "crises" in his patients (who for this purpose sat together around large tubs, or *baquets*, from which protruded fluid-dispensing iron rods), he properly redistributed their share of fluid and cured them. Hence his aphorism: "There is only one illness and one healing."[20]

Mesmer quickly gathered a group of loyal French disciples, and mesmerism became the fashion of the day, with ailing people of all the orders of society flocking to the *baquets*. In certain respects the vogue bore a strong resemblance to the Saint-Médard episode: just as the ability to perform the *oeuvre des convulsions* became a mark of both sanctity and status for the Jansenist sectaries, so too the ability to succumb to *crises* near the *baquet* was prized as the mark of a refined sensibility; the mattress-strewn floor, prepared in expectation of uncontrollable seizures, was a feature of both;[21] and, of course, in both, the convulsions were never solitary experiences but always occurred in a communal setting. Just as the monarchy under Cardinal Fleury had been alarmed by the Saint-Médard convulsionaries, so too, in 1784, a clearly wary Louis XVI appointed a "commission . . . to examine animal magnetism." In their report of their findings (of which the concerned government printed and distributed twelve thousand copies), the commissioners vigorously denied the existence of Mesmer's universal magnetic fluid. But once having done so, they were obliged to offer an alternate, nonmesmeric explanation for the convulsions that routinely shook the patients around the tub. Physical "contact" (*attouchement*) and "imagination" powerfully aided by "mechanical imitation" were, they said, the true causes. "Mechanical imitation" was their version of the concept of moral contagion. They wrote:

The tub is surrounded by a crowd of sick people; sensations are constantly communicated and received; the nerves eventually grow tired of all this exercise; they are irritated, and the most sensitive person gives the signal [i.e., goes into convulsion]. *Then the strings everywhere stretched to the same degree and in unison answer one another*, and the convulsions multiply; they mutually reinforce each other. At the same time, the spectators share these emotions in proportion to their own nervous sensibility, and those whose sensibility is more volatile also have convulsions.[22]

Like Hecquet's model of moral contagion, the commissioners' was materialist, although the putative material transmitters were not aerial corpuscles impinging on nerves but the tautly stretched nervous strings themselves, synchronized and reciprocal in their vibrations in accordance with the laws of physics. The 1784 commissioners were, indeed, familiar with Hecquet's work and cited it in their report.[23] Furthermore, the analogy between Saint-Médard Jansenism and mesmerism, the latter seen as a lay revival of the former, was noted at the time both by journalistic commentators and by the mesmerists themselves, who were convinced that "the tomb of Saint-Médard was a mesmeric tub."[24] This fourth term in our basic "vocabulary" of moral contagion was, then, heavily cross-referenced to the first.

Underlying Motifs

From the welter of detail—often richly colorful detail—of these four stock events, there emerge two central motifs, each crucial for the contextual significance of the medical theory of moral contagion: the role of authority and the expansion and defense of medical-professional prerogatives.

An outbreak of moral contagion was, these events reveal, the occasion for a show of authority. In the first place, authority found the disorder of psychic epidemics distasteful or intolerable; in the second place, authoritarian displays were deemed the effective remedy for moral contagion, the best means for putting a quick halt to it. The Miletian and Haarlem episodes contain the starkest images of authority so employed. An edict of the governing council of Miletus threatens the distraught and suicidal girls with a humiliating posthumous punishment. (Whereas Plutarch sees this strategy as adopted at the suggestion of "wise citizen," Hecquet sees it as solely the work of the magistrates. He revises the story slightly to concentrate and strengthen the image of authority.) In the Haarlem orphanage, authority appears in an even more naked and brute form. Subsequent versions transformed Boerhaave's simple "hot iron" into "a red-hot iron [that would be] applied to the arm rather deeply."[25] The version of Philippe Pinel depicted the "superior" Boerhaave as "surrounding himself with a certain machinery of terror [*appareil de terreur*]."[26] The tactics recommended both by Hecquet and by the royal commissioners of 1784 were somewhat less drastic but equally reliant upon the strong assertion of authority: the group of convulsionaries was to be dispersed and the afflicted individuals, who served as "examples," were to be isolated, "removed to private [*particulier*] places" and "prevented from all commerce" with one another and with the outside world.[27]

What were the nature and source of this intervening "remedial" authority? Was it to be political or medical? An examination of the four events reveals ambiguity on this point, a very significant ambiguity because it points to the confusion and conflation of the medical and political spheres that were, from the outset, inherent in the theory of moral contagion. Boerhaave was clearly a medical authority, but he seems to have recognized that, in his cure by "menace of a hot iron," he was assuming a kind of political authority because he informed the municipal officials of his plan for the orphanage before executing it.[28] Pinel's rendition of Boerhaave, changing the "hot iron" into an "*appareil de terreur*," gives a similar tacit recognition of the political component in the Haarlem cure: writing immediately after the Revolution, Pinel chose words that summon up images of coercive political power—the Jacobin Reign of Terror, through which he had just lived, and the guillotine. The Miletian council was a purely political authority, but Hecquet, in effect, appropriated it as a medical model by citing it in a medical context. Plutarch, after all, intended the Miletian incident not as a medical case history (no physicians even figure in it) but as a moral tale, a reassuring exemplum of the enduring power of the sober virtue of modesty in women. A parallel instance of this kind of appropriation was Hecquet's citation of an incident of a daily outbreak of meowing (*miaulement*) in a convent, quelled only when the nuns were told that "by order of the Magistrates there would appear at the door of the convent a company of soldiers who, at the first sound of this meowing, would enter the convent and whip [each culpable woman] on the spot."[29]

Authoritarian display was not, it should be stressed, an ordinary form of medical treatment in the eighteenth century. Rather, bleedings, emetics, purgatives, and a variety of other drugs and herbal preparations were the standard offerings of the physician—so much so that Pinel saw as one of the most remarkable and praiseworthy aspects of the Haarlem orphanage affair that Boerhaave had "rais[ed] himself above that exclusive confidence" in the "formulae of pharmacy."[30] The extraordinary therapeutics required by moral contagion—and their political resonance—derived from the physicians' conceptualization of the pathology and, in particular, from the role ascribed to the mental faculty of imagination. Materialist models may have been adduced to explain the process of contagion, but a heightened activity of the imagination was held responsible for initially provoking the convulsions, which, in turn, became communicable. According to Hecquet, it was the "inflamed imaginations" of young Jansenist girls, wishing to "see themselves" transformed into "miraculous" manifestations of piety, which acted upon the "nervous fibers" to produce that disequilibrium of solids and fluids that constituted a convulsion.[31] For the royal commissioners of 1784, the profound hope and wish to be cured, the repeated insistence of the mesmerists that cure would come through convulsive crisis, and the intensification of these emotions and expectations when shared by a group of people around a *baquet*—all stimulated "imagination" to so high a degree that "it act[ed] by violent means" and brought forth convulsions.[32] According to Boerhaave's nephew, "fright," an emotion invariably accompanied by a vivid imaginative construction of impending misfortune, had thrown the first of the Haarlem orphans into a convulsive state. The suicidal Miletian women were viewed by Hecquet as so "impelled by the violence of their disturbed imaginations" as to be "swept away by convulsion into hanging themselves."[33]

Throughout this period, and in both Cartesian and sensationalist psychologies, imagination—with its preverbal, concrete pictorial contents, its alleged presence in beasts as well as men, and its intimate connection with visceral passions—was regarded as a mental faculty closely tied to the body, more closely tied than, for example, reason or reflection.[34] It also possessed the power, often depicted as a "terrible power,"[35] to influence bodily functions directly: that the imagination of the mother even influenced the form of the fetus growing in her womb was a scientifically respectable belief.[36] Imagination was thus the intermediary between "*le moral*" and "*le physique*"[37]: it was situated at just the same juncture at which moral contagion, in part a mental and in part a physical malady, was situated. It was, then, to an aggregate of overwrought imaginations that the physician had to minister in an epidemic of moral contagion; his routine remedies, geared to the physical body only, were inappropriate, and he was called upon to innovate.

Now the diseased imagination was, with respect to the images it conjured up and the way those images flowed from one to the other, typically described as "unruly" and "disordered." Even the normal imagination easily eluded the will and was regarded as being "without a master."[38] Hence order, rule, and mastership had to be imposed upon the imagination; and, with this importation of categories from the political realm, medical therapeutics and the exercise of political power began naturally to merge. For how could one reorder, regulate, and master an imagination? One could, in Hecquet's phrase, "strike it" with a new set of images and thereby forcibly banish the old ones: hence the threat of punishment, made as graphic as possible, as a medical procedure. Or one could "calm" an imagination by removing it from the external circumstances that had given rise to and sustained its excitation: hence forced dispersal and isolation as medical procedures.[39] In the more or less uncharted territory opened by moral contagion, a novel "medicine of the imagination" found inspiration in the model of political authority, indeed in a model of fearsome and uncompromising political authority not far removed from the absolutist ideal of the seventeenth and eighteenth centuries. The congruence of styles of authority at different levels of society—and, in particular, of familial, educational, and political authority—has been noted by historians of the family with reference to Old Regime France.[40] The evidence here suggests a congruence between professional and political styles of authority, with the physicians emulating political power. I will have more to say about this theme below.

The merging of the medical and political in the treatment of moral contagion reflects the same merging in the conception of the phenomenon itself. The royal commissioners of 1784 warned the crown of the untoward consequences of the continued application of Mesmer's methods and of the nervous contagion thus set in motion at the *baquets:*

This Art [mesmerism] is baneful, which troubles the functions of the animal economy, pushes Nature into deviations, and multiplies the victims of its irregularities. This Art is all the more dangerous in that it aggravates diseases of the nerves.... If these diseases are contagious, as we have reason to suspect, the practice of inducing nervous convulsions during public treatments is a means of spreading them throughout large cities; and even of afflicting generations to come, since the diseases and the habits of the parents are transmitted to their posterity.[41]

The evil consequences predicted were thus indistinguishably hygienic and political in nature: an urban population in spasm—unhealthy, unproductive, and ungovernable. The commissioners underscored this ambiguity when they noted that the spread of mesmeric convulsions fell into a general category of "the effects of imagination and imitation among assembled people," a category that also included "revolts." "Imagination," they said, "governs the multitude"; when "men [are] gathered in large numbers, [they] are more enthralled by their senses and reason has less power over them." Hence it was necessary to "forbid crowds [*attroupemens*]" in "seditious cities," just as it was necessary to forbid "all public treatment where the means of magnetism are employed" in order to prevent the induced convulsions and their insalubrious propagation.[42] From the perspective of moral contagion theory, there was a generic likeness, almost a continuity, between the pathological phenomenon of convulsive contagion and the political one of revolt. The two were related not metaphorically, but physiologically and structurally.

The second motif that emerges from these events is the use of moral contagion theory as a professional ideology, a theory that enhanced the prerogatives of the medical profession.

When Hecquet articulated the theory with respect to the Saint-Médard convulsionaries, he was self-consciously entering upon a "border dispute" with the Church, extending the purview of medicine into an area traditionally presided over by religion. This was a delicate business in the early eighteenth century, and especially so for a pious man such as Hecquet, and he went about it in a most gingerly fashion. Sometimes he permitted himself the luxury of an exasperated exclamation: "What could be more astonishing than that, in a place as knowledgeable as Paris and in defiance of the so manifest character of the symptoms of this epidemic, people could be so closed to the effects of pure nature . . . in order to treat as theologians or casuists evils that are precisely within the competence of Medicine."[43] But more usually he was careful, when seizing new territory for medicine, to specify that he was leaving much adjoining territory behind for religion, careful to make known that he intended a cooperative and equitable division of labor. His assertions, he said, contained nothing

of supererogation or of indiscreet and presumptuous enterprises of Medicine against Theology; but the Art which cures convulsions, having to lay claim to its rights over and against the enterprises of Theologians . . . , testifies to Theology that it wishes to take nothing away from it, that it entirely surrenders to it the inspection that properly belongs to it of those aspects of illness which concern and which demand the vigilance of Theologians.

With respect to the Saint-Médard convulsions, those "aspects" properly belonging to theological "inspection" were the "impertinent postures, contrary to modesty," which the young women of the sect frequently assumed during their seizures. Hecquet hypothesized that these betrayed a moral failing, a "concupiscence," which coexisted with the purely naturalistic convulsive malady but was logically separable from it; and the responsibility of ministering to this "concupiscence" fell to the clerics.[44]

In the mesmerist episode, the doctrine of moral contagion functioned as a defense of established medicine against the incursions of outsiders. French physicians of the mid- and latter eighteenth century worried about competition from healers without academic training who seduced the public with extravagant promises of cure. A variety of sources attests to this: for example, the *Encyclopédie* article "Charlatan" and the handbills of charlatans self-righteously collected by physicians and sent to the Royal Society of Medicine as proof of their embattlement.[45] The mesmerists' promises certainly qualified as extravagant, and the "sociology" of mesmeric healing likewise gave the movement a distinctly charlatanistic tinge: although both Mesmer and his chief French disciple Charles Deslon were licensed physicians, the general run of lesser mesmerist practitioners had no medical credentials whatsoever.[46] It thus comes as no surprise that the Royal Commission of 1784 arrived at a negative verdict on mesmerism. After all, four of the nine members of the commission were prominent doctors of the Faculty of Medicine of Paris, and the French medical faculties of the Old Regime were not simply teaching institutions but also masterships of guilds and hence, by definition, keepers of monopoly. In the 1784 report, moral contagion theory was the chief instrument of this self-protective professional maneuver. Handily enough, it was able to stigmatize mesmerism in two different ways: it provided an alternate explanation for the mass convulsions at the *baquets* and thus made the universal fluid theory superfluous and expendable; and it raised the specter of the long-term social dangers—generations of spasmodic city dwellers—that would accompany the continued practice of mesmerism.

These two motifs—of authority and of the expansion and defense of medical-professional prerogatives—are clearly related. Because a nervous epidemic was perceived as a potential or actual social disorder and was thereby endowed with political significance, necessitating the intervention of political authority (in style or substance), physicians could, by developing and invoking the theory of moral contagion, tacitly assimilate political authority to themselves. They could then use this "borrowed" authority—as an auxiliary to whatever authority their scientific training bestowed upon them—in their own campaigns for public recognition as professional experts and for the expansion and defense of their profession.

Physical Contagion, Moral Contagion, and the State

How utterly natural it was for eighteenth-century physicians to attempt to assert authority through the doctrine of moral contagion becomes apparent when the place of physical contagion in Old Regime society is considered. The repeated experience of plague epidemics shaped the early modern mentality—"Prescriptions for avoiding plague, in the form of carefully-printed pamphlets, circulated rapidly . . . , so great was the fear of contagion"—and produced the conviction that almost all disease, goiter and scurvy as well as plague, was contagious.[47] Plague also, as Michel Foucault has noted, elicited from municipal magistrates and representatives of the state bureaucracy a strict and minutely detailed regulation of social life in the infested town: citizens forbidden to leave the town and, indeed, their own houses on pain of death; officials and militia stationed on each street, enforcing the quarantine. Significantly, for our purposes, the absolute authority which the magistrates assumed and wielded in the face of the plague was delegated by them to selected members of the medical profession. A physician-in-charge was appointed without whose permission no other practitioner might treat, no apothecary prepare medicine for, no confessor visit a sick person.[48] This unquestioned authority of doctors in time of plague (in part, "borrowed" political authority) was mentioned by Hecquet, together with his "naturalist" corpuscular model of convulsive contagion, to justify his claim that the Saint-Médard convulsions fell within the purview of medicine rather than religion. In other words, writing just a decade after a severe epidemic of plague had ravaged the region of Marseille, Hecquet analogized the plague to moral contagion in order to bolster his contentions about medical power over the latter:

The convulsions become the object of Medicine and fall under its jurisdiction. For what is more established [*de plus acquis*] than the right of this science to examine, judge, make discriminations among and treat epidemics? Nothing more awakens in the minds of men that epidemics belong to the inspection and examination of Medicine than the very first thoughts in places to which the plague comes . . . [that is], to call for doctors, or to send them to the most infected areas.[49]

Plague, then, signified the high-water mark of medical authority and was also the moment of total collaboration between the constituted political authorities and the doctors. But during the seventeenth and especially the eighteenth centuries, that moment became generalized and the object of theoretical discussion and concerted practical action. As the Continental European state aggrandized and centralized its power through an ever-growing bureaucracy, the "science" of state administration—called cameralism in the German lands, mercantilism or *Colbertisme* in France, or, later, enlightened absolutism in both—spawned a branch called "medical

"Moral Contagion" and Psychiatry

police." Although it was in the German cameralist context that *Medizinische Polizei* received its first systematic academic elaboration in the late eighteenth-century treatises of Johann Peter Frank, its precepts had long been well known to French administrators.[50] If, the argument ran, state power depended upon the state's fostering of a vigorous economy and thus required a dense population of subjects to serve as producers, then combating disease—and especially epidemic disease, which took the most dramatic toll in human lives—was a primary political task. An alliance between the state and the physicians, the former supervising and coordinating the activities of the latter so as to improve their effectiveness, was called for.

During the first three-quarters of the eighteenth century in France, this alliance, fitted into the structure of the state bureaucracy created by Louis XIV, was intermittent, coming into being only when an epidemic created an emergency. The intendants (the bureaucratic "fingers" of the king in the provinces) then sent physicians and remedies to the stricken community, and the financial arrangements, including the physicians' emoluments, were handled by the comptroller-general in Paris.[51] Change came during the brief term (1774–76) of Anne-Robert-Jacques Turgot as comptroller-general. Usually classified as an exponent of enlightened absolutism, Turgot tried, in a way consonant with that political label, to rationalize state policy on epidemics and to turn medical police into a constant rather than an intermittent feature of administration. His plan was, first, to gather reports on epidemics from all regions of France and thus to advance medical knowledge on this politically important subject; and second, to expand the bureaucracy further, including within its ranks physicians in all the localities appointed by the intendants and charged with this information-gathering task and with the treatment of epidemics. Only the first part of Turgot's plan survived his speedy fall from power: it evolved into the Royal Society of Medicine, a state-sponsored body given letters patent by the king in 1778. Its special charge was the compilation of data about epidemics and about the geographical and climatological conditions that seemed to foster them; its ultimate goal was the formulation of strategies for coping with epidemic outbreaks. The voluminous correspondence received by the society in response to the questionnaires it sent out between its founding and its dissolution in 1793— some 115 cartons now housed in its archives—is a testament to the magnitude of the project it conceived.[52]

The ideal of an alliance between the medical profession and the state was not discarded by the Revolution, even if the Revolution did dissolve the Royal Society of Medicine as part of a blanket decree against learned societies, all of which were considered tainted by their Old Regime origins. Rather, as that ideal had gotten its first impetus from bureaucratic absolutism, it now got a second impetus from "the period of Utopian daydreaming"[53] that accompanied the Revolution, when revolutionaries foresaw in their new polity not only the reign of social justice and moral rectitude but also the virtual disappearance of disease, epidemic and otherwise. To achieve this last end, the doctor was to become fully integrated into the government. Proposals were put forth in 1790 for a nationalized medical profession, organized along the lines of the clergy and watching over the bodies of the citizenry just as the clergy watched over their souls. One such proposal even suggested dividing the Church lands expropriated by the state equally between the civil parish priests and the doctors.[54]

By the early nineteenth century, these absolutist and revolutionary strands had merged. A new term, "political medicine," had been coined and had percolated down into general usage so that Balzac could speak casually in his novella Z. *Marcas* (1840) of the "political doctor" as one of several types of medical practitioner.[55] "Political medicine" was an umbrella term. It embraced two subfields, both of Old Regime vintage: "medical police," which, as has been noted, meant medical intervention in epidemics and other matters of public sanitation; and "legal medicine," which meant the intervention of medical men as expert witnesses in the courts of law.

Not only had the terminology shifted but so had the locus of advocacy. Whereas the medical police of the eighteenth century arose out of governmental and administrative initiative, doctors as well as administrators pressed for an expansion of "political medicine" in the early nineteenth century. Sometimes doctors even evinced displeasure with the backward state of the project. The article entitled "Médecine politique" (1819) in the *Dictionaire des sciences médicales* defined "that expression" subjunctively as "the series of relations that doctors *ought to have* with governments in the interest of the governed" and observed that most of these "relations" were in fact only cursorily developed.[56] In some respects, "political medicine" had made headway since the Old Regime. The ad hoc system by which the state selected physicians at the time of the outbreak of an epidemic was replaced under Napoleon I by the system once abortively suggested by Turgot: the prior and permanent designation of a *médecin des épidémies* for each *arrondissement* of France, named by the minister of the interior and paid an indemnity by the state.[57] But many doctors regarded the *médecins des épidémies* as an insufficient state commitment to "political medicine." They pointed to the state-designated and state-supported physicians of Germany and Austria, who had much broader responsibilities and were, as one French physician said approvingly, "specially entrusted with all the tasks in which science and the exercise of authority come in contact."[58] A close approximation of this system was found in France only in the department of the Bas-Rhin (Lower Alsace), the cultural frontier between France and Germany, where in 1810 the institution of cantonal physicians was established by one of Napoleon's prefects, an administrator who had studied in Germany and had acquired a full-fledged cameralist outlook.[59] That this institution appealed to a substantial segment of French medical men is clear from the fact that the creation of posts for cantonal physicians throughout France was one of three reforms widely advocated at the time of the first French Medical Congress in 1845.[60]

What, for physicians, constituted the appeal of state collaboration? Why had the physicians become active champions of a program that had originated with the bureaucrats? One clue is to be found in the rhetoric of early nineteenth-century medical writings on political medicine. The physician was not depicted as imparting his technical expertise to the political agency with businesslike detachment. Instead, he was portrayed as participating vicariously in the very being of the magistrate. Momentarily casting off his usual persona, he "assumes the magistrate's sacred character," or literally, "reclothes [*revêtir*] himself as a magistrate," and this constitutes "one of the noblest prerogatives of our profession." "How honorable for our profession," went the rendition of another medical man, "are those circumstances in which he is temporarily obliged to suspend the activity of aid that he brings to the sick and suffering individual, in order to assume the sacred character of the magistrate, of authority without appeal."[61] The fantasy behind such figures of speech is clearly one of status-aggrandizement, of borrowing, if only for a while, the attributes—and, in particular, the authority—of the magistrate, which are perceived as lacking in the ordinary workaday physician.

The fantasy contained in these musings on political medicine, then, indirectly betrays the anxiety of early nineteenth-century physicians about their status, about the degree of authority and public recognition they commanded. This same anxiety was directly expressed in their frequent and rancorous outbursts against the superiority of lawyers to doctors in the professional "pecking order." Lawyers were exempt from the patent, a tax on all income derived from mercantile pursuits, but physicians suffered the ignominy of being *patentables*. Lawyers were more likely to be accepted on intimate terms with aristocrats than were physicians. Lawyers had ready access to political office, whereas physicians were generally excluded. The medical jeremiad went on and on.[62] And indeed it seems to have had a realistic basis in the social mores of the day. Edouard Charton's *Guide pour le choix d'un état* (1842) advised the career-minded young man that the profession of lawyer was "the most alluring today," while that of doctor was the most "subjugating, painful" in terms of the monetary rewards that could be expected and especially in terms of the degree of public esteem in which it was held.[63]

The physicians' deep sense of insecurity in this period was no doubt connected to and compounded by the chaotic condition of their professional organization. The Revolution had abolished the medical corporations in 1791, and, until the tentative efforts at midcentury to create general medical associations, nothing replaced them. By contrast, the legal corporations, also abolished in 1791, had been essentially reconstituted by Napoleon in 1810. Bereft of their corporate identity, comparing themselves invidiously with members of the legal profession (whose status certainly did, in good measure, derive from their constant involvement in affairs of state), physicians naturally saw in the state a repository of status and authority that could be deflected to themselves and logically clamored for the implementation of programs of political medicine.

The tendency was overdetermined—that is, the material conditions of early nineteenth-century medical practice also contributed to and reinforced it. There was a serious "doctor glut" in France, an *encombrement* as contemporaries put it. It appears to have been produced by a combination of factors: the absence, after the abolition of the corporations, of any mechanism regulating the number of new doctors trained and licensed; the pervasiveness of French cultural prejudices against mercantile activity, which encouraged young men to seek their fortunes in the liberal professions in preference to business.[64] Medical unemployment and a sizable "medical proletariat" were stark realities in this period. And in such a situation, French physicians—given the proclivities Alexis de Tocqueville noted in all modern Frenchmen and traced back to the bureaucratic centralization of the Old Regime—focused their attention on the state as a source of salaried positions which could turn their precarious lot into the eminently secure one of the *fonctionnaire*.

Whether the state was being looked to as a source of status or as a source of salaries, the epidemic—the time-honored paradigm of the collaborative relation between the state and the physician, as well as the moment of indisputable medical authority—was certain to come to mind. Outbreaks of "moral contagion" presented physicians with the same social and political possibilities as epidemics of physical disease. And that fact, although inadequate to explain the specific content or internal development of the theory of moral contagion, does help to explain the amount of medical attention lavished on the theory and on its practical applications.

Nor was moral contagion necessarily viewed as a marginal and bizarre occurrence. It could be viewed as the full-fledged counterpart of physical contagion and, if not on a par with physical contagion in seriousness, having a much greater parity than we might expect. In one of the classic texts of early nineteenth-century political medicine, *Rapports de la médecine avec la politique* (1806), the philosophically minded administrator Eusèbe Salverte ascribed to the doctor the task, "entrusted to him by the statesman," of preventing and combating "moral contagion no less than physical contagion." Salverte was thinking here particularly of panics, of the spread of "deadly terrors" and "dangerous frights," often caused by the specter of death during epidemics of physical disease. The doctor was to treat all those afflicted by these tormenting emotions as well as "extending his care to healthy men, in order to preserve them from moral contagion"; and he was to use not only the "resources of the [medical] art" but also public opinion, festivals, and theater—a wide array of "consolations" and "distractions"—to achieve this end.[65] Indeed, precisely the kind of "moral contagion" that Salverte described elicited enough concern from the Napoleonic government that the minister of the interior instructed the prefects to prohibit the sounding of the death knell when mortality rates were rising during an epidemic.[66] Some fifty years later, a basic textbook written by a professor at the Paris Faculty of Medicine routinely included nervous contagion in a typology of contagious diseases. Dr. Eugène Bouchut identified "contagion by imitation" as a variety of "indirect infecto-contagion." Most of the diseases in this group were transmitted by "miasmas." "Contagion by imitation" differed only slightly in being transmitted by "the nervous emanations as subtle as miasmas produced by persons afflicted with nervous disease." Bouchut's classificatory scheme thus placed moral contagion under the same rubric as typhoid fever, yellow fever, and plague—a position that betokened its prominence and absolute legitimacy.[67]

Médecine Mentale and the Elaboration of Moral Contagion Theory

With the emergence of the medical specialty of psychiatry—originally known in France under such compound labels as *médecine des aliénés* and *médecine mentale*—the theory of moral contagion, though by no means entirely abandoned by general medical practitioners, became the special province of the new specialists.

French psychiatry took as its symbolic birthdate Pinel's *grand geste* of striking the chains from the lunatics of Bicêtre in 1793.[68] But a *grand geste* does not a profession make. Even Pinel cared for and studied the insane on a part-time basis only. The first full-time *médecin aliéniste* was his student Jean-Etienne-Dominique Esquirol, who, in turn, trained several dozen students, zealously devoted to him and intent upon plying the "specialty" to the exclusion of other types of medical practice. This "Esquirol circle," coming to maturity in the 1820s and 1830s, should be regarded as the first generation of French psychiatrists. They were also the initiators of the professionalization effort. A thorough account of the strategies they adopted, or of the preconditions for the crystallization of *médecine mentale* out of general medicine, cannot be attempted here. But it must be noted that, in keeping with the emphasis on "political medicine" prevalent among physicians of this period, an emphasis born in part of professional insecurity, these proto-psychiatrists conceived of their specialty not primarily in terms of the depth exploration of individual inner lives gone awry, but in broadly social terms. They sought legitimation through affiliation with the state. First, they explored the possibilities of legal medicine, mounting a campaign in the 1820s to be recognized as expert witnesses in criminal trials and substantiating their claims by reference to a disease entity, monomania—and, in particular, a subspecies of it called homicidal monomania—which they had just discovered. This campaign continued for several decades and engendered a raucous "monomania controversy," but in the end the psychiatrists were, at best, partially successful. Almost simultaneously, they explored the possibilities of medical police, mounting a less highly publicized campaign for the establishment of a nationwide network of state-financed lunatic asylums staffed by psychiatric specialists. Here their efforts at collaboration with the state were crowned with tangible success in the law of 30 June 1838.[69] The theory of moral contagion, then, with its clear social and political implications, fit well with the general orientation and professional goals of early nineteenth-century French psychiatry.

The "founding fathers," Pinel and Esquirol, were familiar with the theory but did little to develop it. In a discussion of "spasmodic ailments" in his architectonic work of general medical classification, the *Nosographie philosophique*, Pinel presented in capsule form the eighteenth-century trio of nervous epidemics—the Saint-Médard convulsionaries, the Haarlem orphanage, and the "sham [*prétendu*] crises of animal magnetism"—and thus contributed to the standardization of these events as the stable tradition, the orthodox canon of moral contagion theory.[70] He was alert to contemporary instances of moral contagion. When a priest hung himself and triggered off a small suicidal epidemic in the vicinity of Etampes, the village on the outskirts of Paris where Pinel had his country home, Pinel eagerly shared this information with his colleagues. Esquirol preserved his teacher's oral account, incorporated it into the written medical record.[71] Esquirol, too, dealt with moral contagion in passing, when it impinged upon subjects that interested him more directly. When writing about suicide, he mentioned epidemics of suicide (which, he believed, could be "propagated by imitation" but could have other causes as well) and included a reference to Plutarch's Miletian women; when writing about demonomania, he mentioned epidemics of demonomania (which he attributed solely to "a sort of moral contagion and the force of imitation") and cited the convulsionaries of Saint-Médard, who "definitely merit to figure among the victims of moral contagion."[72] But the more concerted efforts to elaborate and apply the theory of moral contagion were made in the decades of the 1820s through the 1840s by the first psychiatric generation and, significantly, coincided with the effort to professionalize psychiatry and win public recognition for it.

The first full-scale formulation of the theory of moral contagion and, to my knowledge, the first extended text devoted solely to that subject was the 1833 *thèse de médecine* of the fledgling psychiatrist Prosper Lucas. Although probably read more widely than most productions of this genre[73]—it was, like all French medical dissertations, published—it should be regarded as neither a very influential nor a highly original piece of work. Rather, it codified, gathered in a single place, and, to some extent, cast in the new psychiatric terminology of the 1830s the acccumulated medical wisdom about moral contagion. It was an epitome of the state of medical opinion on that subject in the early decades of the nineteenth century, and therein lies its value for us.

Lucas stressed that observation of the phenomenon of moral contagion was ancient; what was recent was the explanation of that phenomenon by science. Adhering to a roughly Comtean sequence of the progress of knowledge, he noted that "the poets were the first to be struck by it, the historians came after them, followed by the philosophers; the physicians came later." Religious explanations preceded scientific ones. Highlighting a phrase in Plutarch's account of Miletus that had thus far been ignored in the medical literature, Lucas observed that the Miletians, "attached to the fictions of an admirable polytheism," had tended to attribute the suicidal epidemic, especially before it yielded to human remedies, to the anger of the gods.[74] As for the advanced, scientific explanations of his own day, Lucas presented the physiological-mechanistic one of the 1784 Royal Commission report nuanced by the categories for analyzing individual human organisms and their sensory susceptibilities that Pierre-Jean-Georges Cabanis had proposed in his *Rapports du physique et du moral de l'homme* (1802).[75] The basis of moral contagion was the "communication" of the "example": a pattern of heightened nervous vibration in one individual would set up a corresponding pattern in other individuals in proximity. But such a gross formulation required qualification. Just as some individuals had a natural immunity to epidemic physical illnesses (again the analogy between moral and physical contagion), so some resisted the ravages of contagious mental and nervous diseases and did not succumb to the "example" even when exposed to it. The decisive factor, or so Lucas asserted, was the degree of "similitude" between the "example" and the potential sympathetic imitators. Among the pertinent categories of organic similitude were species (humans picked up complex nervous vibrational patterns from other humans, not from lower animals); family, age, and sex (persons of the same family, age, and sex tended to infect one another, and, as a rule, moral contagion occurred much more frequently among females than among males); "temperament" (persons in whom the nervous system predominated, for whom "each sensation is a tremor [*frémissement*] and almost a convulsion," were most likely, when diseased, to emit strong nervous vibrations and, when healthy, to be "impressionable" to such vibrations emanating from others). In addition to these organic similitudes, "acquired" ones—the beliefs, attitudes, and opinions produced by education—could aid the contagion process.[76] Lucas summed up his schema of structural similitude in a vivid image, reminiscent of the image of tensile nerves in the 1784 Royal Commission report: "When the first string [*chanterelle*] of one violin is plucked, it makes the same chord vibrate in another violin which is in unison, while all the others remain motionless."[77]

The disease entity monomania, one of the major discoveries of the first generation of French psychiatry, prompted Lucas to amplify the theory of moral contagion. He insisted upon the highly contagious properties of monomania, so much so that the disease even received special mention in the subtitle of his dissertation: "the sympathetic propagation of nervous disorders and monomanias." The possibility of monomaniacal contagion introduced a new note of gravity into the discussion. Unlike the random motor convulsions of the Saint-Médard Jansenists or the patients in the mesmeric tubs, monomanias had ideational specificity; they could also entail "lesions of the will," causing certain *idées fixes*, often of a criminal nature, to be automatically and blindly translated into action. Thus with the addition of monomania to the list of nervous epidemics, "it is no longer only the sanitary condition of society but also its moral condition that [is] imperil[ed]."[78]

As the foregoing sentence indicates, Lucas was far from regarding moral contagion as a purely academic subject. It had concrete social implications and correspondingly concrete implications for defining the role of the new and still partially undefined profession of *médecine des aliénés*. Cognizant of the social dangers presented by moral contagion, Lucas spelled out the tactics for "opposing" and arresting it. The basic tactic— and here he concurred entirely, if tacitly, with the royal commissioners of 1784—was "the suppression of the example." Afflicted individuals had to be isolated, written accounts that "refreshed the images" of the contagious phenomena had to be banned, and public attention had to be distracted so that the number of oral accounts would likewise diminish. If this tactic failed, recourse was to be had to "the methods of those who suppressed the epidemic . . . of the convulsionaries of the Haarlem hospital"—that is, "to react briskly upon the imagination with great and violent shocks [*secousses*]." In other words, a show of authority was required. The motif is the same as in the stock eighteenth-century accounts of moral contagion—though Lucas, more explicitly pragmatic than his predecessors, indicated that he had in mind the "intervention" of the "administrator" and the "legislator." But this pair of political authorities, though necessary, was clearly insufficient. The uniqueness of each case of moral contagion—the character of the malady, the age, sex, temperament, and "religious or political ideas" that fostered its propagation—precluded the prescription of hard-and-fast tactical rules and made indispensable the presence of an experienced physician at the site of the epidemic. "There is no guide in this matter but the wisdom of the physician."[79] Moral contagion, then, like its physical counterpart, was the occasion for a close collaborative effort between the state and the medical profession. And since they had special expertise about nervous ailments, the *médecins-aliénistes* were to become, in one of their capacities, official epidemic fighters.

Psychiatrists as Political Commentators

The role of official epidemic fighter did not immediately devolve upon the emergent profession of psychiatry. In fact (as will be seen later), only once—in the 1860s and in an obscure Alpine village—were the psychiatrists actually charged by the government to "put down" moral contagion. But from the 1820s on, they assumed an unofficial and purely verbal form of this same role. They used the theory of moral contagion to make pointed policy statements about current affairs and thereby inserted themselves, as commentators, into the political life of the nation.

To interpret or—in more properly medical language—to diagnose a social phenomenon as moral contagion legitimized taking, on sanitary grounds, energetic steps toward its repression. And so, in an era when governments were haunted by the memory and fear of revolutionary upheaval, the psychiatrists became, through the vehicle of moral contagion theory, upholders of the "moral order" and of the state. In two salient episodes, the aftermath of the Henriette Cornier trial and the 1830 incendiarist wave, their diagnoses transformed crime into psychopathology and were accompanied by therapeutic recommendations that were frankly political—and antilibertarian—in nature. With respect to a third episode, the 1848 club movement, the political ramifications of moral contagion theory proved even more extreme, for not only did the remedy counseled by medicine entail a politically partisan stance, but the diagnosis transformed political behavior itself into psychopathology—not a completely novel departure, as the association of "mechanical imitation" and "revolt" by the 1784 royal commissioners shows, but one now made more sophisticated by the expanded nosology of mental disease which the developing psychiatric profession had supplied. Let us look at these three episodes from the period of the constitutional monarchy and the Second Republic in some detail.

Henriette Cornier was a provincial servant girl who confessed to the murder of a neighbor's infant. Her trial in 1826 excited enormous popular interest in France primarily because of its obvious sensationalism but also because it was the occasion for the first enunciation by the nascent Parisian psychiatric community of the concept of homicidal monomania. Called in as expert witnesses, the psychiatrists argued that the crime, utterly senseless and unmotivated, could be explained only by a monomaniacal insanity in the defendant, who ought therefore be absolved of legal responsibility for her act. As the trial wore on, numerous instances were reported of women perversely taking Cornier's behavior as a model for emulation. For example, at a meeting of the Royal Academy of Medicine in August 1826, the chief physician of the general hospital of Amiens told of "a woman who had just given birth [and], having heard of the crime of Mlle Cornier," was seized with a desire to end her infant's life. At first she struggled against her hideous impulses but, finding herself powerless to control them, confessed them to her husband, who "had her locked up. She is not yet cured." Another member of the Academy contributed a comparable case from Languedoc, where "a woman, upon hearing of the Cornier crime . . . conceived the project of killing one of her children." Beset by violent internal conflict over this plan and, at the same time, carrying a razor with her so as to be able to execute it at the favorable moment, she finally appealed for help, and "we were obliged to institutionalize her."[80]

The incendiarist wave broke out in the rural areas of northwestern France in the spring of 1830: during a five-month period, some 250 fires devastated the countryside. Faced with the "scourge of arson," contemporaries offered a wide variety of explanations. Some saw the fires as acts of private vengeance. Others held that the insurance companies were to blame, that their agents were attempting, through this dire tactic, to stimulate business. Still others regarded the fires as politically motivated: this was, after all, the eve of the Revolution of 1830, and political tensions ran high. One theory had it that the fires were set by the opposition party in order to bring the people to a state of desperation that would lead them to support an overthrow of the Bourbon regime; the converse theory maintained that the party in power had set the fires "as a way of terrifying the electorate" and of showing that it intended to stay in power, even by extralegal means. No consensus could be reached—nor, incidentally, has any been reached by modern historians.[81]

For both of these events, the psychiatric explanation was the same: both were instances of the propagation of monomania by imitative contagion, the first on a small scale, the second on epidemic scale. During the Cornier trail, it was *monomanie homicide* that was being transmitted;[82] in the incendiarist wave, the contagious pathology was *monomanie incendiaire* or *pyromanie*, a new subcategory of monomania that had just been added to the nosological scheme.[83] The psychiatric interpreters saw these two events as lessons: it was obviously in the best interests of society to prevent the recurrence of such deleterious moral contagions, and hence the root causes must be ferreted out and prophylactic measures adopted.

According to the psychiatrist Alexandre Brierre de Boismont, public attendance at trials had been particularly responsible for the pathological concomitants of the Cornier affair and ought therefore to be severely curtailed. The right of public attendance at trials was highly controversial at this time: it had been obtained for Frenchmen by the Charter of 1814, but the liberal opposition charged that the Restoration government was abridging it in practice by the requirement that spectators be "pre-screened" and that they come provided with tickets issued by members of the judiciary.[84] Thus Brierre had, through his medical observations, entered the political arena. He was not, he hastened to say, suggesting a full return to the arbitrary justice of the Old Regime or an abandonment of the jury system. He was not suggesting that "it would be necessary to judge all cases behind closed doors; we feel too keenly what latitude such a measure would leave to the passions and to despotism and what grave results it would have for individual liberty." But he did want to see ended the "entirely public pleadings," for these possessed the "serious disadvantage of leading to imitation those weak, unsettled and ill-constituted minds for whom any extraordinary spectacle [and] any strong impression are the cause of mental trouble." All criminal behavior was likely to inspire imitation, and how much more powerful a nervous impression was made by those defendants who harbored the monomaniacal disease! Thus Brierre was "deeply convinced" that a too liberal arrangement in the courtroom would have "bad effects on the social order."[85]

For Prosper Lucas, on the other hand, the press had been the main means of psychopathological transmission both in the proliferation of infanticides à la Cornier and in the incendiarist wave. He expressed this opinion in the context of a more general thesis. Modern society, he said, was bound to be afflicted with epidemics of monomania, which were but the "morbid expression of social movements," an inevitable epiphenomenon which the young psychiatrist grandly labeled "a secondary form of history." This assertion was Lucas's translation into historical terms of his medical theoretical point that "similitude" invites contagion. In modern times, similitudes in nervous and mental configuration were produced in the population by political revolutions and by vast networks of communication which ended the mutual isolation of geographical regions. In the end, there was, "so to speak, a single soul for an entire country, a single center of perception"; and epidemics of monomania raged. In other words, "leveling," the obliteration of social, intellectual, and regional differences, had distinctly psychopathological implications.

The press, Lucas continued, was the leveling agent most responsible for moral contagion "by virtue of the circumstantial details that it recounts of every act of crime and madness." It was more effective in this regard than firsthand attendance at the scene of a crime or at a trial because it could reach a far wider audience: the "sympathetic force" of an actual "spectacle" was exerted "in a narrow circle and had limits of action, time, and place; the press recognizes none of these limits." Furthermore, the "imagination" of the newspaper reader, "reproducing the tableau with a vigor of impression and coloring often superior to that of sight itself," could generate powerful nervous sensations, which amply compensated for the lack of immediacy of their source. While innocuous citizens were casually perusing the daily papers, "a thousand, ten thousand, twenty thousand brains are entering into the same order of ideas and sensations which, in monomaniacs and felons brought about the [fatal and newsworthy] act." They were undergoing mental alterations that rendered them momentarily akin to the subjects of the lurid newspaper stories. The mental health and the safety of the community, the containment of an ever-present tendency for an epidemic outbreak of monomania and crime, thus required surveillance of the press—not, Lucas specified, its "stifling" or "extinguishing" but the expurgation of reports about deviance.[86] Here, too, as in the case of public attendance at trials, the cure for moral contagion had a distinct political signification: during the 1820s and 1830s, the right of press freedom was the liberal cause par excellence, repeatedly fought for against the constitutional monarchy's policy of press censorship.

The menace of moral contagion and repression in the service of prophylaxis: these themes appeared again in the psychiatric response to the 1848 club movement. *Le club*—an institution so fundamentally alien to France that the French took the word directly from the English—was the unmistakable offspring of the 1848 Revolution. Within two months of the February insurrection, some two hundred clubs opened their doors in Paris. Their total membership, which included bourgeois, artisans, unskilled laborers, and students, has been estimated at fifty to seventy thousand. Having roots in the Jacobin and sans-culottes societies of the 1790s and, in some cases, direct progenitors in the underground republican societies of the constitutional monarchy, the clubs were a logical response to the revolution of February 1848, which had mobilized large numbers of people previously excluded from the political process and which, once successful, required a stable form of mass participation. As Adolphe Crémieux said in the Assembly, "With the Republic, it is necessary to grant republican institutions: the clubs are, obviously, a republican institution." Intended for the mutual political edification of their members and for the airing of views on public issues, they were also, by all accounts, prey to "habitual disorder," the combined result of the oratorical inexperience of most *clubistes* and a democratic insistence upon spontaneity, which scorned the traditional etiquette of debate.[87]

Why did the clubs become an area of psychiatric concern? The revolutions of February and June 1848 caused a marked upswing in the incidence of insanity in the capital; such, at least, was the general consensus of opinion in the Parisian psychiatric community.[88] A socially significant statistic of this kind begged for explanation. Brierre de Boismont, who believed that homicidal monomania was being propagated by contagion in France at the time of the Cornier trial, maintained the validity of the contagion model in 1848 as well. As he saw it, society always contained a sizable number of people, "a considerable floating mass," strongly predisposed to or indeed on the verge of insanity. Such people were visible to the trained eye by the "pathognomic signs which foretell their future destiny," including general irritability, flightiness, loosely knit logic, and such an extreme impressionability that, with respect to external sensations, they were "like soft wax." What caused an increased incidence of insanity, then, was the congregation and interaction of these borderline personalities: "One can see how such minds are susceptible to reciprocal inflammation; there is a veritable incitement, a sort of *moral contagion*, which is propagated with electrical rapidity." One revolutionary institution had fostered this moral contagion in 1848: the club. As Brierre put it with wry succinctness: "Persons with the above-named characteristics who enter the clubs out of pure curiosity leave them only to enter insane asylums."[89] His fellow psychiatrist J.-E. Belhomme also deemed the clubs "dangerous for the ideas and the passions" and one of the most important causes of madness during the revolutionary episodes of 1848.[90]

Brierre drew his data from the clientele of his private sanitorium. The February revolution had brought him a rash of new business in the form of bourgeois melancholics, parvenus who were in the grip of a morbid and obsessive fear that their newly acquired social position would be lost in a republican regime. As the revolution veered leftward, culminating in the June Days, this first group of lunatics was followed by a "new series," who, far from being downcast, were manic, having a "proud, exalted, joyous look . . . proclaiming themselves great personages, the saviors of the fatherland." This second group, Brierre suggested, had contracted their illness in the contagious atmosphere of the clubs. To prove his point, he offered case histories of apparently normal men who had become "disordered" in the clubs, both by accepting the notions of social justice purveyed there and by receiving applause and admiration that had raised their self-esteem to pathological, megalomaniacal heights. One such man had been a veritable pillar of bourgeois society, a "manufacturer [*fabricant*] who, by his competence, had succeeded in making a comfortable living." Then, in 1848, he found his way to a club, soon began making ardent speeches "on the lot of the poorer classes . . . and the proper means of alleviating their misery," sought out a printer so that he would be able to disseminate his ideas on a grander scale, and even "threatened" his dismayed parents when they tried to call a halt to this singular turn in his career. "Finally, at a meeting of his club, he gave himself over to such a fit of passion" that nothing could be done but to remove him posthaste to Brierre's sanitorium.[91]

In February 1849, Brierre called for the dissolution of the clubs. He agreed with the "courageous conclusion" of an unsigned editorial in the *Union médicale* (the newspaper devoted especially to the professional interests of French physicians and in which Brierre's own articles on the clubs had appeared) that had also applied the theory of moral contagion to this aspect of republican mass political participation. Said that editorial: "To support such schools [that is, the clubs] or to allow them to survive is to permit isolated diseases to take on the terrible proportions of an epidemic." In this way the "diseases," or, more exactly, "mental aberrations," not only attacked individual "human life" but went on to attack "social life by its root."[92]

Psychiatric Epidemic-Fighting

The nervous epidemic in the tiny Alpine village of Morzine was, in a sense, the culminating moment of the medical and psychiatric theory of moral contagion. All of the separate strands of the eighteenth- and early nineteenth-century discussion came together in this remote setting, and much that had been hypothetical became real.

The epidemic began in 1857, but "nothing serious was attempted, either to observe [its] progress systematically . . . or to oppose a rational medication to it," until the joining of Savoy to France two years later. Almost immediately after the annexation of this Italian province (Napoleon III's reward for aiding Italian unification), the French government sent the asylum doctor Joseph Arthaud, head of the Antiquaille in Lyons, to investigate the situation. In 1861, it took even stronger measures: "Dr. Augustin Constans, inspector-general of lunatics, received from the minister of the interior the commission to study this malady and to apply the means suitable for eradicating it." Constans was successful, but three years later a "grave recrudescence" of the epidemic spurred the government to hurry a new "medical mission" to Morzine, this one led by Philippe Kuhn, psychiatrist at the asylum of Pau.[93]

How can this energetic policy of the French government, all the more remarkable by contrast to the utter laxity of the Italians, be explained? The relationship of the French government to the psychiatric profession, already firmly established by the 1838 asylum law, was becoming even more intimate and prominent under the Second Empire as a result of the activities of the prefect of the Seine, Baron Georges Haussmann. Beginning in 1860, Haussmann undertook a major expansion and administrative overhaul of Parisian psychiatric institutions,[94] which, like the rest of his rebuilding of the capital, was done with an eye to the security of the Bonapartist regime. In short, the utility of psychiatry for the maintenance of social and political order, which had not escaped the leaders of the July Monarchy when they framed the law of 1838, was at least equally apparent to their Imperial successors. Probably, too, the recency of the annexation of Savoy made the Imperial government regard that area as one of particular sensitivity—Napoleon III was, for example, sufficiently concerned about the Savoyards' pride in their "nationality" to refrain from changing the name of the region to "Mont Blanc"[95]—so that a localized epidemic of nervous disease there seemed potentially troublesome. Add to this the fact that the psychiatric profession had, for the past several decades, been identifying itself as a medical police to be deployed in the battle against moral contagion, and the alacrity with which the French government dispatched psychiatrists to Savoy becomes comprehensible.

Morzine was a devoutly Catholic community. But the mountains of Savoy had been one of the seedbeds and centers of the European witch-craze of the sixteenth and seventeenth centuries, and in 1859 Dr. Arthaud noted in the inhabitants of Morzine some of the traits that had characterized their forbears: "an excessive credulity, the facility for accepting as true, by preference, the most marvelous events . . . [and] every story of sorcery, talismans, and magic." Arthaud also observed in the village the proliferation of "popular books treating sorcery and necromancy." Not surprisingly, then, given the history and belief structure of the region, the victims of the epidemic, whose principal symptom was their recurrent convulsions, declared themselves to be the objects of a "diabolical intervention," to be "truly possessed."[96]

The psychiatrists, of course, would have none of this. From their scientific vantage point (as from Hecquet's, when he commented on the Saint-Médard convulsionaries), "the Morzine epidemic manifested nothing that could not be explained by natural causes." The objective symptomatology coupled with the patients' subjective interpretation of it prompted French psychiatrists to diagnose the malady as *hystéro-démonopathie*. The first part of the term referred to the seizures, regarded in this period as the hallmark of hysteria and unmistakable here because they were often accompanied by a telltale sensation of strangulation in the throat, the so-called *boule hystérique*. The second part of the term referred to the victims' preoccupation with the demonic realm as the main intellectual aberration that accompanied the illness. The two aspects of the illness were supposed to interact so as to intensify its force: once the convulsions had been "misinterpreted" as the result of demonic possession, this emotionally charged idea "reacts in turn on the nervous system," multiplying the seizures. Furthermore, *démonopathie* was an "eminently contagious . . . genre of insanity," as Esquirol had noted in 1814; hysterical convulsions, too, were very amenable to "contagion by imitation," especially when they occurred in public.[97]

This closely reasoned psychiatric assessment of the situation was, however, diametrically opposed to the assessment of the most influential authority in the commune—the local clergy. When Dr. Arthaud arrived in Morzine, he had a long conversation with the curé, who, "at the time of my visit, had been discharging the functions of his ministry at this parish for thirty-two years" and who had been "the most usual witness" of the manifestations of the epidemic and the "habitual confidant" of those afflicted. The curé had a clear and unshakable opinion about the epidemic: "He believes in a diabolic intervention as being the only thing able to explain the phenomena observed. He cites in support of [this view] . . . the happy results obtained on a rather large number of patients by exorcism." All the traditional notables of the region seem to have supported this interpretation: observers of the exorcisms who signed official reports verifying the curative effect of these rituals included not only local priests and curés but also two counts.[98]

In attempting to end the epidemic, then, psychiatrists were obliged to set themselves up in the commune as a new, rival authority. As Dr. Arthaud said, the "demonomaniacal delirium" seemed "invincible" because the population "had, unfortunately, not found in its customary guides and counselors the necessary counterweight to its own troublesome tendencies." Help, he continued, had to come from another source: "To the physician belongs the job of imprinting a good direction on the measures to be taken." To effect such a transfer of authority was not easy, for distrust of established medicine was strong in Morzine. Dr. Kuhn reports patients fleeing or hiding at his approach or telling him angrily that "only the holy priests have the power to cure us." When Dr. Constans arrived at Morzine, "the town council, acting almost unanimously, felt obliged in good faith to warn me that, if I was bringing only *natural* remedies, I would never succeed in wiping out the malady." The distrust could assume more virulent forms. The villagers were "strongly inclined to treat as a blasphemer and [diabolic] accomplice" anyone who disputed the supernatural interpretation of the events. One such man "almost perished in a riot," and "it was loudly proclaimed that until three or four such impious individuals had been burned in the town square, the malady would not be eradicated."[99] In fact, the psychiatrists were able to influence the situation only because they came with the backing of the central government.

Dr. Constans's task force, which immediately followed Dr. Arthaud's brief preliminary investigation, made full use of the coercive power of the government to implement the "standard" anticontagion program sketched by the royal commissioners of 1784 and described at greater length by Prosper Lucas. The "suppression of the example" was the key. Constans removed from Morzine (and into various hospitals in the department of the Haute-Savoie) a large number of victims of the epidemic whose continued presence would, according to medical theory, have perpetuated the contagion. This evacuation was accomplished with the aid of "a small detachment of infantry and a brigade of *gendarmerie*" specially requested by the psychiatric doctor. He also replaced the curé and the vicars, who had, by their assent, so powerfully reinforced the pathological idea of demonic possession. The military remained in the town and had the salutary effect that Constans intended: "general intimidation" and "the conviction that the authorities were firmly decided to have recourse to all means to attain the goal."[100] At Morzine, then, Boerhaave's "hot iron," Hecquet's admonition to the clergy about the scope of medical power, and the fantasy of political medicine—of the physician's "assuming the sacred character of the magistrate, of authority without appeal"—all reappeared in new guise and coalesced around a single event.

Conclusion

Dr. Bouchut, not himself a psychiatrist, wrote in his medical textbook of 1857: "There ought to be in society a sort of moral lazaretto where could be hidden away, as soon as they manifest themselves, the mental and nervous disorders of man whose contagious properties have been established."[101] A more forceful summation of the early nineteenth-century theory of moral contagion can hardly be imagined. It includes, by allusion, the historical roots of that theory in the experience of plague and quarantine, the authoritarian tendencies of the theory, and the evolution of a form of medical authority modeled on political authority in which physicians are not only healers but also allies of the state and repressive guardians of social order. None of the psychiatrists of the early nineteenth century made quite so stark a statement of the theory of moral contagion, and only in their actual epidemic-fighting at Morzine did they have the opportunity to "hide away" the contagious examples. But the measures they advocated bore witness to an implicit ideal of a "moral lazaretto," or at least to a comparable situation of reduced public contact and participation—courtrooms closed, clubs closed, the press expurgated—which they deemed hygienic.

By the criteria of its own day, moral contagion must certainly qualify as a scientific theory. It pieced together accepted medical views on nervous vibration, the faculty of imagination, and the nosology of mental illness in an attempt to provide a coherent explanation of a puzzling phenomenon. But the drive for rational explanation is only part of the story. This essay has argued that, against the background of the seventeenth- and eighteenth-century tradition of "medical police," the impetus to develop the theory of moral contagion came as well from the social circumstances of the medical profession and its new psychiatric specialty—and, in particular, from the variety of factors that caused medical men to have, in their own estimation, an insufficient degree of authority and status.

As the theory was successively elaborated and applied, its antidemocratic implications became clear, so that there is, in this respect, a striking continuity between the use of moral contagion by early nineteenth-century French psychiatrists and its use by fin-de-siècle crowd psychologists. The other face of the theory, its anticlerical, or at least secularizing aspect, was apparent from the outset in Hecquet's discussion of Saint-Médard, and it continued to be relevant in the nineteenth century, as the case of Morzine shows.[102] In fact, the very emergence of the theory of moral contagion can be correlated with this latter aspect—that is, with the termination of witchcraft trials, at the insistence of the state, in the late seventeenth century.[103] When state pressure was exerted to secularize a phenomenon once conventionally identified as "demonic possession," the way was smoothly paved for the medical assumption of theoretical jurisdiction over that phenomenon. Redefined, it passed from the hands of the witch-prosecuting judicial magistrates into the hands of physicians and, later, psychiatrists. It thus passed out of the ideological repertory of one profession and into that of another.

Notes

1. On the 1885 elections, see Jean-Marie Mayeur, *Les débuts de la Troisième République, 1871–1898* (Paris, 1973), pp. 162–64.
2. Letter to Minna Bernays, 3 December 1885, in Ernst L. Freud, ed., *Letters of Sigmund Freud*, trans. Tania and James Stern (New York, 1964), pp. 187–88. For Freud's awareness of French electoral turmoil, see his account of the *deuxième tour*, the second round of voting, later in October in a letter to Martha Bernays, 19 October 1885, p. 174. After accurately identifying the contending factions, Freud commented, "The yelling of the newspaper vendors was deafening."
3. Gabriel Tarde, "Qu'est-ce qu'une société?" *Revue philosophique* 18 (1884): 491; Gustave Le Bon, *The Crowd* (New York, 1960), p. 30; Emile Durkheim, *Suicide: A Study in Sociology*, trans. John A. Spaulding and George Simpson (New York, 1951), Book 1, chap. 4, entitled "Imitation," and p. 132 for the use of the term "moral contagions."
4. Philip Rieff, "The Origins of Freud's Political Psychology," *Journal of the History of Ideas* 17 (1956): 235–49; Leon Bramson, *The Political Context of Sociology* (Princeton, 1961), chap. 3; Robert A. Nye, *The Origins of Crowd Psychology: Gustave Le Bon and the Crisis of Mass Democracy in the Third Republic* (Beverly Hills, 1975); and Reba N. Soffer, *Ethics and Society in England: The Revolution in the Social Sciences, 1870–1914* (Berkeley and Los Angeles, 1978), chaps. 10–11.
5. Le Bon, *Crowd*, pp. 37, 75, 182; and Introduction by Robert K. Merton, pp. xx–xxv.
6. For a full account of this debate, see Steven Lukes, *Emile Durkheim: His Life and Work* (New York, 1972), pp. 302–13.
7. Durkheim, *Suicide*, pp. 132, 140, italics added.
8. Lukes, *Durkheim*, pp. 57–58.
9. Le Bon, *Crowd*, pp. 31, 39, 40; Tarde, "Qu'est-ce qu'une société?" p. 509; Sigmund Freud, *Group Psychology and the Analysis of the Ego*, chap. 2, and "The 'Uncanny'" (1919), trans. Alix Strachey, in *Collected Papers*, 5 vols. (London, 1948–50), 4:399.
10. Durkheim, *Suicide*, bibliographical footnotes on pp. 57, 123.
11. See, e.g., the error on this point in Nye, *Origins of Crowd Psychology*, p. 68. According to Nye, "the origins of the term mental contagion stem from the definition of the mid-[nineteenth-]century clinical psychologist Despine," and French psychiatrists picked up the concept from Despine at an even later date.

"Moral Contagion" and Psychiatry 217

12. B. Robert Kreiser, *Miracles, Convulsions, and Ecclesiastical Politics in Early Eighteenth-Century Paris* (Princeton, 1978), pp. ix–xiii, 175–76, 257–58, 279.
13. On Hecquet's biography, see "Hecquet," in *Encyclopédie méthodique, ou par ordre des matières*, Series: Medicine, 13 vols. (Paris, 1787–1830), 7:77–87; and "Hecquet," in J.-E. Dezeimeris, *Dictionaire historique de la médecine ancienne et moderne*, 4 vols. (Paris, 1828–39), 3:79–80.
14. Philippe Hecquet, *Naturalisme des convulsions dans les maladies de l'épidémie convulsionnaire* (Soleure, 1733), pp. 1, 2–5, 10 (for use of term "epidemic"), 30 (for use of term "contagion"). While Hecquet cites one prior medical source that foreshadows his idea—the work of the early seventeenth-century Dutch physician and naturalist Bontius on the East Indies—he clearly regards his own formulation as a strikingly novel addition to medical theory: "But, it will be said, what a bizarre idea this convulsionary epidemic is!" (p. 177).
15. Ibid., pp. 28–30.
16. Ibid., p. 28.
17. Philippe Hecquet, *Réponse à la "Lettre à un confesseur, touchant le devoir des médecins et des chirurgiens au sujet des miracles et des convulsions"* (Paris, 1733), pp. 29–30.
18. Owsei Temkin, *The Falling Sickness: A History of Epilepsy from the Greeks to the Beginnings of Modern Neurology*, 2d ed. (Baltimore, 1971), pp. 225–26, gives Boerhaave's skeletal account and the additional information provided by Kaau Boerhaave.
19. The word *convulsionnaires*, with its connotations of Saint-Médard, seems not to have been used at the time but was applied in the early nineteenth century. See A. J. de Montègre, *Du magnétisme animal et de ses partisans* (Paris, 1812), p. 4. But, as will be noted below, the parallel with the Saint-Médard affair was explicitly drawn.
20. On Mesmer and mesmerism, see Henri Ellenberger, *The Discovery of the Unconscious: The History and Evolution of Dynamic Psychiatry* (New York, 1970), pp. 55–74, and Robert Darnton, *Mesmerism and the End of the Enlightenment in France* (New York, 1970), esp. chap. 2.
21. Kreiser, *Miracles*, p. 258; and Montègre, *Magnétisme animal*, p. 4. For the mattress-strewn floor, see the illustration in Darnton, *Mesmerism*, p. 9.
22. *Rapport des commissaires chargés par le roi de l'examen du magnétisme animal* (1784), pp. 41–42.
23. Ibid., p. 41 note g.
24. Darnton, *Mesmerism*, pp. 61–62, quote on p. 36.
25. Joseph Lieutaud, *Précis de la médecine pratique*, 4th ed., 3 vols. (Paris, 1776), 1:309.
26. Philippe Pinel, *Nosographie philosophique, ou la méthode de l'analyse appliquée à la médecine*, 2 vols. (Paris, 1798), 2:57–58.
27. Hecquet, *Naturalisme*, p. 194; *Rapport des commissaires*, p. 41 and note g (which cites Hecquet for corroboration).
28. Kaau Boerhaave, *Impetum faciens dictum Hippocrati*, as quoted in French trans-

lation in Eugène Bouchut, *Nouveaux éléments de pathologie générale et de séméiologie*, 2d ed. (Paris, 1869), p. 172.
29. Hecquet, *Réponse*, pp. 30–31.
30. Pinel, *Nosographie philosophique*, 2:57–58.
31. Hecquet, *Naturalisme*, pp. 14–15.
32. *Rapport des commissaires*, pp. 39, 43, 45.
33. Hecquet, *Naturalisme*, pp. 174–75.
34. A full survey of the theories of imagination current in the eighteenth century is obviously impossible here. My generalizations derive from the article "Imagination" in the *Encyclopédie, ou dictionnaire raisonné des sciences, des arts et des métiers*, 36 vols. (Lausanne and Berne, 1778–81), 18:358–670; Etienne Bonnot de Condillac, *Essai sur l'origine des connaissances humaines* (1746) in *Oeuvres de Condillac*, 23 vols. (Paris, 1798), 1: chaps. 2, 3, 4, 9; and, on the Cartesian Malebranche, Emile Bréhier, *The History of Philosophy: The Seventeenth Century*, trans. Wade Baskin (Chicago, 1966), pp. 204–8.
35. *Rapport des commissaires*, p. 43.
36. See Nicolas Malebranche, *La recherche de la vérité* (1675), Bk. 2, pt. 1, chap. 7, sec. 3. The *Encyclopédie* article "Imagination" denied the validity of the belief but only on the grounds that the proper physical links between the brain of the pregnant woman and the brain of the fetus, necessary to give imagination its usual efficacy, were lacking (p. 365). At the beginning of the nineteenth century, Pierre-Jean-Georges Cabanis refused either to affirm or deny the belief and asserted that there was much empirical evidence in support of it. See *Rapports du physique et du moral de l'homme* (1802), Mémoire XI, in *Oeuvres philosophiques de Cabanis*, 2 vols., ed. Claude Lehec and Jean Cazeneuve (Paris, 1956), 1:605.
37. Cabanis, *Rapports du physique et du moral*, p. 604.
38. For usage of these terms, see, e.g., Hecquet, *Naturalisme*, p. 174; Condillac, *Essai*, pp. 119, 130, 141–42; "Imagination," pp. 359, 362.
39. Hecquet, *Naturalisme*, pp. 30, 193–94; *Rapport des commissaires*, p. 41.
40. Philippe Ariès, *Centuries of Childhood: A Social History of Family Life*, trans. Robert Baldick (New York, 1962), pp. 171, 356; and David Hunt, *Parents and Children in History: The Psychology of Family Life in Early Modern France* (New York, 1970), pp. 191–94.
41. *Rapport des commissaires*, p. 46.
42. Ibid., pp. 39–40, 46.
43. Hecquet, *Naturalisme*, p. 10.
44. Ibid., pp. 19, 21.
45. *Encyclopédie, ou dictionnaire raisonné des sciences, des arts et des métiers*, 7:396–99. The handbills are in the archives of the Société Royale de Médecine; see Harvey Mitchell, "Rationality and Control in French Eighteenth-Century Medical Views of the Peasantry," *Comparative Studies in Society and History* 21 (1979):99 n. 46.
46. Darnton, *Mesmerism*, pp. 58–59.

47. Robert Mandrou, *Introduction to Modern France, 1500–1640: An Essay in Historical Psychology*, trans. R. E. Hallmark (New York, 1977), pp. 34–35.
48. Michel Foucault, *Discipline and Punish: The Birth of the Prison*, trans. Alan Sheridan (New York, 1977), pp. 195–96. Foucault is here paraphrasing the regulations promulgated in a late seventeenth-century town; the document, conserved in the Archives militaires de Vincennes, "is broadly similar to a whole series of others that date from the same period and earlier" (p. 316).
49. Hecquet, *Naturalisme*, p. 181. For details on the Marseille plague, see Jean-Noël Biraben, "Certain Demographic Characteristics of the Plague Epidemic in France, 1720–1722," *Daedalus* 97 (Spring 1968):536–45.
50. See George Rosen, "Cameralism and the Concept of Medical Police," *Bulletin of the History of Medicine* 27 (1953):21–43; Rosen, "Mercantilism and Health Policy in Eighteenth-Century France," *Medical History* 3 (1959):259–77; and Marc Raeff, "The Well-Ordered Police State and the Development of Modernity in Seventeenth- and Eighteenth-Century Europe," *American Historical Review* 80 (1975):1221–43.
51. See Caroline C. Hannaway, "The Société Royale de Médecine and Epidemics in the Ancien Régime," *Bulletin of the History of Medicine* 46 (1972):259–61; and Archives Nationales, F15 230, for examples of requests addressed to the comptroller-general for payments, and sometimes pensions, for doctors who had served in local epidemics.
52. Hannaway, "Société Royale," pp. 258, 262–65.
53. Jean Starobinski, Review of Foucault, *Birth of the Clinic*, *New York Review of Books*, 22 January 1976.
54. Michel Foucault, *Naissance de la clinique: Une archéologie du regard médical*, 2d ed. (Paris, 1972), pp. 31–32.
55. *Oeuvres complètes*, 28 vols. (Paris, 1956–63), 13:412.
56. 60 vols. (Paris, 1812–22), 31:535, 543. The author of the article, Cadet de Gassicourt, was a medical professional but a pharmacist rather than a physician; for a capsule biography, see Dora Weiner, "Public Health under Napoleon: The Conseil de Salubrité de Paris, 1802–1815," *Clio Medica* 9 (1974):273.
57. Jacques Léonard, *Les médecins de l'Ouest au XIXème siècle*, thesis, Université de Paris IV, 1976, 3 vols. (Lille, 1978), 1:447–48.
58. See, for quotation, U. Coste, Review of *Dictionnaire abrégé des sciences médicales* in *Journal universel des sciences médicales* 43 (1826):61; and Théophile Archambault, Review of Jean-Baptiste Cazauvieilh, *Du suicide* in *Annales médico-psychologiques* 1 (1843):171–72.
59. George D. Sussman "Enlightened Health Reform, Professional Medicine and Traditional Society: The Cantonal Physicians of the Bas-Rhin, 1810–1870," *Bulletin of the History of Medicine* 51 (1977):566–69.
60. George D. Sussman, "The Glut of Doctors in Mid-Nineteenth-Century France," *Comparative Studies in Society and History* 19 (1977):290.
61. C.-V.-F.-G. Prunelle, *De la médecine politique en général et de son objet* . . .

(Montpellier; 1814), p. 2; N. P. Gilbert, *Quelques réflexions sur la médecine légale et sur son état actuel en France* . . . (Paris, an IX), p. 6.
62. This point is developed at length in my "French Psychiatry in Social and Political Perspective: The Formation of a New Profession, 1820–1860," (Ph.D. dissertation, Columbia University, 1978), pp. 46–60.
63. Edouard Charton, *Guide pour le choix d'un état* (Paris, 1842), pp. 47–48, 389, 393.
64. Sussman, "Glut of Doctors"; and Goldstein, "French Psychiatry," pp. 22–28.
65. Eusèbe Salverte, *Rapports de la médecine avec la politique* (Paris, 1806), pp. 202–3.
66. See the ministerial circular of 24 January 1806, described in Léonard, *Médecins de l'Ouest*, 1:450 note 116.
67. Eugène Bouchut, *Nouveaux éléments de pathologie générale et de séméiologie* (Paris, 1857), pp. 184–88. The text was a standard one and went through three more editions in the nineteenth century: 1869, 1875, 1882.
68. Recent scholarship has revealed that this date, always part of a legendary history of French psychiatry created and recited by the psychiatrists themselves, is erroneous. The event occurred in 1797. See Dora B. Weiner, "The Apprenticeship of Philippe Pinel: A New Document," *Clio Medica* 13 (1978): 125.
69. Goldstein, "French Psychiatry," chaps. 1–3. The emergence and legitimation of a psychiatric profession in France in the period from the late eighteenth through the late nineteenth centuries is treated at length in the book I am currently preparing.
70. Pinel, *Nosographie philosophique*, 2:56–58.
71. Jean-Etienne-Dominique Esquirol, "Suicide," in *Dictionaire des sciences médicales*, 60 vols. (Paris, 1812–22), 53:247.
72. Esquirol, "Suicide," pp. 246–47, and "De la démonomanie" (1814), reprinted in his *Des maladies mentales*, 2 vols. (Paris, 1838), 1:501–2.
73. See C.-C.-H. Marc, "Considérations médico-legales sur la monomanie," *Annales d'hygiène publique et de médecine légale* 10 (1833):483–84, an article by a senior psychiatrist, forensic expert, and the physician to Louis-Philippe which cites and praises it; and Durkheim, *Suicide*, p. 123 n. 1.
74. Prosper Lucas, "De l'imitation contagieuse, ou de la propagation sympathique des névroses et des monomanies" (Thesis, Faculty of Medicine, Paris, 1833), pp. 3, 48.
75. Lucas did not credit these sources directly for his explanation but comments elsewhere in the thesis indicate his familiarity with the 1784 report (p. 14) and his sense of indebtedness to Cabanis (p. 50).
76. Lucas, "Imitation contagieuse," pp. 54–56. A comparison of Lucas's categories with the topics of Mémoires IV (age), V (sex), VI ("temperaments"), and XII ("acquired temperaments") of Cabanis's *Rapports du physique et du moral de l'homme* indicates the latter's influence.

77. Lucas, "Imitation contagieuse," p. 57.
78. Ibid., p. 21.
79. Ibid., pp. 75–76.
80. *Globe*, 15 August 1826.
81. For rural speculations on the causes of the incendiarism, see the anonymous letter printed in the *Gazette des tribunaux*, 25 May 1830; for the most recent assessment by a historian, see John M. Merriman, "The Norman Fires of 1830: Incendiaries and Fear in Rural France," *French Historical Studies* 9 (1976):452–66.
82. Alexandre Brierre de Boismont, *Observations médico-légales sur la monomanie homicide* (Paris, 1827), p. 43.
83. Marc, "Considérations sur la monomanie," pp. 398–403.
84. André-Marie-J.-J. Dupin, *Observations sur plusieurs points importans de notre législation criminelle* (Paris, 1821), pp. 129–30.
85. Brierre de Boismont, *Observations sur la monomanie homicide*, pp. 41–42, 42 n. 1.
86. Lucas, "Imitation contagieuse," pp. 68, 71–72, 74. Brierre also mentioned the contagious psychopathological effect of the press but gave it far less emphasis; see *Observations sur la monomanie homicide*, p. 42 n. 1.
87. Peter Amann, *Revolution and Mass Democracy: The Paris Club Movement in 1848* (Princeton, 1975), pp. 33–40, 67–68; for Crémieux, see *Moniteur universel*, 21 March 1849, p. 951.
88. The only vocal dissenter appears to have been Jules Baillarger. See his comments at the Academy of Medicine reprinted in J.-E. Belhomme, *Influence des événements et des commotions politiques sur le développement de la folie* (Paris, 1849), pp. 23–24.
89. Alexandre Brierre de Boismont, "Des folies épidémiques," *Union médicale*, 13 February 1849.
90. Belhomme, *Influence des commotions politiques*, p. 27.
91. Alexandre Brierre de Boismont, "De l'influence des derniers événements sur la folie," *Union médicale*, 20 July 1848.
92. Brierre de Boismont, "Folies épidémiques"; and Unsigned, "Les clubs et les fonctions cérébrales," *Union médicale*, 3 February 1849.
93. Dr. Joseph Arthaud, *Relation d'une hystéro-démonopathie épidémique observée à Morzine* (Lyons, 1862), pp. 11, 77; Dr. C. Chiara, "Les diables de Morzine, ou les nouvelles possédées," pt. 1, *Gazette médicale de Lyon*, 1 November 1861, p. 488; Philippe Kuhn, "De l'épidémie hystéro-démonopathique de Morzine," pt. 1, *Annales médico-psychologiques*, 4th ser., 5 (1865):400, 408. After I had completed this essay, two short monographs on the Morzine episode appeared almost simultaneously in France. They are Jacqueline Carroy-Thirard, *Le mal de Morzine: De la possession à l'hystérie, 1857–1877* (Paris, 1981), primarily a collection of documents from the departmental and diocesan archives of the Haute-Savoie; and Catherine-Laurence Maire, *Les possédées de Morzine, 1857–1873* (Lyons, 1981).

94. See Gérard Bleandonu and Guy Le Gaufey, "Naissance des asiles d'aliénés (Auxerre-Paris)," *Annales ESC* 30 (1975):93–121.
95. *Courrier des Alpes*, 11 July 1861.
96. Arthaud, *Relation d'une hystéro-démonopathie*, pp. 8–9, 47; H. R. Trevor-Roper, Title essay of *The European Witch-Craze of the Sixteenth and Seventeenth Centuries and Other Essays* (New York, 1956), p. 106.
97. L.-J.-F. Delasiauve, Minutes of the Sociéte Médico-psychologique, "Rapport sur la candidature de M. Constans," *Annales médico-psychologiques*, 4th ser., 6 (1865):126; and Arthaud, *Relation d'une hystéro-démonopathie*, pp. 68–70, 72.
98. Arthaud, *Relation d'une hystéro-démonopathie*, pp. 12–13.
99. Ibid., pp. 67–68, 72; Kuhn, "Epidémie de Morzine," pt. 1, p. 410; Constans, *Relation sur une épidémie d'hystéro-démonopathie en 1861*, 2d ed. (Paris, 1863), p. 43; Delasiauve, "Rapport sur la candidature de Constans," p. 123.
100. Constans, *Relation sur une épidémie*, p. 111.
101. Bouchut, *Nouveaux éléments* (1857), p. 142.
102. Morzine is not the only nineteenth-century example. Among others, the massive work of the psychiatrist L.-F. Calmeil, *De la folie considérée sous le point de vue pathologique, philosophique, historique et judiciaire . . . ; description des grandes épidémies de délire . . . qui ont atteint les populations d'autrefois et régné dans les monastères*, 2 vols. (Paris, 1845), deserves to be mentioned. Calmeil's purpose was to reveal the many centuries of misinterpretation of madness and moral contagion as religious phenomena.
103. See Robert Mandrou, *Magistrats et sorciers en France au XVIIe siècle* (Paris, 1968). I wish to thank Lawrence Stone for calling my attention to this connection.

PART THREE
Medical Monopoly, Professional Power, and Political Cultures

5
MATTHEW RAMSEY

The Politics of Professional Monopoly in Nineteenth-Century Medicine: The French Model and Its Rivals

Of all the professions, medicine enjoys the tightest legal monopoly. The reasons for its success seem obvious: on the one hand, the public cares deeply about its health and wishes to ensure that medical practitioners are qualified to treat patients; on the other hand, modern medical science and education have given physicians demonstrable superiority over all unlicensed rivals. The result is a social consensus.

Sociological studies of the professions have generally accepted this common-sense functionalism. Eliot Freidson, for example, in *Profession of Medicine*, argues that "a significant monopoly could not occur until a secure and practical technology of work was developed." This new technology dates from the last third of the nineteenth century, starting with the pioneering contributions of Louis Pasteur and Robert Koch. From then on, the "distinction between physician and so-called quack needed no longer to rest on the academic certification of the superiority of one superstition over another." And only then "was licensing widely established in the United States and based on uniform standards for medical education."[1]

Not all accounts have attached so much weight to the triumph of medical science. Some sociologists have also stressed collective social and economic action by physicians, for whom monopoly is an essential part of the "professional project."[2] Historians, for their part, have argued increasingly in recent years that professional "power" preceded technical prowess—a theme implied, for example, in the very title of Jacques Léonard's last book on nineteenth-century French medicine, *La médecine entre les pouvoirs et les savoirs*.[3] Nearly all these interpretations, however, share a common assumption: that medicine, the medical profession, and professional monopoly followed a predictable path of progress—from pseudoscience to science, from an ineffectual learned profession to a competent consulting profession, from guild privileges to a uniform licensing system—as Western societies moved from preindustrial to industrial forms of economic organization and from "traditional" to "modern" politics. Although these trends proceeded at varying rates, and at somewhat different times in different places, they all somehow came together at the end of the nineteenth century, when modern medicine and the modern medical profession were established throughout the West.

In its rough outlines, this account of medicine's professional success is plausible enough: around the end of the nineteenth century and the beginning of the twentieth, reforms in medical education, major advances in medical science, the creation of social insurance schemes and other forms of third-party payments—all these and related developments helped raise the prestige, status, and income of physicians in the industrialized countries to levels never before attained.[4] It seems intuitively apparent that medicine and the medical profession underwent a simultaneous, overdetermined modernization, producing the medical institutions we know today.

The late nineteenth and early twentieth centuries also saw a new wave of medical legislation in the United States, Latin America, parts of Europe, and even Japan. This development at first glance appears to belong to the same long-term trend. But a closer look at the history of de jure monopoly in the West suggests that it fits the paradigm only imperfectly. Some monopolies of the "modern" type antedate Pasteur and the social success of the profession. And then instead of even progress, one sees discontinuities; instead of a neat correlation between science, modernity, and monopoly, one finds several "advanced" countries in which professional monopoly was absent or defective, and a number of "backward" countries which, however limited the means of enforcement, possessed strong medical practice legislation.[5]

In a sense, this pattern should not be surprising. As all the sociological studies recognize, legal monopoly is a political institution. Unlike the market for medical services and the cultural prestige of medicine, which have grown slowly but fairly steadily, professional monopoly can in principle be legislated into existence and just as easily legislated out again, depending on the power of the interested parties and the political climate

The Politics of Medical Monopoly

of the moment. The vagaries of state regulation are startling only if one assumes that control of medical practice has been outside politics and that the profession, once its scientific preeminence had justified its claims to special protection, would necessarily receive it. But this assumption is unjustified. On the contrary: there was nothing inevitable about the development of professional monopoly. The various forms it took and in some instances its very existence were problematic, and to understand what happened in each case it is necessary to look at political life and institutions and at the larger political cultures in which they functioned.

Though we already have a sizable body of literature on certain aspects of this problem—particularly licensure in England and America—it has not yet received the systematic study that it deserves; even the bare outlines of the legislative history are in large part unknown to sociologists and historians alike. The reasons for this neglect are understandable: institutional history has fallen out of favor, and it can be argued that medical practice laws are not historically interesting—that they were only a symbol, a kind of badge conferred on an interest group that had already achieved power in a real struggle conducted on other terrains; or that they were ineffectual and played only a small part in securing what Freidson calls a "significant" monopoly (by which he presumably means de facto control over all of medical practice). Such arguments show, however, not that de jure monopoly is an unimportant part of the history of the professions but rather that it is only one part. It is in fact a singularly interesting one for reasons that can only be suggested here. Medical practice laws both express and help shape the profession's relationship with the state; because they are not entirely of the physicians' own making, they can constrain as well as confirm the growth of professional power. They contribute both to the public's perception of the profession and to the profession's perception of itself; the question of regulation was one about which doctors cared deeply, and it was often the single professional issue that most preoccupied them outside the daily routines of patient care. Finally, although regulation failed to extirpate parallel medicine, it helped determine its form and scope. It is almost a truism that prohibitory legislation is of no practical consequence because it does not eliminate the activity that it outlaws. But if it is enforced, it can matter a good deal, and not simply to the individuals singled out for prosecution and punishment. The old antifornication statutes that remained on the books in twentieth-century America may have been socially irrelevant; antiabortion laws and Prohibition clearly were not.

A history of de jure monopoly in the medical profession must adopt a broadly comparative approach, essentially for two reasons. First, and more obviously, there is no one profession but rather a diversity of national professions, widely different in their present-day structures and even more so in their histories; even a division into, say, Anglo-American and Continental types will not do. Freidson's study concerns American medicine, in which the organization of a comprehensive licensing system coincided (roughly) with the Pasteurian era; but the American experience, as will be shown in this essay, was highly unusual. The second reason is that in the course of the nineteenth century the question of regulating medical practice became the subject of a transatlantic debate; by the early twentieth century, international conferences were devoted to it. Even members of American state legislatures or of Swiss cantonal councils (two groups not necessarily noted for cosmopolitanism or wide learning) were at least vaguely aware of the major foreign models. It simply is not possible to do justice to the topic by considering only one or two national cases in isolation.

It will be necessary here to focus on the most widely discussed cases of the nineteenth century: the French monopoly and the four rival models that appeared in Britain, the United States, Germany, and parts of Switzerland. Although the rivals collectively take up the greater bulk of the essay, it begins with France, and the French model provides the framework for understanding all the later developments. For it was France, during the Revolution, that first legally abolished preexisting professional privileges in medicine. But it was also France, at the very beginning of the nineteenth century, that developed what most later jurists considered to be the first "modern" professional monopoly—at the time probably the tightest de jure monopoly in the world. And France then proceeded, in the Napoleonic wars, to impose its model by force in the conquered territories annexed to the Empire and to disturb established medical institutions in the much larger area subjected to French control. In later years, French doctors would no doubt have been surprised to learn that they enjoyed rigorous legislation and a tight monopoly. They regularly complained that their law was an ill-designed stopgap measure, that enforcement was lax, and that regimes (like the Bourbon Restoration) that were highly sympathetic to the Catholic Church readily allowed priests and nuns to give medical advice and dispense drugs. When Charles X revived the use of the royal touch for scrofula, the head of state himself could be said to practice medicine illegally.[6] For all the doctors' jeremiads, though, a highly visible group of offenders was fined and in some cases jailed for "illegal medical practice"; and to foreigners, French legislation remained synonymous with a strict "police" of the medical field.

The Politics of Medical Monopoly

The rival models that emerged in territories outside the French sphere of influence also have an importance that transcends national boundaries. Although opponents of strict regulation succeeded in only a handful of cases, they won a surprisingly sympathetic hearing from a minority of intellectuals, politicians, and even some physicians in a number of countries (including a few in France itself). Moreover, just as the other legislative models defined themselves in part against the French, so medical reformers in France in the latter part of the nineteenth century rejected alternative foreign models (as well as France's own revolutionary past). The significance of the French case cannot be fully understood in isolation from this larger context.

The discussion that follows falls into three unequal parts. The first introduces the major terms and concepts used in the study, outlines the principal institutions regulating medical practice in the Old Regime, and summarizes the collapse and reorganization of medical regulation brought on by the French Revolution. The second moves from the early years of the nineteenth century and the Napoleonic settlement through the middle decades of the century, when the strongest new rivals to the French model appeared; the third more briefly pursues the history of these rivals into the twentieth century.

The argument of the first section, in its barest outlines, is that professional monopoly had emerged by the end of the eighteenth century as a political issue—still inchoate on much of the Continent but rapidly given new substance and urgency by the events of the French Revolution. The individual case histories in the second section suggest that the profession's degree of control over entry into medical practice in the nineteenth century depended on a set of constraints deriving from the French revolutionary assault on Old Regime institutions and from a more pervasive liberal challenge to regulatory institutions, both state and corporate, that climaxed in the 1850s and 1860s in many parts of the Western world. Briefly, where laissez-faire liberalism flourished, de jure monopoly was generally weak or nonexistent; where mainstream liberalism was strongly committed to reform from the center, monopoly was only weakly challenged; and where liberalism failed, professional monopolies were at their tightest. Other political factors must be considered as well; but the key point is that neither a high level of professional organization nor the successful development of medical science guaranteed a strict monopoly. No unitary model of increasing professional power accumulated through collective social action or the exploitation of scientific prestige will work for the nineteenth century. The final section addresses the question whether, by the early twentieth century, the regulation of medical practice was in some sense depoliticized—whether a consensus indeed developed that the claims of scientific medicine were so strong, and the demands of public health so compelling, that monopoly need not be a politically divisive issue. In the case of France (as of the United States), this might appear to be the case; but the discussion here will point to several counterexamples to the watershed theory and suggest that although the influence of scientific prestige cannot be entirely discounted, the comparative success of professional monopoly in a country such as France may reflect acceptance of government regulation as much as confidence in technological medicine. Medical practice has remained, if only tacitly, a political issue.

From the Old Regime to the French Revolution

Basic Concepts

The argument presented here depends on a set of interrelated concepts concerning professional controls and freedom. It is important to bear in mind, first of all, the basic forms of regulation of medical practice. Every state now has some system for identifying and certifying trained practitioners. Licensing can be either voluntary or mandatory; the two forms are sometimes known as "definitive" (because licensing simply defines qualified practitioners) and "restrictive." The latter system normally imposes criminal sanctions for unauthorized practice.[7]

The forms as well as the degree of control over medical practice have varied widely, and for the purposes of this study it would be useful to think of four, rather than two, basic models. (1) Corporate monopolies: the exclusive right to practice in certain regions is granted to members of chartered medical bodies and those persons they choose to co-opt as members or licensees. Since these bodies were often urban and local, their jurisdiction in some cases failed to blanket the territory of a state, leaving holes in the smaller towns and the countryside. This pattern characterized Old Regime France, Britain before 1858, and early regulation in the United States. (2) Bureaucratic regulation: a state-appointed medical board or some other state agency identifies qualified individuals, who alone have the right to practice medicine. This was the Prussian model and the basis for French regulation in the nineteenth century. (3) The radical free field, in which every man might be his own or another's physician. This situation existed in the nineteenth century in outlying areas that had few trained physicians and no history of regulation—Alaska, a number of Latin American states, large parts of Africa, and (arguably) parts of the Russian Empire. It was created, however, in two countries with a prior history of regulation: in France during the Revolution and in the United States during the middle decades of the nineteenth century. (4) The modified free field, with strict certification. Trained practitioners are identified by a professional body, university, or government agency. They do not enjoy a legal monopoly, and unauthorized practice is not penalized; but the false use of an official title is strictly punished. Moreover, qualified practitioners enjoy certain privileges such as the exclusive right to give an expert opinion in legal cases, to sign a death certificate, to hold government appointments or commissions as military medical officers, or to be reimbursed by a national health insurance program. The United Kingdom, Germany, and three Swiss cantons adopted this system in the second half of the nineteenth century. (A similar arrangement appeared in Norway in 1871 and in Sweden in 1915, but these cases will not be discussed here—in part because they did not figure in the nineteenth-century debates, in part because unqualified practitioners were hemmed in from the outset by so many restrictions that authorized personnel wound up with a partial but still substantial de jure monopoly.)[8] For convenience the radical and modified free fields will sometimes be referred to here simply as "free fields."

Each of these models carried political implications and associations. The radical free field was traditionally considered republican or even revolutionary and was connected historically with assaults on hierarchy and privilege: Nicholas Culpeper's attack on monopolies during the Puritan Revolution; Benjamin Rush's vision of a republican medicine that would embody the spirit of the American Revolution; the French Revolution's assault on the learned societies and faculties, which crippled medical education for two years and virtually suspended certification and licensing for a decade.[9] Echoes of this tradition were heard in central Europe in 1848; in Spain following the September Revolution; and in Russia after the Revolution of 1917. The modified free field followed the liberal model for economic activity; laissez-faire implied confidence in the ability of the public, aided by education and correct information about the qualifications of practitioners, to discriminate between the good and the bad. In the eyes of medical liberals, special protection both stifled initiative and violated the citizen's right to free choice of occupation; and many would have rejected on political grounds alone any interference by the state in a private citizen's choice of a healer. The remaining two models can loosely be characterized as authoritarian, but they pointed in different directions. The corporate model, which can be traced back to the efforts of the medieval universities to establish monopolies for their faculties, evoked a society of estates, orders, and privileges. It primarily protected the traditional rights of a private interest group; like guild regulations, it also served, in principle, to guarantee the quality of services offered to the public. It seemed, in addition, to offer a bulwark against the anarchy that would result if members of the various trades left their appointed niches. Bureaucratic regulation, finally, affirmed the police powers of the state—its right in this case to protect a naive public that could not perceive its true interest and therefore had to be subjected to some degree of administrative tutelage. It also served, of course, to promote *la raison d'état*; not surprisingly, it was most closely associated in the eighteenth century with Enlightened absolutism and in the early nineteenth century with Napoleon.

The Old Regime

How were these institutions distributed in the eighteenth century? To some extent they overlapped, but, broadly speaking, corporate institutions remained strongest in western Europe and became weaker as one proceeded east. The system in Britain and Ireland was too complex to describe fully here, but it depended essentially on an uncoordinated network of privileged licensing bodies, some of which had a local monopoly over medical practice. The Royal College of Physicians (chartered in 1518) enjoyed a legal monopoly in London and its outskirts, and in theory (though this provision was never successfully enforced) had the right to examine anyone, except graduates of Oxford and Cambridge, who wished to practice in England.[10] To complicate matters further, the Anglican episcopate was entitled to examine and license practitioners (though this right was not actively exercised after the seventeenth century), and the crown sometimes issued warrants to individual practitioners and remedy vendors.[11] France, in contrast, did produce a national law on medical practice, the royal Edict of Marly (1707), which required all practitioners in cities and towns to hold the degree of *licencié* from one of the medical faculties; but the edict specifically affirmed the rights and privileges of the corporations—the local *facultés* and *collèges*. The greatest threat to corporative regulation came, instead, from a parallel system of special warrants and permissions, issued by authorities ranging from the crown on down to local nobles and municipal officials. The closest approximation to a royal medical bureaucracy, the Société Royale de Médecine, which received its letters patent in 1778, was primarily concerned with epidemics and the regulation of secret remedies; it had no power to license physicians.[12]

The bureaucratic model could be found in Prussia, where the Royal Obercollegium Medicum, established in 1685, was empowered to license physicians, apothecaries, barbers, surgeons, oculists, herniotomists, toothpullers, and midwives.[13] In Spain, the Royal Protomedicato, or medical board, licensed physicians, surgeons, barbers, and pharmacists and dealt with cases of malpractice and empiricism. In many places, practitioners also had to belong to local corporations—*gremios, colegios, cofradías*—but these chartered institutions were not licensing bodies; they functioned as mutual aid organizations, religious confraternities, and the like.[14] In late medieval Italy, regulation of medical practice belonged to appointed commissions in the south; in the northern and central states guildlike colleges enjoyed the right to issue licenses. By the sixteenth century, though, a number of colleges (outside the north) had evolved into virtual organs of the state. At Florence, the grand duke in 1560 established a separate self-perpetuating state board with licensing powers.[15] In the New World, the principle of state regulation came early to the French and Spanish colonies, later to English settlements, where the first specific requirement for a government license to identify the qualified was adopted for New York City in 1760. In 1772, New Jersey, in response to pressures from the provincial medical society, passed legislation requiring all medical men, except for those already in practice, to be examined by two judges of the Supreme Court and the advisers of their choice; unlicensed practitioners who accepted fees for their services would be fined.[16] In the New World, then, the few systems of mandatory licensing depended on government certification.

During the eighteenth century the liberal model was most fully realized in England's North American colonies, where hostility to monopoly was strong and the power of the colonial governments to charter medical corporations was restricted under common law. The Massachusetts Medical Society (founded in 1781) could give letters testimonial, so that "a just discrimination should be made between such as are duly educated, and properly qualified for the duties of their profession, and those who may ignorantly and wickedly administer medicine whereby the health and lives of many valuable individuals may be endangered, or perhaps lost to the community." No penalty, however, was attached to unlicensed practice.[17]

The patents and charters that created or recognized medical boards and corporations typically contained explicit prohibitions of unauthorized practice and of specific forms of empiricism and remedy vending such as hawking medicines from a stage in a public square. In addition, special ordinances might regulate medical practice, renew or modify old privileges, fulminate against quacks, and add or modify penalties for illegal practice. In Prussia, for example, various royal ordinances denied the right to practice to medical students, preachers, chemists, distillers, Jews, shepherds, quacks, old wives, soothsayers, and others who encroached on the medical domain.[18] This sort of legislation was rarely consistent and was not always well known at the local level. It often left in limbo certain types of practice (such as special branches of surgery) or practice in areas outside the jurisdiction of established faculties, corporations, or *collegia medica*; to confuse matters still further, individuals often received special authorizations to sell remedies or practice some part of medicine or surgery in apparent contradiction to the statutes. In addition, the rival claims of the various grades of physicians, surgeons, and apothecaries clouded the entire issue of medical regulation: an "unauthorized" practitioner might well be licensed to practice in a closely related field.[19] The Old Regime so clearly lacked a uniform professional monopoly that it would be an anachronism to apply the current concept of "illegal practice" to the eighteenth century.

Whatever their form, professional privileges were never uncontroversial. The first systematic critique, however, emerged from the liberal Enlightenment (most clearly the Scottish school), which attacked guild privileges in medicine as in other domains. Adam Smith specifically addressed the question of medical practice in a famous letter to the physician William Cullen, in which he argued that "in every profession the fortune of every individual should depend as much as possible upon his merit, and as little as possible upon his privilege."[20] Monopoly encouraged sloth, complacency, and hostility to new ideas; competition would lower prices and keep practitioners on their toes. The primary justification for an open field, then, was utilitarian; but freedom of practice was also consistent with two broad liberal goals, which were to assume greater prominence in the nineteenth-century debates: minimizing government interference and allowing the individual to do as he pleases.[21] These doctrines attracted a smaller following on the Continent, where a more authoritarian school also attacked the corporations but wished to vest extensive powers in a medical bureaucracy, which would serve as an arm of the reformist state. Turgot, appropriately, was godfather to the Société Royale de Médecine.

The French Revolution and Napoleon

In the French Revolution, medical regulation collapsed under a double assault, aimed at barriers to economic freedom and at the special privileges of the "aristocratic" corporations. A law of March 1791 held that anyone could practice the profession of his choosing upon payment of a tax known as the *patente;* a decree of August 1792 suppressed the faculties (although instruction continued on a reduced scale at a few institutions). The Société Royale de Médecine was abolished a year later, together with the other learned societies and academies. As a result, regular certification of practitioners was ended, the police of empirics' remedies suspended, and medical education severely crippled. Regular instruction returned at the beginning of 1795, following the establishment of three special schools of medicine (a move considerably facilitated by the army's urgent need for trained personnel); but the regulation of medical practice was not so easily reestablished, even after Thermidor, although the Directory Constitution explicitly authorized it. Local officials struggled to control empiricism as best they could through prefectoral decrees and police measures; at the national level, the late 1790s saw only a series of debates and unsuccessful proposals, with relatively liberal solutions advocated by Pierre-Claude-François Daunou and Claude-Antoine Prieur-Duvernois (Prieur of the Côte d'Or) and less liberal systems by the physician legislators Jean-Marie Calès, Louis Vitet, and Jean-François Baraillon. Pierre-Jean-Georges Cabanis suggested a compromise between freedom of industry and protection of the public interest; although his arguments produced no immediate results, they provided the ideological underpinnings for the bill subsequently presented, under the more favorable political conditions of the Consulate, by Antoine François de Fourcroy. The proposal emanated from the Conseil d'Etat, and a compliant Corps législatif passed it without difficulty. The Ideologue interpretation of medical politics, voiced by Cabanis and reflected in this law of 19 Ventôse Year XI (10 March 1803), rejected the liberals' faith in the patient's ability to identify a good physician and insisted on mandatory state certification as a guarantee against charlatanism.[22]

One of the catchwords of republican medicine during the Revolution had been "medical liberty," a concept more ominous to physicians than the more familiar doctrine of free trade. Some Jacobins, moreover, were overtly hostile to the profession. For most physicians and many laymen at the beginning of the nineteenth century, the idea of a free field was tainted by recollections of a decade of "medical anarchy" and of a period of persecution that they considered the medical equivalent of the Terror.[23] In a country where it is still possible to be passionately for or against the Revolution, a memory of this sort carried enormous weight.

The law of Ventôse did not mean a return to the *status quo ante;* in this as in other domains, the Napoleonic settlement did not restore the privilege system of the Old Regime. Equality before the law remained; the old corporations were not revived. Indeed, under the Le Chapelier Law of 1791 on professional associations, physicians were not even able to organize as an interest group; medical syndicates were not formally legalized (and invested once more with the right to initiate prosecutions of unauthorized healers) until 1892.

The paradoxical legacy of the Revolution was visited by *la grande nation* upon the conquered territories of Europe. First, the revolutionary pressure for economic freedom undermined the old corporations and promoted the concept of careers open to talent. Not that revolutionary France directly exported medical republicanism to any significant extent. Except in territories actually annexed to the Republic, older antiquack regulations remained in effect (in the Helvetic and Batavian republics, for example), and new ones were adopted. One illustration: the Dutch town of Dordrecht issued an ordinance in 1801 ("the seventh year of Batavian freedom") that banned medical practice by quacks and the sale of secret remedies; the text appeared under the transposed revolutionary slogan "Equality, Liberty, Fraternity."[24] When the Dutch Revolution officially abolished the guilds in 1798, the *collegia medica* survived—there were no true guilds in medicine—and medical regulation was subsequently reorganized through health commissions and councils.[25] But the broad principle of professional privilege had been shaken.

Then after 1803, the Napoleonic bureaucracy promoted a uniform system of state control that granted licenses to individuals, rather than privileges to exclusive bodies. In the annexed *départements*, Napoleon imposed the law of Ventôse.[26] The satellite kingdoms enacted comparable legislation, although they usually conserved the outlines of local medical institutions.[27] These political upheavals recast the regulation of medical practice in a large part of western Europe. The influence of the Ventôse law lingered on, notably in Belgium, where a court decided only in the middle of the century that it had been abrogated and not merely supple-

The Politics of Medical Monopoly 237

mented by later enactments.[28] And even where new legislation supplanted French or French-inspired laws—as in Modena, which after the return of the House of Este attempted a medical restoration to expunge the legacy of French occupation[29]—it was difficult to reestablish Old Regime institutions intact.

Regulation in the Nineteenth Century

The events of little more than a decade, then, are crucial to understanding the history of professional monopoly in the nineteenth century. France had provided the paradigm both of medical liberty and of strict regulation, the Scylla and Charybdis between which most nineteenth-century legislators tried to steer a course. In order to make sense of the later events, it will be necessary to follow the development of medical regulation in each country. No set of static models can sufficiently convey how the various solutions emerged over time; no single narrative can do justice to the variety of national institutions. A fully historical comparative analysis must emerge from a series of parallel narratives. Each of the major cases (France and the four free fields) will therefore be discussed separately. The various forms that monopoly took outside France are of course important, too; they comprised the great majority of cases. But they can be only briefly summarized here, following the section on France.

France

The law of Ventôse reorganized the medical profession, creating the titles of doctor of medicine or surgery, which required a doctorate from a medical school, and health officer (*officier de santé*), which required simpler and more practical training and then approval, after examination, by a departmental medical board (*jury médical*). Special provisions were made for licensing physicians and surgeons admitted under the Old Regime and those who had set up a practice following the collapse of regulatory institutions during the Revolution. The law limited the practice of medicine to these authorized personnel and strictly protected their titles. By contemporary standards, the definition of illegal practice was broad; as the courts interpreted the law, any medical act by an unlicensed person, apart from routine first aid, constituted a violation. Penalties were light compared with most European antiquack ordinances, although the law prescribed a more severe punishment for offenders who "usurped" an official title—a nod in the direction of the liberal definitive model. Despite subsequent concessions made by administrative decree to the medical and pharmaceutical activities of the clergy, the law stood out in the eyes of jurisconsults as a "modern" statute because it imposed a clear, uniform national licensing system, marred only by provisions needed to accommodate personnel already in practice; declared that anyone not on the official list of licensed personnel who practiced medicine was ipso facto in violation of the law; implicitly rejected all special privileges; and ignored all extenuating circumstances such as the relative harmlessness of an offender's activities, his apparent success in curing illness, or his willingness to treat the poor gratis.[30]

As a weapon against illegal practice, the Ventôse law rapidly proved inadequate, and defects in its construction drew criticism from the jurists who had to interpret it. Physicians denounced a grandfather clause that allowed unlicensed practitioners to be admitted as *officiers de santé* merely by obtaining a certificate from their mayor and two local notables attesting that they had established a practice after the suppression of the old corporations. Controversial from the outset, the lower order of practitioners—originally intended to meet the medical needs of the countryside—met with increasing opposition from both doctors and government officials. The only solution seemed to be new legislation. Several efforts, notably in the 1840s, yielded no results. No ministry was strong enough to push through a bill; governments (and even regimes) had an awkward way of collapsing when a promising draft was under consideration.[31] In the 1880s a series of new proposals included one bill, strongly supported by the organized profession and physician deputies in the legislature, that finally led in 1892 to a new law; it cut off production of new *officiers de santé*, consolidated the doctorates in medicine and surgery, and reinforced the provisions for the enforcement of professional monopoly. Henceforth a medical doctorate would be obligatory for the practice of medicine and surgery; dentistry would for the first time require a special diploma. Penalties for illegal practice were stiffened, although it was now necessary to show that the defendant practiced medicine "habitually." More important, the act imparted a neocorporate twist to medical regulation by legalizing professional *syndicats* and empowering them to initiate criminal prosecutions of unauthorized practitioners, as well as civil suits for damages. The law of 1892 was extended to Algeria four years later and copied with only slight changes by Monaco (1894) and Luxemburg (1901). Outside the French legal pale it offered a refurbished model for strict regulation, with no distinction made between charitable and mercenary practice.[32]

At no time in nineteenth-century France did professional monopoly suffer a serious challenge. Only scattered and isolated republican critiques appeared; the work of the anarchist physician Ernest Coeurderoy, who called for a "war unto death" against monopoly, produced no echoes.[33] Nor did the liberal critique fare much better, although it occupied a far more central place in French medical politics. Even during the Enlightenment, medical freedom had fewer proponents in France than across the Channel, and with the Ideologues it nearly vanished from the mainstream liberal agenda. Cabanis specifically excluded medicine from his program for industrial freedom. Jean-Baptiste Say, although a disciple of Adam Smith, was silent on the subject of medicine; so was Antoine-Louis-Claude Destutt de Tracy, although he asked for "entire and absolute freedom in all kinds of industry." Even at the height of the laissez-faire movement during the Second Empire, liberals in the tradition of Say ignored medical freedom. Edouard Laboulaye called for allowing the individual to develop his faculties and for freedom of work, but his long list of abusive monopolies omitted medicine. Jules Simon actually wrote a sympathetic preface to a book that assailed quackery, justified monopoly, and called for harsher laws and stricter enforcement.[34]

The key exceptions appeared early in the century in the entourage of Saint-Simon. The young Auguste Comte and the liberal political economist Charles Dunoyer denounced the state monopoly on education, and their consistent opposition to restrictions on freedom of industry led them to oppose legislation reserving the practice of certain occupations to qualified persons: such prohibitions, they wrote, accredited ignorance and bestowed titles on charlatanism, while favoring corporatism and the growth of state authority. Even they, however, bowed to what they saw as popular expectations: "Many imaginations would become acutely alarmed if it were once again permitted to call oneself a physician, pharmacist, [or] lawyer without having defended theses and paid for diplomas."[35] Indeed, the only systematic defense of medical liberty came from a small circle of Comte's physician disciples, among them Georges Audiffrent, one of Comte's executors. The Comteans wished to give physicians a special role in the reorganization of society; they opposed the existing monopoly, however, because they saw in it a remnant of medieval restraints on science which the revolutionary principle of freedom of conscience had still not entirely suppressed.[36]

A less systematic but more pervasive critique of professional monopoly emerged during the Restoration and July Monarchy in the debates over the various proposals to reform medical practice and education.[37] The great national medical congress of 1845 and the legislation subsequently proposed by the minister of education, the comte de Salvandy, brought matters to a head. The key issue was not corporate privilege but the growing power of the state; the bulk of the criticism came from liberal Catholics opposed to the government monopoly over education. The state, they argued, had succumbed to fears of ultramontanism and had not fully respected freedom of instruction as guaranteed in the Charter of 1830. Many Catholics also hoped to protect the medical activities of the religious orders, whose conflict with the official personnel was, after the role of the *officiers de santé*, the most hotly disputed issue in the nineteenth-century French debates on medical practice. The primary legislative spokesman for the liberal Catholic point of view was the comte de Montalembert, whose speech to the Peers on 5 June 1847 was and remains a classic brief for the liberal field. Montalembert appealed both to the French traditions of 1789 and 1830 and to British laissez-faire models. It seemed paradoxical, he suggested, that France should have achieved political liberty, which was normally the last freedom to be won, "and that our natural and social liberty should be so limited and so nearly destroyed."[38]

In the second half of the century, the profession and the Church worked out an uneasy *modus vivendi*. The Catholics established their own medical faculty at Lille in 1877, although the state retained the exclusive right to confer medical degrees.[39] A different critique of monopoly appeared during the Second Empire within the ranks of the physicians themselves: a vocal minority rejected the law of Ventôse as an unnecessary and even undesirable crutch. The law had never been well accepted by the population and was impossible to enforce; harsher penalties would only make the law more hateful and were an anachronism in an era that was adopting industrial, commercial, and professional liberty.[40]

The rank and file of the medical corps were not, however, won over in great numbers to the liberal model. Whatever their qualms about government interference in the medical domain—which made French physicians wary, for example, of proposals for a medical order patterned after the Order of Lawyers established by Napoleon in 1810—the doctors remained protectionists, fearful of competition from empirics, foreign physicians, and even their French colleagues.[41] In a sense, the medical profession had the best of both worlds. Although the state administration oversaw education and admission to practice, the medical practitioner, once established, was free from corporate or bureaucratic oversight. The profession did not have to give up antiquack laws in return for its liberty (as happened in Germany, in the view of some German physicians); nor did it sacrifice its independence in return for monopoly. Only the empirics had reason to fear *gendarmes* looking over their shoulders.

The failure of medical liberty in France reflected not so much the strength of the profession, whose institutions remained comparatively weak for most of the century, as the strength of the state and the relative weakness of the liberal challenge. True, nineteenth-century France has often been characterized as a bourgeois liberal society, and the broad principle of free enterprise was never really in question. The state did not attempt to direct the development of the economy, although it occasionally made loans and encouraged the development of certain industries; and it was slow to enact labor legislation or public health measures that might have restricted industrial freedom. But it did retain a highly centralized and powerful administration, together with a welter of regulations that impinged directly on economic life. Laboulaye complained, with only some exaggeration, that "complete, open, and sincere" liberty had long existed in Holland, England, and America, whereas in France it was a "stranger." In the name of the public interest the state continued to regulate certain occupations. In large towns, for example, the number of butchers was fixed by ordinance; the number of bakeries was limited until 1863.[42] Why should medicine suddenly have been singled out as a field for untrammeled free enterprise—especially when, for most French liberals, a strong commitment to public health made the medical field a *noli me tangere?*

Many physicians, not surprisingly, remained dissatisfied. Several years after the law of 1892 went into effect, one of them even managed to envy the Germans, who, without the benefit of mandatory licensing, had convicted a licensed but quackish physician of swindling and manslaughter and had sentenced him to more than four years in prison; in France he would have been covered with honors and would probably be a deputy in the National Assembly.[43] Perhaps; but Germany also possessed a large body of full-time, professional, unqualified healers, whose activities were allowed and virtually sanctioned by the law. In France, de jure monopoly was at no point seriously in question. Though the forms of regulation have changed, since 1803 only state-certified personnel have been authorized to practice medicine; their uncertified rivals have been subject to prosecution for illegal medical practice.

Other Monopolies

The French model was exceptionally conspicuous, but it needs to be understood as one among various systems of mandatory licensing. Two general points should be kept in mind. First, except for the three countries and parts of a fourth that explicitly adopted the liberal model, along with a few places where medicine was basically unregulated (such as Honduras, San Salvador, Colombia, and parts of Argentina), every Western state in the nineteenth century had some form of de jure monopoly in medicine and penalties for unauthorized practice. But although regulation was the norm, and bureaucratic regulation at that, it was rarely carried out on the French model. Second, despite widespread awareness of the free field, particularly after Germany introduced it at the beginning of the Second Reich, it rarely won extensive support; aside from the few cases in which the liberal model was actually adopted, it seems not even to have come close to winning acceptance, with only one or two exceptions.

On the first point: outside the United Kingdom (before 1858) and the United States (in the early nineteenth century), bureaucratic regulation was the accepted model for policing the medical field, as in France; indeed, in most of Europe the principle of controlling medical practice through state-appointed commissions or *collegia medica* had been well established at a time when France still retained its medical corporations. Despite some stirrings of neocorporatist sentiment at the end of the century (in Italy, for example),[44] the broad principle of state regulation received no serious challenges. And yet medical practice legislation diverged in significant ways from the French model.

Perhaps the most startling feature, in some states lying outside the French sphere of the revolutionary and Napoleonic era, is the long persistence of Old Regime legislation, which characteristically included both antiquack ordinances and provisions for granting special privileges to practitioners with exceptional talents who were not regularly qualified. In Denmark, a royal ordinance of 1672, though modified by an Enlightenment antiquack ordinance of 1794 and a law of 1854, remained on the books until 1934.[45] In Sweden, the antiquack provisions of an ordinance on apothecaries (1683), a medical ordinance (1688), and a royal decree on the Collegium Medicum (1698) remained in force until the passage of a liberal statute in 1915. The old Scandinavian legislation had allowed the king to award special authorizations to healers who showed unusual ability, and this archiac and distinctly un-French provision reappeared in the liberal Norwegian law of 1871 and the Swedish act of 1915.[46] It was used; in Denmark, for example, at the beginning of the present century, one family was said to have enjoyed such a permission for almost two hundred years.[47]

More generally, despite penalties that were often severe, legislation outside France contained critical loopholes—frequently tolerating charitable healing, for example, or taking into account the results of the en-

The Politics of Medical Monopoly

counter between patient and healer. In their concern with the harm done to a privileged profession and to the patient, such statutes recall the patents and antiquack ordinances of the Old Regime; they contrast with the modern French law, which concerns only the fact of practice by an unauthorized person.

Toleration appeared in more extreme form, for obvious practical reasons, in frontier areas where university-trained physicians were rare. In Russia, for example (where unauthorized practice was not specifically penalized until 1845), a law of 1864 stipulated that an empiric would be punished only when he had used "strong remedies"; an out-and-out ban was considered in 1903 but rejected as unwise in view of the dearth of trained personnel.[48] Similarly, in the New World, Colombia and Ecuador, even after accepting the basic principle of regulation, made exceptions for regions without physicians.[49]

Finally, many states (especially in the Americas) tolerated or even recognized certain special forms of irregular practice that in Europe would either have been co-opted into medicine or dismissed as quackery. The Dominican Republic, for example, admitted electromagnetic healing and homeopathy; Brazil recognized special diplomas for homeopathy and magnetism. So, too, in Canada, despite a tradition of regulation that consistently diverged from the British laissez-faire model; British Columbia made special provisions for homeopathy, osteopathy, and nature healing.[50]

An overview of the various cases suggests widespread reluctance to adopt the French model in full, even when the principle of state regulation was unquestioned. Some legislation comparable to the French did appear (the Italian public health law of 1888, for example);[51] but the departures are more striking. The reasons are complex; in some cases the weakness and disorganization of the profession played a role, together with the success and popularity (even among political elites) of alternative forms of healing. But it is equally apparent that medical practice legislation tended to conform to indigenous legal and institutional practices, whatever the changing prestige of medicine or the organizational strength of the profession. The Ventôse law has to be understood as part of the vast reorganization of the French legal system that included the Code Napoléon; a similar observation applies elsewhere.

As for the liberal model, Adam Smith and the Manchester school found disciples in political economy in many parts of western Europe and America; yet medical libertarianism, except in a handful of cases, failed to thrive. This failure stemmed in part from the relative weakness of liberalism as a political force, even during its mid-nineteenth-century heyday; but it also reflected divergences and some fundamental ambiguities within the liberal agenda.

On the issue of corporate privilege all liberals could agree, and medical reformers sometimes denounced the guild spirit in medicine—in the Netherlands, for example, during the debates of the 1850s and 1860s on professional reorganization.[52] In a sense, though, this was an academic issue: outside the United Kingdom and the United States, professional monopoly was enforced by the state rather than by corporations. Moreover, in conservative Catholic societies such as Austria, Spain, and most of Latin America, the obvious "corporate" enemies of the liberals were the Church and the military rather than Anglo-American-style corporations or the professions, in whose ranks the liberals were themselves disproportionately represented.[53]

As for the role of the state, liberals found themselves caught in a classic and now famous bind. Though they hoped to promote individual liberties and free enterprise, it also seemed essential, as Jeremy Bentham had argued, for the state to use its police powers in certain domains to protect the social welfare. Public health was invariably one such domain. Its importance can be seen, for example, in the Netherlands, where liberals were arguably stronger than in France but where the key medical practice legislation was passed during the second cabinet of Jan Rudolf Thorbecke, the great liberal leader. As premier he supported free trade, but he was eager to see the state intervene in the fields of health, education, and welfare.[54] A fortiori, progressive intellectuals living in what they saw as more backward societies looked to the state as a motor of social and economic progress. Perhaps the most revealing case is that of Spain (which gave liberalism its name); the ideal government of Spanish liberals was not that which governed least but a bureaucratic machine centered in Madrid.[55] The one real challenge to professional monopoly came with the September Revolution, which established freedom of instruction, of the press, of association, and of religion and seriously considered the question of freedom of occupation. But even then, although the control of medical practice deteriorated between 1868 and 1874, the principle of professional monopoly prevailed; proposals for medical liberty failed during the discussions on the constitution in 1869 and during three subsequent sessions of the Cortes.[56]

Apart from Spain, where it took a revolutionary republican episode even to challenge monopoly, one ambiguous case stands out from the rest. In Mexico, as in parts of western Europe, professional freedom appeared on the liberal agenda in the second half of the nineteenth century. In a sense it prevailed, but essentially by default. Mexican liberals in the decades following independence (1821) were on the whole Benthamite utilitarians for whom the public welfare was the decisive test of any policy.[57] In keeping with these principles, the liberal constitution of 1857 guaranteed freedom of instruction but provided that the law could determine which occupations required a qualification. In theory, an organic law was to resolve this question, and medicine would surely have been included among the regulated professions, but despite several abortive efforts over the next half-century, it failed to materialize. If the legislative debates are any indication, concerns about intrusions on professional and even more especially educational freedom played a role in the defeat of national legislation. Some states interpreted the constitution to mean that practice remained free in the interim; others, together with the Federal District, held that old legislation remained in effect, in some cases adopting new measures to improve enforcement. And so, although regulation continued to take place at the local level, Mexico remained without a uniform professional monopoly.[58]

In a handful of other cases the free field was explicitly adopted. It remains to see why.

The United Kingdom

Medical practice in the United Kingdom during the first half of the nineteenth century (1801–58) was subject in theory to a bewildering regulatory network that in many ways recalls the institutions of Old Regime France. The legislation of Great Britain and Ireland gave licensing powers to some twenty institutions and to the archbishop of Canterbury. The licensing bodies included the universities of England, Scotland, and Ireland, together with the colleges and corporations in London, Edinburgh, Glasgow, and Dublin that governed practitioners of the three traditional branches of medicine: the physicians, surgeons, and apothecaries. The London surgeons had separated from the barbers in 1745 and organized as an independent City company, which in 1800 was elevated to the status of a royal college. (A new charter in 1843 renamed it the Royal College of Surgeons of England and authorized it to appoint fellows.) The Society of Apothecaries had existed as a London guild since 1617. At the beginning of the century neither institution had a monopoly or coercive powers comparable to those of the Royal College of Physicians, but each jealously guarded the privileges of its special sphere, maintaining the tripartite division of the medical field more or less intact in the capital. In the provinces, however, these distinctions had become increasingly blurred—after about 1730 the terms "surgeon" and "apothecary" were often used interchangeably—and medical practice outside the urban seats of the licensing bodies was essentially unregulated.[59]

The early nineteenth century saw several proposals for a new form of medical organization that would coordinate the activities of the various branches of medicine on a national scale. The Royal College of Physicians hoped to see all practitioners subjected to its control. A rival proposal by the Scottish-educated physician Edward Harrison urged creating a single medical register that would blur the old distinctions of rank. He also placed great emphasis on policing the activities of unqualified practitioners; the College took a broader view of the subject, arguing that it was necessary to distinguish between quacks and the imperfectly qualified, whose ministrations were preferable to domestic medicine or popular remedies.[60]

In 1813 the London apothecaries drafted a bill that was a compromise between the College's and Harrison's versions. Although much weakened through the intervention of the College, it passed in 1815 and extended the authority of the Apothecaries' Company from London to all of England and Wales. Although the apothecaries lacked coercive powers, it nevertheless became a punishable offense to practice the profession without certification.[61]

Licensees of the Society of Apothecaries had been entitled to attend patients as well as to dispense since the Rose case went against the Royal College of Physicians in 1703/4. They also performed minor surgery. (They were not permitted, however, to charge for medical advice.) Surgeons treated internal as well as external diseases; if they took the license of the Society of Apothecaries (L.S.A.), they were also entitled to dispense. By the 1830s, holders of the L.S.A. typically became members of the Royal College of Surgeons as well. Even in London, the old corporate lines were breaking down, and the men who practiced medicine and surgery increasingly became known as "general practitioners." But the law did not recognize a professional monopoly in general practice; and the College of Surgeons still lacked monopoly of title and repressive powers.[62]

The gaps and defects in the existing legislation greatly impeded the prosecution of unqualified practitioners. Under common law, anyone might practice medicine, though at his own risk. Prosecutions for unauthorized practice under statute law were infrequent and ineffectual, and they often

The Politics of Medical Monopoly 247

involved encroachment by trained personnel on a corporate monopoly. The Royal College of Physicians, which had long ago ceased to prosecute empirics, brought its last case in 1828 against Dr. Edward Harrison. The Society of Apothecaries prosecuted eighty-six persons in England and Wales between 1820 and 1832—an average of fewer than seven a year (and this number included some qualified surgeons).[63]

Medical men agreed on the need for reform. Legislative action was hindered, however, by the sharp conflict between two major interest groups: general practitioners and modest provincial physicians (usually graduates of the Scottish faculties) on the one hand, and the medical elite on the other—the London fellows and licentiates of the Royal College and medical graduates of Oxford and Cambridge.[64] The former would have liked to see medical practitioners included on a single list for the entire kingdom, ignoring or even abolishing the old hierarchy; their rhetoric abounds in denunciations of corporate privilege. They were also the most eager to suppress practice by the unqualified. Most argued for state control; some, for a ministry of medicine.[65] The Royal College of Physicians naturally wished to retain its prerogatives, and although it hardly favored quackery, it opposed the device most often suggested for combating it: the single national mandatory certification, enforced by the state. In the late 1840s, the College yielded some ground on the question of unqualified practice, accepting in principle that it should be repressed by the civil magistrate, but it continued to the end to object to the single minimum standard for qualification.[66]

Practitioners outside London recognized the need for a professional association that would represent their interests in this conflict and serve as a political counterweight to the London corporations. The key organization was the Provincial Medical and Surgical Association (founded in 1832), which in 1856 became the British Medical Association. It issued a strong call for prohibiting all medical and surgical practice by any but legally qualified persons, and in 1851 it formed a Committee on Quackery, which campaigned against homeopathy, proprietary medicines, and government patents for remedies.[67]

During the 1840s and 1850s, Parliament considered seventeen projects for medical reform; the bill finally adopted as the Medical Act of 1858 was the sixteenth. The act created a General Council of Medical Education and Registration, whose members would include representatives of the existing licensing bodies, together with practitioners nominated by the crown. Regional licenses were abolished, and all legally qualified personnel would be included in a single medical register. The old licensing bodies, however, continued to certify practitioners, and they did so in the separate fields; not until 1884 did the two colleges establish a conjoint board for examinations in medicine and surgery.[68]

The 1858 legislation eliminated all penalties for unauthorized practice; after abolishing corporate monopolies, Parliament could not stomach the notion of creating a new crime called illegal medical practice. It did, however, impose certain disabilities on practitioners whose names did not appear in the Medical Register. In addition to not being able to style themselves "physician," "surgeon," "apothecary," or "doctor," they could not serve as military medical officers or hold appointments in the poor or sanitary administrations or any similar government office; they could not sue for fees. Only the registered could deliver legal attestations; only they would be exempt from ordinary military, community, and jury duties. The law prescribed a penalty for falsely assuming a title or falsely claiming to be listed in the Register and a much stiffer penalty for securing a place in the Register through fraud. This was the essence of the definitive model: all practitioners must identify themselves correctly. The government would be free to choose its official physicians, and it would choose the certified.

Not surprisingly, the Medical Act of 1858 has given rise to diverse and sometimes conflicting interpretations. The key point here, though, is that the corporations lost the privilege of conferring an exclusive right to practice and the power to prosecute empirics. Indeed, the law was a liberal victory in the sense that it abolished the last vestiges of corporate monopoly while instituting only the weakest form of bureaucratic regulation—even if, as a concession to vested interests, it left the corporations in place and allowed them to retain their powers of certification. The act obviously stopped far short of the radical reforms of the French Revolution; where the French had slain the monster of privilege, the English were content to draw its teeth.

The discussion so far has emphasized the conflicting interests of rival groups of practitioners; this disunity indisputably weakened the profession's ability to act as an effective lobby for protective legislation and resulted in an enactment that was wholly satisfactory to neither side. But the debates over medical reform also reflected more general political cleavages. The "Whig" position strongly favored reform, and particularly a restructuring of the old hierarchy; any state health council would have to include representatives from all parts of the profession. At the same time, it held that the principle of laissez-faire precluded restrictive measures against empirics so long as they did not misidentify themselves. (Further to the left, some medical republicans could be found among British radicals—including a few qualified practitioners who were particularly hostile to the old monopolies). The "Tory" position was that the corporations should be retained with their privileges as the governing bodies for any new system of medical regulation. As David Cowen argued in a seminal article more than a decade ago, the contests can best be understood in the context of the larger debate over liberty and laissez-faire.[69]

To a far greater extent than the French, the British developed a critique of professional monopoly that borrowed from two strands of liberal thought: the attacks on special privilege and on excessive state power. The first theme figured most prominently in the debates that preceded adoption of the Medical Act in 1858; with the elimination of corporate monopolies the issue of state interference naturally came to overshadow it. Although the General Medical Council in fact had no powers to act against unqualified practice, compulsory public health measures showed the state's willingness to intervene in at least some medical affairs, and, as medical libertarians were well aware, the rank and file of the profession continued to prefer stricter regulation. The antistatist position found its classic expression in the 1840s in a series of articles that Herbert Spencer wrote for *The Nonconformist* (most appropriately, since unorthodox medicine had long been linked to religious dissent); as restated in his celebrated *Social Statics* (1851), the argument for "equal freedom" in medicine, as in other domains, received wide attention in both Britain and the United States. Perhaps the only radical liberal statement to rival Spencer's in its sustained invective against regulation appeared in the work of the physician and publicist James John Garth Wilkinson, editor of Blake, translator of Swedenborg, antivivisectionist, and, for most of his career, a convinced homeopath. Spencer and Wilkinson, though, are only the most prominent examples of a large medical libertarian school in Britain that passionately advocated "free trade" in medicine and suspected even such mainstream liberals as Gladstone (who believed that every patient should be free to choose his own physician) of selling out to the profession. On the other side, even some of the harshest critics of medical empiricism hesitated to call for repressive legislation. The middle road in Britain lay far to the left of its French counterpart.[70]

The debate in the United Kingdom flared up with renewed intensity in the 1870s, in part because three proposals, all unsuccessful, were made to reform medical licensing. Wilkinson issued a new tract entitled *A Free State and Free Medicine*, which argued against the Contagious Diseases Prevention Acts of 1866–69, as well as against professional monopoly. In

1871, the Mancunian school of medical political economy established (in Manchester, naturally enough) a quasi-official organ, *Medical Freedom: The National Free Medical Adviser*, which supported a libertarian and homeopathic program. During the following decade the principle of medical liberty held firm. T. H. Huxley, who served in 1882 on a Royal Commission on the Medical Acts, expressed the general sentiment even of many reformers when he deemed a strict monopoly "impracticable." Economic protection of qualified practitioners did not raise a question of public interest; as for protecting the public, Huxley wrote, "I think it is very much wholesomer for the public to take care of itself in this as in most other matters; and, although I am not such a fanatic for the liberty of the subject as to plead that interfering with the way in which a man may choose to be killed or cured is a violation of that liberty, yet I do think that it is far better to let everybody do as he likes."[71]

The United States

Although the beginnings of bureaucratic regulation had appeared in two American colonies not long before the Revolution, regulation during the early national period depended heavily on state and local societies established by special incorporation laws. This arrangement of course somewhat resembles corporate regulation in Old Regime France. In America, though, penalties were either light or (in New England) nonexistent; it has been argued that the license of the medical society was essentially honorific. By 1800, thirteen of the sixteen states had a corporate licensing system, and this regime persisted in the Northeast and in parts of the old Northwest. In the South, however, state licensing boards were created, and penalties were harsher than elsewhere. (The Louisiana territory, with a strong tradition of regulation under French and Spanish rule, established a licensing board in 1808.) In addition to licensing legislation, some states also passed antiquack laws (New Jersey, for example, in 1813 and 1818). Regulation, then, was the general rule; among the older states, only Pennsylvania, North Carolina, and Virginia lacked medical practice statutes. It is important to keep in mind, however, that a number of states attached no penalty to illegal practice or simply barred the unqualified from suing for fees. The legislation also contained significant loopholes; New York, for example, during much of the time its regulatory legislation was in effect, opened the medical field to domestic practitioners using "any roots or herbs, the growth of the United States." Finally,

Massachusetts and Connecticut made special concessions to medical graduates of Harvard and Yale, respectively, and other states later came to accept a diploma from any chartered medical school in lieu of a license.[72]

Starting in the early 1830s, penalties for unlicensed practice were abolished; in some states the entire regulatory system disappeared. By 1845, at least eight states lacked licensing legislation; some ten others had repealed it; and Ohio had even revoked the incorporation of the state medical society. By 1849, it was said that only New Jersey and the District of Columbia retained any effective control of medical practice. In 1854, New Jersey suspended the licensing privileges of the state society, and thereafter it sufficed to possess a medical diploma from any institution. Though some remnants of a licensing system remained, the American medical field was the freest in the Western world. Europeans who looked to America saw a pilot model of democratic medicine.[73] Americans who looked to Europe could find nothing to compare with it. "Even in Switzerland," wrote a contributor to the *National Quarterly Review* in 1861, "there is no such liberty as that which allows the ignorant speculator to put the credulous to death with impunity." France and Germany (it seemed to him) had strict and zealously executed laws; no wonder that shoemakers, tailors, and liquor dealers left the Old World and set up as doctors in the "land of liberty."[74]

Why was medical practice legislation so seriously weakened or even discarded in the quarter-century preceding the Civil War? The arguments for repeal were various. A poor record of enforcement, coupled with popular resistance, convinced many legislators and some physicians that the laws were unworkable. The provision that the unqualified could not sue for fees meant simply that unlicensed practitioners would demand payment in advance. Heavier penalties turned them into martyrs and aroused popular support. Moreover, the increasing importance of medical diplomas and the corresponding decline of professional society licenses had rendered many statutes almost meaningless. In a number of states, finally, the Thomsonian botanical medical sect proved a powerful lobby.[75] In New York, for example, the Thomsonians bombarded the state assembly with thousands of petitions—"more . . . than on any other subject which has occupied the attention of the present Legislature," a committee report noted in 1840.[76] One indication of the sect's influence: in Maryland, an 1838 law whose effect was to allow anyone to practice medicine for pay was actually entitled "An Act to Authorize Thompsonians [sic] to Charge and Receive Compensation for their Services and Medicine."[77]

But the issue was also politically charged. Indeed, the attack on medical licensing laws formed part of a larger leveling campaign against monopoly, special privilege, and chartered corporations, a campaign infused with the rhetoric of democracy and the American revolutionary tradition. One New York State legislator, an advocate of repeal, charged that "the people of this state have been bled long enough in their bodies and pockets" and declared that it was time that "they should do what the men of the Revolution did: resolve to set down and enjoy the freedom for which they had bled."[78] The Thomsonians, whose explicit slogan was to make "every man his own physician," were closely associated with Jacksonianism. In their attack on the licensing laws, some Thomsonians emphasized free trade and called for repeal of the "medical tariff." More commonly they assailed defenders of licensing as "aristocrats" and descendants of the Tories. Some voiced a distrust of formal learning.[79] When Alexis de Tocqueville visited the United States in 1831, he observed that lawyers constituted America's closest equivalent of an aristocracy, "the only counterbalance to democracy in that country";[80] he might have added a footnote on physicians had he talked to a member of one of Samuel Thomson's Friendly Botanical Societies.

The republican challenge to medical aristocracy was not new in the 1830s; it was a product of the American Enlightenment, which had accepted Smith's critique of professional privilege in medicine and carried it several steps further. The most cogent statement of this position appears in the work of Benjamin Rush, who saw in the American Revolution a "disorganizing force" in the tradition of primitive Christianity and the Protestant Reformation. Just as the Revolution had diffused political knowledge beyond a narrow elite by establishing a republican form of government, so medical knowledge would be widely disseminated. In Rush's medical utopia, medicine and surgery would occasionally be needed, but for the most part health care would be domestic, and "fathers will instruct their sons, and mothers their daughters, in the principles of medicine."[81]

When Rush expressed these views in a lecture delivered in 1796, a similar vision had been largely discredited in France. In America, which had experienced no medical Terror, medical republicanism lived on, though primarily among nonphysicians. By the 1830s, political radicalism had combined with religious revival and medical empiricism into the strange hybrids that were the first medical sects. Elias Smith, who served Thomson for a while as a general agent, was a Baptist preacher who hated ministers, physicians, and lawyers. Wooster Beach, the founder of Eclecticism (an offshoot of the botanical movement), was a medical school graduate who abominated "King-craft, Priest-craft, Lawyer-craft, and Doctor-craft" and assisted the Workingmen's party in New York in its opposition to medical licensing. The Thomsonians attacked the "idle rich" and paper money and praised workingmen as the "producers of wealth."[82]

To the emotional attacks on despotism and class interest, the Thomsonians added a soberer argument based on fundamental legal principles. The interweaving of the various legal and political appeals can be seen, for example, in an 1830 tract by an Ohio Thomsonian named William Hance. Like most of his fellow sectarians, Hance saw in medical practice legislation a threat to "the liberties of a free people"; but he couched his critique in broad constitutional terms, comparing medical liberty several times to freedom of religion and pleading for toleration. He denounced the Ohio law that allowed only practitioners licensed by the state medical society to accept compensation, arguing that it established special legal privileges in violation of the Constitution. The consequences of abusive medical regulation, Hance suggested, could be seen in France, where it had degraded the profession; and he cited with approval a comment by the *American Lancet*, which called French medical legislation "a mere excuse for undermining the civil rights of a large class of the people, and annihilating the liberties of their neighbors."[83]

The exact nature and extent of the connections between medical libertarianism and the Jacksonians have been a subject of dispute. In New York, for example, a higher proportion of Whigs than of Democrats voted for repeal of licensing legislation, probably in an attempt to expand their electoral support. But the actual party alignments are less important than the general sympathetic hearing accorded antimonopoly rhetoric and the alacrity with which many legislators responded to Thomsonian petitions. Without a widely persuasive political argument espoused by an active lobby, the laws on unqualified practice, whatever their defects, would have remained on the books.[84]

In the middle decades of the century, two related factors helped firmly establish the free field in America. To a far larger extent than in Europe, dissident sects (chiefly the homeopaths and Eclectics) won converts among the ranks of the medical doctors, making it increasingly difficult for physicians to present a united front against their unqualified rivals. Moreover, the United States, unlike Europe, truly enjoyed freedom of medical education. In the period 1810–40, twenty-six new medical schools were created and from 1840 to 1875, forty-seven more.[85] The proliferation of proprietary medical colleges, some of them notorious "diploma mills," made it extremely difficult to standardize qualifications. In the middle decades of the century, proponents of regulation faced formidable obstacles.

Germany

The history of professional monopoly in nineteenth-century Germany, as in France, must begin with the French revolutionary wars and Napoleon, for the French invaders brought with them a double message: the law of Ventôse and abolition of the guilds.

Napoleon directly imposed the French legislation of 1803 in the annexed territories of the Rhineland. In the German context, the new French model was not of course a radical innovation: bureaucratic control of medicine had been commonplace in the various states of eighteenth-century Germany, and indeed in France the most vigorous enforcement of the Ventôse law, carried out by a system of cantonal physicians in the Bas-Rhin, owed much to the German model of medical police.[86] Moreover, outside French-administered territory Old Regime antiquack ordinances remained in effect, and some states adopted new ones. Penalties were characteristically harsh, and a few regulations (Baden and Saxe-Weimar) actually called for punishing patients who had resorted to quacks during epidemics.[87]

Anticorporatism and the notion of freedom of trades (*Gewerbefreiheit*) were more novel, however, and they were to have far-reaching implications. In the annexed and French-dominated territories, including Jerome Bonaparte's Kingdom of Westphalia, guilds were abolished. French influence was also visible elsewhere. Prussia allowed free practice of certain trades in some provinces in 1806, and an edict of 1810 granted all subjects *Freizügigkeit*—the right, upon receipt of an appropriate license, to practice their trade anywhere in the kingdom. Though the guilds were left standing, obligatory membership and special corporate privileges were abolished. The history of Prussian guild legislation after 1815, when the defeated French ceded the Rhenish provinces, is complex. In 1845, though, a general Ordinance on Trades established that freedom of occupation could be limited only in the public interest, although it retained forty closed occupations and still allowed handicraft workers to organize in corporations. Under pressure from craftsmen, compulsory membership returned in 1849, but in the 1860s a few ordinances somewhat widened freedom of occupation again. In other German states the old guild system largely prevailed, and some states that had abolished guilds under French influence restored them in 1815. In the years after 1848, however, the trend was toward accepting the more liberal Prussian model.[88]

At the same time that Germany was edging toward occupational freedom, the various states adopted a series of new measures against medical empiricism; unlike the eighteenth-century regulations, which usually appeared in state medical ordinances, the nineteenth-century versions were generally incorporated in comprehensive state penal codes. The first code to punish quackery as such was adopted in Saxony in 1838; it treated charlatanism as one of several "deceptive" trades, lumping medical practitioners together with solicitors, notaries, and jobbers. More specific provisions subsequently appeared in the codes of Württemberg, Baden, Hannover, Hesse, Prussia, Saxony, Brunswick, and Bavaria. The codes generally defined the offense as unauthorized practice motivated by greed. Thus despite some measure of occupational freedom, the practice of medicine was far from free.[89]

Moreover, the profession itself, unlike its American or French counterparts, was "unfree": everywhere the state controlled the licensed physician's activities to some degree. For a period in Hesse-Nassau he was a state civil servant, paid a stipend (which he could supplement through private practice), and told where to settle. In Bavaria the municipality could veto his decision to marry. Even where medical practitioners were not automatically civil servants, a large proportion in fact held state appointments—in Prussia in 1827, for example, 49 percent of university-trained physicians and an even larger percentage of surgeons first class. What was more, functionaries and nonfunctionaries alike could typically be disciplined like civil servants, and they could lose their official approbation for reasons entirely unrelated to professional competency—as happened after 1848, for example, to many practitioners who had compromised themselves in the *Vormärz* (pre-1848) period through membership in *Burschenschaften*, or student clubs. In Prussia, the physician's position of dependency was symbolized by an obligatory official oath, in which he not only promised to practice to the best of his ability but also pledged loyalty to the king.[90]

The free medical field was introduced in Prussia and the North German Confederation by a rider attached to a much more general measure, the *Gewerbeordnung* (GO), or trades ordinance, of 1869. In a sense it was an afterthought. The Prussian "emergency" trades legislation of July 1868, which suspended the old legislation on corporations and certification of competency in the trades, said nothing about abandoning mandatory certification in medicine. The drafters of new legislation for the Confederation had rejected such a move, and the government trades bill in 1869 expressly provided for examinations and mandatory licensing of medical personnel (section 29). Debate in the Reichstag developed only after the second reading of the bill, prompted by a petition from the Berlin Medical Society and a belated motion by several deputies, who asked for *Kurierfreiheit* (freedom of healing). Their leader was a physician, Wilhelm Loewe (Loewe-Kalbe), the last president of the German revolutionary parliament of 1848–49, who had been much influenced by his experiences as a young man in America; with Rudolf Virchow, he was one of the leading proponents of democractic-liberal reforms in medicine.[91] Loewe denounced the existing restrictions on practice as puerile and unnecessary. They were ineffective; they protected privileges which the beneficiaries were prepared to renounce; and they were unworthy of the education and good judgment of the people, who were mature enough not to require such leading strings.

The president of the Chancellery, Rudolf von Delbrück, was caught unprepared; at the next reading of the bill, he returned prepared to voice the government's opposition to amending section 29. Like Thorbecke in the Netherlands, this liberal leader of a free-trade government opposed *Kurierfreiheit* in the name of public health. The free field, however, carried the day and was included in the trades ordinance. Shortly after the creation of the Reich in 1871, the GO was extended to the entire empire; in 1889 it took effect in Alsace-Lorraine, where the law of Ventôse had applied for the better part of a century and where, thanks to German influences, professional monopoly had probably been more strictly enforced than anywhere else in the French provinces.[92]

It is apparent that without support from the medical profession, *Kurierfreiheit* would have failed; indeed the subject might not even have been broached. Later in the century, to explain the peculiar behavior of the Berlin Medical Society, proponents of regulation often suggested that the doctors had followed a conscious "*do ut des*" strategy: they gave up the quack ban as a concession in order to win repeal of section 200 of the Prussian penal code, which compelled physicians to assist persons in urgent need of medical attention, under threat of a 20–500-thaler fine. Physicians considered this *Kurierzwang* oppressive; if they gave up monopoly, this and other forms of state control might be lifted as well, producing a consistently liberal arrangement with extramural freedom for the unlicensed and intramural freedom for the doctors—above all, the right to choose their own patients. This interpretation, though plausible, is untrue. Although it was hostile to government interference, the Society

The Politics of Medical Monopoly

insisted that the *Kurierzwang* should not be seen as a *quid pro quo* for the quack ban, since the latter, just as much as the former, was intended to protect the public rather than physicians. Professional monopoly seemed both impracticable and (as an apparent form of special privilege) politically unpopular; and so the doctors pronounced themselves ready to abandon it. Their renunciation of this "anachronism" was not a cynical means to an end, a "Paris is worth a Mass"; if anything this revolution of the professionals recalls the night of 4 August 1789, when the French Second Estate renounced its "feudal" rights.[93]

The most that can be said to diminish the significance of the Berlin Medical Society's intervention is that the signers of the petition did not represent the German medical profession as a whole.[94] The Society's membership was largely drawn from an academic medical elite, who, like the fellows of the Royal College of Physicians in London, had little direct experience of competition with unqualified practitioners. Although proposals for *Kurierfreiheit* had emerged elsewhere (for example, at a convention of scientists in Dresden in September of 1868) and although the Society had been joined in its petition by physicians from Verden, Neisse, and Tiegenhof and by the Union of Hessian Physicians, its proposal most clearly reflected the concerns of the Berliners.[95] A Bavarian commentator writing in 1871 recalled that physicians in southern Germany were taken by surprise when the North German Confederation adopted the free field.[96] It is even possible, had Germany possessed a unified professional organization comparable to the strongly antiquack British Medical Association, that the Berlin proposal might have failed; German medical organization was confined, however, to fragmentary local societies, which were mostly concerned with scientific rather than professional issues.[97]

The GO introduced a classic liberal model for the medical field. The state retained privileges of certification; only the authorities of a *Land* with a university could confer licenses, and then only on persons who had taken a state examination at a German university. The license could be withdrawn only for deontological offenses unless the qualifying examination could be shown to have been invalid. It would be possible to practice without a license, but the unqualified would be legally responsible for the consequences, and usurpation of a medical title would be punishable with a 300-mark fine or imprisonment. In addition, the unlicensed were subject to certain restrictions (extended in a new redaction of 1883): they could not hold government offices that required qualified physicians; they could not work as itinerant healers or practice midwifery professionally; they could not run sanitariums, insane asylums, or maternity hospitals.

The free field survived a series of reforms of the legislation on trades toward the end of the century. The new redaction of 1883 exempted a number of occupations and businesses from the general principle of *Gewerbefreiheit*, including fishing, apothecaries' shops, teaching, practice as a lawyer or notary, professional emigration agencies, underwriters, railway entrepreneurs, public ferryboat operators, and the merchant marine—but not medicine. Even when a dance teacher, a gymastics instructor, the proprietor of a bathing establishment, or a secondhand dealer could be put out of business if he were shown to be "unreliable" (1900), no medical practitioner could be prevented from plying his "trade."[98] Moreover, when the GO became law for the entire Reich, it superseded all other legislation; the individual *Länder*, although they had the right to oversee public health and regulate the activities of medical practitioners, could not prohibit unlicensed practice as such. (A post-GO ordinance in Württemberg that prohibited unlicensed practitioners from treating cancer and other "dangerous" diseases had to be rescinded.) Except for some restrictions imposed by military order during the war of 1914–18, *Kurierfreiheit* remained an unaltered fact of professional life until the National Socialists finally ended its seventy-year reign.[99]

Kurierfreiheit emerged from a proposal by liberal intellectuals, and its origins can best be understood if seen in the larger context of German liberalism. Progressive physicians of the *Vormärz* period, like most liberals, would have embraced the values expressed in Alexander von Humboldt's essay on the limits of state activity. Humboldt rejected the authoritarian and paternalist state (*Obrigkeitsstaat*) and with it state control of religion, the press, manners, economic enterprise, and social behavior—though at the same time he held that the state should protect its own rights and those of its subjects and that it had a role to play in encouraging the development and welfare of the individual.[100] This latter proviso was consistent with state repression of unqualified practice; and yet implicit in the liberal critique of "tutelage" (*Bevormundung*) is an argument against medical practice legislation: if the people are sufficiently enlightened, it would be possible—and worthier of their dignity as individuals—to allow them to discriminate on their own between good and bad healers. This position emerged in the radical liberal critique of medical regulation that developed after 1848 (most clearly in Virchow's writings); proponents of medical freedom attacked special privileges but emphasized even more strongly the political implications of excessive state power. Virchow called for equal rights for all citizens and criticized quack bans as the means through which "the sick are placed under the tutelage of the guardian police state."[101]

As the thrust of German liberalism shifted after midcentury, it displaced some of the ideological underpinnings of the free field. Liberalism before 1848 had been basically philosophical, divorced from interest groups, and relatively unconcerned with free trade; in the 1850s the emphasis moved from an attempt to use political change for economic reform to a program that retained some of the old concern with education and enlightenment but urged using economic change for political reform. (The Congress of German Economists in 1858 exemplifies many of these trends.) The ideas of Adam Smith had become common coin; three decades of experience with rival and then gradually consolidated trade unions—partly directed against foreign competition but also intended to promote free trade within Germany—had encouraged proponents of laissez-faire. At the end of the 1850s, the first major concessions to industrial freedom appeared. By 1865, sixteen states in the German Confederation, with a population of 34 million, had industrial freedom; seven, with 7 million, were moving toward it; and only twelve, with 3.5 million inhabitants, retained the old controls in full. Despite opposition from handicraftsmen, who condemned industrial freedom as "the child of the red republic," the principle prevailed; in the North German Confederation, Bismarck, who would not grant the middle classes full political freedom, gave the industrial bourgeoisie laissez-faire (July 1868). In 1869, the GO confirmed the specific principle of professional freedom in its opening words: "The practice of an occupation is permitted to everyone." Though the guilds were not abolished, the rescission of their privileges sharply reduced their powers, and the government encouraged their voluntary dissolution and made arrangements for transforming them into free associations.[102]

The free medical field must be seen in the context of the campaign against guilds and for freedom of trade and occupation that was central to the successful liberal economic program of the 1860s. Support for *Kurierfreiheit* owed something, too, to the more timid liberal critique of state paternalism. In the end, it was intervention by the Berlin medical elite that ensured repeal of professional monopoly: but the Society acted at a favorable moment and appealed to a legislature already hostile to special privilege and state control of occupations.

Switzerland

This last case illustrates very clearly the constraints that politics can impose on professional monopoly—but only because of exceptional institutions, at the other extreme from France's Paris-centrism. Swiss liberalism followed a path not very different from that taken in Germany, supporting constitutional reform, equality of opportunity, free trade, and industrial freedom. Yet neither the liberals of the middle decades of the century nor the radicals who came to form the dominant party at the end of the century (Freisinnig-demokratische Partei) seem to have advocated *Kurierfreiheit* as an official program;[103] and although some physicians (in Vaud, for example)[104] argued that the profession should renounce its privileges, their influence on the Confederation was not comparable to that of the Berlin Medical Society in the North German Confederation. But what happens in Swiss national politics says relatively little about Swiss political life; it is only by considering the situation at the cantonal level, together with the role of direct democracy in the legislative process, that it is possible to understand the fate of medical monopoly.

During the French Revolution and Empire, many Swiss medical institutions remained intact despite major disruptions of local sovereignty and political life: annexation of the bishopric of Basel, the Valtellina, and Geneva; the creation of the Helvetic Republic (1798); and Napoleon's Act of Mediation (1803, annulled in 1813), which created a federal republic under French control (and in theory guaranteed freedom of settlement and occupation). Geneva, following the revolutionary example, adopted the principle of professional freedom in 1798, although the municipality continued to examine and approve medical practitioners as before. After 1803, annexed territories (including Geneva) were subjected to the law of Ventôse; elsewhere Old Regime medical practice laws remained in effect.[105]

At the end of the eighteenth century and during the first few decades of the nineteenth, the different cantons adopted new medical laws or penal codes containing provisions for regulating medical practice. They varied widely in severity. At one extreme, a Zurich law of 1836 required all practitioners to obtain a government patent; Geneva, at the other extreme, was highly tolerant of unqualified practice. Somewhere in between stood Vaud, where legislation allowed the cantonal health council to issue one-month authorizations to practitioners who wished to perform surgical operations and where the Council of State could authorize a healer to practice in one region upon proof of "practical knowledge."[106] Without the law of Ventôse or comparable legislation at the national level, the Swiss in the first two-thirds of the nineteenth century could not even agree on a definition of a qualified practitioner. In 1867, the federal council ratified a concordat, accepted by most cantons, which provided that examinations at a Swiss university would suffice for legal recognition in any of the cantons that were parties to the agreement. This arrangement solved the problem of identifying trained personnel, but it offered no uniform procedure for dealing with the unqualified.[107]

The political debate over medical liberty in Switzerland came into its own only in the second half of the century. The climate in the first decades of the century was hardly propitious: official guilds, which had been abolished in 1798, were reintroduced in 1803 outside the annexed territories and flourished later under the restoration imposed by the Congress of Vienna. Although the strength of economic regulation varied from canton to canton, many of them closely controlled prices, limited the number of people in a given trade, and imposed strict guild obligations. (One of the few striking exceptions was Geneva, which since the end of the eighteenth century had enjoyed full freedom of trade.) Theoretical liberalism opposed such corporative and state restrictions on commerce; Christoph Bernoulli fueled the debate with his essay *On the Disadvantageous Influence of the Guild System on Industry* (1822). In practice, however, liberal economics, which was almost always unpopular among artisans, began to win wider support only with the "regeneration" movement of 1830–31, and even then liberals proceeded much more cautiously in all spheres than had the Helvetic Republic.[108]

Social and political liberalism gained a tentative foothold with the Regeneration. Constitutional commissions established representative democracy in the various cantons, and moderate liberals came to hold power in most of them. It has been estimated, however, that only a fifth of the electorate actually voted. In January 1848, Tocqueville could still argue (with some justification) that "Switzerland is one of the countries of Europe in which the Revolution went least deep, and the following restoration was most complete." Apart from the cantons that practiced direct democracy, freedom of religion, speech, the press, and association were as much or more unknown than to subjects of most of the monarchies; "liberty" in Switzerland meant primarily privilege or independence.[109]

In the two or three decades after Tocqueville wrote, however, Switzerland emerged as a stronghold of liberalism, where economic and social (as well as political) freedoms were consecrated in the federal constitutions of 1848 and 1874. The first, adopted in the wake of the Sonderbund War of 1847–48 (which pitted the Radical majority in the federal diet against a league of reactionary Catholic cantons), proclaimed intercantonal economic freedom; it did not guarantee freedom of occupation, although it allowed the individual cantons to do so. Some, such as Baselstadt, retained the old guild restrictions; but most, including the larger and industrialized cantons, embraced industrial freedom. During the 1860s, the cantons began to turn to direct popular democracy, introducing the popular legislative referendum and initiative. In 1874, the new federal constitution (article 31) guaranteed freedom of commerce and industry throughout the Confederation, with certain restrictions, among them the proviso that the cantons could decide when to require a government patent for the practice of the scientific professions. In addition, during the 1870s, various cantonal constitutions guaranteed freedom of religion, of the press, of speech, and of occupation. The constitutions were to be essentially bills of rights: "Through the constitution, full freedom is given fundamental recognition." Perhaps nowhere else in Continental Europe was liberty so pervasive a commonplace of political culture.[110]

The second half of the century, particularly after the German GO, saw a series of proposals to abrogate the earlier restrictions on medical practice, based in part on a sense that the laws could not be enforced but in part, too, on the conviction that the laws went against the grain of Swiss political institutions and offended public opinion.[111] Debates flared up during the 1870s and 1880s in Appenzell Ausser-Rhoden, Glarus, Graubünden, Schaffhausen, Baselland, Neuchâtel, and Geneva. Although in several cantons the liberals succeeded in building up enough momentum to present bills before cantonal councils and assemblies, their efforts were rarely successful. In 1878, for example, the Great Council of Thurgau rejected a bill that would have opened medical practice to all adult citizens. As late as 1904, the cantonal council of Zurich considered and rejected by a huge majority (158 to 5) a proposal for an open field. When through a legislative initiative the question was submitted to a popular referendum, it failed by a proportionally smaller but still substantial margin (51,319 to 22,881). The great majority of cantons retained their ban on medical practice by unqualified persons.[112]

In Neuchâtel the free field had the support of a substantial part of the medical profession, hostile to the old German conception of the medical civil servant and fascinated by the freedom of teaching and practice evident in England and the United States. (In America especially, it seemed exceptionally easy to embark on a chosen career or switch to a new one; one liberal cited with approval the varied, not to say checkered, career of Ulysses S. Grant.) Under the Swiss constitution, all citizens were equal before the law; was not medical liberty as fundamental as freedom in religion, politics, education, and science? The best model to follow would be not the French but the current English and German one: freedom of practice but full legal responsibility for any torts committed.[113] In April

1875 the Great Council of Neuchâtel adopted just such a measure in a new law on public health: official titles would be protected, and only legally qualified personnel would be allowed to hold government appointments, but no restriction was placed on unlicensed practice as such.[114]

Neuchâtel's discreet decision to reject the regulatory model of its French neighbor attracted little international attention. Not so the introduction of the free field into two German-speaking cantons in the northeastern part of the Confederation: Glarus and one-half of the old canton of Appenzell, which had been divided in 1597 for religious reasons. Both Glarus and Appenzell Ausser-Rhoden were small, mountainous, sparsely populated, and largely Protestant; both were "pure democracies," among the handful of cantons that possessed the *Landsgemeinde*, or annual assembly of voters (adult male citizens). (In contrast, the tiny half-canton of Appenzell Inner-Rhoden was almost exclusively rural and Catholic; indeed, the constitution officially recognized Catholicism, although religious freedom was in theory guaranteed. Although the canton had the lowest literacy rate in Switzerland, it seems not to have been unusually hostile to professional medicine.) Neither Glarus nor Appenzell Ausser-Rhoden had remained entirely bucolic; both included textile manufacturing centers, and Glarus in particular boasted a well-developed cotton-printing industry. Not surprisingly, industrial freedom had come relatively early, in the Regeneration era—although the abolition of Old Regime restrictions on enterprise did not mean unbridled laissez-faire; Glarus was a pioneer in social legislation and was the first state in Europe to impose a ten-hour work day.[115]

In Glarus, the *Landsgemeinde* of 1874 passed a resolution opening every branch of medical practice to all citizens, who would be restrained only by civil responsibility for any errors they committed. A subsequent ordinance limited civil service appointments and medico-legal functions to qualified personnel.[116]

Appenzell Ausser-Rhoden adopted at the outset a more restricted free field for citizens with full civic rights. "Higher surgery" and obstetrics were excluded. Only qualified physicians could give testimony in legal cases; positions in public health and government service were similarly open only to the qualified. The principle of legal responsibility was severe: if a healer caused physical or mental injury to his patient, he could be fined up to 1,000 francs; for a second offense he could be barred from practicing. But anyone could call himself a physician (a departure from the German/English model), and Appenzell, unlike Germany, imposed no ban on itinerants.[117]

The case of Appenzell is of particular interest because it clearly reveals a split between a loosely organized popular movement against professional monopoly and a local government much more favorable to official medicine. A public health ordinance of 1865 required a special examination for physicians except, after 1867, for those who had been approved under the federal concordat. In 1870, a movement originated in the town of Waldstatt that would have extended the right to practice medicine to persons who were not legally qualified but were solid citizens of the canton. Proponents of the free field submitted a petition to this effect, which the Great Council refused to bring before the *Landsgemeinde* on the grounds that free practice was not "useful and good" for the fatherland. A blacksmith of Waldstatt, however, used the popular initiative to bring the question before the *Landsgemeinde* of 1871, where the people supported him. In anticipation of this outcome, the Great Council had prepared the measure that limited surgery, obstetrics, legal medicine, and government appointments to qualified physicians; the *Landsgemeinde* accepted this amendment.

The abolition of professional monopoly reflected both the liberal conviction that everyone should be free to choose a medical adviser and a deep-seated popular distrust of professionals, experts, and academics that recalls the sans-culotte mentality in the French Revolution. Like other opponents of government intervention, notably their libertarian counterparts in England, the Appenzellers also found it difficult to accept public health regulations. A new health law was submitted, in accordance with the provisions of the cantonal constitution, to the *Landsgemeinde* of 1882; the crux of the measure was the appointment of local health commissions and of three district physicians for the canton. Although the law respected the principle of free practice, it was criticized for sneaking medical coercion in through the back door, and the assembly of voters rejected it "with a shout of joy." The voters subsequently refused a federal measure on compulsory immunization, repealed a cantonal ordinance on vaccination dating from a smallpox epidemic of 1865, and voted down a new health law, although the drafters had taken great care to exclude any mention of district physicians. On the question of compulsory immunization, the Appenzellers were joined by a majority of their fellow citizens in the confederation, but on health reform in general they proved an exceptionally consistent and stubborn lot; a very liberal sanitation ordinance, which of course respected free medical practice, finally won approval in 1887.[118]

The Swiss experience does not simply reflect the power of empirics or the weakness of the medical profession. Some rural areas, it is true, lacked

The Politics of Medical Monopoly

qualified personnel until early in the twentieth century; in Valais, for example, peasant and artisan healers played a large role, especially as bonesetters, until they eventually yielded to the arrival of more physicians, panel practice, and X-rays. Homeopathy was popular in Baselland, and in several regions members of religious sects practiced lay homeopathy. In the larger cities and areas where Protestant medical sects were strong, patients were attracted to Christian Science and healing through prayer; many parallels could be drawn with the United States. But empirics were not conspicuously more numerous than elsewhere. Nor were they better organized; it was only in the 1920s that a group of healers, primarily from Appenzell Ausser-Rhoden and Baselland, formed an Organization for the Free Practice of Medicine.[119]

Switzerland's distinguishing characteristic—in contrast not only to France but also to Germany and even the United States—was the extreme diversity of its legislation on medical practice. A drive for medical freedom throughout the confederation would undoubtedly have failed. But Swiss political institutions made a few pockets of *Kurierfreiheit* possible, for two reasons. The first was of course the high degree of political autonomy granted the culturally and religiously disparate units of the confederation; views held by only a minority in the confederation at large could predominate locally. The second factor was the system of direct democracy, in the form of the popular initiative and (in a few cantons) the legislative powers vested in the annual assembly of voters. *Kurierfreiheit* emerged, not so much because the unqualified healers fought for it effectively or because the medical profession failed to oppose it but because the local citizenry insisted on it.

The Fate of the Free Fields

The last two decades of the nineteenth century and the first decade of the twentieth saw a coordinated movement against medical empiricism whose influence was felt throughout the Western world and beyond. New medical practice legislation appeared not only in France, the United States, and elsewhere in Europe and the Americas but also (for example) in Egypt and Japan. Physicians, joined in some cases by laymen, formed antiquack societies in the United States and Europe; in 1905, following a suggestion from Dr. J. M. van Elk of the Dutch antiquackery organization, several interested national societies created an international league against charlatanism.[120] Probably no other period has seen so concerted an effort to eradicate illegal practice. To many observers, medical liberty appeared a thing of the past. By the second quarter of the century, only a handful of de jure free fields remained; in 1927, a report on 197 countries and territories revealed that only 19 lacked a clear ban on empiricism: 12 "primitive" countries, the United Kingdom and four of its colonies, Appenzell, and Germany. (Some jurists would have added Sweden and Norway.)[121]

Was the nineteenth century, then, an exceptional era for medical politics, a period when the old privilege system broke down without being replaced by a monopoly securely based on the indisputable superiority of medical science? Was medicine subsequently depoliticized at the end of the nineteenth century and the beginning of the twentieth, deciding the issue once and for all? Certainly the liberal wave had crested. No major new free fields emerged, unless one counts Sweden in 1915 and a brief interlude in the Soviet Union that followed the adoption in 1922 of new penal legislation that failed to prohibit unqualified practice. (In May 1925, a decree of the People's Commissariat for Health and Justice introduced a firm quack ban.)[122] But a review of the four free fields inherited from the nineteenth century raises doubts about the presumed association between post-Pasteurian "scientific" medicine and professional monopoly.

Great Britain

In Britain, as in most of western Europe, pressure mounted in the first decade of the twentieth century for stricter regulation of medical practice and the sale of proprietary remedies, which were widely advertised in the popular press. In a prominent series of articles for *Vanity Fair*, Henry Sewill criticized the weakness of the General Medical Council and called for a government commission to investigate the subject. The council itself felt hobbled by existing legislation; in 1907 it appointed a committee to investigate medical practice laws in the colonies and in foreign countries. Its report showed, to no one's surprise, that many states had much stronger statutes. The following year the council passed a resolution calling for the appointment of a royal commission "to inquire into the evil effects produced by the unrestricted practice of medicine and surgery by unqualified persons." All that emerged in the end was a report, published in 1910 under the aegis of the Local Government Board, that carefully documented widespread unqualified practice by persons ranging from chemists and herbalists to faith healers and witches but offered no specific recommendation for stronger action against them.[123]

In subsequent years, the registered practitioner's exclusive right to participate in state-financed panel practice further widened the gap between the licensed and unlicensed, and the unqualified were subjected to additional disabilities: they could not dispense dangerous drugs or certain therapeutic substances; they could not treat venereal disease.[124] And yet, even though such professionals as dentists (1921) and opticians (1959) have won a monopoly, the modified free field has remained in British medicine; it was embodied in the Medical Act of 1956, which replaced the 1858 statute, and in subsequent legislation adopted in 1969.[125] State prosecution for illegal practice on the French model went against the grain of English legal and political traditions, even after the "nineteenth-century revolution of government" and even during the era of the full-blown welfare state. Many would doubtless have agreed with the author of the 1880 Cobden Prize Essay at Oxford when he argued that Britain had had "too much laissez-faire" and that it needed "more paternal government—that bugbear of the old economists."[126] But medical liberty was another matter. If anything, medical libertarianism gained new ground in the campaign against coercive public health measures: in 1909, while the investigation of the "evil effects" of unauthorized practice was in progress, Parliament passed a law that all but ended compulsory vaccination, dismantling the system that had been erected during the middle decades of the nineteenth century.[127] Even if a suitable medical practice law had been passed, new institutions would have been needed to enforce it; the General Medical Council had refused from the outset to assume the burden of prosecuting even persons who falsely used a protected title, forcing private physicians to form a Medical Defense Association to combat abuses.[128] Scotland had a public prosecutor, but it was difficult to envisage anything in Britain even remotely comparable to the French bureaucratic network of prefects, subprefects, and *procureurs*. National restrictive legislation was about as likely in the United Kingdom as definitive regulation in France—as likely, in other words, as the upheaval in political culture that would have made it possible.

Switzerland

In Switzerland, the regulation of medical practice continued to depend on local legislation, despite an unsuccessful effort in the 1920s, on the part of a number of physicians, to include a quack ban in the proposed new federal code.[129] The only instrument available at the intercantonal level was an agreement accepted by all but three cantons for the evaluation of secret remedies. The limited free field survived in Neuchâtel until 1919[130] and in Glarus until 1920, when it yielded to a concerted campaign by the medical profession, led by the director of the cantonal hospital. The physicians quickly won the support of the local authorities; in a passionate speech to the *Landsgemeinde* of that year, the cantonal president urged that in the future professional practice of medicine be allowed only to persons who had received a federal diploma, with the exception of those who had practiced for ten or more years in the canton and could prove sufficient capacity to win the authorization of the government council. The *Landsgemeinde* adopted the resolution—with the result, according to one physician, that unlicensed healers either gave up their practice or moved to Appenzell.

The Appenzellers persisted in their resistance to official medicine and hygiene. In 1906, the canton did accept a federal pure food and drug law, but the first inspector was not appointed until 1910. The 1907 *Landsgemeinde* rejected a law on the sale of poisons, and new public health bills failed in 1911 and 1912. The libertarian sanitation ordinance of 1887, although revised in 1924, was not replaced until 1965—and even then the free field remained. "The population," one physician noted, "considers this permission to doctor freely, when and where the opportunity presents itself, as an old popular right, which it tenaciously supports." With the defection of Glarus in 1920, Appenzell reigned supreme as the Swiss capital of medical empiricism. In 1928, this tiny canton with a population of 55,000 had 84 full-time healers, or one unqualified practitioner for every 655 inhabitants.[131]

One other case from the 1920s suggests how vulnerable medical practice laws could be to popular hostility. A Catholic priest of St. Gallen, who practiced "poison-free" herbal healing (he was popularly known as the *Kräuterpfarrer*, or herb priest), attracted so wide a following through his practice and publications that the cantonal authorities decided to intervene. He responded by moving to Graubünden, where he abandoned the priesthood and devoted himself exclusively to herbal healing. Fearing a new intervention by the authorities, his supporters used the popular initiative to propose a revision of the medical practice law, and the voters of Graubünden passed it by a large majority. The amendment lifted the previous quack ban and allowed nonphysicians to use "poison-free" herbal methods, but only if they possessed full civic rights, demonstrated sufficient knowledge of medical botany, and passed an examination by a government-appointed commission that would include one physician. This provision was far from full *Kurierfreiheit*, and the *Kraüterpfarrer* seems to have been the only person to take advantage of it. But the case does illustrate the power of direct democracy. A somewhat similar situation obtained in Baselland, where the empirics successfully used the popular initiative to organize a referendum on the free field. Although their draft measure went down to defeat, it was said to have resulted in laxer enforcement of the medical practice laws.

Germany

The German case presents an apparent paradox: the free field survived well into the twentieth century, despite advances in medical science (in which Germany was the acknowledged world leader) and a marked decline in liberalism. Several reasons could be cited to explain the failure of professional monopoly, including the vitality of the health movement and the extraordinary popularity of the various forms of parallel medicine, from Prießnitz's hydroptherapy to baunscheidtism (which used a form of acupuncture). The interpretation here, however, will point to the relative political effectiveness of the two major interest groups concerned: the qualified professionals and their unqualified rivals.

The liberal consensus that provided such favorable conditions for the introduction of *Kurierfreiheit* in 1869 began to erode soon afterward, following the economic crisis of 1873. Free trade ended in 1879; the next few years saw a reversal of the liberal Reich, the end of the *Kulturkampf* that had united Bismarck with the liberals against the Catholics and the Center party (who were hostile to laissez-faire), and the first of the measures on labor and social security that were to make Germany a leader in social legislation. In 1884, the old National Liberal leader Johannes Miquel remarked on the passing of laissez-faire individualism: "We no longer recognize that kind of liberalism which defines progress as the diminution of the state's role, an exclusive reliance on self-help, and the rejection of all public social and economic organizations; which identifies free trade with political freedom; and which will not let the state do anything in economic affairs, because the state cannot do everything."[132] Among other things, the state now adopted regulatory measures that infringed on professional liberty. As was noted earlier, revisions of the GO allowed licensing in a number of critical occupations (though not medicine). In the medical field, a series of innovations curtailed the freedom that physicians might have expected under a liberal regime. The health insurance system (1883) undermined the principle of free choice of physician and the "liberal" honorarium paid directly by the patient. A Prussian medical ordinance enjoined physicians not to charge the poor for their services and to compensate by raising fees for the rich. In addition, new institutions with disciplinary powers emerged, among them elected but official chambers of physicians; licensed practitioners guilty of unethical conduct could be tried by "courts of honor" (*Ehrenräte*).[133]

Although an undercurrent of medical libertarianism persisted among physicians, it seemed increasingly out of place in an era of social Catholicism, state social welfare, new restrictive public health laws, and tighter controls over professional conduct. Germany, moreover, had a long tradition of medical police and more generally of state regulation; it was a land where, as one opponent of *Kurierfreiheit* pointed out, there was a law against jumping off a streetcar before it had come to a full stop.[134] How, then, to account for the survival of the free field?

In order to make sense of *Kurierfreiheit*'s seventy-year career, it would be helpful to divide it into two roughly equal phases. In the last three decades of the nineteenth century, the free field was not seriously challenged. The crisis came in the first decade of the new century. By then the healers were well entrenched and politically stronger than the doctors, who failed to dislodge them or even to place serious restrictions on their activities; and they sustained this advantage for the next several decades.

Opposition to the GO built up only slowly at the end of the nineteenth century, in large part because many physicians, who remembered the German profession's traditional subordination to the state, feared that any new legislation would bring more obligations than rights. Although by the late 1880s a number of medical organizations and congresses (including the Berlin Medical Society) had called for legislative reform,[135] it was still possible to argue at the end of the century that the profession stood to lose *Freizügigkeit* and what remained of the free choice of patients. More generally, physicians remained wary of taking on a political battle that they might well lose; colleagues who refused to accept their status under the GO, one resigned Bavarian physician wrote, were like Frenchmen who would not accept the loss of Alsace-Lorraine: it was perfectly acceptable to feel this way, so long as one just went on quietly hoping.[136] Pragmatists pointed to the various options for prosecution under existing legislation: the worst offenders could be tried for manslaughter or injury through negligence; for deception or swindling; or (after 1901) for the unauthorized sale of secret remedies. A law of 1909 on unfair competitive practices could be applied to members of any occupation who knowingly made untrue and misleading statements to win customers—though it was necessary to prove economic injury, a prospect the doctors found distasteful. At the local level, the *Länder* (although they could not restrict medical practice as such) could bar activities that were not "objectively" healing—oneiromancy and cartomancy, for example; they could regulate empirics' publicity, force them to register, oblige them to declare their methods and type of practice, or even to keep a register that would be open to inspection.[137]

By the first decade of the twentieth century, however, a consensus had emerged in the profession that favored restrictive legislation at the national level;[138] on this point the physicians remained firm, even while their British, Swedish, and Norwegian colleagues resigned themselves to accepting unsatisfactory but politically popular legislation.[139] The government, under pressure to propose a medical practice law, submitted two drafts of a bill to the Reichstag, in 1908 and 1910. This legislation would not have prevented unlicensed persons from practicing; the idea was to contain them. The second draft provided that they would have to register and provide information about their training, type of practice, and methods and that they would have to keep books and show them periodically to the authorities. More important, they would be forbidden to give medical advice by correspondence; to employ "mysterious" therapies; to treat socially dangerous diseases, diseases of the sexual organs, or cancer; to use hypnosis or narcotics; to administer injections; to deliver remedies; and in general to treat any patient whose life was in danger. Finally, the Federal Council would have the right to issue other restrictions.[140]

The failure of even this moderate bill suggests how little support the physicians enjoyed. It was soon buried in committee; new elections intervened, and no new draft was subsequently presented. The minutes of the Reichstag debates show wide sympathy for *Kurierfreiheit*. The Social Democrats, traditionally hostile to the medical elite, led the opposition to the bill; their speaker ridiculed the restrictions (what was a harmful substance?—even water could be harmful in certain circumstances) and defended the nature healers, to wild applause from his socialist colleagues. Gustav Stresemann, speaking for the National Liberals, also had a kind word for the nature healers; and a member of the Center party argued that the limitation on *Kurierfreiheit* curtailed civic freedom (though a good deal of other social and economic legislation obviously did the same).[141]

Neither the Reich in its last years nor the Weimar regime abolished the free field, though subsequent legislation did somewhat narrow the permissible range of action for unlicensed practitioners. Starting in 1917, work on "pathogenic agents" required special authorization. The insurance ordinance of 1924 eliminated nonphysicians entirely from panel practice, putting them on the same footing as their British counterparts. The following year, the various parties in the Reichstag hopefully declared public health "neutral territory," arousing new expectations of medical regulation or at least restriction of unqualified practice along the lines of the 1910 bill. The results were modest: in 1927, a law barred all but licensed practitioners from treating venereal diseases and diseases of the genitals.[142]

Why did the physicians fail when they finally united in opposition to *Kurierfreiheit*? Their scientific prestige was not in doubt; but they faced a formidable political force in the unlicensed healers, who had emerged almost as a distinct profession, the *Heilpraktikerberuf*. The statistics on nonphysician healers diligently complied by some of the *Länder* show an extraordinary growth in the number of full-time unqualified practitioners under the GO. Although these figures can be criticized, the order of magnitude is clear, and these materials should be required reading for anyone who seriously believes that medical practice legislation is a mere symbol. In Berlin, the period 1879–1903 saw an increase of more than 3,500 percent in the number of empirics, as compared with a 120 percent increase in population. The ratio of full-time empirics to physicians was 1:34 at the beginning of the period, 1:3.25 at the end. In Bavaria in 1879, the number of empirics actually exceeded the number of physicians.[143]

The healers proved exceptional masters of publicity and political action. They organized conferences, gave lectures (in Berlin alone in 1928, the "biochemists" were said to give forty a month), and published innumerable tracts and books, one of which, Friedrich Eduard Bilz's work on "the new method of natural healing," was said to have sold a million copies. In some cases the healers hired academic political economists to defend their position. More than that, they organized their own institutes and a variety of professional associations and pressure groups (from the Central League for the Parity of Healing Methods to the National Syndicate for Defense Against Compulsory Laws in Medicine), which coordinated their publicity campaign throughout the Reich.[144] Apart from their own organizations, the healers enjoyed the political support of the local nature clubs, almost nine hundred strong at the beginning of the century. These organizations enjoyed extensive influence among legislators and officials, in part because they shrewdly practiced what would now be called single-issue politics. Though their strongest allegiance was to the

The Politics of Medical Monopoly

Social Democrats, they rejected any SPD candidate who favored a quack ban. In some cases they ran their own nature-cure candidates on a platform denouncing the doctor, "whose wealth is the sickness of his fellow man."[145]

As for the physicians, they had professional organizations but not effective political pressure groups. The Ärztevereinsbund, founded in 1873 as an umbrella organization for medical societies, sponsored annual conferences that regularly debated the *Kurierfreiheit* issue but rarely passed from talk to action.[146] The single most active lobby was a society for the suppression of quackery (Deutsche Gesellschaft zur Bekämpfung des Kurpfuschertums, or DGBK), founded by a group of physicians in 1903.[147] But even this organization remained largely ineffectual. It stressed education and public health over direct defense of the profession's material interests as practiced by the French *syndicats*: it published an official journal for popular consumption (the *Hygienische Blätter*), sponsored public lectures, and published tracts on the evils of charlatanism.[148] These tame activities aroused little enthusiasm among physicians; nor did the society's attempt to enlighten the public—in imitation of the temperance movement's direct appeal to the people—win many converts. The working class was equally hostile to antiquack and temperance propaganda; although it was said, somewhat improbably, that the *Maandblad* of the Dutch antiquack society was read in workers' circles, German workers—and the Social Democrats—sneered at the physicians' proselytizing.[149] Nor was this all. The DGBK was badly troubled by internecine quarrels, organizational problems, and a chronic lack of funds, exacerbated after the war by inflation. In the end its achievements were modest: it persuaded one deputy, the dermatologist Peter Rudolf Wilhelm Struve, to defend the 1910 bill in the Reichstag (unsuccessfully); it occasionally won administrative actions against unlicensed practitioners; and it successfully fought an attempt by nonphysicians to win recognition as forensic experts.[150]

Given the well-entrenched political position of the healers, it seems most unlikely that *Kurierfreiheit* could have been ended in a parliamentary regime. It was the rise to power of the Nazis that doomed *Kurierfreiheit*—ironically, because their leadership included some of the nature healers' most ardent devotees.[151] As early as 1933 the National Socialists proposed to regulate the healers at the national level for the first time by organizing them into a single corporation, the Heilpraktikerbund Deutschlands, in which membership would be obligatory. After reorganizing the medical profession, the Third Reich in 1939 adopted a crucial penal law that specifically punished unauthorized practice of medicine. Henceforth anyone other than a licensed physician who wished to practice medicine would need special permission, and this authorization would be granted only in exceptional cases; those who received it would be allowed to use the title "practitioner of natural medicine." *Kurierfreiheit* thus ended—but not quite. The law defined medical practice as the treatment of diseases, suffering, and injuries, leaving open to question whether purported treatments (or treatment of imaginary diseases), preventive medicine, and cosmetic surgery constituted medical practice. Moreover, a grandfather clause ensured that anyone who had practiced as a healer before the code was adopted could continue to do so, though he had to join the Registered Union of German Healers. (Schools for healers were outlawed, however; the new generation of nonphysician practitioners was to be nipped in the bud.)[152]

The National Socialists settled the long controversy over *Kurierfreiheit*, not out of deference to physicians (who now received only an imperfect monopoly) but as part of the program of *Gleichschaltung*—literally "putting into the same gear"—the reorganization of society and institutions to serve the National Socialist state, which completely politicized cultural and social life. *Kurierfreiheit* was the product of a "liberal democratic ideology"; in the National Socialist *Weltanschauung*, the duty of maintaining health was to replace the liberal idea of the right to one's own body. The prestige of scientific medicine did not prevent the Nazis from according state recognition to the *Heilpraktikerberuf*—in part because it already had some of the characteristics of a self-regulating profession, in part because of the *volkisch* allure of nature healing.[153] In the nineteenth century, Prussia had led the way in establishing a single medical title when it abolished the rank of surgeon second class and joined medicine and surgery (1852); now in the twentieth century, Germany had become a center for a new type of less well-trained (when not completely untrained) practitioner.

The United States

Of the major free fields, only the American was reversed in the nineteenth century: by the century's end, every state and territory except Alaska had some form of medical regulation, though generally much less stringent than the French law of 1892. Does this one case show the decisive influence of scientific medicine?

Regulation returned slowly and unevenly to the United States over a

The Politics of Medical Monopoly 275

period of two decades. The provisions of the first statutes varied widely; most states initially required only that practitioners register their diplomas—a far cry from professional monopoly. The model for strong legislation was the Illinois statute of 1877, which created a state board of health with the power to examine candidates or certify diplomas; unapproved practitioners would be prosecuted. The trend toward restrictive legislation accelerated during the 1880s and culminated in a major burst of legislative activity between 1887 and 1893. Most states either established a special board of examiners or empowered an existing board of health to examine candidates. In growing numbers they refused to accept a diploma, even from a recognized institution, as a license to practice; by 1898, twenty-two states required both a medical degree and an examination.[154]

As a concession to sectarian medicine, some states gave homeopathic physicians joint representation on the boards, together in a few cases with the Eclectics; others created separate boards. Nonregulars had a hand in licensing in all but three states at the end of the century. A few legislatures also exempted other irregulars and certain nonphysician practitioners from the licensing requirement: in Connecticut, for example the senate tacked onto the 1893 medical bill an amendment in favor of Christian Scientists and other drugless healers.[155] Many of these compromises were politically crucial; if the German profession had been willing to show similar flexibility, *Kurierfreiheit* would probably have ended much sooner than it did.

The reinstatement of mandatory licensure gave rise to a national political debate that has received surprisingly little attention.[156] In some ways the rhetoric of this period recalls the controversies of the Jacksonian era. The cast of advocates was different, however, the Thomsonians having been replaced by homeopaths, hydropaths, spiritualists, and others; and a new pattern of discourse appeared. The opponents of monopoly threw out the Thomsonians' more radical social arguments; when they criticized "class legislation," they generally meant a legal rather than a social class. The rhetoric appealed to God and Nature and to Spencer's more pragmatic arguments on the virtues of free competition; but mainly it evoked America, American law, and the American Constitution, with increasing attention to technical legal arguments. Within these limits, the antimonopolists revived the old plea for republican medicine; the emphasis wavered between an attack on special privilege and a critique of state power—of "French police [and] *gendarmerie*," as one of them put it.[157]

The contest over medical legislation pitted the regulars' professional associations (chiefly the state and county medical societies)[158] against the often well-organized lobbies of the sectarians and nonphysicians. The homeopaths had the American Institute of Homeopathy and a number of journals, such as George Winterburn's *American Homeopath*, which promoted a radical libertarian position. The Eclectics had the National Eclectic Medical Society and their own journals. Supporters of sectarian medicine founded the National Constitutional Liberty League in Boston in 1888, under the titular leadership of Joseph Rhodes Buchanan, former president of the Eclectic Medical Institute of Cincinnati; it led the fight against medical practice legislation in several eastern states.[159] Opposition was strongest in the Northeast, where the irregulars were well entrenched and where Christian Science and spiritualist healing enjoyed strong support among local elites. Three New England states were the last to yield, in 1895.[160]

After licensing legislation won passage in the state assemblies, its opponents took to the courts. Judicial review as practiced in America had no real counterpart elsewhere, and nowhere else did proponents of the free field rely so heavily on the argument that medical practice statutes violated some more fundamental law. Some irregulars maintained that they had been deprived of a property in their practice without due process, as guaranteed by the Fourteenth Amendment (1868) or that they had been denied freedom of contract or equal protection under the laws. In 1888 the Supreme Court finally ruled on a medical practice law in *Dent* v. *West Virginia* and upheld the principle that a state might make licensing mandatory.[161] Some faith healers, especially Christian Scientists, invoked Christ's injunction to heal the sick and hoped that their activities would enjoy constitutional protection under the freedom of religion clause. The state courts, however, consistently found against them when they accepted fees ("the exercise of healing for compensation . . . cannot be classed as an act of worship"). In the end, the Supreme Court affirmed that religious freedom could not override the basic criminal statutes of the land.[162] Other avenues of escape were closed as the courts and legislatures redefined "the practice of medicine" to include a broad range of activities—pretended as well as "actual" treatment, spiritual healing as well as the use of medicine and drugs.[163]

The American experience of regulation was in many ways as disappointing as the French. But the state medical practice laws in place by the beginning of the century, together with the later use of federal alcohol regulations and postal fraud statutes against purveyors of patent remedies, the initial prosecutions under the Pure Food and Drugs Act, and the vigorous voluntary efforts of the Propaganda Department (later the Bureau of Investigation) of the American Medical Association (AMA) all established the United States, not as an outpost of medical freedom but as one possible model for regulation. In Germany, where proponents of *Kurierfreiheit* had always cited free America as the example to follow, physicians turned with interest to the new developments across the Atlantic. True, America did not provide an ideal professional monopoly; various states allowed limited licenses for osteopaths, chiropractors, eclectics, mechanotherapists, magnetopaths, clairvoyants, nature healers, and others who in Germany would have been considered unqualified; in some states they had their own training programs and certifying examinations. Still, the American experience suggested that it was possible to reverse a free field, even where irregular medicine was very strong and the political culture had long been hostile to professional privilege.[164]

American's return to the restrictive model cannot be wholly explained by the growth of professional organizations or the development of a generally recognized paradigm of medical science or therapeutics. The profession was far better organized in the early twentieth century than in the second third of the nineteenth, but the most important developments occurred after the new legislation had been passed. As for the growing prestige or unity of medicine, the return to monopoly began slightly before the first major applications of microbiology in the 1890s, and medicine remained conspicuously "preparadigmatic" into the early twentieth century; one of the most difficult issues to resolve, when the licensing bodies were set up, was how unorthodox medical views were to be represented among the examiners. The most that can be said is that the gap between homeopath and "allopath" had begun to close, as the number of doctrinaire followers of Samuel Hahnemann's system declined.[165]

The success of medical practice legislation owed a good deal to another trend, external to the discipline; medicine was only one of a number of fields that moved toward tighter organization and closer regulatory supervision in the decades after Reconstruction. Twenty-four licensing statutes existed in 1870 for a total of five occupations; most concerned teachers or attorneys. Over the next three decades the states passed 171 licensing laws covering twenty occupations.[166] Other enactments involved government more deeply than ever before in America's economic life, starting with the railroads. The regulatory legislation of the late nineteenth century has been a subject of controversy; but whether such measures primarily benefited consumers or producers who wished to control or rationalize the market, they reflected a growing fear that untrammeled competition could threaten the public welfare and even liberty itself. Starting in the 1870s, a new generation of economists, many of them trained in Germany, attacked laissez-faire; where "[Adam] Smith called upon private enterprise to check and circumscribe government activity," wrote Edmund James of the Wharton School, "we are forced to call upon government to circumscribe and regulate private enterprise."[167] More generally, as Robert Wiebe has argued, the "search for order" implied greater acceptance of scientific expertise, professionals, bureaucracy, and government supervision of everyday affairs.[168] By the Progressive Era, the United States had installed a modest (and still largely decentralized) version of *la police*, which Americans had long viewed as typically French, un-American, and inimical to liberty. Unlike Britain in the nineteenth century, but somewhat like France in the period from the Convention to the Consulate, the country underwent enough of a shift in political culture to make the rhetoric of medical republicanism, briefly persuasive in the early part of the century, increasingly marginal later on. As in France, corporatism was followed by a strong anticorporatist reaction, which was followed in turn by a repudiation of "medical anarchy." Like the French medical restoration, the American sidestepped the issue of corporate privilege by vesting licensing powers in a state bureaucracy. The growing legalism of the irregulars' arguments and their appeal to the courts reflect their recognition of how far medical libertarianism had moved from political center; in a sense it was now they, not the physicians, who required protection from the will of the majority.

As a political phenomenon, the return to monopoly has puzzled some commentators. Jeffrey Berlant, in his stimulating discussion of professional monopoly in British and American medicine, finds it paradoxical that regulation should have been reestablished at the height of the antitrust movement (the Sherman Act was passed in 1890); his explanation emphasizes that the antitrust reformers were sympathetic to privileges in restraint of trade for local enterprises and small businesses, as opposed to interstate behemoths. It was not clear, though, (until the recent penetration of large corporations into the health care field) how to distinguish small from big business in medicine; some opponents of monopoly attacked the entire profession as a "trust" and compared it to the railroads. It is more important to recognize that the state medical practice laws, like the Pure Food and Drugs Act of 1906 (also a restraint on trade, and hardly favorable to small producers), answered to a version of Cabanis's argument that when the consumer cannot tell good from bad, the state must intervene to protect him.[169] Only when the public safety has been assured does the principle of minimizing restraints on trade come into play. Actions by organized medicine that have hindered free competition by li-

The Politics of Medical Monopoly

censed practitioners have been treated differently from unqualified practice. In 1889, for example, when Kansas adopted its first general legislation on trusts, it prohibited price setting and fee schedules for lawyers and physicians. At the federal level it has been difficult to prosecute under the Sherman Act because medicine is not a form of interstate commerce; but in 1943 the Justice Department won a suit that charged the AMA and the local medical society with restraint of trade in Washington, D.C., after the society expelled members who had agreed to participate in a prepaid health plan and worked with the AMA to get their hospital privileges revoked.[170]

The American case, like the German, suggests that a free field could be reversed only in a political climate that favored state intervention. The issue of monopoly was not depoliticized.

The general argument developed here is that shifts in political culture in the century and a half after 1789 had a large and perhaps dominant role in shaping legislation on medical practice and in fixing the official privileges of the profession. Monopoly was not an automatic concomitant of "modernization," and a review of the national cases would suggest that it correlates imperfectly with such indexes of modernity as economic development, literacy and mass education, scientific advance, and the therapeutic prowess of medicine. Even good professional organization did not ensure a closed field.

The French case is particularly revealing: well before the Pasteurian era, France adopted an exceptionally tight de jure monopoly. The law of 1803 is best seen as part of the postrevolutionary Napoleonic settlement, which restored order to the medical field but on new terms: no regional differences, no privilege system, no corporations. The state would grant licenses to practitioners as individuals rather than as members of a *corps*. The principle of state-enforced professional monopoly has remained a given in French political life ever since, surviving all changes in political regime, the structure of the profession, and the profession's larger relationship with the state.

Medical freedom appeared in the nineteenth century in several countries with a prior history of regulation, where liberals succeeded in challenging corporate privilege (the United States and Britain) or bureaucratic regulation (Germany and Switzerland—although here, too, antiguild sentiment played a role). The free fields had different origins and took various forms: a modified free field introduced from above in Germany and the United Kingdom; a more democratic free field, promoted from below, in the United States and Switzerland—though in the latter case the elites succeeded in introducing restrictions that brought it closer to the Anglo-German model. What the four cases have in common is that they appeared during the heyday of laissez-faire. Two of the free fields and a part of a third persisted well beyond the Pasteurian era, for essentially political reasons, in countries that had well-established medical professions and major centers of medical education and research. One free field was reversed at the end of the nineteenth century but more out of disenchantment with laissez-faire than in deference to the prowess of the new medicine.

Why did the free fields appear where they did? This essay has not attempted to develop a global interpretation, which would require a comparative history of liberalism, but any such metahistorical inquiry might begin by looking at religion. Not only was a good deal of unofficial medicine religious but medical libertarianism also echoed religious attitudes toward authority and views on the autonomy of the individual. In England and the United States, especially, medical freedom was linked to religious dissent and sectarianism; a radical Protestant tradition going back to the seventeenth century joined rejection of medical authority to distrust of the clerical hierarchy. The evangelical and revivalist movements of the eighteenth and nineteenth centuries took seriously the Christian injunction to heal the sick; John Wesley wrote a celebrated popular medical handbook, *Primitive Physick,* which proposed (as its title suggests) to restore medicine, like religion, to the laity.[171] More generally, medical liberty appears to have had links to Protestantism. All the states that adopted the free field after the French Revolution had predominantly Protestant populations (counting Prussia as the originator of the *Gewerbeordnung* and setting aside the ambiguous case of Mexico). Conversely, the free field for a time dominated the Protestant world.[172] Finally, in addition to specific religious convictions, a history of pluralism and political toleration for confessional diversity helped bolster support for the open field; medical libertarians everywhere took freedom of conscience as a model.

Monocausal explanations in history are rarely satisfactory, and an ideological interpretation of professional monopoly will be no exception if it is pushed too far. This essay has already pointed to the political role of competing interest groups and medical institutions. Some weight should also be assigned to the prestige of medical science and public health during the period when the program for professional monopoly was at its acme; the theme appears, for example, in some of the Swiss debates of the early twentieth century. (In an earlier period, inversely, the connections between therapeutic skepticism and medical libertarianism deserve to be explored further.) What is disturbing, however, about invoking the "advance of science" as the sole or prime explanation of the modern professional monopoly is that it is not easy to show that either lawmakers or the public moved from mass disbelief to mass acceptance of the physician's superiority. Even in the early modern period, "quacks" were blamed for depopulating states whose rulers considered men, like bullion, a measure of national wealth.[173] It is a mistake to suppose that educated practitioners received privileges simply as a favor because they belonged to the same social stratum as the political elites.[174]

It is not even certain that the issue of professional privilege has been resolved once and for all. True, by the 1930s, the outlook for medical liberalism was fairly bleak; after World War II it barely survived as an ideology, although a very consistent proponent of laissez-faire such as Milton Friedman could still justify free enterprise in medicine in terms very similar to those used by Adam Smith almost two centuries ago.[175] It is conceivable, though, that a society hostile to the tyranny of the experts may whittle away at professional privileges, even while the consumption of medical technology continues to grow. The current American trend toward the deregulation of economic activities threatens to extend to medical practice, that last untouchable, first for the libertarian left and now for the libertarian right. A recent volume of papers on policy for the 1980s published by the Hoover Institution contains an essay on health care that recommends replacing mandatory licensing with voluntary certification and encouraging consumers to seek cheaper "substitutes" for physicians and dentists.[176] In France, a strong current of opposition has developed to the Order of Physicians (created by Vichy and reestablished after the Liberation on terms more favorable to the profession), to which all legal practitioners theoretically must belong; the more radical critics plead for *la médecine libre*.[177]

One can only speculate about the future of free enterprise in medicine. To the historian, the course of monopoly says something both about the development of professional power and about the fortunes of liberalism. It confirms, at the end of the nineteenth century, what most French physicians saw after the Revolution—a failure of liberal optimism, of the sense that free citizens could learn to recognize their own true interest. It also suggests the limits of professional power and reminds the historian of France that the relatively favorable position of the French profession was not the rule, even on the Continent. Control over the medical domain had to be fought for and could be lost. Not only competing interest groups but also political and legal institutions and even ideological pressures could impede the professional project. Any model of professional power must take into account such contextual constraints.

Notes

This essay is a substantially revised version of a paper presented to the Davis Center seminar, 25 January 1980. A fellowship year at the Center, funded by the National Endowment for the Humanities, provided the opportunity to undertake this project; a Davis Center travel grant enabled me to complete the bulk of the research at the New York Academy of Medicine, the College of Physicians of Philadelphia, and the National Library of Medicine in Bethesda. I would also like to acknowledge a grant-in-aid from the American Council of Learned Societies, which made possible a six-week research trip to Paris and London. I have greatly profited from the constructive criticisms of the other Davis Center fellows and participants in the seminar, especially Gerald Geison and Charles Rosenberg, and from suggestions offered by Stanley Katz, John Womack, Jr., and Barbara Rosenkrantz. Mårten Liander helped with materials in Scandinavian languages. Special thanks to Linda Burcher Ramsey, who read and commented on several versions of the paper. Responsibility for errors remains, of course, my own.

Unless otherwise indicated, all translations are mine.

1. Eliot Freidson, *Profession of Medicine: A Study of the Sociology of Applied Knowledge* (New York, 1970), pp. 16, 21. See also Magali Sarfatti Larson, *The Rise of Professionalism: A Sociological Analysis* (Berkeley and Los Angeles, 1977), pp. 23–24, 36–37.
2. For the argument that the professions have promoted credentials as an instrument of social stratification, see Randall Collins, *The Credential Society: An Historical Sociology of Education and Stratification* (New York, 1979), pp. 138–47 (on medicine) and passim; the *locus classicus* is Max Weber, *Economy and Society: An Outline of Interpretive Sociology*, ed. Guenther Roth and Claus Wittich, trans. Ephraim Fischoff et al. (New York, 1968), p. 1000 and passim. On professions, the state, and social elites, see also Freidson, *Profession of Medicine*, pp. 72–73, and Larson, *Rise of Professionalism*, p. xii (leaning heavily on Freidson); on the "professional project": Larson, pp. 50–51 and passim. For a Weberian approach that specifically rejects Parsonian functionalism and develops a political model of "monopolization strategies," see Jeffrey L. Berlant, *Profession and Monopoly: A Study of Medicine in the United States and Great Britain* (Berkeley and Los Angeles, 1975). Berlant's study has the merit of clearly emphasizing the political context of monopoly and the importance of constraints such as antimonopolistic legislation (e.g., p. 128). His argument emerges, however, as a sort of whig history in reverse, decrying the expansion of professional power. Even the British Medical Act of 1858,

which created a free field in medicine, appears as an alternative "monopolization strategy," devised in response to liberal pressures; and the modernization thesis appears in political guise: "The rise of the medical profession did not occur in either [the United States or Great Britain] until certain traditional political relationships passed away" (p. 302). Recently, Paul Starr has argued for an interpretation of professional authority more complex than either the functionalist or the "power theorist" approach (*The Social Transformation of American Medicine: The Rise of a Sovereign Profession and the Making of a Vast Industry* [New York, 1982], introduction and pp. 143–44). Authority arises from lay deference and from what he calls "institutionalized forms of dependence," which derive from changes in the society as a whole. Starr is only incidentally concerned with the problem of legal monopoly, but his work is of interest for the present study because it offers an analysis of the ways in which professional power and autonomy may be weakened by larger social and economic trends.

3. Paris, 1981. This is the title as it appears on the cover and spine; on the title page it reads *La médecine entre les savoirs et les pouvoirs: Histoire intellectuelle et politique de la médecine française au XIXe siècle*. But the text makes clear that what Léonard calls *le bio-pouvoir* did not depend on technical efficacy.

4. See, for example, Jacques Léonard, *Les médecins de l'Ouest au XIXe siècle*, thesis, University of Paris IV, 1976, 3 vols. (Lille, 1978), pp. 932–33 and chaps. 11–12; James G. Burrow, *Organized Medicine in the Progressive Era: The Move toward Monopoly* (Baltimore, 1977); Noel Parry and Jose Parry, *The Rise of the Medical Profession: A Study of Collective Social Mobility* (London, 1976); and Henry E. Sigerist, "From Bismarck to Beveridge: Developments and Trends in Social Security Legislation," *Bulletin of the History of Medicine* 13 (1943): 365–88.

5. A useful survey is Henry Graack, *Kurpfuscherei und Kurpfuschereiverbot: Eine rechtsvergleichende, kriminalpolitische Studie* (Jena, 1906). For the texts of the major legislation (in German translation), see Graack, comp., *Sammlung von deutschen und ausländischen Gesetzen und Verordnungen, die Bekämpfung der Kurpfuscherei und die Ausübung der Heilkunde betr.* (Jena, 1904); also the various volumes of the *Annuaire de législation étrangère* (Paris, 1874–).

6. On this point see Jacques Léonard, "La Restauration et la profession médicale," *Historical Reflections/Réflexions historiques* 9 (1982):81.

7. On the general history of licensing and regulation: Sigerist, "The History of Medical Licensure," *Journal of the American Medical Association* 104 (1935): 1057–60; Richard H. Shryock, *Medical Licensing in America, 1650–1965* (Baltimore, 1967); and Benjamin Spector, "The Growth of Medicine and the Letter of the Law," *Bulletin of the History of Medicine* 26 (1952):512–20.

8. Norwegian law of 1871 in Graack, *Sammlung*, pp. 108–9; the restrictions (including limits on diseases that could be treated by nonprofessionals) were tightened further by a law of 19 June 1936 (*Norsk lovtidende* [Oslo, 1936], 19 June, no. 9, pp. 366–68). For Sweden: *Svensk författningssamling för 1915*

(Stockholm, 1916), no. 362, pp. 893–95. The current law (30 June 1960) eliminates the right of the crown to issue special authorizations but still does not penalize unlicensed practice as such; see *Svensk författningssamling för 1960* (Stockholm, 1961), no. 408, pp. 1099–1101.

9. Nicholas Culpeper, *A Physicall Directory, or a Translation of the London Dispensatory Made by the Colledge of Physicians in London* (London, 1649); Benjamin Rush, "Introductory Lecture on Imposture in Medicine" (1796), The Library Company of Philadelphia in the Pennsylvania Historical Society, ms. Yi 2/7400 f.5. On Culpeper, see Christopher Hill, *The World Turned Upside Down* (New York, 1973), p. 240; and Charles Webster, *The Great Instauration: Science, Medicine and Reform, 1626–1660* (New York, 1975), pp. 267–71 (and pp. 256–62, on the critique of monopoly during the Puritan Revolution). For an overview of French medical institutions during the Revolution: Michel Foucault, *The Birth of the Clinic: An Archaeology of Medical Perception*, trans. A. M. Sheridan Smith (New York, 1973), chap. 3.

10. Sir George N. Clark, *A History of the Royal College of Physicians*, 3 vols. paginated continuously [vol. 3 by A. M. Cooke] (Oxford, 1964–72), pp. 54–66, 77–78, 507. See also Bernice Hamilton, "The Medical Profession in the Eighteenth Century," *Economic History Review*, 2d ser., 4 (1951):141–69.

11. John R. Guy, "The Episcopal Licensing of Physicians, Surgeons, and Midwives," *Bulletin of the History of Medicine* 56 (1982):528–42; Leslie G. Matthews, "Licensed Mountebanks in Britain," *Journal of the History of Medicine and Allied Sciences* 19 (1964):30–45.

12. Paul Delaunay, *La vie médicale aux XVIe, XVIIe, XVIIIe siècles* (Paris, 1935), chap. 9; text of law in François André Isambert et al., *Recueil général des anciennes lois françaises, depuis l'an 420 jusqu'à la Révolution de 1789*, 29 vols. (Paris, 1821–33) 20:508–17. Caroline C. Hannaway, "The Société Royale de Médecine and Epidemics in the Ancien Régime," *Bulletin of the History of Medicine* 46 (1972):257–73; Matthew Ramsey, "Traditional Medicine and Medical Enlightenment: The Regulation of Secret Remedies in the Ancien Régime," *Historical Reflections/Réflexions historiques* 9 (1982):215–32.

13. Reinhold August Dorwart, "The Royal College of Medicine and Public Health in Brandenburg-Prussia, 1685–1740," *Medical History* 2 (1958):13–23; Dorwart, *The Prussian Welfare State before 1740* (Cambridge, Mass., 1971), pt. 5, esp. chap. 16. See also Manfred Stürzbecher, *Beiträge zur Berliner Medizingeschichte: Quellen und Studien zur Geschichte des Gesundheitswesens vom 17. bis zum 19. Jahrhundert*, Veröffentlichungen der Historischen Kommission zu Berlin beim Friedrich-Meinecke-Institut der Freien Universität Berlin, vol. 18 (Berlin, 1966), pp. 27–34 (text of 1685 Brandenburg ordinance) and passim. Cf. the discussion of bureaucratic regulation in Old Regime Switzerland in Eugène Olivier, *Médecine et santé dans le pays de Vaud au XVIIIe siècle, 1675–1798* (Lausanne, 1939), pp. 13, 32–33, 41–42.

14. José María López Piñero, "The Medical Profession in Sixteenth-Century Spain," in Andrew W. Russell, ed., *The Town and State Physician in Europe*

from the Middle Ages to the Enlightenment, Wolfenbütteler Forschungen, vol. 17 (Wolfenbüttel, 1981), pp. 85–98; Michael E. Burke, *The Royal College of San Carlos: Surgery and Spanish Medical Reform in the Late Eighteenth Century* (Durham, N.C., 1977), chap. 3.

15. Carlo Cipolla, *Public Health and the Medical Profession in the Renaissance* (Cambridge, 1976), pp. 8, 70–73; Richard Palmer, "Physicians and the State in Post-Medieval Italy," in Russell, ed., *Town and State Physician*, pp. 47–61, esp. pp. 49–51, 56–57.
16. Shryock, *Medical Licensing*, pp. 8, 14, 17–18; David L. Cowen, *Medicine and Health in New Jersey: A History* (Princeton, 1964), pp. 12–14.
17. Berlant, *Profession and Monopoly*, pp. 191–203; Joseph A. Kett, *The Formation of the American Medical Profession: The Role of Institutions, 1780–1860* (New Haven, 1968), p. 14, citing *Massachusetts Special and Private Statutes* 1 (1781): 25.
18. Dorwart, "Royal College," pp. 13, 21.
19. See, for example, Matthew Ramsey, "The Repression of Unauthorized Medical Practice in Eighteenth-Century France," *Eighteenth-Century Life* 7 (1982):118–35.
20. The text of Smith's letter to Cullen (20 September 1774) is printed in Ernest Campbell Mossner and Ian Simpson Ross, eds., *The Correspondence of Adam Smith* (Oxford, 1977), pp. 173–79 (quotation p. 178). See Manfred S. Guttmacher, "The Views of Adam Smith on Medical Education," *Bulletin of the Johns Hopkins Hospital* 47 (1930):164–75. Smith was replying to a memorial written by Cullen, who was president of the Edinburgh College of Physicians, for the duke of Buccleugh, who had just been elected an honorary fellow. For the text, see John Thomson, *An Account of the Life, Lectures and Writings of William Cullen, M.D.* (Edinburgh, 1859), pp. 468–72. No direct rebuttal to Smith's letter has been found, but Cullen explained his opposition to free competition in medicine more fully in a Latin discourse pronounced two years later at the University of Edinburgh; Thomson gives an English translation, pp. 482–86.
21. On the development of liberal thought, Guido de Ruggiero's tribute to the liberal tradition, written during the early years of Fascism, is still a useful overview: *The History of European Liberalism*, trans. R. G. Collingwood (1927; reprint, Boston, 1959).
22. Matthew Ramsey, "The Ideology of Medical Power: The Program for Professional Monopoly in France, 1770–1830," paper delivered at the annual meeting of the American Historical Association, Dallas, 30 December 1977; see also David M. Vess, *Medical Revolution in France, 1789–1796* (Gainesville, 1975), on military medicine and medical education. On the law of Ventôse: René Roland, *Les médecins et la loi du 19 ventôse an XI* (Paris, 1883).
23. See Merlin of Thionville's denunciation of physicians, 18 Frimaire II (8 December 1793) in *Archives parlementaires de 1787 à 1860*, 1st ser. (1862–), vol. 81, p. 128. For a physician's response to the "medical terror," see, for

example, Archives Nationales (Paris) (hereafter AN) F⁸ 165, Serrières, "Discours sur l'influence de la Révolution," and F⁸ 153, memoir by Denicastro, former member of the College of Medicine of La Rochelle.
24. *Bekendmaking*, Dordrecht, 4 July 1801, broadside, no. 78,759, Wellcome Historical Medical Library, London.
25. Surgical guilds were abolished, however. On the guilds: Simon Schama, *Patriots and Liberators: Revolution in the Netherlands, 1780–1813* (New York, 1977), pp. 259–60 and passim; Dr. M. A. van Andel, *Chirurgijns, vrije meesters, beunhazen en kwakzalvers: De chirurgijnsgilden en de pratijk der heelkunde, 1400–1800*, 2d ed. (Amsterdam, 1946), p. 188 on abolition; Arie Querido, *The Development of Socio-Medical Care in the Netherlands* (London, 1968), chap. 2. On subsequent developments (ordinance of 1800, local health commissions, 1804 statute on departmental health councils): Joannes Henricus Tersteeg, *De strafbepalingen in der Nederlandsche geneeskundige wetten*, Leyden law thesis, 1870 (n.p., n.d.), p. 5; Graack, *Kurpfuscherei*, pp. 46–47. Text of 1800 ordinance in Graack, *Sammlung*, pp. 96–98.
26. See, for example, AN F¹⁷ 2455, extract from the minutes of the Ministry of the Interior, 3d division, Napoleon to king of Italy, ordering that the law of Ventôse be published in the jurisdiction of Genoa, 27 November 1806; the Ligurian Republic, including Genoa, had been annexed to France in 1805.
27. In Milan, for example, Napoleon published a decree in 1806 that established administrative departments of medical police corresponding to the Kingdom of Italy's faculties at Pavia, Bologna, and Padua, together with departmental health commissions. The departments would grant licenses for the practice of medicine, surgery, and pharmacy; the commissions would authorize the practice of phlebotomy and midwifery, as well as the sale of drugs (*Della polizia medica*, 5 September 1806, folio pamphlet, no. 51,800, Wellcome Historical Medical Library).
28. Jules Sauveur, *Histoire de la législation médicale belge* (Brussels, 1862), p. 150; see also *Pandectes belges: Encyclopédie de législation, de doctrine, et de jurisprudence belges*, 136 vols. in 149 (Brussels, 1878–1949), s.v. "Art de guérir," and Emile Brunet et al., *Répertoire pratique de droit belge* . . . , 17 vols. (Brussels, n.d.), s.v. "Art de guérir."
29. Luigi di Florio, "La regolamentazione dell'esercizio della professione medica in Modena dopo la restaurazione estense del 1814," *Pagine di storia della medicina* 12 (1968):88–91.
30. For the text of the law: *Bulletin des lois*, 3d ser., 7 (Year XI):567–76. See also Roland, *Loi du 19 ventôse*.
31. George Weisz, "The Politics of Medical Professionalization in France, 1845–48," *Journal of Social History* 12 (1978–79):3–30; Léonard, *Médecins de l'Ouest*, pp. 725–822.
32. Léonard, *Médecins de l'Ouest*, pp. 1084–1124; René Roland, *Les médecins et la loi du 30 novembre 1892* (Paris, 1893); Graack, *Kurpfuscherei*, p. 35.
33. Ernest Coeurderoy, *Jours d'exil* (London, 1854; reprint, 3 vols., Paris, 1910–

11), 1:388–90, 435, quotation p. 390. A few republicans published works advocating medical self-help. See the physician J. Morel de Rubempré's *Véritable médecine sans médecin, ou sciences médicales mises à la portée de toutes les classes de la société* (Paris, 1826), and, for his medico-political ideas, *De la liberté chez les peuples anciens et modernes, ou tableau des droits naturels et des facultés physiques et morales de l'homme* (Paris, 1828); also François-Vincent Raspail's *Manuel annuaire de la santé* (e.g., 1854 ed., p. viii), and *Procès et défense de F.-V. Raspail, poursuivi le 19 mai 1846, en exercice illégal de la médecine* (Paris, 1846). And cf. Dr. Edouard Lemaître, *Catéchisme républicain, ou code des droits du citoyen: Dialogue entre un docteur, un ouvrier et un conservateur rallié à la République* (Le Hàvre, 1848). The doctor in the dialogue defines liberty in good liberal fashion as "the right which every person has to do what he pleases, without harming public morality, [or] the interests and liberty of others" (p. 3); the author advocates state salaries for physicians and pharmacists to forestall popular fears of exploitation but stops short of attacking professional privileges.

34. Pierre-Jean-Georges Cabanis, *Rapport fait au nom de la Commission d'Instruction Publique et projet de résolution sur un mode provisoire de police médicale* . . . , in *Oeuvres philosophiques de Cabanis*, ed. Claude Lehec and Jean Cazeneuve, 2 vols. (Paris, 1956), 2:391; Jean-Baptiste Say, *Traité d'économie politique* (Paris, 1803); Antoine-Louis-Claude Destutt de Tracy, *Elémens d'idéologie*, 5 vols. (Brussels, 1826–27), vol. 4; see also "Quels sont les moyens de former la morale d'un peuple?" appended to his *Commentaire sur L'Esprit des lois de Montesquieu* (Paris, 1828), p. 426: "I ask again for complete and absolute freedom to engage in any kind of industry." Edouard Laboulaye, *L'Etat et ses limites* (Paris, 1865); Laboulaye, *Le parti libéral: Son programme et son avenir* (Paris, 1863); Jules Simon, preface to Camille Delvaille, *De l'exercice de la médecine: Nécessité de réviser les lois qui la régissent en France* (Paris, 1865).

35. Auguste Comte and Charles Dunoyer, "Des garanties individuelles dues à tous les membres de la société," *Le censeur européen* 9 (1818):41–42. Later, in his massive *De la liberté du travail*, 3 vols. (Paris, 1845), Dunoyer argued more strongly for a system without required training or diplomas, in which practitioners, if challenged, would have to defend their competence in court; but even here he spoke of the need to proceed with caution in applying such principles (3:47–55).

36. Georges Audiffrent, *Appel aux médecins* (Paris, 1862), pp. 151, 155, 158–59; Jean-François-Eugène Robinet, *Considérations sur la répression de la médecine illégale et sur le projet de l'Association Générale des Médecins de France* (printed as a supplement to the Audiffrent), pp. 188, 190–91.

37. See, for example, AN CC 473, dossier 127, no. 164, Vincent Minot, property owner at Saint-Etienne, to Chamber of Peers (1826), on the patient's "natural right" to treat himself, and on the analogy between medical and religious freedom; and the article by the liberal physician J. P. Tessier in *Le correspondant* 17 (1847):939–41.

38. AN CC 473, *liasse* 622, no. 137, Comité Central des Pétitions en Faveur de la Liberté d'Enseignement, to Chamber of Peers. For the debates in the Peers, see *Journal des débats*, 6 and 9 June 1847. The full texts of the pleas for medical freedom by the prince de La Moskowa (Ney) and the marquis de Barthélemy, together with Montalembert's speech, can be found in *Le moniteur universel*, 1847, pp. 1438–39, 1474–77, 1439–42. Montalembert's address soon appeared in an anonymous English translation: *Speech of the Count de Montalembert in the House of Peers of France, the 5th June 1847, on the Subject of Medical Reform* (London, 1847). The translator appended some observations on the English situation, in which he attacked both medical empiricism and corporate privileges and called for a strict definitive system. Quotation from *Speech*, p. 9.
39. Léonard, *Médecins de l'Ouest*, pp. 960–65, 1238–1350; Léonard, "Femmes, religion et médecine: Les religieuses qui soignent en France au XIXe siècle," *Annales: Economies, sociétés, civilisations* 32 (1977):887–907.
40. See, for example, P. Diday, "Lettre sur le projet de répression du charlatanisme par l'action en dommages-intérêts," *Gazette médicale de Lyon* 9 (1857): 134–36; and M.-H. Benoît, "De la liberté d'exercice de la médecine," *Gazette médicale de Strasbourg* 25 (1865):129–43 *(feuilleton)*.
41. Léonard, *Médecins de l'Ouest*, chaps. 18, 20.
42. Claude Fohlen, "Bourgeoisie, liberté et intervention de l'Etat," *Revue économique*, 1956, pp. 414–28; Adeline Daumard, "L'Etat libéral et le libéralisme économique," in *Histoire économique et sociale de la France*, ed. Fernand Braudel and Ernest Labrousse, vol. 3, *L'avènement de l'ère industrielle: 1789–années 1880* (Paris, 1976), pp. 137–41, and Daumard, "Caractères de la société bourgeoise," ibid., pt. 3, chap. 3, p. 831; Laboulaye, *Le parti libéral*, p. viii and passim.
43. See *Journal de médecine de Paris*, 2d ser., 8 (1896):605.
44. See E. Pittaluga, "La necessità di una legge che regoli l'esercizio della professione medica e la istituzione di un Consiglio dell'Ordine," *Bollettino della R. Accademia Medica di Genova* 10 (1895):339–41.
45. Graack, *Kurpfuscherei*, pp. 48–49; "Königliche-dänische Verordnung gegen die Quacksalber," *Medicinisch-chirurgische Zeitung* 1 (1798):78; Søren Hansen, *Haandboog i den danske medicinallovgivning*, 2d ed. (Copenhagen, 1905), p. 257. For the 1934 legislation: Knud Sand, *Medicinallovgivning og socialmedicin i udtog*, 6th ed. (Copenhagen, 1945), pp. 16–27.
46. Graack, *Kurpfuscherei*, p. 49; and see n. 8, above. On the persistence of the privilege system, see comment by Herwart Fischer in *Ueber die Mißstände auf dem Gebiete der Kurpfuscherei und Maßnahmen zu ihrer Beseitigung: Bericht über die Verhandlungen eines zusammengesetzten Ausschußes des Landesgesundheitsrates am 9 und 10 März 1927*, Veröffentlichungen aus dem Gebiete der Medizinalverwaltung, no. 235 (Berlin, 1927), pp. 107–8.
47. See Povl Heiberg, "Om kvaksalveri," *Dansk tidsskrift* 5 (1902):297–300.
48. Graack, *Kurpfuscherei*, pp. 37–39. See W. Horsley Gannt, *Russian Medicine*

(New York, 1937); Nancy Frieden, "Physicians in Pre-Revolutionary Russia: Professionals or Servants of the State?" *Bulletin of the History of Medicine* 49 (1975):20–29; and Frieden, *Russian Physicians in an Era of Reform and Revolution* (Princeton, 1981).

49. Fischer, *Ueber die Mißstände*, p. 107. Cf. the tolerant Panamanian law: "Medical-Practice Law in Panama," *Journal of the American Medical Association* 43 (1904):214.
50. Fischer, *Ueber die Mißstände*, pp. 106–7. On the Canadian experience of regulation, see John Joseph Heagerty, *Four Centuries of Medical History in Canada*, 2 vols. (Toronto, 1928) 1:316–27; H. E. Macdermot, *One Hundred Years of Medicine in Canada* (Toronto, 1967), pp. 19–20; and Joseph F. Kett, "American and Canadian Medical Institutions, 1800–1870," in S.E.D. Shortt, ed., *Medicine in Canadian Society: Historical Perspectives* (Montreal, 1981), pp. 189–205. The Canadians seem to have associated medical empiricism with political radicalism imported from the south; see, for example, the *Toronto Patriot*, editorial of 12 October 1838, cited in William Canniff, *The Medical Profession in Upper Canada, 1783–1850* (Toronto, 1894), p. 111.
51. Text of law of 1888 in *Raccolta ufficiale delle leggi e dei decreti del regno d'Italia (parte principale)*, ser. 3a (Rome, 1888), no. 5, 849. See P. S. Mancini, ed., *Enciclopedia giuridica italiana*, 16 vols. in 45 (Milan, 1884–1916), 10:315–17; and Luigi Lucchini, ed., *Il digesto italiano*, 24 vols. in 49 (Turin, 1884–1921), s.v. "medico-chirurgo." Also Donato Constanzo Eula, *L'esercizio abusivo della medicina e della farmacia* (Milan, 1898). On the Italian medical profession in the nineteenth century: Paolo Frascani, "Il medico nell'Ottocento, *Studi storici* 3 (1982):617–37.
52. See, for example, *Gedachten over geneeskundige wetten en gepromoveerde geneesheeren, in verband met het natuurlijk regt en het belang der ingezetenen* (Antwerp, 1858); and *De medische wets-ontwerpen, III, art. 9, en IV, art. 1: Een dwangjuk voor de burgerlijke vrijheid; een slagboom tegen den vooruitgang der geneeskunde; een nieuw monopolie ten nadeele der arbeidende klassen* (Utrecht, 1863). Laissez-faire doctrines were common coin by midcentury, diffused, for example, by David Abraham Portielje, *De handel van Nederland in 1844* . . . (Amsterdam, 1844). See Gerlof Verwey, *Geschiedenis van Nederland: lebensverhaal van zijn bevolking* (Amsterdam, 1976), pp. 738–39; and on the earlier influence of Adam Smith, Schama, *Patriots and Liberators*, p. 259.
53. See, for example (on Austrian liberalism), C. A. Macartney, *The Habsburg Empire, 1790–1918* (New York, 1969), pp. 321, 519–20, and passim.
54. On the reform of Dutch medical legislation: Tersteeg, *Strafbepalingen*, pp. 7–8; Sauveur, *Législation médicale belge*, title 3. For the texts of the 1865 laws: *Staatsblad van het Konigrijk der Nederlanden, 1865* (The Hague, 1866), nos. 58–61. On Thorbecke's role: Jan Jacob Moll, *Onbevoegde uitoefening der geneeskunde* (The Hague, 1899), p. 9; Gerald Newton, *The Netherlands: An Historical and Cultural Survey, 1795–1977* (London, 1978), pp. 69–70.
55. See Raymond Carr, *Spain, 1808–1939* (Oxford, 1966), pp. 53, 69, 184, 201,

and passim. One strand of liberal doctrine, derived from Adam Smith, emphasized the virtues of competition and attacked guilds as obstacles to progress (they were abolished in 1834). A translation (adaptation, really) of *Wealth of Nations* by Josef Alonso Ortiz appeared in 1794; Say's *Traité d'économie politique* (1803) was translated almost immediately. See also the treatise by Alvaro Flórez Estrada, *Curso de economía política* (1828).

56. On the development of Spanish medical legislation: Rafael Muñoz Garrido and Carmen Muñiz Fernández, *Fuentes legales de la medicina española (siglos XIII–XIX)* (Salamanca, 1969); Agustín Albarracín Teulón, "La titulación medica en España durante el Siglo XIX," *Cuadernos de historia de la medicina española* 12 (1973):15–79; and Ricardo Oyuelos y Pérez, *Legislación de medicina y farmacia* . . . , (Madrid, 1903), pp. 593–94, 600–601, 604–5, for the jurisprudence of the late nineteenth century. On the September Revolution: Carr, *Spain*, chap. 8; Albarracín Teulón "Titulación," pp. 61–64; *El siglo médico* 21 (1874):69–71, 125–26.

57. Charles Adams Hale, *Mexican Liberalism in the Age of Mora, 1821–1853* (New Haven, 1968), esp. chap. 8.

58. José María Gamboa, ed., *Leyes constitucionales de Mexico durante el siglo XIX* (Mexico City, 1901), p. 529; Daniel Cosío Villegas, ed., *Historia moderna de Mexico*, vol. 4, *El Porfiriato: La vida social*, by Moisés González Navarro (Mexico City, 1957), pp. 538–43; Ramón Rodríguez, *Derecho constitucional*, 2d ed. (Mexico City, 1875), pp. 346–59 (includes defense of liberal position). In 1910, a diploma from a recognized medical school sufficed for practice in Mexico, except in Mexico City and the state of Veracruz (American Medical Association, *Laws [Abstract] and Board Rulings Regulating the Practice of Medicine in the United States and Elsewhere*, 16th ed. [Chicago, 1910], p. 125).

59. See John Davies, *An Exposition of the Laws Which Relate to the Medical Profession in England* . . . (Edinburgh, 1844); Edwin Lee, *The Medical Profession in Great Britain and Ireland, with an Account of the Medical Organization of France, Italy, Germany and America* (London, 1857); Sir Zachary Cope, *The Royal College of Surgeons of England: A History* (Springfield, Ill., 1959), chaps. 1, 2, 4; Cecil Wall and H. Charles Cameron, *A History of the Worshipful Society of Apothecaries of London*, vol. 1, *1617–1815*, ed. E. Ashworth Underwood (London, 1963); and Joseph F. Kett, "Provincial Medical Practice in England, 1730–1815," *Journal of the History of Medicine and Allied Sciences* 19 (1964):17–29. For background on the profession and medical reform, see the summaries in Berlant, *Profession and Monopoly*, chap. 4; Parry and Parry, *Rise of the Medical Profession*, chap. 6; and M. Jeanne Peterson, *The Medical Profession in Mid-Victorian London* (Berkeley and Los Angeles, 1978), chap. 1.

60. Clark, *Royal College*, pp. 627–32. See box 4, envelope 41, Archives of the Royal College of Physicians (henceforth RCP).

61. S.W.F. Holloway, "The Apothecaries' Act, 1815: A Reinterpretation," *Medical History* 10 (1966):107–29, 221–36.

62. See Peterson, *Medical Profession*, pp. 11–12, 17–18. On the Rose case: Clark, *Royal College*, pp. 476–79.
63. On common and statute law: John William Willcock, *The Laws Relating to the Medical Profession* . . . (London, 1830), chaps. 3–4; Earl of Halsbury et al., *The Laws of England*, 31 vols. (London, 1907–17) 20:334–44. On prosecutions: Clark, *Royal College*, pp. 664–66; Harrison to Royal College, 28 September 1830, box 4, envelope 41, RCP, demanding that the College's charter be revised to preclude further harassment; Holloway, "Apothecaries' Act," p. 229. Davies estimated that only a dozen unlicensed practitioners were prosecuted during the first twenty-nine years the act was in force (*Exposition*, p. 80), but this figure is probably too low.
64. On the controversies over medical reform, see Charles Newman, *The Evolution of Medical Education in the Nineteenth Century* (London, 1957), chap. 4; Clark, *Royal College*, chap. 35; Parry and Parry, *Rise of the Medical Profession*, pp. 117–26; and William L. Burn, *The Age of Equipoise: A Study of the Mid-Victorian Generation* (New York, 1965), pp. 202–11.
65. Ernest M. Little, *History of the British Medical Association*, (London, 1932), pp. 62–65. For a defense of state control, see, for example, Robert E. Grant, *On the Present State of the Medical Profession in England* (London, 1841). Grant was president of the first British Medical Association, (an organization formed in London in 1836 and not the direct ancestor of the present BMA).
66. Committee to Investigate the Several Grievances Complained of in the Several Petitions to Parliament for Medical Reform, grievance no. 7, "The Absence of Some Restrictions upon Quacks and Vendors of Quack Medicines" (n.d., ca. 1845–50), box 4, envelope 17, RCP; 1858 draft of petition on minimum standard, 2027/1, ibid.
67. Little, *British Medical Association*, pp. 273–74.
68. Medical Act of 1858: 21 & 22 Vic., chap. 90. The relevant debates can be found in *Hansard's Parliamentary Debates*, 3d ser., vol. 149. The Medical Act Amendment Act of 1884 later allowed the profession to elect a representative at large to sit on the General Medical Council with the representatives of the corporations and the universities. See Cooke, *Royal College*, pp. 804–14; Berlant, *Profession and Monopoly*, pp. 153–67; and on the conjoint board, Cooke, chap. 38, and Newman, *Medical Education*, pp. 298–300.
69. Explicit liberal justifications of the 1844 and 1858 bills were offered by their sponsors (Graham and Cowper). On political and ideological conflicts: David L. Cowen, "Liberty, Laissez-Faire, and Licensure in Nineteenth-Century Britain," *Bulletin of the History of Medicine* 43 (1969):30–40 (with Kett, the best available discussion of the political context of medical regulation in a single country). See also Newman, *Medical Education*, pp. 139–40; and Berlant, *Profession and Monopoly*, pp. 153–67. On medical radicalism: Francis Barrymore Smith, *The People's Health, 1830–1910* (London, 1979), pp. 347–48. The surgeon Matthew Fletcher supported the Chartists; the general practitioner

William Price was a physical force man. Others attacked monopoly and called for a medical republic—though the monopoly they had in mind was that of the corporations rather than the profession.

70. Herbert Spencer, "The Proper Sphere of Government," Letter 9, *Nonconformist* 2 (1842):779–80; Spencer, *Social Statics* (London, 1851), chap. 28, "Sanitary Supervision." J.J.G. Wilkinson, *Unlicensed Medicine*, reprinted from the *British Journal of Homeopathy* (London, 1855); *The Human Body and Its Connection with Man* (Philadelphia, 1851), which calls for diffusing medical knowledge; *War, Cholera, and the Ministry of Health: An Appeal to Sir Benjamin Hall and the British People* (Boston, 1855), which calls for "free trade" in medicine (p. 24); and, for his homeopathic sympathies, "An Address Read before the Congress of British Homeopathic Practitioners, Held at London, July 4th, 1855," *British Journal of Homeopathy* 13 (1855):529–60. For a defense of liberal legislation by strong opponents of quackery, see Davies, *Exposition*, p. 84, and "An Attempt to Develop the Fundamental Principles which should Guide the Legislature in Regulating the Profession of Physic," *Edinburgh Medical and Surgical Journal* 14 (1818):1–26.

71. Cowen, "Liberty, Laissez-Faire, and Licensure," p. 39; Wilkinson, *A Free State and Free Medicine* (London, 1870); "Objects of Our Paper," *Medical Freedom*, 4 February 1871; T. H. Huxley, "The State and the Medical Profession," *Nineteenth Century*, no. 84 (1884), pp. 228–38 (quotation pp. 228–29).

72. Shryock, *Medical Licensing*, pp. 24–26; Kett, *American Medical Profession*, pp. 14–30; Berlant, *Profession and Monopoly*, pp. 203–17; William G. Rothstein, *American Physicians in the Nineteenth Century: From Sects to Science* (Baltimore, 1972), pp. 72–80. On Louisiana: John Duffy, *The Rudolph Matas History of Medicine in Louisiana*, 2 vols. (n.p. [Baton Rouge], 1958–61), 1: chap. 9, and 2: chap. 4; and Stanford E. Chaillé, "History of the Laws Regulating the Practice of Medicine, etc., in Louisiana, 1808 to 1878," *New Orleans Medical and Surgical Journal*, n.s., 5 (1877–78):909–26. On New York, Charles B. Coventry, "History of Medical Legislation in the State of New York," *New York Journal of Medicine* 4 (1845):152–59; and James J. Walsh, *History of Medicine in New York: Three Centuries of Medical Progress* (New York, 1919), chap. 6. The list of early licensing legislation in Rothstein, Appendix 2, is incomplete but more reliable than Berlant's Table 2, pp. 210–13.

73. Henry B. Shafer, *The American Medical Profession, 1783–1850* (New York, 1936), pp. 208–14; Shryock, *Medical Licensing*, p. 30; Berlant, *Profession and Monopoly*, pp. 218–21; Rothstein, *American Physicians*, pp. 104–8; Cowen, *New Jersey*, p. 69.

74. *National Quarterly Review* 2 (1861):354–55.

75. Kett, *American Medical Profession*, chap. 4; Rothstein, *American Physicians*, chap. 7. On Thomsonianism, see Alex Berman, "The Thomsonian Movement and Its Relation to American Pharmacy and Medicine," *Bulletin of the History of Medicine* 25 (1951):405–28, 519–38.

76. State of New York, in Assembly, no. 354, 12 May 1840, *Report of the Minority of the Select Committee, to Which was Referred Numerous Petitions Asking a Change of the Law towards Thomsonian Physicians,* p. 1 (quotation) and passim. See also New York State Assembly, *Reports of the Majority and Minority of the Select Committee on Several Petitions Relative to the Repeal of the Law Restraining Botanic Practice,* 16 February 1835.
77. John R. Quinan, "President's Address on the Chartered Right of the Medical and Chirurgical Faculty of Maryland to Exact Licenses to Practice in This State," in *Transactions of the Medical and Chirurgical Faculty, State of Maryland, at its Eighty-Seventh Annual Session* (Baltimore, 1885), p. 69.
78. Shafer, *American Medical Profession,* citing *Albany Evening Atlas,* quoted in New York Medical Society, *Proceedings,* 1844–46 (Albany, 1846), App., p. 71.
79. Kett, *American Medical Profession,* pp. 110–12.
80. Alexis de Tocqueville, *Democracy in America,* trans. George Lawrence, ed. J. P. Mayer and Max Lerner (New York, 1966), p. 247. Tocqueville went on to suggest that lawyers formed "the only enlightened class not distrusted by the people" (p. 248)—in contrast, presumably, to doctors.
81. Rush, "Imposture in Medicine," fols. 24–25, 41. Rush, like the Committee on Public Instruction of the French Revolutionary Convention, admired B. C. Faust's medical handbook, *Catechism of Health.* (For the French: AN D XXXVIII 3, dossier 46.)
82. Kett, *American Medical Profession,* pp. 103–6, 109. On the aftermath of Thomsonianism: Alex Berman, "Neo-Thomsonianism in the United States," *Journal of the History of Medicine and Allied Sciences* 11 (1956):133–55.
83. William Hance, *An Appeal to the Citizens of Ohio, Showing the Unconstitutionality, Injustice, and Impolicy of the Medical Law* . . . (Columbus, 1830), p. 19 and passim. Cf. D. F. Nardin, *A Memorial to the Legislature of South-Carolina, Praying for a Repeal of the Medical Law, to Which is Appended Arguments Showing its Unconstitutionality, and Oppressive Bearing upon the Followers of the Thomsonian System of Medicine* (Charleston, 1837).
84. Kett, *American Medical Profession,* p. 115 (New York State). On the general question of connections with Jacksonianism: ibid., p. 31, and Berlant, *Profession and Monopoly,* pp. 216–21.
85. Rothstein, *American Physicians,* chaps. 5–6; Shryock, *Medical Licensing,* p. 28.
86. Matthew Ramsey, "Medical Power and Popular Medicine: Illegal Healers in Nineteenth-Century France," *Journal of Social History* 10 (1976–77):560–87.
87. Graack, *Kurpfuscherei,* pp. 8–12.
88. Fritz Stier-Somlo and Alexander Elfter, *Handwörterbuch der Rechtswissenschaft* (Berlin, 1927), s.v. "Gewerbefreiheit"; J. H. Clapham, *The Economic Development of France and Germany, 1815–1914,* 3d ed. (Cambridge, 1928), pp. 84, 322–23.
89. Graack, *Kurpfuscherei,* pp. 12–14; Alfons Fischer, *Geschichte des deutschen Gesundheitswesens,* 2 vols. (Berlin, 1933) 2:410.

90. Wolf Becher, "Geschichte des ärztlichen Standes," in Max Neuburger and Julius Pagel, eds., *Handbuch der Geschichte der Medizin*, 3 vols. (Jena, 1901–4) 3:1001–22; Claudia Huerkamp, "Ärzte und Professionalisierung in Deutschland: Überlegungen zum Wandel des Arztberufs im 19. Jahrhundert," *Geschichte und Gesellschaft*, vol. 6 (1980), no. 3, *Professionalisierung in historischer Perspektive*, ed. Hans-Ulrich Wehler, pp. 349–82, esp. pp. 360–61. (The most comprehensive survey of the development of the German profession can still be found in Fischer, *Geschichte*, pending the appearance of Huerkamp's dissertation on the profession in the nineteenth century.) On the question of government interference in the affairs of the profession, see, for example, "Ein Wort für die Freiheit der Aerzte in Nassau," *Deutsche Zeitschrift für die Staatsarzneikunde*, n.s., 19 (1862):3–8.
91. On medical reform and politics, see Erwin H. Ackerknecht, *Beiträge zur Geschichte der Medizinalreform von 1848* (Leipzig, 1932); and Paul Diepgen, "Politik und Zeitgeist in der deutschen Medizin des 19. Jahrhunderts," *Historischen Jahrbuch der Görresgesellschaft* 55 (1935):439–52.
92. Graack, *Kurpfuscherei*, pp. 12–17; Berliner Medicinische Gesellschaft, *Petition die Gewerbe-Ordnung betreffend* (Berlin, [1869]). Section 29 is in Graack, *Sammlung*, pp. 145–46. For the debates, see *Stenographische Berichte über die Verhandlungen des Reichstages des Norddeutschen Bundes*, 1869 session (Berlin, 1869), 1:301–7, 327–33.
93. Otto Neustätter, "Kurierzwang und Kurpfuscherfreiheit: Die nochmalige Zerstörung einer Legende," *Archiv für die Geschichte der Naturwissenschaften und der Technik* 6 (1913):272–82; *Verhandlungen der Berliner Medicinischen Gesellschaft*, 1867–68, pp. 105, 110–11. See also Albert Guttstadt, *Zur Revision der Gewerbe-Ordnung vom 21 Juni 1869* . . . , serialized in *Medicinal-Gesetzgebung* 5 (1879).
94. It was even suggested that several key medical authorities were not present at the meetings of 24 and 31 March 1869, when the Society debated the petition; their signatures appeared on the petition only because they belonged to the board of directors, who had to endorse any resolution adopted by the Society. See Albert Guttstadt, "Die ärztliche Gewerbefreiheit im Deutschen Reich und ihr Einfluß auf das öffentliche Wohl," *Zeitschrift des Königlich Preußischen Statistischen Bureaus* 20 (1880):219.
95. Hermann Eberhard Richter, *Das Geheimmittel-Unwesen, nebst Vorschlägen zu dessen Unterdrückung* (Leipzig, 1872), p. 71; Guttstadt, "Zur Revision," p. 98.
96. T. L. W. von Bischoff, *Der Einfluß des norddeutschen Gewerbegesetzes auf die Medicin* (Munich, 1871), p. 3.
97. Huerkamp, "Ärzte und Professionalisierung," pp. 363–66.
98. Heinrich Joachim and Alfred Korn, *Grundriß des deutschen Ärzterechts* (Jena, 1914), pp. 130–31; J. Grosse, *Die Bestimmungen der Reichs-Gewerbeordnung* (Leipzig, 1895); Gaston Vorberg, *Kurpfuscher! eine zeitgemäße Betrachtung* . . . (Leipzig, 1905), p. 70, on 1900 law.

99. Joachim and Korn, *Grundriß*, p. 131; Helmut Tegetmeyer, *Die nichtärztlichen Heilbehandler: Ihre Rechtslage und deren Weiterentwicklung* (Leipzig, 1934), pp. 21–22; Moritz Fürst, "Kurpfuscherei und Kurpfuschereigesetze," *Zeitschrift für ärztliche Fortbildung* 15 (1918):605–11, 634–39; Edgar Lion, *Die strafrechtliche Behandlung der Kurpfuscherei* (Leipzig, 1910), pp. 46–52.
100. On German liberalism, see Leonard Krieger, *The German Idea of Freedom: History of a Political Tradition* (Chicago, 1957).
101. Rudolf Virchow, "Der Staat und die Ärzte," *Die medicinische Reform*, 16 March 1849. Virchow was the one strong proponent of medical liberty who was also a major political figure: he was a leader of the Progress party and later of the opposition to Bismarck.
102. Krieger, *German Idea of Freedom*, p. 407 and passim; James Sheehan, *German Liberalism in the Nineteenth Century* (Chicago, 1978), pp. 85–86; Theodore S. Hamerow, *The Social Foundations of German Unification, 1858–1871*, 2 vols. (Princeton, 1969–72) 1:96–98, 120–24; 2:338, 340, and passim.
103. Ernst Steinmann, *Geschichte des schweizerischen Freisinns im Auftrag der Zentralleitung der Freisinnig-demokratischen Partei der Schweiz . . .* , vol. 1, *Der Freisinn als Gründer und Gestalter des Bundestaates, 1830–1918* (Bern, 1955); see also William E. Rappard, *L'individu et l'Etat dans l'évolution constitutionnelle de la Suisse* (Zurich, [1936]).
104. When the Vaudois medical society sent a petition in 1882 to the Great Council asking for better enforcement and new laws on medical practice, only half the members signed; some of the dissenters believed that unpopular professional privileges were one of the reasons for the lack of respect shown physicians. See André Guisan, *Le charlatanisme dans le canton de Vaud de 1834 à 1882, d'après les archives du service sanitaire*, Veröffentlichungen der Schweizerischen Gesellschaft für Geschichte der Medizin und der Naturwissenschaften, vol. 7 (Zurich, 1930), pp. 136–41.
105. Edouard Chapuisat, comp., *La municipalité de Genève pendant la domination française: Extraits de ses registres et de sa correspondance, 1798–1814*, 2 vols. (Geneva, 1910), 1:163, 268–69, 353; 2:18–19, 28, 130, 142, 144. For regulation before 1798, see Léon Gautier, *La médecine à Genève jusqu'à la fin du dix-huitième siècle* (Geneva, 1906).
106. Graack, *Kurpfuscherei*, p. 43; Dunoyer, *De la liberté du travail*, 3:48; Guisan, *Le charlatanisme*, p. 11.
107. "Concordat touchant le libre établissement du personnel médical suisse, conclu le 22 juillet 1867," in *Recueil officiel des lois et ordonnances de la Confédération Suisse* 9 (1869):97–112. A federal law of 1877 created a federal diploma and prohibited the cantons from requiring a patent of anyone who possessed it (*Recueil systématique des lois et ordonnances, 1848–1947*, 15 vols. [Bern, 1949–57] 4:303–4). For federal regulation under the constitution of 1874, see Ludwig Rudolf von Salis, comp., *Schweizerisches Bundesrecht: Staatsrechtliche und verwaltungsrechtliche Praxis des Bundesrates . . .* , 4 vols. (Bern, 1891–93) 1:366–

67, 407–21; for legislation and ordinances, F. Schmid, *Tableau systématique des lois, ordonnances, règlements, prescriptions, et autres dispositions concernant l'hygiène publique en Suisse* (Bern, 1891).

108. Eduard His, *Geschichte des neuern schweizerischen Staatsrechts*, vol. 2, *Die Zeit der Restauration und der Regeneration, 1814 bis 1848* (Basel, 1929), chap. 12. Christoph Bernoulli, *Über den nachtheiligen Einfluß der Zunftverfassung auf die Industrie* (Basel, 1822).

109. E. Bonjour, H. S. Offler, and G. R. Potter, *A Short History of Switzerland* (Oxford, 1952), pp. 252–54, 299. Tocqueville, *Democracy in America*, Appendix 2, "Report Given before the Academy of Moral and Political Sciences on January 15, 1848, on the Subject of M. Cherbuliez' Book Entitled *On Democracy in Switzerland*," p. 712 and passim.

110. Eduard His, *Geschichte des neuern schweizerischen Staatsrechts*, vol. 3, *Der Bundesstaat, von 1848 bis 1914* (Basel, 1938), chap. 12; Bonjour, Offler, and Potter, *Switzerland*, pp. 299–300; Félix Bonjour, *Real Democracy in Action: The Example of Switzerland*, trans. C. Leonard Leese (London, 1920). *Recueil des constitutions fédérale et cantonales* (Bern, 1891), p. 56 (art. 31) and passim. Quotation is art. 2 of the constitution for Appenzell Inner-Rhoden, p. 660.

111. See, for example, Morthier and Cornaz, *Le libre exercice de la médecine dans le canton de Neuchâtel: Mémoires présentés à la Société d'Emulation* (Neuchâtel, 1869); Ladame, "Examen du projet de loi sanitaire fondé sur la libre pratique de la médecine pour le canton de Schaffhouse," *Correspondenzblatt für Schweizer Aerzte* 4 (1874):57–63; Guisan, *Le charlatanisme*, pp. 140–41.

112. Graack, *Kurpfuscherei*, p. 43; Georges-Denis Weil, *De l'exercice illégal de la médecine et de la pharmacie* (Paris, 1886), p. 10; "Zur Volksabstimmung im Kanton Zürich vom 27 November über die sogenannte Kurpfuscherei-Initiative," *Schweizerische Blätter für Gesundheitspflege* 19 (1904):241–50.

113. On the Neuchâtel debates, see Morthier and Cornaz, *Le libre exercice*, and Dr. Morax, "De l'exercice de la médecine," *Bulletin de la Société Médicale de la Suisse Romande* 6 (1872):219–28.

114. "Loi sur la police sanitaire," 7 April 1875, chap. 3, "De l'exercice de la médecine et des professions qui s'y rattachent," *Recueil des lois, décrets et autres actes du gouvernement de la République et Canton de Neuchâtel*, 15 vols. (Neuchâtel, 1849-83) 13:66–69.

115. Graack, *Kurpfuscherei*, p. 44; Walter Schläpfer, *Appenzell Außerrhoden, von 1597 bis zur Gegenwart*, 2 vols. (n.p., 1972); Bonjour, Offler, and Potter, *Switzerland*, p. 308; Irving B. Richman, *Pure Democracy and Pastoral Life in Inner Rhoden* (London, 1895), chap. 10; Bonjour, *Real Democracy*, p. 71. Both Appenzell Ausser-Rhoden and Glarus adopted economic freedom in the 1830s (His, *Geschichte des Staatsrechts* 3:593); the constitutions for the two cantons during the period considered here give identical guarantees of economic freedom within the limits imposed by the common good (*Recueil des constitutions*, art. 12 in each case).

116. *Landsbuch des Kantons Glarus, zweiter Theil, enthaltend die Gesetze, Beschlüße, Uebereinkünfte, und Verordnungen administrativer Natur* (Glarus, 1878), p. 132.
117. "Gesetzliche Bestimmungen betreffend die Freigebung der ärztlichen Praxis" (30 April 1871), *Gesetzbuch für den Kanton Appenzell A.Rh.* (Herisau, 1883), pp. 65–66.
118. Schläpfer, *Appenzell* 2:537–39. Sanitary ordinance of 24 April 1865 in *Gesetzbuch für den Kanton Appenzell der äußern Rhoden*, vol. 2, *Die vom großen Rathe erlaßenen Verordnungen und Reglemente* (Trogen, 1867), pp. 114–20 (on medical personnel); health ordinance of 23 March 1887 in *Sammlung aller im Kanton Appenzell A.Rh. gegenwärtig (Juli 1889) in Kraft bestehenden Verordnungen, Reglemente, Regulative, Instruktionen, etc.* (Herisau, 1889), pp. 185–89. On public health legislation in other cantons: His, *Geschichte des Staatsrechts* 3:971-72.
119. H. Hunziker, "Der Kampf gegen das Kurpfuschertum in der Schweiz," in *Der Kampf gegen die Kurpfuscherei: Zehn Vorträge herausgegeben von der Deutschen Gesellschaft zur Bekämpfung des Kurpfuschertums*, Veröffentlichungen aus dem Gebiete der Medizinalverwaltung, no. 252 (Berlin, 1928), pp. 11–12.
120. Graack, *Kurpfuscherei*, p. 55, and *Sammlung*, p. 92. *Hygienische Blätter* 2:41–42, 117–21; L. Eisenstadt, "Bemerkungen zu einer internationalen Bekämpfung des Kurpfuschertums," *Aerztliche Sachverständigen-Zeitung* 14 (1908): 48.
121. Fischer report, *Ueber die Mißstände*, p. 104. On the persistence of the free field, see also F. Decourt, "L'exercice 'libre' de la médecine en certains pays" [report to Congrès International pour la Répression de l'Exercice Illégal de la Médecine et du Charlatanisme, Paris, 7 July 1937], *Le concours médical* 59 (1937):3324–28.
122. Marmann, "Die Einstellung des Staates zur Kurpfuscherei," in *Der Kampf gegen die Kurpfuscherei*, p. 60.
123. Henry Sewill, articles reprinted in *Quackery (Quack Remedies and Quack Practice) and Medical Law Reform: A Plea for a Royal Commission* (London, 1910). Great Britain, Local Government Board, *Report as to the Practice of Medicine and Surgery by Unqualified Persons in the United Kingdom* (London, 1910), p. 2 and passim.
124. See Leonard Le Marchant Minty, *The Legal and Ethical Aspects of Medical Quackery* (London, 1932); and William I. S. Rawson, *The Law, the Public, and the Non-Registered Health Practitioner* (London, 1950).
125. On contemporary British legislation, see C. R. A. Martin, *Law Relating to Medical Practice*, 2d ed. (Tunbridge Wells, 1979). Text of 1956 act in *Halsbury's Statutes of England*, 3d ed., 39 vols. (London, 1968–72) 21:624–73.
126. A. N. Cumming, *On the Value of Political Economy to Mankind* (Glasgow, 1881), cited by Harold Perkin, *The Origins of Modern English Society, 1780–1880* (London, 1969), p. 450. See Oliver MacDonagh, "The Nineteenth-Century Revolution of Government: A Reappraisal," *Historical Journal* 1 (1958):58–61.
127. R. M. MacLeod, "Law, Medicine, and Public Opinion: The Resistance to

Compulsory Health Legislation, 1870–1907," *Public Law*, 1967, pp. 107–28, 189–211. On the sources of opposition to vaccination, see Ann F. Beck, "Issues in the Anti-Vaccination Movement in England," *Medical History* 4 (1960):310–21.

128. Sewill, *Quackery*, p. 31; W. E. Steavenson, *The Medical Act (1858) Amendment Bill and Medical Reform* (London, 1880), pp. 9–11; Robert Forbes, *Sixty Years of Medical Defence* (London, 1955).

129. The following account is based primarily on Hunziker, "Der Kampf," pp. 8–15.

130. Practice was limited to persons holding a federal diploma: "Loi sur l'exercice des professions médicales," 23 April 1919, in *Recueil officiel des lois, décrets et arrêtés de la république et canton de Neuchâtel*, 3d ed., 3 vols. (Neuchâtel, 1924–26) 3:407–11.

131. Schläpfer, *Appenzell Außerrhoden*, pp. 538–39; Hunziker, "Der Kampf" (quotation p. 9). On the contemporary situation in Appenzell: Notker Kessler, *Die freie Heiltätigkeit im Gesundheitsgesetz des Kantons Appenzell Außerrhoden*, Zürcher medizingeschichtliche Abhandlungen, n.s., no. 146 (Zurich, 1981).

132. Sheehan, *German Liberalism*, p. 189 (Miquel). On the free trade issue in the decade after the GO, see Ivo Nikolai Lambi, *Free Trade and Protection in Germany, 1868–1879*, Vierteljahrschrift für Sozial- und Wirtschaftsgeschichte, supplement no. 44 (Wiesbaden, 1963).

133. Becher, "Geschichte des ärztlichen Standes," pp. 1009–11; Huerkamp, "Ärzte und Professionalisierung," pt. 3.

134. Otto Neustätter, "Medical Charlatanism in Germany," *British Medical Journal*, 1906, vol. 1, p. 1348.

135. *Aerztliches Vereinsblatt für Deutschland: Organ des Deutschen Aerztevereinsbundes* 14 (1887):118–34, 155–58, 235–53, 267–90. "Feuilleton: Zur Frage des Kurpfuschereiverbots," *Berliner klinische Wochenschrift*, 1887, pp. 501–4, 536–38; *Verhandlungen der Berliner Medicinischen Gesellschaft aus dem Gesellschaftsjahre 1879–80* (Berlin, 1881), pp. 123–92. *Verhandlungen des XXV. Deutschen Aerztetages zu Eisenach am 10. und 11. September 1897*, supplement to *Aerztliches Vereinsblatt*, no. 362; see also ibid. 24 (1897):131–33, 539–43, 578–82, 636, 652–58 (Eulenburg, report to Aerztekammer für Brandenburg-Berlin). The national congress at Eisenach adopted a resolution that called for removing medicine from the GO and regulating it instead through a special ordinance on physicians.

136. Arno Krüche, "Wie sind Kurpfuscherei und Geheimmittelschwindel auf gesetzlichem Wege zu bekämpfen?" *Aerztliche Rundschau* 6 (1896):50, 65–67.

137. Keferstein, "Bekämpfung der Kurpfuscherei auf gerichtlichem und polizeilichem Wege," *Zeitschrift für Medizinal-Beamte* 16 (1903):585–91; Lion, *Die strafrechtliche Behandlung*; Heinrich Schopohl, *Kurpfuscherei und die rechtlichen Bestimmungen zu ihrer Bekämpfung*, Veröffentlichungen aus dem Gebiete der Medizinalverwaltung, no. 206 (Berlin, 1926); J. Biberfeld, "Das Gesetz zur Bekämpfung des unlauteren Wettbewerbs in seiner Anwendung auf die

Kurpfuscherei," *Deutsche medicinische Wochenschrift* 29 (1903):932–34. A few physicians still hoped for regulation at the local level. See J. Biberfeld, "Zur Bekämpfung der Kurpfuscherei: Ein Versuch mit untauglichen Mitteln," *Deutsche medicinische Wochenschrift* 28 (1902):688–89 (on a plan submitted to the Royal Saxon Medical College); and Julian Marcuse, "Der badische Gesetzentwurf zur Bekämpfung des Kurpfuschertumes," *Aerztliche Sachverständigen-Zeitung* 10 (1904):137–38.

138. See, for example, Oskar Schwartz, "Die Notwendigkeit eines Verbotes gewerbsmäßiger Kurpfuscherei durch die staatliche Strafgesetzgebung," *Die Heilkunde* 7 (1903):301–3; L. Eisenstadt, "Ueber die neueren Vorschläge zur Bekämpfung des Kurpfuschertums," *Aerztliche Sachverständigen-Zeitung* 10 (1904):35–38; and the debates of the 1905 Hauptversammlung des Preussischen Medizinalbeamten-Vereins, reported in Carl Reissig "Die gerichtsärztliche Beurteilung der Kurpfuschereidelikte: Ein Referat," *Hygienische Blätter* 3 (1906):34–39 (transcripts in Preussischer Medizinalbeamten-Verein, *Offizieller Bericht über die Hauptversammlung*, no. 22 [1905]:70–106).

139. Decourt, "L'exercice 'libre,' " pp. 3326–27.

140. Schopohl, *Kurpfuscherei*, p. 31; Curt Wachtel, *Vor dem Ende der Kurierfreiheit?* (Berlin, 1930), p. 70. Text of bill and statement of grounds for legislation in *Verhandlungen des Reichstags: Anlagen zu den stenographischen Berichten*, 12th legislative period, 2d session, no. 535. On the physicians' role and their reactions to the 1908 draft: Theodor Rumpf, "Über den vorläufigen Entwurf eines Gesetzes betreffend die Ausübung der Heilkunde durch nichtapprobierte Personen und den Geheimmittelverkehr," *Soziale Medizin und Hygiene* 4 (1909):20–28.

141. *Verhandlungen des Reichstags: Stenographische Berichte*, vol. 262, 12th legislative period, 2d session, 90th and 91st meetings (30 November–1 December 1910).

142. Walter Lustig, *Die Bekämpfung des Kurpfuschertums* (Berlin, 1926), pp. 33, 48, and passim; Wachtel, *Vor dem Ende?* pp. 59, 62, and passim. See also Karl Heinrich Müller, *Kurierfreiheit und Kurpfuschertum* (Cuxhaven, 1929).

143. Guttstadt, "Die ärztliche Gewerbefreiheit," pp. 220–32 (on trends in the supply of qualified personnel), and pp. 232–42 (on empirics); Graack, *Kurpfuscherei*, pp. 61–62 (on Berlin and Bavaria). See also Abraham Flexner, *Medical Education in Europe* (New York, 1912), pp. 311–14.

144. Graack, *Kurpfuscherei*, p. 64; E. Lehmann, "Hygienische Volksbelehrung durch öffentliche Vorträge," in *Der Kampf gegen die Kurpfuscherei*, pp. 113–18; Friedrich Eduard Bilz, *Das neue Naturheilverfahren* (numerous editions; title varies). Among the publications on medical freedom, "so-called quackery," and related questions, see Deutscher Verein der Naturheilkundigen, *Die Kurierfreiheit: Ein heiliges Gut des deutschen Volkes* (Berlin, 1908); Bund für freie Heilkunst E.V., Zentralband für die Parität der Heilmethoden, Schriften über Wesen und Bedeutung der Kurierfreiheit, 1st ser., Alexander de Corti, *Das Kurpfuschertum als Problem*, and Martin Beradt, *Die gesetzlichen Handhaben gegen Auswüchse der Kurierfreiheit* (Berlin, 1910). (The Bund was in theory to

provide a neutral forum for discussion of *Kurierfreiheit*, but in its efforts to distinguish between "quackery" and alternative forms of "healing" it generally served the interests of the unlicensed practitioners.) On the proliferation of healer organizations and the alliances they formed, see Wachtel, *Vor dem Ende?* p. 77.

145. Neustätter, "Medical Charlatanism," p. 1471 and passim. On single-issue politics, see *Hygienisches Volksblatt* 4 (1903):151.
146. Huerkamp, "Ärzte und Professionalisierung," pp. 366–67.
147. Rumpe, "Die Deutsche Gesellschaft zur Bekämpfung des Kurpfuschertums," in *Gedenkboek van de Vereeniging tegen de Kwakzalverij, 1880–1905* (Amsterdam, 1906), pp. 156–64. See opening speech by T. Sommerfeld, 9 March 1903, *Hygienisches Volksblatt* 4 (1903):78–82.
148. Otto Neustätter, "Die Einstellung der Deutschen Gesellschaft zur Bekämpfung des Kurpfuschertums zur Kurpfuschereibekämpfung, 1904–24," in *Der Kampf gegen die Kurpfuscherei*, pp. 98–103; Lehmann, "Hygienische Volksbelehrung." Among the publications, see Wilhelm Back, ed., *Das Kurpfuschertum und seine Bekämpfung: Sieben Vorträge gehalten auf der 1. Jahresversammlung der Deutschen Gesellschaft zur Bekämpfung des Kurpfuschertums* (Strasbourg, [1903]), and *Ueber Kurpfuschertum und seine Bekämpfung: Eine Vortragsreihe herausgegeben von der Deutschen Gesellschaft zur Bekämpfung des Kurpfuschertums*, Veröffentlichungen aus dem Gebiete der Medizinalverwaltung, no. 220 (Berlin, 1927).
149. A. Dührssen, "Die Jahresversammlung der Gesellschaft zur Bekämpfung des Kurpfuschertums," *Medicinische Woche* 5 (1904):27–28 *(Feuilleton); Hygienische Blätter* 2 (1906):120.
150. Neustätter, "Einstellung der Deutschen Gesellschaft," pp. 100–101; Wachtel, *Vor dem Ende?* p. 73.
151. See, for example, the statements in defense of nature healing by Rudolf Hess (who says that scientific medicine has entered a blind alley) and by Dr. Gerhard Wagner, the National Socialist health director (both 1933), in Tegetmeyer, *Die nichtärztlichen Heilbehandler*, pp. 51–52.
152. Ibid., pp. 55–56; Paul Bockelmann, *Strafrecht des Arztes* (Stuttgart, 1968), pp. 1–4; Rudolf Ramm, *Ärztliche Rechts- und Standeskunde: Der Arzt als Gesundheitserzieher*, 2d ed. (Berlin, 1943), pp. 59–63. All the National Socialist legislation can be found in Detlof, freiherr von Schwerin and Johann Mang, eds., *Gesundheitsrecht*, 3 vols. (Munich, 1939–40), vol. 1, pt. B.
153. Ramm, *Ärztliche Rechts- und Standeskunde*, pp. 59–60. For background (social and economic policy): Karl Dietrich Bracher, *The German Dictatorship: The Origins, Structure, and Effects of National Socialism*, trans. Jean Steinberg (New York, 1970).
154. Shryock, *Medical Licensing*, pp. 47–49, 51–56; Reginald H. Fitz, *The Legislative Control of Medical Practice* (Boston, 1894), pp. 37–40; American Medical Association, *Laws (Abstract)*. The most complete and useful list of medical legislation is in Ronald Hamowy, "The Early Development of Medical Licensing Laws in the United States, 1875–1900," *Journal of Libertarian Studies* 3 (1979):73–119, Appendix I. On the Illinois law, see H. O. Johnson, "The

Regulation of Medical Practice by State Boards of Health, as Exemplified by the Execution of the Law in Illinois," *Transactions of the American Medical Association* 30 (1879):293–98. One anomalous case: in North Carolina, a law of 1859 required the state medical society to examine and license all practitioners. This act was a tardy example of the legislation that characterized the first third of the century, rather than an adumbration of later measures; practice by unauthorized persons was not made a punishable offense until 1885 (see *Abstract of Laws Regulating the Practice of Medicine in the Various States and Territories, Compiled by a Member of the Suffolk Bar* [Boston, 1889], pp. 16–17, and *Laws Regulating the Practice of Medicine in North Carolina* [n.p., n.d., ca. 1889]).

155. Rothstein, *American Physicians*, pp. 305–10; Connecticut Medical Society, report of the Committee on Legislation, *Proceedings of the Connecticut Medical Society*, 1893, p. 27.

156. A brief discussion appears in Shryock, *Medical Licensing*, pp. 59–60, and Starr, *Social Transformation*, pp. 102–6. Two more extended treatments are Hamowy, "Early Development," and Samuel Lee Baker, "Medical Licensing in America: An Early Liberal Reform" (Ph.D. dissertation, Harvard University, 1977), which attempts to explain why the various laws were adopted when they were and then looks more closely at the case of Massachusetts.

157. See, for example, *An Earnest Appeal for Medical Freedom* (Boston, 1877); *The Doctors' Plot Exposed, or Civil, Religious, and Medical Persecution* . . . (Boston, 1877); *Medical Freedom: Arguments of J. H. Benton, Jr., Esq., Prof. C. W. Emerson, Dr. J. R. Buchanan, Against Medical Legislation in Massachusetts, together with Gov. Long's Veto Message and Extract from Herbert Spencer's "Social Statics"* (Boston, [1885]); Henry Wood, "Medical Slavery through Legislation," *Arena* 8 (1893): 680–89. For a summary of the opposing arguments: Champe S. Andrews, "Medical Practice and the Law," *Forum* 31 (1901):542–51.

158. On the AMA: James G. Burrow, *AMA: Voice of American Medicine* (Baltimore, 1963), chaps. 1–2. For the role of a state medical society, a particularly rich source is J. B. Roberts, comp., scrapbook on licensure in Pennsylvania, 1884–93, Cage 210c/16, Library of the College of Physicians of Philadelphia; Roberts was secretary of the Committee on Medical Legislation of the Medical Society of the State of Pennsylvania. The scrapbook includes several circulars from the National Constitutional Liberty League. (For further background on Pennsylvania legislation, see Harold Freed Alderfer, "Legislative History of Medical Licensure in Pennsylvania," *Pennsylvania Medical Journal* 64 [1961]: 1605–9.) The regulars could also draw on the support of public interest organizations closely identified with their cause, such as the health committee of the American Social Science Association. See the society's petition to judiciary committee, Massachusetts legislature, on a draft of a medical practice law (n.p., n.d. [after 1877]), copy in Library of the College of Physicians of Philadelphia, Pam 5377, no. 15.

159. On the homeopaths: Martin Kaufman, *Homeopathy in America: The Rise and*

Fall of a Medical Heresy (Baltimore, 1971), chap. 10. On the National Constitutional Liberty League: see the materials in the Roberts scrapbook; Fitz, *Legislative Control*, pp. 58–64; and *Proceedings of the Connecticut Medical Society*, 1893, pp. 286–91.

160. The exact chronology has been a subject of disagreement, largely because some early legislation (such as the 1894 statute in Massachusetts) did not actually penalize unlicensed practice; see Baker, "Medical Licensing," chap. 2. On the opposition to regulation in New England, see George Lewis Collins, *State Control of Medical Practice: An Address Delivered at the Annual Meeting of the Rhode Island Medical Society, June 9, 1889* (n.p., 1889); *The Doctors' Plot; Medical Freedom*; Fitz, *Legislative Control*; and Charles Johnson Noyes, *Argument of Hon. Charles J. Noyes before the Committee on the Judiciary of the House of Representatives of Massachusetts, Against a Bill to Regulate the Practice of Medicine, February 18, 1889* (Boston, 1889).

161. Jethro K. Lieberman, *The Tyranny of the Experts: How Professionals Are Closing the Open Society* (New York, 1970), pp. 180–81; *West Virginia v. Frank M. Dent*, opinion by Judge Green, 1 November 1884; *Dent v. West Virginia*, 129 U.S. 114 (1888). See also Collins, "State Control," pp. 19–20; and "Are Laws Regulating the Practice of Medicine Constitutional?" *Philadelphia Medical Times* 15 (1884–85):240–41. For a full survey of court cases (presented from the profession's point of view), see American Medical Association, Medico-Legal Bureau, *A Digest of the Case Law on the Statutory Regulation of the Practice of Medicine* (Chicago, 1915). For the arguments on economic due process: Lawrence M. Friedman, "Freedom of Contract and Occupational Licensing, 1890–1910: A Legal and Social Study," *California Law Review* 53 (1965):487–534 (esp. pp. 490–92).

162. Roy M. MacLeod, "Medico-Legal Issues in Victorian Medical Care," *Medical History* 10 (1966):45, citing Nebraska decision of 1894. Cf. AMA, *Digest*, pp. 103–6.

163. They also made it easier to try an unqualified practitioner for a common-law offense such as manslaughter, rejecting the precedent established early in the century when Thomson himself was acquitted on such charges. See Andrews, "Medical Practice and the Law," pp. 544–46; and William Archer Purrington, "Manslaughter, Christian Science, and the Law," *Medical Record* 54 (1898):757–61.

164. James Harvey Young, *The Toadstool Millionaires: A Social History of Patent Medicines in America before Federal Regulation* (Princeton, 1961), pt. 4; Young, *The Medical Messiahs: A Social History of Health Quackery in Twentieth-Century America* (Princeton, 1967); and see also Burrow, *AMA*, chaps. 4 and 6, and Morris Fishbein, *Fads and Quackery in Healing . . .* (New York, 1932). Otto Neustätter, "Der Kampf gegen die Kurpfuscherei in Amerika," *Archiv für soziale Medizin und Hygiene* 2 (1905):289–308; Neuburger, "Das Kurpfuschertum in den Vereinigten Staaten von Nordamerika," in *Der Kampf gegen die Kurpfuscherei*, pp. 17–54; W. A. Puckner, "Die Bekämpfung des Geheimmit-

telschwindels in Amerika durch die Abteilung für Pharmakologie und Chemie der American Medical Association," trans. P. zum Busch, *Deutsche medizinische Wochenschrift*, 6 October 1922. (Puckner was director of the AMA's Council on Pharmacy and Chemistry.)

165. On professional organization: Burrow, *AMA*, chaps. 4 and 6; Burrow, *Organized Medicine*, chap. 2; Rothstein, *American Physicians*, chap. 16. On the evolution of homeopathy: Kaufman, *Homeopathy*, chap. 8.

166. Council of State Governments, *Occupational Licensing Legislation in the United States* (Chicago, 1952), pp. 1, 22–23, 78–80.

167. "The Relation of the Modern Municipality to the Gas Supply," American Economic Association, *Publications* 1 (1886):54, cited in John Arthur Garraty, *The New Commonwealth, 1877–1890* (New York, 1968), p. 326. Garraty provides a useful overview of the decline of laissez-faire; see esp. chap. 8. On economic regulation and the police powers of the state, see also Morton Keller, *Affairs of State: Public Life in Late Nineteenth-Century America* (Cambridge, Mass., 1979), chap. 11.

168. Robert H. Wiebe, *The Search for Order, 1877–1920* (New York, 1967). This is Wiebe's general argument; his specific discussion of medicine, though, invokes a form of technological determinism, suggesting that the collapse of licensing owed something to the doctors' "harsh remedies and feeble results" and that the United States lagged in rejecting quackery following the discoveries of Pasteur and Koch because the country was "too far from the centers of early discovery" (pp. 113–15; quotations, p. 114). For a contemporary analysis of the growth in the role of government, in a newly complex society in which "the development of applied science has tremendously augmented man's power both to assist and to injure his fellow man," see Abraham Flexner, "Medical Colleges," *World's Work* 21 (1911):14,238–39.

169. Berlant, *Profession and Monopoly*, pp. 238–40. On the "medical trust," see, for example, Eugene Christian, *The Crime of Medical Legislation* (New York, n.d. [1908?]), p. 47: "The medical trust is one of the most dangerous foes to freedom under our flag, for the reason that it has not yet come to be recognized as a trust by any anti-trust political party." Gabriel Kolko's discussion of regulatory legislation in *The Triumph of Conservatism: A Reinterpretation of American History, 1900–1916* (Glencoe, 1963), although it exaggerates the role of big business in promoting such measures as the Pure Food and Drugs Act, indicates some of the ways in which state regulation was inimical to small enterprise (see pp. 108–10 on the pure food measure). On big business and health care in more recent times: Starr, *Social Transformation*, book 2, chap. 5.

170. Burrow, *Organized Medicine*, pp. 106–7; "The American Medical Association: Power, Purpose, and Politics in Organized Medicine," *Yale Law Journal* 63 (1954):990–91, 1019 (on *AMA v. United States*, 317 U.S. 519); section 3 of the Sherman Act allowed the federal government to enforce its provisions in Washington, D.C. (Berlant also cites this case, pp. 243–44.) On the AMA's

role, see Morris Fishbein, *A History of the American Medical Association, 1847 to 1947* (Philadelphia, 1947), pp. 534–50.
171. *Primitive Physick, or an Easy and Natural Method of Curing Most Diseases* (1747 and numerous later editions).
172. The exceptions include the English-speaking Canadian provinces, South Africa, the majority of predominantly Protestant Swiss cantons, the half-Catholic Netherlands, and Russian-dominated Finland. In Finland, starting in the 1860s, the Liberals succeeded in reducing government control over trade and industry (Eino Jutikkala and Kauko Pirinen, *A History of Finland*, trans. Paul Sjöblom [New York, 1974], p. 215), but medical regulation remained in effect; for the legislation see the various volumes of *Finlands medicinal-författningar* (1846–70, Helsinki, 1874; 1871–86, Helsinki, 1888, and others). On South Africa, see E. H. Cluver, *Medical and Health Legislation in the Union of South Africa* (n.p., 1949), pp. 3–4, 21; and L. Herman, "New Medical Bill for the Orange Free State," *South African Medical Journal* 1 (1893–94): 235–37. South Africa was in some ways a borderline case. After the creation of the Union in 1910, it was necessary to consolidate the laws in force in the four provinces; it took until 1928 to accomplish this task, largely because of staunch resistance from unorthodox practitioners, including osteopaths, chiropractors, naturopaths, and cancer curers. In 1923, an amendment that would have exempted faith healers, hydropaths, naphrapaths, neuropaths, and other sectarians received serious consideration but was eventually rejected by the select committee considering the bill. Several members of Parliament hoped to exempt herbal healers in backveld areas where their ministrations were needed by the local populations; their amendments were also defeated. The main obstacle to legislation until 1927 was a clause that prohibited medical practice by unqualified persons "for gain, hire or reward, direct or indirect, or for the expectation thereof." The bill that finally passed penalized only practice "for gain" and usurpation of a medical title.
173. See, for example, André Du Breil, *La police de l'art et science de médecine* . . . (Paris, 1580), "Epître au Roi," which asked the king to control the abuses "that are perpetrated [in medicine] in your Kingdom, under the pretext of charity toward one's neighbor . . . by those who maliciously cause your subjects to perish [and] ruin and depopulate your Republic."
174. As Larson does, for example, in *Rise of Professionalism*, p. 24.
175. Milton Friedman, *Capitalism and Freedom* (Chicago, 1962), chap. 9, esp. pp. 149–60. Cf. Berlant's critique in *Profession and Monopoly*, pp. 182–84.
176. Rita Ricardo Campbell, "Your Health and the Government," in Peter Duignan and Alvin Rabushka, eds., *The United States in the 1980s*, Hoover Institution Publication no. 228 (Stanford, 1980), pp. 285–341, esp. pp. 306–10, 336.
177. On the origins of the Order, see Jacques Reynaud, *L'Ordre des Médecins*, law thesis, University of Lyons (Lyons, 1943). For approaches to alternative

medicine, see, for example, the special issues of *Autrement*, no. 9, *Francs-tireurs de la médecine*, May 1977; no. 15, *Panseurs de secrets et de douleurs*, September 1978; and no. 26, *La santé à bras-le-corps*, September 1980.

Index

Abria, Jeremie-Joseph-Benoit, 80
Academic institutionalization of science, 70
Academic reform movement, 71–72, 85–101, 119–21
Academic scientists: dependence on state, 5; struggle for autonomy, 5–6; to 1850, 72–85
Académie des Inscriptions et Belles-Lettres, 91
Académie des Sciences, 81–84, 105–6
Académie des Sciences Morales et Politiques, 91
Académie Française, 91
Academy, defined, 66
Academy of Surgery (France), 162–63, 166
Ackerknecht, Erwin, 172
Administration des Travaux Publics, 29, 32–35
Aerztevereinsbund, 273
Agrégation, 87, 98, 130 n.75, 142 n.176; in the sciences, 74–76, 83, 87
Alésia, 90, 132 n.87
Alglave, Emile, 95
American Homeopath, 276
American Institute of Homeopathy, 276
American Lancet, 253
American Medical Association, 277, 279
American Revolution, 231, 250–52
American Social Science Association, 301 n.158
Anglican Church, and medicine, 232
Annalen der Physik, 106
Annales de chimie et de physique, 94
Apothecaries, 150, 175 n.5; in Great Britain, 245–50

Apothecaries' Company, 246
Appenzell, Switzerland, 263–65, 268
Apprenticeship, for surgeons, 158
Arago, François, 27, 73, 78, 82–84, 89, 125 n.32
Architects, 52
Argentina, 242
Arthaud, Joseph, Dr., 211–14
Association Française pour l'Avancement des Sciences, 107–18, 120
Association Philotechnique, 51
Association Polytechnique, 51
Association Scientifique de France, 141 n.169
Asylum law (1838), 212
Attributions libres, 38
Audiffrent, Georges, 239
Austria, medical profession in, 169–70, 199–200, 244
Authority: and epidemic control, 196–201, 205, 213; and moral contagion, 190–95
Autonomy, of professionals, 1–2

Baccalauréat-es-lettres: classes of, 59 n.53; as educational requirement, 124 n.24; history, 17–24; limit on number awarded, 22–23; and military service, 144 n.190; power of, 19–28, 52–55; in engineering professions, 4; role in social stratification, 17–24; as unifying device, 22–23
Baccalauréat-es-sciences, 57 n.8, 89, 132 n.84
Baillarger, Jules, 221 n.88
Balard, Antoine-Jérôme, 129 n.72, 130 n.72
Ballière, Germer, 95
Balzac, Honoré de, 171, 198

307

Baquets, 189–90, 192–93
Barber-surgeons. *See* Surgeons
Barrot, Odilon, 91
Bastiat, Frédéric, 22
Baudrimont, Alexandre, 80
Bazard, Saint-Amand, 49
Bazin, Pierre-François-Aman, 80
Beach, Wooster, 252
Belhomme, J.E., 210
Bentham, Jeremy, 244
Berlant, Jeffrey, 278
Berlin Medical Society, 256–57, 270
Bernard, Claude, 102, 108, 138 n.136, 140 n.164
Bernheim, Hippolyte, 183
Bernoulli, Christoph, 261
Berryer, Antoine, 91
Bert, Paul, 115
Berthellot, Marcellin, 118
Berthollet, Claude-Louis, 85–86
Bertin, Pierre-Auguste, 106
Besançon, 116
Bicêtre lunatic asylum, 202
Bichat, Ernest, 113
Bifurcation, 87, 89, 98, 130 n.75, 132 n.84
Bilz, Friedrich Eduard, 272
Biot, Jean-Baptiste, 73, 78, 81–84
Bischoffsheim, Louis-Raphael, 100
Bismarck, Otto von, 259
Bizuthage, 29, 40
Blanchard, Emile, 89, 96, 136 n.107
Blanchard, Raphael, 119
Bloodletting, 164, 171, 177 nn.42–43
Bobin, A., 25, 59 n.8
Boerhaave, Hermann, 185–88, 190–92
Bonaparte, Pierre, 137 n.133
Bontius, Jacobus, 217 n.14
Bordeaux, support of science in, 80, 109, 112, 126 n.43
Boucart, Henry, 43
Boucher de Perthes, Jacques, 102
Bouchut, Eugène, Dr., 201, 214
Boulanger, Georges (General), 181–82
Bourbon restoration, 77
Bourdieu, Pierre, 16
Bourgeois, Léon, 116
Brazil, 243
Bréal, Michel, 94, 139 n.145

Brenier, Casimir, 113, 116
Brierre de Boismont, Alexandre, 207–8, 210
Brillouin, Marcel, 106, 140 n.150
British Association for the Advancement of Science, 92–93, 107–8
British Medical Association, 247, 257, 291 n.65
Broca, Paul, 108
Broglie, Duc de, 91
Brongniart, Adolphe, 89, 130 n.72
Brothier, Léon, 39
Brunel, Isambard, 37
Buchanan, Joseph Rhodes, 276
Buchner, Ludwig, 95
Bureau des Longitudes, 73
Bureaucracy: and medicine, 303 n.169; in professions, 1–2; role of *baccalauréat*, 22–24; and social stratification, 17. *See also* Ministry of Public Instruction
Burschenschaften, 255

Cabanis, Pierre-Jean-Georges, 204, 218 n.36, 239, 278
Canada, medical regulation in, 170, 243, 304 n.172
Cantagruel, Louis, 34, 62 n.90
Capitalism and professions, 2
Catholic Church: and medical profession, 228, 240; and science, 86–89, 92, 95, 97–98, 103, 110, 130 nn. 70, 72–75, 136 n.116
Caumont, Arcisse de, 92–93, 110
Central League for the Parity of Healing Methods, 272
Certificat d'études physiques, chimiques et naturelles, 79, 125 n.39
Chaptal, Jean-Antoine, 37
Charcot, Jean-Martin, 181, 183
Charlatanism, 195
Charles X, 228
Charme, 25
Charras, Adolphe, 34
Charter of 1814, 207–8
Charton, Edouard, 39, 200
Chassaignac de Latrade, Louis, 34
Chemistry, 104–7, 139 n.151
Christian Science, 275–76

Index

Cipolla, Carlo, 167
Civil engineers: career expectations, 38–40; dependence on state, 4–5; educational requirements, 38–40; origin, 35–40; prestige of, 45–52; and social stratification, 35–37; state domination of, 51–52
Class. *See* Social stratification
Classical education, 52–53, 139 n.145; and engineering profession, 4; entrenchment of, 23–24
Clausius, Rudolf, 94
Clement, Nicolas, 37
Clermont, 113, 143 n.184
Club movement (1848), 206, 209–11
Code universel, 19
Code universitaire, 19–21
Coeurderoy, Ernest, 239
Colbertisme, 196–97
Collective psychology, 182–85
Collège de France, 73
Collège Royal, 78
Collèges communaux, 74
Collèges royaux, 75
Collegial element in medicine, 166, 168, 171
Colombia, 242
Combes, Charles, 108, 140 n.164
Comité des Travaux Historiques, 90–92
Commission de l'Instruction Publique, 124 n.21
Communautés, 6, 152–53, 158
Commune (1870), 105–6
Communities of the competent, 1–2
Comptes rendus, 82
Comte, Auguste, 239
Conducteurs auxiliaires, 33
Conducteurs des ponts et chaussées, 4, 32–34, 128 n.63
Conducteurs embrigadés, 33–34
Congrès Archéologiques, 92
Congrès Scientifiques, 92
Congress of German Economists, 259
Conseil de l'Instruction Publique, 75, 86, 98–99, 119, 130 n.71, 145 n.196
Conservatoire des Arts et Métiers, 37
Constans, Augustin, Dr., 211–14
Contagious Diseases Prevention Acts (1866–1869) (Great Britain), 249

Contestations, 162–63
Convulsions: and moral contagion theory, 185–90
Cornier, Henriette, 206–7
Corporate idiom, 3
Corps des Ingénieurs des Ponts et Chaussées, power of, 53–55
Corps des Mines, 35
Corps des Ponts et Chaussées, 39; and Ecole Centrale, 42; military motif in, 30–31; origins, 28–30; rivalry with civil engineers, 51–52; and social stratification, 52–55; and Société Centrale des Ingénieurs Civils, 49–51; rivalry with civil engineers, 51–52. *See also* State engineers
Corps d'état. *See* Corps des Ponts et Chaussées; State corps of engineers
Corps of *conducteurs*. *See* Conducteurs des ponts et chaussées
Corps of engineers, 17, 51–52. *See also* Corps des Ponts et Chaussées
Corps of Mining Engineers, 60 n.61
Corps of Royal Engineers (Great Britain), 54
Corréard, Alexandre, 62 n.98
Cournot, Antoine-Augustin, 19, 78
Cousin, Victor, 78, 130 n.74
Cowen, David, 249
Crémieux, Adolphe, 209
Criminology, 182–83, 202, 206
Culpeper, Nicholas, 231
Culture: and *baccalauréat*, 25; science and, 80; and social stratification, 16–17; and unification of elite, 17–28
Cumul, 68, 77, 85, 119–21, 129 nn.66–67, 138 n.136
Currency and exchange rates, 66
Cuvier, Georges, 66, 71, 78, 81, 119, 125 n.32

d'Almeida, Charles, 107
DeDaineville, R.P., 22
Delaunay, Charles, 108, 138 n.138
Denmark, medical regulation, 242
Dent v. West Virginia, 276
Dentists, 267
Desains, Paul, 106
Deschanel, Emile, 100

Description scientifique, 90–91, 132 n.89
Deshayes, Gérard-Paul, 129 n.67
Deslon, Charles, 195
Despine, 216 n.11
Destutt de Tracy, Antoine-Louis-Claude, 239
Deutsche Gesellschaft zur Bekämpfung des Kurpfuschertums, 273–74
Deville, Henri Etienne Sainte-Claire, 105, 138 n.136
Dictionaire des sciences médicales, 198
Dictionnaire archéologique de la Gaule, 91
Dictionnaire topographique, 91
Diocesan seminaries, *baccalauréat* requirement, 19
Doctorat degree, 19
Doctorat-ès-sciences, 76
Doctrine of Saint-Simon: An Exposition, The, 49
Dollfus, Charles, 43, 94
Dollfus, Jean, 43
Dombale, Mathieu de, 37
Dominican Republic, 243
Dubois, Paul-François, 27
Dufour, Leon, 102, 135 n.107
Duhem, Pierre, 119, 145 n.198
Dulong, Pierre, 77, 125 n.29
Dumas, Jean-Baptiste, 48–50, 78, 89–90, 96, 104, 110, 130 n.72, 132 n.84
Dunoyer, Charles, 239
Dupanloup, Felix, 87, 91, 97
Dupin, Charles (Baron), 34
Dupuytren, Guillaume, 173–74
Duras, Duchesse de, 78, 125 n.32
Durkheim, Emile, 3, 182–84
Duruy, Victor, 71–72, 96–103, 136 n.116, 138 n.138

Eclecticism, 252–53, 275–76
Ecole Centrale: and civil engineers, 20, 39–40; Council on Studies, 42; ideology, 40; influence of *baccalauréat*, 53, 58 n.23; and professional institutions, 45–46; social background of students, 42–45; student organization, 40
Ecole Centrale des Arts et Manufactures, 28, 37, 39, 53
Ecole de l'Artillerie et du Génie, 73

Ecole des Mines, 73
Ecole des Ponts et Chaussées, 32, 62 nn.105–6; science in, 73; state dominance of, 39–45; student ranking, 40
Ecole Municipale de Physique et de Chimie Industrielles, 110
Ecole Normale Supérieure, 67, 87; clerical reform, 87–88; Napoleonic reform, 74; origins, 123 n.15; physics at, 107; science curriculum, 83; student unrest, 101
Ecole Polytechnique: *baccalauréat* requirement, 52–53; and civil engineers, 38; and conducteurs, 32, 34–35; Council of Instruction, 27; Council on Improvements, 27; entrance requirements, 24, 26–28; science curriculum, 73, 128 n.63; social background of students, 42–45; student ranking in, 29–30, 40
Ecole Pratique des Hautes Etudes, 97
Ecole Supérieure d'Eléctricité, 110
Ecole Vétérinaire, 73
Ecoles secondaires, 18
Edict of Marly, 232
Education: engineering, 24–25; financial support of, 112–18, 120, 145 n.201; French medical practitioners, 158; industrial, 104–18; medical, 162–63, 172–73, 253–54; nonclassical, 23–24; scientific posts in, 67–70; and social stratification, 15–17, 55 n.4, 79–80, 99–101; student rankings, 60 n.61; for surgery, 152–53. *See also* Classical education
Edwards, Henri Milne, 89, 96, 110, 138 n.136, 141 n.169
Eiffel, Gustave, 63 n.111
Electrical industry, 110, 142 n.175
Elias, Norbert, 165
Elite: *baccalauréat*, 23–24; cultural unification of, 17–28; enrollment in engineering schools, 43–45; medical, 160–63, 166–71; in nineteenth century, 15–17; scientific, 66–73, 82–84, 107, 109, 111, 118, 144 n.195; state-created, 17, 56 n.7; technological, 41–45
Emmery, Henri-Charles, 33
Enfantin, Prosper, 49
Engineers: *baccalauréat* as educational requirement, 25–28; career expectations,

Index

30–31; commercial activities, 31, 60 n.75; educational requirements, 24–25; ethos of, 31–32; marriage habits, 31; military, 29–30; pensions, 30–31, 60 n.67; salaries, 30–31, 60 n.66; social stratification of, 16–17, 56 nn.6–7. *See also* Civil engineers; Corps of engineers
Enlightenment, 239
Enseignement secondaire, 17–18, 22, 53–54
Epidemics, 186–201. *See also* Psychic epidemics
Erudits, 78, 90–92
Esquirol, Jean-Etienne-Dominique, 202
Etampes suicide epidemic, 203
Examen impartial des contestations etc. (Quesnay), 163
Examinations: for *baccalauréat*, 5, 18–19, 77; for surgical degrees, 152–53. *See also* Agrégation

Fabré, Jean-Henri, 118
Faculties of science: courses for medical students, 79–80; duties of, 77; educational backgrounds, 83–84; in higher education, 67–70; scientific-industrial relations, 104; and Second Empire reform, 85–86
Failure, scholastic, 41, 63 n.116
Falloux Law, 18, 86–87, 129 n.70
Faye, Hervé, 104
Feldshers, 150, 175 n.5
Ferry, Jules, 101, 119
Financial support of education, 112–18, 143 nn. 182, 184
Finland, medical regulation in, 304 n.172
Fizeau, Hippolyte, 107
Flammarion, Camille, 89, 118
Flexner, Abraham, 170
Fortoul, Hippolyte, 71, 86–89, 90–91, 95
Foucault, Michel, 11 n.7, 150, 172, 174 n.3, 196, 219 nn. 48, 54, 284 n.9
Fourier, Joseph, 82
François I, 78
Franco-Prussian War (1870), 105, 108–9
Frank, Johann Peter, 197
Free field model in medicine, 8, 231–32; France, 19th century, 239–41, 287 nn.

33, 37; future prospects, 281–82; in Germany, 254–59, 269–74; in Great Britain, 248–50, 266–67; in Switzerland, 259–65, 267–69; in United States, 251–54, 274–80; twentieth-century prospects, 265–66
Free State and Free Medicine, A, 249
Freidson, Eliot, 167, 225, 227
Freizügigkeit, 254, 270
French Medical Congress (1845), 199, 239
French Revolution, 197–98, 229–31, 284 n.9
Freud, Sigmund, 181, 184
Friedman, Milton, 281
Functionalist school of sociology, 1–2

Gay-Lussac, Joseph-Louis, 78, 129 nn. 66–67
Gayon, Ulysse, 113
Gazette spéciale de l'instruction publique, 24, 26, 52
General Council of Medical Education, 247–50
General Medical Council (Great Britain), 267, 291 n.68
General practitioners, 6–7, 169–74
Geneva, Switzerland, 260–61
Geology, 67
Gerhardt, Charles, 80, 85, 126 n.42, 129 n.67
Germ theory of disease, 171
Germany: academic life in, 67, 70–71, 93–95, 97, 101, 105, 133 n.97; cameralism in, 196–97; medical profession in, 8–9, 169–70, 179 n.69, 199, 231–32, 240, 254–59, 269–74; physics in, 105; politics, 3; professions in, 3; research on professions, 11 n.9
Gewerbeordnung, 255–59, 269–74
Girardin, Emile de, 95
Girardin, Saint-Marc, 20–21, 100
Giraud, Léopold, 98, 136 n.115
Gladstone, William Ewart, 249
Glarus, Switzerland, 263–65
Gleichschaltung, 28
Goblet, René, 116
Godron, Alexandre, 104
Goubert, Jean-Pierre, 153

Grant, Robert E., 291 n.65
Grant, Ulysses S., 262
Great Britain: academic life in, 67, 70–71; engineering in, 4, 41, 46, 54; medical profession in, 8, 170, 173, 175 n.5, 179 n.68; medical regulation in, 245–50, 266–67; physics in, 106; science in, 93
Great Council of Neuchâtel, 262–63
Great Council of Thurgau, 262
Greene, Franklin, 41
Grenoble, 113, 142 n.178, 143 n.184
Group Psychology and the Analysis of the Ego, 184
Guide pour le choix d'un état, 39, 200
Guilds, medical, 254–55, 286 n.25
Guizot, François, 43, 78, 83, 128 n.60

Haarlem orphanage convulsion outbreak, 185–88, 190–92
Hance, William, 253
Harrison, Edward, 246–47
Health insurance, 270
Health officers, 169–70, 240
Hecquet, Philippe, Dr., 186–88, 190–92, 196
Hegel, Georg Wilhelm Freidrich, 97
Heilmann, Jean-Jacques, 43
Heilpraktikerberuf, 272–74
Heilpraktikerbund Deutschlands, 273–74
Helvetic Republic (1798), 260–61
Les héritiers, 16
Herriot, Edouard, 113
Herschel, John, 93–94
Hillebrand, Karl, 94
Hippocratic medicine, 164
Historiography of professions, 1–4
Homeopathic medicine, 253–54, 268, 275–77
Honduras, 242
Hospitals, 172
Humboldt, Alexander von, 93, 238
Huxley, T.H., 250
Hygienische Blätter, 273
Hystéro-démonopathie, 213

Imagination, and moral contagion, 192–95
Incendiarist wave (1830), 206–8
Industrial capitalism, 37–38, 41, 172, 180 n.78

Industrial engineering, 37–38, 141 n.170
Industry, support of science, 101–18
Infanticide, 206–8
Ingénieur. *See* Engineers
Ingénieurs civils. *See* Civil engineers
Institut Chimique, 116
Institut de France, 66, 133 n.91
Institut des Provinces, 92
Institut Eléctro-technique, 113, 116
Institution of Civil Engineers, 45–46
Intellectual freedom, 85–101
International collaboration in science, 93–97
International Congress of Students (Liège 1865), 98
Italy, medical profession in, 167, 243, 286 n.27

Jacksonianism, 252–53
Jacques le Fataliste (Diderot), 157
Jamin, Jule, 100
Jansenist movement, 185–88
Jardin du Roi, 73, 78
Jews, 98, 109
Joule, James Prescott, 94
Journal de physique théorique et appliqué, 107
Journal des chemins de fer, 47
Journal du génie civil etc, 36–37, 45–47, 51
July Monarchy, 71, 73, 81, 93, 212

Kirchhoff, Gustav, 106
Koch, Robert, 225
Koechlin, Eugénie, 43
Kuhn, Phillippe, 212–14
Kurierfreiheit, 256–60, 265, 269–75
Kurierzwang, 256–59

La Martinière, Germaine Pichaut de, 157
Laboulaye, Edouard, 100, 239, 241
Laissez-faire theory and medicine, 165, 229–30. *See also* Free field model in medicine
Lamblardie, 28
Lamennais, H.F. Robert de, 75
Land-registry administration, 21
Landsgemeinde, 263–65, 268
Laplace, Pierre Simon de, 66, 71, 73, 82, 85, 119
Lapparent, Albert de, 119, 145 n.198

Index 313

Laprade, Victor de, 88, 131 n.82
Latin, as educational requirement, 28, 52, 59 n.55
Laurens, Camille, 49
Laurent, Auguste, 80, 126 n.42
Law, *baccalauréat requirement*, 19, 22
Lawyers, 199–200
Le Bon, Gustave, 182–84
Le Chapelier Law (1791), 28
Le Verrier, Urbain, 89–90, 96, 110, 130 n.72, 132 n.84, 138 n.138
Lebesgue, Victor-Amédée, 80
Lecoq, Henri, 102
Lectures, 78, 99–101, 125 n.32, 137 nn. 126, 128
Léon, Alphonse, 34
Léonard, Jacques, 225
Liard, Louis, 113, 116, 124 n.19
Libri, Guglielmo, 82–84
Licence, 19, 142 n.176
Licensing, medical: in France, 152–53, 158, 230, 232–37; in Germany, 257–59; in Great Britain, 230–32, 247–50; and medical monopolies, 226–30; in United States, 227–28, 230–32, 250–54, 275–77. See also Medical legislation; Medical regulation
Lichtheim, George, 56 n.7
Littré, Emile, 39
Loewe, Wilhelm, 256
Lorain, Paul, 102
Lovejoy, Arthur O., 184
Lucas, Prosper, 203–5, 208, 214
Lycées: and *baccalauréat-es-lettres*, 18; classical curriculum, 4; reform of, 74, 87–88, 131 n.79

Magendie, François, 102
Marceau, Jane, 15
Marrast, Armand, 50
Marriage, 31, 55 n.1, 60 n.71
Marxism, 2, 10 n.5, 56 n.7
Mathematics, and engineering education, 28
La médecine entre les pouvoirs et savoirs, 266
Médecine mentale. See Psychiatry
Médecins-aliénistes. See Psychiatry
Medical Act Amendment Act of 1884 (Great Britain), 291 n.68

Medical Act of 1858, 247–50
Medical Act of 1956 (Great Britain), 267
Medical Defense Association, 267
Medical Freedom: the National Free Medical Adviser, 250
Medical legislation, 226–30. See also Licensing, medical; Medical regulation
Medical police, 196–98, 202, 215
Medical profession, and state, 2, 6, 9
Medical regulation, 8; basic concepts, 230–32; French, 233–37, 241–45; in Germany, 254–59, 269–74; in Great Britain, 245–50, 266–67; in Switzerland, 259–65, 267–69; in United States, 250–54, 274–80
Medical students, 153, 175 n.10
Medicine, autonomy in, 9; in pre-Revolutionary France, 149–51; professional monopoly in, 7–8; student unrest in, 97; *baccalauréat* requirement, 19. See also Nonlicensed practitioners
Merchants, 179 n.65
Meritocracy, 3, 15, 25–26, 53, 166
Mesmer, Franz Anton, 189
Mesmerism, 189–90, 192–95
Meunier, Victor, 96, 100
Mexico, medical regulation in, 244–45
Michelet, Jules, 93
Miletian suicide outbreak, 185, 190–92, 203
Military corps, salaries, 30
Military engineers, 39, 60 n.61
Military service, 117–18
Millardet, Alexis, 113
Ministry of Commerce, 142 n.174
Ministry of Public Instruction: and Ecole Polytechnique, 27; and engineering education, 25; domination of science, 5, 71, 81, 83–84, 92, 119–20, 128 n.59, 142 nn. 174, 176; Duruy administration, 96–101; financial support of education, 112
Miquel, Johannes, 269
Moigno, Abbé, 144 n.195
Moleschott, Jacob, 95
Monarchy, and medical professions, 163, 165–69, 172
Monge, Gaspard, 26
Monod, Gabriel, 94
Monomania theory, 202–8
Monopolies, medical, French model, 225–

Monopolies—*continued*
30; in Great Britain, 247–50; and moral contagion, 193–95, 201; in Switzerland, 259–65
Montalembert, Comte de, 240
Moral contagion, 7; definition and usage, 181–82; as professional ideology, 194–95; and psychiatry, 201–5; underlying motifs, 190–95; vocabulary, 185–90
Moralia, 185
Morzine convulsion epidemic, 211–16
Mouquin-Tandon, Alfred, 86
Muel, Leon, 43
Mulhouse business community, 23

Napoleon I: and *baccalauréat*, 20; and Corps des Ponts et Chaussées, 32; and education, 73–74, 86; and engineers, 29; and medical profession, 6, 8, 198–200; and science, 72
Napoleon III: and Catholic church, 96; and Duruy, 101; and Savoyard nationalism, 212; and science, 90, 95, 119, 132 n.87, 137 n.132, 138 n.136
Napoleon's Act of Mediation (1803), 260
National Constitutional Liberty League, 276
National Eclectic Medical Society, 276
National Quarterly Review, 251
National Socialists (Nazis) and medicine, 273–74
National Syndicate for Defense Against Compulsory Laws in Medicine, 272
National workshops for engineers, 49–51
Nationalism, 90–91, 108–10, 132 n.89, 133 n.90
Nationalization of medicine, 198–201
Naturalism, and moral contagion theory, 187–88, 196
Nefftzer, Auguste, 94
Netherlands, medical regulation in, 244, 304 n.172
Neuchâtel, Switzerland, 262–63, 268
Nisard, Désiré, 90, 96–97
Noir, Victor, 137 n.133
Nonconformist, The, 249
Nonlicensed medical practitioners, 152–53, 167, 228–29. *See also* Quackery
Normaliens, 87–88, 127 n.56, 131 n.77

North German Confederation, 257, 259
Norway, medicine in, 231
Notables, 84–85, 166; scientific, 67; defined, 121 n.1

Odysse-Barot, 95
Old Regime, medicine in, 230–37; social vocabulary of, 3
Olivier, Théodore, 42
On the Disadvantageous Influence of the Guild System on Industry, 261
Opticians, 267
Order of Lawyers, 240
Ordinary practitioners, model of, 150–52, 169–72
Organization for the Free Practice of Medicine, 265
Orthodox Church, 98

Parallel medicine, 269
Pâris, François de, 186
Paris Observatory, 73
Parsons, Talcott, 1–2
Passeron, Jean-Claude, 16
Pasteur, Louis, 97, 101–4, 110, 137 n.130, 138 n.136, 225
Patient's rights, 163–65, 177 n.48, 287 n.37. *See also* Free field model in medicine
Patronage: and medical profession, 152, 161–63, 165–69, 172; and science, 5
Patronats, 15
Pensions, for engineers, 29–30
Perronet, Jean-Rodolphe, 28
Petits seminaires, 18
Phlebotomy. *See* Bloodletting
Physical contagion. *See* Epidemics
Physicians: geographic distribution, 154–56; glut of, 200; in Great Britain, 245–50; numerical strength and population density, 154, 167, 169–70; and practice, 159; relations with patients, 171; relations with surgeons, 159–63; social stratification, 155, 157. *See also* Ordinary practitioners
Physics, 105–7
Picard, Emile, 118
Pinel, Phillippe, 190–92, 202–3
Plague, 196–97
Plutarch, 185, 188, 190–92, 203

Index   315

Poincaré, Henri, 144 n.195
Poisson, Denis, 27, 73, 127 n.54
Political medicine, 7–8, 198–202, 214
Political repression, and moral contagion, 206, 209–11
Politics: and authority, 196–201; and Ecole Centrale, 42–43; of engineers, 31–32; and epidemic control, 197–201; and German medical regulations, 271–74; and medical monopolies, 225–30; and moral contagion theory, 181–82, 214–16; and psychiatry, 7, 205–14; of scientists, 5, 71–75, 84, 94–95; in Switzerland, 262–65; and United States medicine, 252–54, 274–80
Popularization of science, 77–84, 99–101, 103, 117–18, 125 n.32, 127 n.47, 144 n.195
Pouchet, Félix, 96–97, 135 n.107
Power in medical profession, 8, 173–74, 213–14, 283 n.2
Premier surgeon, 152–53, 166
Press, and moral contagion theory, 208–11
Primitive Physick, 280
Prizes, scientific, 92, 133 n.91
Profession: Anglo-Saxon definition and usage, 3; French definition and usage, 3, 10 n.7
Profession of Medicine, 225
Professional associations: engineering, 45–52; medical, 200–201, 275–76, 301 n.158; scientific, 92–93, 96, 104–7, 110–18, 120, 140 n.158; surgical, 152–53
Professional unification, 149–50
Professionalization: and moral contagion, 184–85; modern concepts, 1–3, 10 n.7, 149–50, 165–66, 168–69
Propriétaires, and engineering schools, 45
Protestants, 41, 98, 109, 280
Provincial Medical and Surgical Association, 247
Provincial scientists, 78–88, 96–98, 120–21, 135 n.107, 142 n.178, 145 nn. 200–201; salaries, 85–86
Prussia. *See* Germany
Psychiatrists: and moral contagion theory, 201–5; origins, 202–5
Psychic epidemics, 181–82, 184, 202–5, 211–14

Psychopathology, 206–8
Public health, 244, 267
Publishing, 19
Pure Food and Drug Act, 276, 278–79
Puritan Revolution, 231

Quackery: in Germany, 254–59, 272–74; in Great Britain, 246–50; in United States, 250–54, 275–77. *See also* Mesmerism
Quatrefages de Bréau, J.L. Armand de, 79–80, 85, 108–9, 126 n.40, 140 n.164
Quesnay, François, 163–65
Quet, Jean-Antoine, 106
Quinet, Edgar, 93

Rabanis, Joseph-François, 88
Ramsey, Matthew, 2, 10 n.7, 179 n.69
Rapports de la médecine avec la politique, 201
Rapports du physique et du moral de l'homme, 204
Raulin, Victor, 80
Regnault, Victor, 89, 107
Reingold, Nathan, 107
Religion: and medicine, 280; and moral contagion theory, 185–88, 194; and psychiatry, 212–14
Renan, Ernest, 93, 97
Rendu, Ambroise, 20, 24
Rentiers, and engineering schools, 45
Répertoire archéologique, 91
Research: parochialism in, 95, 121; and Second Empire reform, 94; versus practical application, 103–9, 115–18
Revolution of 1830, 27, 207–8
Revolution of 1848, 34, 49, 209–11
Revue des cours litteraires, 95
Revue des cours scientifiques de la France et de l'étranger, 95
Revue des deux mondes, 82, 93
Revue germanique, 94–95
Revue international de l'enseignement, 103
Richet, Charles, 118
Robin, Charles, 98–99
Rollier, Constant, 81
Rouland, Gustave, 71, 86–89, 90–91, 95–96
Royal College of Physicians (Great Britain), 232, 245–47, 257
Royal Society of Medicine, 197–98
Royer-Collard, Pierre Paul, 21, 75

Rush, Benjamin, 231, 252
Russia, medicine in, 231, 243

Sacy, Antoine Silvestre de, 91
Sainte-Beuve, Charles-Augustin, 131 n.82, 137 n.132
Saint-Médard convulsion outbreak, 186–88, 203, 215–16
Saint-Simon, Henri, 26
Salaries: of engineers, 30–31; of scientists, 85–86, 129 nn.64–66, 138 n.136, 145 nn.200–201
Salvandy, Comte de, 130 n.149, 239–40
Salverte, Eusebe, 201
San Salvador, 242
Sarcey, Francisque, 88
Savants: as elites, 73, 82–84, 107, 109, 111, 118, 144 n.195; political power of, 5; as public servants, 84, 90–92, 94, 97, 99, 117; rhetorical style, 78, 125 n.30; salaries, 85
Say, Jean-Baptiste, 239
Schneider, Ignace Léon, 43
Science: academic versus utilitarian, 103–18; decline of, 6; educational requirements, 101–3; industrial support of, 101–18; parochialism in, 93–97; Second Empire reform of, 85–101; and social stratification, 85–86; state domination of, 70–72, 81–84, 109–10, 119–21; student enrollment, 74–75, 77–79, 113–16, 123 n.16, 125 n.36
Sciences pratiques, 104
Scientists: as elites, 66–72; career patterns, 67, 70–75, 101–3, 122 n.2, 127 n.56, 139 n.141; educational backgrounds, 76; educational requirements, 73–85; publishing activities, 80–81; salaries, 85–86, 129 nn.64, 66, 138 n.136, 145 nn.200–201. *See also* Academic scientists; Provincial scientists
Second Empire, 71–72; scientific reform in, 5, 85–101
Séguin, Marc, 37
September Revolution (Spain), 231, 244
Sewill, Henry, 266
Sexual attraction, and moral contagion, 186–88
Sherman Act, 278–79

Simon, Jules, 88, 100, 239
Skocpol, Theda, 56 n.7
Smith, Adam, 243
Smith, Elias, 252
Social Statics, 249
Social stratification: and *baccalauréat*, 19–20, 22–24; and bureaucracy, 17; and culture, 16; and education, 15–17, 55 n.4, 79–80, 99–101; and 18th-century physicians, 151–52; and engineering, 16–17, 42–45, 53–55, 56 nn.6–7; and French medical practitioners, 155, 157; and industrial development, 106; and medical profession, 159–63, 171–74, 199–201, 225–30, 281, 282 n.2; and professions, 3; and science, 85–86; in Great Britain, 54; of patients, 159, 176 n.32; psychiatrists, 7; state role in, 4; surgeons, 155, 157, 163–65
Société Centrale des Ingénieurs Civils, 48–52
Société Chimique de Paris, 104, 106
Société d'Encouragement pour l'Industrie Nationale, 37
Société Française de Physique, 106–7, 111
Société Internationale des Eléctriciens, 111
Société pour l'Etude des Questions d'Enseignement Supérieur, 103
Société Royale de Médecine, 233, 235
Société Zoologique de France, 141 n.172
Society of Apothecaries, 245–47
Sociology, 182–83
Solvay, Ernest, 116
Sonderbund War, 261
Soult, Marshal, 27
South Africa, medical regulation in, 304 n.172
Spain, medical regulation in, 231, 244
Spencer, Herbert, 249
State: and British medicine, 248–50; and German medical regulations, 255–59, 270–74; and medical monopolies, 226–30; and medical regulation, 240–41; and moral contagion theory, 195–201; and psychiatry, 211–14; and social stratification, 56 n.7; and United States medicine, 276–79; definition of, 57 n.7; domination of engineering, 17, 53–55; domination of science, 5, 70–72, 81–84, 102–10, 119–21; political medicine, 7; professional de-

Index

pendence on, 3–4; role in professions, 1–2; role in social stratification, 4. *See also* Bureaucracy; Monarchy
State corps of engineers, 4, 35–52; rivalry with civil engineers, 35. *See also* Corps des Ponts et Chaussées
Stresemann, Gustav, 271–72
Struve, Peter Rudolf Wilhelm, 273
Student enrollment, in science, 74–75, 77–79, 113–16, 123 n.16, 125 n.36
Students. *See* Medical students
Suicide, 182–85, 203
Suicide, 182–84
Surgeons: and practice, 6, 158–59; family origins, 157, 176 n.22; in France, 150–52; geographic distribution, 154–57; in Great Britain, 245–50; legal status, 152–53; numerical strength and population density, 153–54, 167–68; power of, 163–65; relations with patients, 163–65; relations with physicians, 159–63; social stratification, 155, 157
Sweden, medicine in, 231, 242
Switzerland, medical regulation in, 8, 231–32, 259–65, 267–69, 304 n.172

Tarde, Gabriel, 182–84
Tardieu, Auguste-Ambroise, 137 n.133
Teachers, salaries, 30
Terror, and moral contagion, 191
Thenard, Louis-Jacques, 78, 86
Therapeutic efficacy, 173
Thierry, Amédée, 96
Thierry, Pierre-Boniface, 79
Third Republic, 72, 181; scientists in, 5–6
Thomas, Emile, 49
Thomas, Léonce, 49
Thomson, Samuel, 252
Thomson, William, 94
Thomsonian botanical medical sect, 251–54, 275–77
Thorbecke, Jan Rudolf, 244, 256
Thurston, Robert, 41
Tocqueville, Alexis de, 39–40, 200, 252, 261
Tour de France, 160–61, 176 n.28
Trials, public attendance at, 207–8
Tudesq, Jean, 122 n.1
Turgot, Anne-Robert-Jacques, 197–98

Unconscious, theory of, 183–84
Union des Ingénieurs Civils et Industriels de l'Ecole Centrale, 48
Union médicale, 211
Union of Hessian Physicians, 257
United Kingdom. *See* Great Britain
United States, medical regulation in, 8, 170, 250–54, 274–82
Universitaires: career patterns, 74; defined, 66; discontent of, 79–81, 92–93, 96, 104, 139 n.145; as elites, 91, 99–101; as lecturers, 117–18; as public servants, 84; political activity, 85–86, 110; purge of, 75, 87–89; and reform movement, 71–72; state corps of, 70–71
Université de France: and *baccalauréat*, 27–28; classical curriculum, 52–53; international relations, 97; Napoleonic reform, 20; provisional phase, 73–76; science faculty, 5; scientific reform, 98, 119, 128 n.58; Second Empire reform, 100
Upward mobility, and engineering, 15–17, 55 nn.2–4

Valeriani, Luchino, 42
Vaud, Switzerland, 260
Ventôse law, 240, 243, 260
Verdet, Emile, 94, 107, 134 n.98
Veron, Eugène, 132 n.83
Version latine, 24
Vie de Jésus, 97
Villemain, Abel, 21–22, 52, 77–78
Virchow, Rudolf, 256, 295 n.101
Vocabulaire de la langue française, 38
Vogt, Carl, 95

Waitz, George, 134 n.99
Weiss, John, 4, 10 n.7
Wesley, John, 280
Wilkinson, James John Garth, 249
Wine industry, 113, 115–16, 143 n.186
Winterburn, George, 276
Work ethic, in engineering, 41–42
Wundarzt, 150, 175 n.5
Wurtz, Adolphe, 94, 102, 104, 108–9, 134 n.98

Yung, Eugène, 95

Zaharoff, Basil, 116
Zurich, Switzerland, 260, 262

Notes on Contributors

ROBERT FOX has taught at the University of Lancaster since 1966. A past-president of the British Society for the History of Science, he was recently elected to a British Academy Readership in the Humanities. He is the author of *The Caloric Theory of Gases from Lavoisier to Regnault* (1971) and of a critical edition of Sadi Carnot's *Réflexions sur la puissance motrice du feu* (1978), and has co-edited (with George Weisz) *The Organization of Science and Technology in France, 1808–1914* (1980).

GERALD L. GEISON is associate professor of history and history of science at Princeton University. He is the author of *Michael Foster and the Cambridge School of Physiology* (1978) and editor of *Professions and Professional Ideologies in America* (1983).

TOBY GELFAND is Hannah Professor of the History of Medicine and associate professor in the Department of History at the University of Ottawa. He is the author of *Professionalizing Modern Medicine: Paris Surgeons and Medical Science and Institutions in the 18th Century* (1980).

JAN GOLDSTEIN is assistant professor of modern European history at the University of Chicago. She has published articles on the development of psychiatry and psychoanalysis and is presently completing a book on the emergence of the psychiatric profession in nineteenth-century France.

MATTHEW RAMSEY is assistant professor of history at Harvard University. He is the author of several articles on the social history of medicine in eighteenth- and nineteenth-century France, and of a forthcoming book on popular medicine, the medical profession, and the French state, 1770–1830.

Contributors

JOHN WEISS is associate professor of history and Director of the Western Societies Program at Cornell University. He is the editor of *Technology and Social History* (1971), and author of *Little Injustices: Small Claims Courts and the American Consumer* (1972) and of *The Making of Technological Man: The Social Origins of French Engineering Education* (1982).

OHIO UNIVERSITY LIBRARY

Please return this book as soon as you have finished with it. In order to avoid fine it must be returned by the latest date